Revision Checklist

WORTHWHILE CONTENT

The essay's main point is clear and sharply focused.
- ☐ Does the title attract attention and give a forecast? (45)
- ☐ Is the topic limited enough? (22)
- ☐ Do you get to your main point quickly? (46)
- ☐ Is the thesis definite, informative, and easy to find? (23)

The discussion delivers on the promise made in the thesis.
- ☐ Will readers learn something new and useful? (80)
- ☐ Do you support every assertion with enough details? (79)
- ☐ Does everything belong, or can anything be cut? (84)
- ☐ Have you used only your best material? (31)

SENSIBLE ORGANIZATION

The essay has a definite introduction, body, and conclusion.
- ☐ Will your introduction make readers want to read on? (10)
- ☐ Does each body paragraph develop *one* supporting point? (90)
- ☐ Does the order of body paragraphs reveal a clear line of thought and emphasize what is most important? (10)
- ☐ Does the conclusion give a real sense of an ending? (10)
- ☐ Is everything connected? (15)
- ☐ If you varied this organization, was it for good reason? (155)

Except for paragraphs of transition or special emphasis, each body (or support) paragraph usually is a mini-essay.
- ☐ Does the paragraph have a topic (or orienting) statement? (92)
- ☐ Does the topic statement come at the beginning or end, depending on your emphasis? (92)
- ☐ Does everything stick to the point (unity), and stick together (coherence)? (94, 95)
- ☐ Is the paragraph developed enough to support the point? (83)

READABLE STYLE

Sentences are clear, concise, and fluent.
- ☐ Can each sentence be understood the first time it is read? (110)
- ☐ Is the information expressed in the fewest words possible? (119)
- ☐ Are sentences put together with enough variety? (126)

Each word does its job.
- ☐ Is a real person speaking, and is the voice likable? (133)
- ☐ Is everything in plain English? (140)
- ☐ Is your meaning precise, concrete, and specific? (134)
- ☐ Is your tone appropriate for this situation and audience? (138)

Numbers in parentheses refer to the first page of major discussion in the text.

Canadian Edition

The Writing Process

A Concise Rhetoric

John M. Lannon

University of Massachusetts, Dartmouth

David B. Parsons

Lakehead University

PEARSON
Longman

Toronto

National Library of Canada Cataloguing in Publication

Lannon, John M.
  The writing process : a concise rhetoric / John M. Lannon, David B. Parsons. —
Canadian ed.

Includes index.
ISBN 0-201-74223-3

1. English language—Rhetoric. 2. Report writing. I. Parsons, David B., 1943– II. Title.

PE1408.L35 2004   808'.042   C2003-901698-6

ISBN 0-201-74223-3

Vice President, Editorial Director: Michael J. Young
Acquisitions Editor: Marianne Minaker
Supervising Developmental Editor: Suzanne Schaan
Marketing Manager: Toivo Pajo
Production Editor: Cheryl Jackson
Copy Editor: Valerie Adams
Proofreader: Ann McInnis
Senior Production Coordinator: Peggy Brown
Formatter: Jansom
Art Director: Julia Hall
Interior Design: David Cheung
Cover Design: David Cheung
Cover Image: PhotoDisc

1 2 3 4 5 08 07 06 05 04

Printed and bound in Canada.

PEARSON
Longman

BRIEF CONTENTS

SECTION FOUR

The Research Process   317

APPENDIX A

Editing for Grammar, Punctuation, and Mechanics   453

APPENDIX B

Format Guidelines for Submitting Your Manuscript   479

APPENDIX C

Useful Web Sites and Electronic Library Resources   482

DETAILED CONTENTS

SECTION TWO

SPECIFIC REVISION STRATEGIES   73

C H A P T E R   5

REVISING THE CONTENT: WRITING SOMETHING WORTHWHILE   77

C H A P T E R   6

REVISING THE PARAGRAPHS: SHAPING FOR READERS' ACCESS   89

C H A P T E R   7

REVISING THE SENTENCES: WRITING WITH STYLE   109

SECTION FOUR

THE RESEARCH PROCESS

C H A P T E R **19**

PREFACE

This text promotes rhetorical awareness by treating the writing process as a set of deliberate and recursive decisions. It promotes rhetorical effectiveness by helping develop the problem-solving skills essential to reader-centred writing. Practical guidelines, accessible models, and case studies enable students to produce writing that works.

ORGANIZATION OF *THE WRITING PROCESS*

Section One, "THE PROCESS," covers planning, drafting, and revising. Students learn to invent, select, organize, and express their material recursively. They see how initial decisions about purpose and audience influence later decisions about what will be said and how it will be said. They see that writing is essentially a "thinking" process, and they also learn to work collaboratively.

Section Two, "SPECIFIC REVISION STRATEGIES," focuses on top-down revision: content, organization, and style. Students learn to support their assertions; to organize for the reader; and to achieve prose maturity, precise diction, and appropriate tone.

Section Three, "ESSAYS FOR VARIOUS GOALS," shows how the strategies (or modes) of discourse serve the particular goals of a discourse; that is, how description, narration, exposition, and argument are variously employed for expressive, referential, or persuasive ends. The opening chapter explains how reading and writing are linked and offers strategies for reading and responding to essays by others. Subsequent chapters cover each rhetorical mode, using a balance of student and professional writing samples to touch on current and lasting issues. Beyond studying the samples and case studies as models, students are asked to respond to the issues presented; that is, to write in response to a specific rhetorical situation.

Section Four, "THE RESEARCH PROCESS," approaches research as a process of deliberate inquiry. Students learn to formulate significant research questions; to explore a selective range of primary and secondary sources; to record, summarize, and document their findings; and, most important, to evaluate sources and evidence and interpret findings accurately.

Finally, for easy reference, Appendix A is a concise handbook, with exercises. Appendix B—an additional, brief appendix—offers advice on formatting a manuscript. Appendix C lists useful Web sites and electronic information resources for writing students.

THE FOUNDATIONS OF *THE WRITING PROCESS*

- Writers with no rhetorical awareness overlook the decisions that are crucial for effective writing. Only by defining their rhetorical problem and asking the important questions can writers formulate an effective response to the problem.
- Although it follows no single, predictable sequence, the writing process is not a collection of random activities; rather it is a set of deliberate decisions in problem solving. Beyond emulating this or that model essay, students need to understand that effective writing requires critical thinking.
- Students write for audiences other than instructors and purposes other than completing an assignment. To view the act of writing as only a mere display of knowledge or fluency, an exercise in which writer and reader (i.e., "the instructor") have no higher stake or interest, is to ignore the unique challenges and constraints posed by each writing situation. In every forum beyond the classroom, we write to forge a specific connection with a specific audience.
- Students at any level of ability can develop audience awareness and learn to incorporate within their writing the essential rhetorical features: worthwhile content, sensible organization, and readable style.
- As well as being a fluent communicator, today's educated person needs to be a discriminating consumer of information, skilled in the methods of inquiry, retrieval, evaluation, and interpretation that constitute the research process.
- As an alternative to reiterating the textbook material, classroom workshops apply textbook principles by focusing on the students' writing. These workshops call for an accessible, readable, and engaging book to serve as a comprehensive resource. (Suggestions for workshop design are in the Instructor's Manual.)
- Finally, writing classes typically contain students with all types of strengths and weaknesses. The Writing Process offers explanations that are thorough, examples and models that are broadly intelligible, and goals that are rigorous yet realistic. The textbook is flexible enough to allow for various course plans and customized assignments.

The Writing Process proceeds from writer-centred to reader-centred discourse. Beginning with personal topics and a basic essay structure, the focus shifts to increasingly complex rhetorical tasks, culminating in argument. Within this cumulative structure, each chapter is self-contained for flexible course planning. The sample essays represent a balance of student and professional authorship. Application exercises in each chapter offer various levels of challenge. (All material has been class-tested.)

KEY FEATURES

- **Student-written model essays.** Although professional examples enhance skills in reading and responding, reviewers agree that students are more comfortable emulating essays written by other students.
- **Case studies throughout.** Concise case studies show student writers at work as they read, plan, draft, and revise.
- **Guidelines for writing and research.** Boxed "Guidelines" help students synthesize and apply the information in each chapter.
- **Collaborative projects.** This text features collaborative projects throughout, including guidelines for computer-mediated collaboration.
- **Coverage of computers and the Internet.** Fully integrated computing advice is supplemented by end-of-chapter applications and Appendix C, listing useful Web sites and electronic resources for student writers and researchers.
- **Emphasis on information literacy.** Information-literate people are those who know how to organize information, how to find information, and how to use information to influence others. Critical thinking—the basis of information literacy—is covered intensively in Section Four.

SUPPLEMENTS

- **Instructor's Manual** (0-201-74224-1). The Instructor's Manual for the Canadian edition provides suggested answers to Applications as well as additional Applications, options for essay writing, and further discussion of some key points from the text.
- **Companion Website** (www.ablongman.com/lannonwriting). This site created for the American edition of the text includes additional exercises and links to online samples and resources.

ACKNOWLEDGMENTS FOR
THE SEVENTH AMERICAN EDITION

Much of the improvement in this edition was inspired by helpful reviews from Jan Coulson, Okmulgee State University; Marie Garrett, Patrick Henry Community College; Frederic Giacobazzi, Kirtland Community College; Jeanne Ann Graham, Ivy Tech State College; Lee Ann Hodges, Tri-County Community College; Kathleen Kelly, Northeastern University; Catherine Rahmes, Cincinnati State Technical and Community College; Denise M. Rogers, University of Southwestern Louisiana; Kathleen M. Sole, University of Phoenix; Esther A. Stinnett, Montana State University, Great Falls; Todd Travaille, Buena Vista University; John Wolff, West Shore Community College. I am also grateful to the reviewers of the last edition: Dan Damerville, Tallahassee Community College; Suzanne Forster, University of Alaska—Anchorage; Lynn Goya, Leeward Community College; Paula Guetschow, University of Alaska—Anchorage; Judith Hinman, College of the Redwoods; Edward Klein, University of Notre Dame.

For examples, advice, and support, I thank colleagues and friends at the University of Massachusetts–Dartmouth, especially Tish Dace, Barbara Jacobskind, Louise Habicht, and Richard Larschan. As always, Raymond Dumont helped in countless ways.

A special thanks to my students who allowed me to reproduce versions of their work: Al Andrade for "The Old Guy," Joe Bolton on toys of violence, Mike Creeden on physical fitness, Wendy Gianacoples for "Confessions of a Food Addict," Liz Gonzales on rap music, Shirley Haley for "Life in Full Colour," Cheryl Hebert on single-sex schools and standardized testing, Pam Hebert on summer beaches, Jeff Leonard for "Walk but Don't Run," John Manning for "Is Online Education Taking Us Anywhere?" Maureen Malloy for "Cars R Us," Cathie Nichols for "A First-Week Survival Guide for Commuters," and the rest of the student writers named in the text.

I thank my publisher for excellent editorial support. Lynn Huddon's and thoughtful suggestions inspired most of the improvements in this edition. Dave Munger's invaluable help at every stage has essentially redefined my notion of "developmental editor." I continue to enjoy the extreme good fortune of Janet Nuciforo's expertise in project management.

For Chega, Daniel, Sarah, and Patrick—without whom not.

JOHN M. LANNON

ACKNOWLEDGMENTS FOR THE CANADIAN EDITION

Thanks to Canadian reviewers Mary Keating, University College of Cape Breton; Pam Stimpson, University of Alberta; Julia Denholm, Langara College; Jean Clifford, Capilano College; and Kent Walker, Humber College.

At Lakehead University, a special thanks to my students who allowed me to reproduce versions of their work: Skye Lantinga for "Spring Bear Hunt," John K. Anthony for "Being a Mature Student," Brian Yantha for commentary on Muskoka, and Terry-Lynn Fero and Mike Dahlquist for their research essays. As well, a special thanks to Anne McCourt for "The Heart of My Neighbourhood" and to Kim Fedderson for "'Scutwork': The Marginalization of Writing within Canadian Universities."

At Pearson Education Canada, I thank especially Marta Tomins, Developmental Editor, and also Marianne Minaker, Acquisitions Editor, who were with me throughout; Cheryl Jackson, Production Editor; and Paula Druzga, Assistant Editor, all who provided that guidance so important to creating an effective student-centred text.

DAVID PARSONS

SECTION ONE

The Process—Decisions in Planning, Drafting, and Revising

Introduction

WRITING AS DECISION MAKING

People who succeed usually are those who make the right decisions—about a career, an investment, a relationship, or anything else. Like any decision making, good writing requires hard work. If we had one recipe for all writing, our labours would be small. We could learn the recipe ("Do this; then do that"), and then apply it to every writing task—from love letters to lab reports. But we write about various subjects for various audiences for various purposes—at home, at school, on the job. For every writing task, we make our own decisions.

Writing has no recipes

Still, most of us face identical problems: in deciding on who our audience is and how to connect with it; in deciding on what goal we want to achieve and on how to make the writing achieve that goal. This book introduces strategies that help us succeed as writers.

Most writers face problems like these

Most writing is a conscious, deliberate *process*—not the result of divine intervention, magic, miracles, or last-minute inspiration. Nothing ever leaps from the mind to the page in one neat and painless motion—not even for creative geniuses. Instead, we plan, draft, and revise. Sometimes we know right away what we want to say; sometimes we discover our purpose and meaning only as we write. But our finished product takes shape through our decisions at different stages in the writing process.

Writing can be hard work for anyone

NOTE *This book shows you how to plan, draft, and revise in a suggested sequence of activities. But just as no two people use an identical sequence of activities to drive, ski, or play tennis, no two people write in the same way. How you decide to use this book depends on your writing task and on what works for you.*

HOW WRITING LOOKS

The neat and ordered writing samples throughout this book show the products of writing—not the process. Every finished writing task begins with messy scribbling, things crossed out, lists, arrows, and fragments of ideas, as in the section from the first draft of this introduction shown in Figure I.1.

Just as the writing process has no one recipe, the finished products have no one shape. In fact, very little writing published in books, magazines, and newspapers looks exactly like the basic college essay discussed in this book's early chapters (an introductory paragraph beginning or ending with a thesis statement; three or more support paragraphs, each beginning with a topic sentence; and a concluding paragraph). But all effective writers use identical skills: they know how to discover something worthwhile to write about, how to organize their material sensibly, and how to express their ideas clearly and gracefully.

Writing appears in many shapes

Academic essays offer a good model for developing these skills because they provide you with a basic structure for shaping your thinking. They also supply an immediate, helpful audience—your instructor and

Why academic essays are important

FIGURE I.1
Part of a typical first draft

Messiness is a natural and often essential part of writing in its early stages

*Wouldn't it be nice if there were a formula for writing:
*"this is the way you do it"? *Any kind of decision-
(USE) + (DEVELOP) making is hard

Introduction

-buy a car
-a house
-getting married
-having children
(CHANGE THESE)

In writing, as in the rest of life, decisions are important

Later you will write all kinds of documents for all kinds of purposes: -letters to the school board

all goals that need a plan →
-job application letters
-love letters
-requests for pay raises
-apologize for mistakes
-memos or reports for clients and colleagues
-poetry, fiction,?
-computer documentation
? (Transitional writing)?

All these are designed to get the reader to do something or at least to like you

Those who succeed generally are those who make good decisions

(NO)

Instead of just letting things happen

(?) So, what ~~does writing~~ do college essays have to do with these varied tasks? "Why am I doing this?" is a
(MAYBE) question asked by ~~many~~ people who find themselves in a composition class. ~~And this question deserves an answer.~~
(If there were I could write this section in a couple of hours,)
There is no one way of "doing it right." (instead of a week)
(USE) But all writers in all situations face certain ~~comm~~ common problems: they need to ~~figure out~~ decide what to say; they need to ~~figure out~~ decide why they're saying it; they need to organize to make their thinking clear; they need to express themselves line of

classmates. Unlike many audiences who read only your final draft and from whom you could not reasonably expect helpful and sympathetic advice, your teacher and classmates can give you valuable feedback as you continue to shape and rework drafts of your writing.

What any reader expects

Like any audience, your classroom readers will expect you finally to give them something worthwhile—some useful information, a new insight on some topic, an unusual perspective, or an entertaining story—in a form easy to follow and pleasing to read.

HOW WRITING MAKES A DIFFERENCE

Surface reasons for writing

Deeper reasons for writing

All through school, we write too often for surface reasons: to show we can grind out a few hundred words on some topic, cook up a thesis, and organize paragraphs; to show we can punctuate, spell, and use grammar; or to pass the course. These surface reasons mask the deeper reasons we write: to explore something important to us, to connect with our readers, to make a difference—as students, as employees, as citizens, or as friends.

Differences writing can make

What kind of difference can any writing make? It might move readers to act or reconsider their biases; it might increase their knowledge or win their support; it might broaden their understanding. Whether you're giving instructions for running an electric toothbrush or pouring out your feelings to a friend, effective writing brings writer and reader together. As you read the essays in this book, you will see how student and professional writers in all kinds of situations manage to make a difference with their readers. These models, along with the advice and assignments, should help your writing make a difference of its own.

DECISIONS IN COLLABORATIVE WRITING

Many of the Applications in this book ask you to collaborate with peers. Especially now that the Internet simplifies collaborative work, countless documents in the workplace are produced collaboratively; effective collaboration enables a group to synthesize the *best* from each member. Collaboration allows us to:

Benefits of collaboration

- Share in new perspectives.
- Test and sharpen ideas.
- Recognize our biases and assumptions.
- Get feedback from group members.
- Enjoy group support instead of working alone.

But like all writing, collaborative work demands decisions. Group members have to find ways of expressing their views persuasively, of accepting constructive criticism, of getting along and reaching agreement with others who hold different views. Collaborators may face these potential problems:

Things that go wrong in collaborative work

- Differences in personality, working style, commitment, standards, or ability to take criticism.
- Disagreements about exactly what or how much the group should accomplish, who should do what, or who should make the final decisions.
- Feelings of intimidation or reluctance to speak out.

Guidelines in the following chapters will help make collaborative projects useful for you.

DECISIONS ABOUT WRITING WITH COMPUTERS

Like collaborative writing, computers can provide tremendous advantages if you understand their limitations. Here are some of the decisions you will be making about computers as you progress through this book:

1. *How should I use computers to write my papers?* Working directly on the computer screen reduces the drudgery of writing and revising. You can brainstorm, develop different outlines, and design countless versions of a document without retyping the entire piece. You can also insert, delete, or move blocks of text; search the document to change a word or phrase; or have your document examined automatically for correct spelling, accurate word choice, and readable style. You then can file your finished document electronically, for easy retrieval.

2. *How should I use computers to enhance my research?* Instead of thumbing through newspapers, journals, reference books, or printed card catalogues, you can do much of your research at the computer terminal. See Chapter 19 for detailed descriptions of computerized research and reference tools (card catalogues, online databases, Internet resources, and so on).

3. *How should I use computers for collaborative projects?* Computers facilitate collaborate writing. For instance, group members might review, edit, or proofread your writing directly from a disk you have provided. The latest software even enables readers to comment on your writing without altering the text itself. Finally, using electronic mail, you can transmit copies of your writing to classmates and they can respond.

But your decisions about these issues should take the following cautions into account:

Limitations of writing with a computer

- Messages still need to be *written*. The task of sorting, organizing, and interpreting information still belongs to the writer.
- No computerized device can convert bad writing to good. Moreover, the ease of "fixing" our writing on a computer might encourage minimal revision. (Sometimes the very act of rewriting an entire page in longhand or type causes us to rethink that whole page or discover something new.)
- A computer is not a substitute brain. Shabby thinking produces shabby writing.

The following chapters will help you make thoughtful decisions about the part computers can play in your work.

APPLICATION **A**

Identify a situation in which your writing (or someone else's) has made a difference. Be prepared to describe the situation in class.

APPLICATION **B**

Locate a piece of nonfiction writing that you think "makes a difference." Bring a copy to class and be prepared to explain why this particular piece qualifies.

CHAPTER 1

Decisions in
the Writing Process

uring the writing process you transform the material you discover—by inspiration, research, accident, or other means—into a message that makes a difference for readers. In short, writing is a process of making deliberate decisions.

For example, consider a Dear John or Jane letter, an essay exam, a job application, a letter to a newspaper, a note to a sick friend, or your written testimony as a witness to a crime. In each of these writing situations, you write because you feel strongly enough to have a definite *viewpoint* and to respond or speak out.

But merely expressing a viewpoint doesn't tell readers very much. To understand your ideas, readers need *explanations* that have been shaped so that readers can follow them. In any useful writing, whether in the form of a book, a news article, a memo, a report, or an essay, writers decide on a sensible line of thinking, often in a shape like this:

Much of your writing will have this basic shape.

> ### INTRODUCTION
> The introduction attracts attention, announces the viewpoint, and previews what will follow. All good introductions invite readers in.
>
> ### BODY
> The body explains and supports the viewpoint, achieving *unity* by remaining focused on the viewpoint. It achieves *coherence* by carrying a line of thinking from sentence to sentence in logical order. Bodies come in all different sizes, depending on how much readers need and expect.
>
> ### CONCLUSION
> The conclusion sums up the meaning of the piece, or points toward other meanings to be explored. Good conclusions give readers a clear perspective on what they have just read.

Writers also make decisions about whom they're writing to (their *audience*) and what they want to sound like: whether they want to sound formal, friendly, angry, or amused.

DECISION MAKING AND THE WRITING PROCESS

Composing words on paper or your computer screen is only one small part of the writing process. Your real challenge lies in making decisions like those in Figure 1.1:

FIGURE 1.1
Typical decisions during the writing process

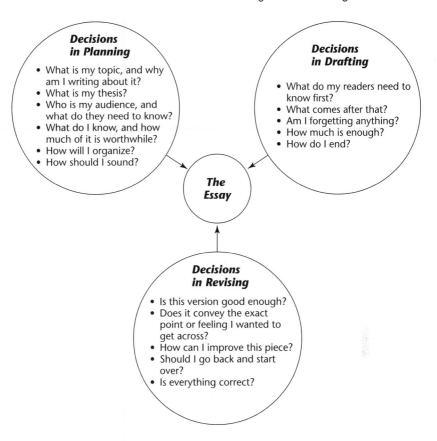

Decisions in Planning
- What is my topic, and why am I writing about it?
- What is my thesis?
- Who is my audience, and what do they need to know?
- What do I know, and how much of it is worthwhile?
- How will I organize?
- How should I sound?

Decisions in Drafting
- What do my readers need to know first?
- What comes after that?
- Am I forgetting anything?
- How much is enough?
- How do I end?

The Essay

Decisions in Revising
- Is this version good enough?
- Does it convey the exact point or feeling I wanted to get across?
- How can I improve this piece?
- Should I go back and start over?
- Is everything correct?

CASE STUDY

ONE WRITER'S DECISION-MAKING PROCESS

To appreciate writing as a deliberate process, let's follow one student through two approaches to the same writing situation. We'll see how decisions about planning, drafting, and revising like those shown in Figure 1.1 distinguish this writer's quickest effort from her best effort.

Shirley Haley has been assigned an essay on this topic: How do you want your life to be different from (or similar to) that of your parents? Haley's twofold goal is to explore her feelings about this topic and to share that exploration with us. Her first response, a random piece of freewriting, took about 30 minutes:

Haley's freewriting

When my mother was my age, life was simple. Women really didn't have to study in university. They came primarily to find a husband, and they majored in liberal arts or teaching. They knew they were going to be wives and mothers. My mother says she got an education so she would have "something to fall back on" in case something ever happened to my father—which was a good thing, I suppose. Maybe it was her attitude about "family first, me second" that made our home life so stable.

I appreciate the fact that my parents have given me a stable home life, and I want parts of my life to turn out like theirs. But my parents are slaves to their house; they never go anywhere or do anything with their spare time. They just work on the house and yard. They never seem to do anything they want to do—only what other people expect of them. I wish my parents would allow themselves to enjoy life, have more adventure. They go to the same place every year for their vacation. They've never even seen a country outside Canada.

I'll have a family some day, and I'll have responsibilities, but I never want to have a boring life. When I'm on my own, I want my life to be full of surprises. And even though I want to provide a stable home life for my children and husband someday, I hope I never forget my responsibility to myself as well.

Discussion of Haley's freewriting

Freewriting is a valuable invention tool—but only a first step. Haley's draft has potential, but she hints at lots of things in general and points at nothing in particular. Without a thesis to assert a controlling viewpoint, neither writer nor reader ever finds an orientation. Lacking a definite thesis, Haley never decided which material didn't belong, which was the most important, and which deserved careful development.

At first, the essay seems to be about a change in women's roles, but the end of the first paragraph and the beginning of the second suggest that Haley's topic has shifted to ways in which she wants her life to resemble her parents'. But the second, third, and fourth paragraphs discuss what Haley dislikes about her parents' lives. The final sentence adds confusion by looking back to a now-defunct topic in the first paragraph: stable family life. The lack of an introduction and conclusion deprives us of a way of narrowing the possible meanings of the piece and of finding a clear perspective on what we have just read. The paragraphs also either lack development or fail to focus on one specific point. And some sentences (like the last two in paragraph 1) lack logical connections. Finally, we get almost no sense of a real person speaking to real people. Haley has written only for herself—as if she were writing a journal or diary.

A quick effort (as in a journal or diary) offers a good way to get started. But when writers go no further, they bypass the essential stages of *planning* and *revising*. In fact, putting something on the page or screen is relatively easy. But in order to get the piece to *succeed*, to make a difference for readers, tougher decisions need to be made.

Now let's follow Haley's thinking as she struggles through her planning decisions.

*Haley's planning
decisions*

What exactly is my topic, and why am I writing about it? *My intended
topic was "How I Want My Life to Be Different from That of My Parents,"
but my first draft got off track. I need to focus on the specific differences!*

*I'm writing this essay to discover my own feelings and to help readers
understand these feelings by showing them specific parts of my parents'
lifestyle that I hope will be different for me.*

What is my thesis? *After countless tries, I think I've finally settled on my
thesis: "As I look at my parents' life, I hope my own will be less ordinary,
less duty-bound, and less predictable."*

Who is my audience, and what do they need to know? *My audience
consists of my teacher and classmates. (This essay will be discussed in
class.) Each reader already is familiar with this topic; everyone, after all, is
someone's son or daughter! But I want my audience to understand specifically the differences I envision.*

What do I know about this topic? *A better question might be, "What
don't I know?" I've spent my life with this topic, and so I certainly don't
have to do any research.*

**Of all the material I've discovered on this topic, how much of it is
worthwhile (considering my purpose and audience)?** *Because I could
write volumes here, I'll have to resist getting carried away. I've already
decided to focus on the feeling that my parents' lives are too ordinary,
duty-bound, and predictable. One paragraph explaining each of these supporting points (and illustrating them with well-chosen examples) should
do. How will I organize? I guess I've already made this decision by settling
on my thesis: moving from "ordinary" to "duty-bound" to "predictable."
Predictability is what I want to emphasize, and so I will save it for last.*

How do I want my writing to sound? *I'm sharing something intimate
with my classmates, so my tone should be relaxed and personal, as when
people talk to people they trust.*

In completing her essay, Haley went on to make similar decisions for drafting and revising. Here is her final draft.

*Haley's final draft
Introductory para-
graph (leads into
the thesis)*

LIFE IN FULL COLOUR

I'm probably the only person I know who still has the same two
parents she was born with. We have a traditional Canadian family: we go
to church and hockey games; we watch the Olympics on television and
argue about politics; and we have Thanksgiving dinner at my grandmother
Clancy's and Christmas dinner with my father's sister Jess, who used to let
us kids put pitted olives on our fingertips when we were little. Most of my
friends are struggling with the problems of broken homes; I'll always be

Thesis statement

grateful to my parents for giving me a loving and stable background. *But sometimes I look at my parents' life and hope my life will be less ordinary, less duty-bound, and less predictable.*

Topic sentence and first support paragraph

I want my life to be imaginative, not ordinary. Instead of honeymooning at Niagara Falls, I want to go to Paris. In my parents' neighbourhood, all the houses were built alike about twenty years ago. Different owners have added on or shingled or painted, but the houses basically all look the same. The first thing we did when we moved into our house was plant trees; everyone did. Now the neighbourhood is full of family homes on tree-lined streets, which is nice; but I'd prefer a condo in a renovated brick building in Winnipeg. I'd have dozens of plants, and I'd buy great furniture one piece at a time at auctions and dusty shops and not by the roomful from the local furniture store. Instead of spending my time trying to be similar to everyone else, I'd like to explore ways of being different.

Topic sentence and second support paragraph

My parents have so many obligations, they barely have time for themselves; I don't want to live like that. I'm never quite sure whether they own the house or the house owns them. They worry constantly about taxes, or the old furnace, or the new deck, or mowing the lawn, or weeding the garden. After spending every weekend slaving over their beautiful yard, they have no time left to enjoy it. And when they're not buried in household chores, other people are making endless demands on their time. My mother will stay up past midnight because she promised some telephone voice 3 cakes for the church bazaar, or 5 dozen cookies for the Girl Guide meeting, or 76 little sandwiches for the women's club Christmas party. My father coaches soccer, wears a clown suit for the Lions' flea markets, and both he and my mother are volunteer firefighters. In fact, both my parents get talked into volunteering for everything. I hate to sound selfish, but my first duty is to myself. I'd rather live in a tent than be owned by my house. And I don't want my life to end up being measured out in endless chores.

Topic statement and third support paragraph

Although it's nice to take things such as regular meals and paycheques for granted, many other events in my parents' life are too predictable for me. Every Sunday at five o'clock we dine on overdone roast beef, mashed potatoes and gravy, a faded green vegetable, and sometimes that mushy orange squash that comes frozen in bricks. It's not that either of my parents is a bad cook, but Sunday dinner isn't food anymore; it's a habit. Mom and Dad have become so predictable that they can order each other's food in restaurants. Just once I'd like to see them pack up and go away for a weekend, without telling anybody; they couldn't do it. They can't even go crazy and try a new place for their summer vacation. They've been spending the first two weeks in August at Falcon Lake since I was two years old. I want variety in my life. I want to travel, see this country and see Europe, do things spontaneously. No one will ever be able to predict my order in a restaurant.

Concluding paragraph

Before long, Christmas will be here, and we'll be going to Aunt Jess's. Mom will bake an apple pie, and Grandpa Frank will say, "Michelle, you sure know how to spoil an old man." It's nice to know that some things never change. In fact, some of the ordinary, obligatory, predictable things in life are the most comfortable. But too much of any routine can make life seem dull and grey. I hope my choices lead to a life in full colour.

—*Shirley Haley*

Here are some of Haley's major improvements:

Discussion of Haley's final draft

- The distinct shape (introduction, body, conclusion) enables us to organize our understanding and follow the writer's thinking.
- The essay no longer confuses us. We know where Haley stands because she tells us, with a definite thesis; and we know why because she shows us, with plenty of examples.
- She wastes nothing; everything seems to belong and everything fits together.
- Now each paragraph has its own design, and each paragraph enhances the whole.
- We now see real variety in the ways in which sentences begin and words are put together. We hear a genuine voice.

All good writing has these qualities

Because she made careful decisions, Haley produced a final draft that displays the qualities of all good writing: *content* that makes it worth reading; *organization* that reveals the line of thinking and emphasizes what is most important; and *style* that is economical and convincingly human.

Writers rarely struggle with these decisions about planning, drafting, and revising in a predictable sequence. Instead, writers choose sequences that work best for them. Figure 1.2 diagrams this looping ("recursive") structure of the writing process.

NOTE   *Rarely is any piece of writing ever strictly "finished." Even famous writers have returned to a successful published work years later in order to revise it once again.*

APPLICATION 1-1

The essay that follows (a third draft) was written in response to this assignment:

Identify a personal trait that is so strong you cannot control it (a quick temper, the need for acceptance, a fear of failure, shyness, a bad habit, a phobia, an obsession, or the like). In a serious or humorous essay, show how this trait affects your behaviour. Provide enough details for readers to understand clearly this part of your personality.

FIGURE 1.2
The looping struc-
ture of the writing
process

Decisions in the
writing process are
recursive; no one
stage is complete
until all stages are
complete.

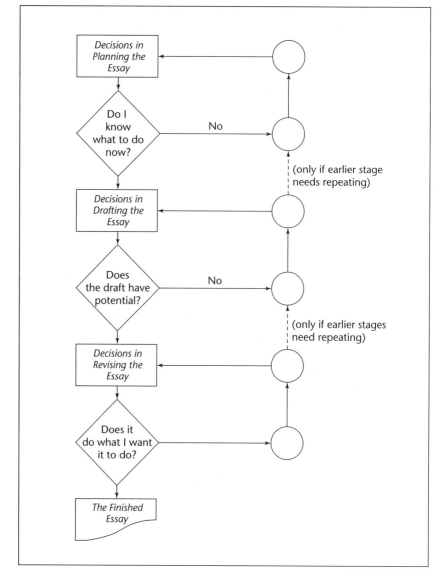

(only if earlier stage
needs repeating)

(only if earlier stages
need repeating)

A writer might
even revisit the
"finished" essay for
additional revision.

Our writer, Wendy Gianacoples, decided to explore a personal obsession:
food.

Read Wendy's essay once or twice. Then read it again, using the questions that follow the essay for your analysis.

Essay for analysis

CONFESSIONS OF A FOOD ADDICT

Like many compulsive eaters, I eat to fill a void—an emptiness within.
I feed my feelings. Food can be my best friend, always there when I need
it. This friend, however, actually is a tyrant that dominates my life through
endless cycles of need, indulgence, and guilt.

Thanks to my food obsession, I seem to have two personalities: the respected, self-controlled Wendy who eats properly all day, and the fat Wendy who emerges after dark to gobble everything in sight. Lying in bed, I wait for the house to be silent. Feeling excited and giddy, I sneak to the kitchen and head straight for the freezer to begin my search. My initial prize is an unopened pint of Häagen-Dasz chocolate chip ice cream. I break the container's seal, dig in with my spoon, and shovel down massive gobs. (I have a love/hate relationship with food: I want all or nothing.) Next thing I know the container is empty.

Stashing the empty container deeply in the trash, I continue my rampage. From the cookie drawer, I snatch a nearly full package of Fig Newtons. As I tiptoe toward the milk, I ask myself what the folks at Weight Watchers would say if they could see me standing half-awake in my ice cream splattered Lanz nightgown, popping down Fig Newtons and swigging milk from the carton. After pushing the few remaining cookies to the front of the package so it looks fuller, I rummage around for my next "fix."

Beneath a bag of frozen Green Giant vegetables, I find a frozen pizza—the ultimate midnight snack. The oven will take too long but the microwave is too noisy—all that beeping could get me busted. Feeling daring, I turn on the kitchen faucet to drown out the beeps, place the pizza in the microwave, set the timer, grab the last handful of Fig Newtons, and wait.

By the time I polish off the pizza, it's 1:00 a.m. and I crave Kraft Macaroni and Cheese. Standing on a chair I reach for a box from the overhead cabinet. Trying to be quiet, I dig out a spaghetti pot from a pile of pots and pans. Grabbing the handle, I hold my breath as I pull the pan from the clutter. While the water boils and the macaroni cooks, I fix a bowl of Rice Krispies. Just as I finish chowing down "Snap, Crackle, and Pop," the macaroni is ready. After eating the whole package, I bury the box in the trash.

After a binge, I panic: "What have I done?" Setting a hand on my bulging stomach, I think of the weight I'll gain this week. Climbing the stairs to my bed, I feel drained, like a person on drugs who is now "coming down." In my bedroom, I study myself in the full-length mirror, looking for visible signs of my sins. Lying in bed, I feel fat and uncomfortable. Although I usually sleep on my stomach, on "binge" nights, I assume the fetal position, cradling my full belly, feeling ashamed and alone, as if I were the only person who overeats and uses food as a crutch. When the sugar I've consumed keeps me awake, I plead with God to help me overcome this weakness.

The next morning I kick myself and feel guilty. I want to block out last night's memories, but my tight clothes offer a painful reminder. My stomach is sick all day and I have heartburn. During the following week, I'll eat next to nothing and exercise constantly, hoping to break even on the scale at Weight Watchers.

Most people don't consider compulsive eating an addiction. Substance abusers can be easy to spot, but food addicts are less obvious. Unlike drugs, one can't live without food. People would never encourage a drug addict or alcoholic to "have another hit" or "fall off the wagon." However, people constantly push food on overeaters: "Come on, one brownie won't hurt. I made them especially for you," says a friend. When I decline, she scowls and turns away. Little does she know, while she was in the bathroom, I had four.

—Wendy Gianacoples

Questions about the writing

Does the Content of the Essay Make It Worth Reading?

- Can you find a definite thesis that announces the writer's viewpoint?
- Do you have enough information to understand the viewpoint?
- Do you learn something new and useful?
- Does everything belong, or should any material be cut?

Does the Organization Reveal the Writer's Line of Thinking?

- Is there an introduction to set the scene, a middle to walk us through, and a conclusion to sum up the meaning?
- Does each support paragraph present a distinct unit of meaning?
- Does each paragraph stick to the point and stick together?

Is the Style Economical and Convincing?

- Can you understand each sentence the first time you read it?
- Should any words be cut?
- Are sentences varied in the way they're put together?
- Is the writer's meaning always clear?
- Can you hear a real person speaking?
- Do you like the person you hear?

Write out your answers to these questions and be prepared to discuss them in class.

APPLICATION 1-2

Collaborative Project: In class, write your "quickest effort" essay about a personal trait, or about this subject: "Important Differences or Similarities Between My Life and That of My Parents." Exchange papers with a classmate, and evaluate your classmate's paper, using the questions from Application 1-1. In one or two paragraphs, give your classmate advice for revising. Don't be afraid to mark up (with your own questions, comments, and suggestions) this paper you're evaluating. Discuss with your classmate your evaluation of his or her work. At home, read the evaluation of your paper carefully, and write your "best" version of your original essay. List the improvements you made in moving from your quickest effort to your best effort. Be prepared to discuss your improvements in class.

Also, in two or three paragraphs, trace your own writing process for this essay by describing the decisions you made. Be prepared to discuss your decisions in class.

Note: Don't expect miracles at this stage, but do expect some degree of frustration and confusion. Things will improve quickly, though.

APPLICATION **1-3**

Collaborative Project: Out of class (drawing on your personal experience with group work if possible), write down one thing you look forward to in working with peers, and one potential problem you find especially important. In class, share your expectations and concerns with a small group. Do group members raise similar issues, or does everyone have different concerns? As a group, craft these issues and concerns into a list of group goals: benefits you hope to achieve and pitfalls you hope to avoid.

APPLICATION **1-4**

Computer Application: Familiarize yourself with your school's computer labs. What are their hours? Learn to use your school's e-mail system. Make sure your account is active.

OPTIONS FOR ESSAY WRITING

The following topics offer ideas for essays to get you started. People write best about things they know, and so we begin with personal forms of writing. You might want to return to this list for topic ideas when essays are assigned throughout the early chapters of this book.

1. What major effects has television had on your life (your ambitions, hopes, fears, values, consumer habits, awareness of the world, beliefs, outlook, faith in people, and so on)? Overall, has television been a positive or negative influence? Have you learned anything from TV that you couldn't have learned elsewhere? Support your thesis with specific details.

2. How do advertising and commercials shape our values (notions about looking young, being athletic, being thin, smoking, beer drinking, and so on)? Does advertising present an unrealistic view of life? In what ways? What kinds of human weaknesses and aspirations do

commercials exploit? Support your viewpoint with examples your readers will recognize.

3. If you could repeat your high school years, what three or four things would you do differently? Write for a younger brother or sister entering high school, and provide enough detail to get your viewpoint across.

4. Do some music videos communicate distorted and dangerous messages? If so, what should be done? Discuss specific examples and their effect on viewers.

5. Canadians are often criticized for their lack of identity and lack of patriotism. Is this criticism valid? Do Canadians, and do you as a Canadian, have a distinct Canadian identity and demonstrate patriotism?

6. Our public schools have been accused of failing to educate Canada's students. Does your high school typify the so-called failure of Canadian education? Why or why not? How well did your school prepare you for college or university—and for life?

7. University students commonly are stereotyped as party animals. Explain to a skeptical nonstudent audience that university life is harder than people imagine—but don't sermonize or complain. For instance, if you attend a university, you might write members of parliament who want to cut the budget.

8. Write about a job you've had and explain what you liked and disliked about the job. Show readers exactly what the job was like. Would you recommend this job to a friend? Why or why not?

9. Describe the good and bad points of being a "nontraditional" student (returning to school after employment, raising a family, or the like). Write for readers in a similar situation who are thinking about returning to school. What are the most important things they should know?

10. Explain to a skeptical audience the benefits of an alternative lifestyle choice you or someone you know has made (vegetarianism, co-housing, nontraditional family, male homemaker, back-to-nature, or the like). Dispel the negative stereotypes.

11. As a part-time student who balances work and school, give advice to a friend in your situation who wants to follow your example but feels fearful or discouraged. Explain how you manage to cope.

CHAPTER 2

Decisions in Planning

Writing is a battle with impatience, a fight against the natural urge to "be done with it." Effective writers win this battle by *planning*: analyzing their writing situation, exploring their assets, and finding a voice. Of course, planning continues throughout the writing process, but an initial plan gives you a place to start and a direction for your decisions.

DECIDING ON A TOPIC, PURPOSE, THESIS, AND AUDIENCE

Your earliest planning decisions will require that you analyze your writing situation:

Questions for Analyzing a Writing Situation

- *What, exactly, is my topic?*
- *Why am I writing about it?*
- *What is my viewpoint?*
- *Who is my audience?*

Of course, you won't always follow a single order in making these decisions; in Chapter 1, Shirley Haley discovers her thesis before brainstorming for material. The key is to make all the decisions—in whichever order works best for you.

As with any stage in the writing process, you might have to return again and again to your plan.

Decide on Your Topic

In most out-of-school writing ("Why I deserve a promotion"; "Why you should marry me"; "How we repaired the computer"), topics are decided for you by the situation. But when you are asked to choose your own topic, remember one word: *focus*.

"What, exactly is
my topic?"

Sometimes, afraid we'll have too little to say, we mistakenly choose the broadest topic. But a focused topic actually provides more to write about by allowing for the nitty-gritty details that show readers what we mean.

For instance, if you wanted to know the "personality" of a particular town, walking around and talking with the people would show a lot more than flying over the place at 10 000 feet. A *focused topic*, then, is something you know and really can talk about, something that has real meaning for you.

Decide on Your Purpose

"Why am I
writing?"

Finding a *purpose* means asking yourself, "Why am I writing this piece?" Each writing situation has a specific goal. Perhaps you want audience members to see what you saw, to feel what you felt, or to think differently. To achieve your goal, you will need a definite *strategy*.

Goal plus strategy equals purpose. Consider one writer's inadequate answers to the familiar questions, "Why am I writing this paper?"

Inadequate
Statements of
Purpose

(a) I'm writing this essay to pass the course.

(b) My goal is to write an essay about student life.

(c) My goal is to describe to classmates the experience of being a non-traditional student.

Responses **a** and **b** above tell nothing about the specific goal. Response **c** defines the goal, but offers no strategy. Here, finally, is our writer's purpose statement (goal plus strategy):

A Useful Statement
of Purpose

My purpose is to describe to classmates the experience of being a nontraditional student. I'll focus on the special anxieties, difficulties, and rewards.

Sometimes you will be unable to define your purpose immediately. You might need to jot down as many purposes as possible until one pops up. Or you might need to write a rough draft first or make an outline. In any case, the purpose statement should provide the raw material for your thesis.

NOTE *While the purpose statement is part of the discovery process, the thesis is part of the finished essay. (See pages 52–53.)*

Decide on Your Thesis

"What is my
viewpoint?"

In your purpose statement, you identify exactly what you want to *do*. In your thesis, you announce exactly what you want to *say*. Your thesis statement makes a definite commitment. It tells readers what to expect by making your viewpoint absolutely clear. Here are some different ways of expressing your viewpoint:

As an opinion	Starting university after age 30 hasn't been easy, but the good points definitely outweigh the bad.
As an observation	My high school education was mostly a waste of time.
As a suggestion	Computer literacy should be required for all applicants.
As an attitude	I want my life to be better than that of my parents.
As a question	Should university be for everyone?

Each of these thesis statements creates a clear expectation. They don't keep readers guessing. They make their points fast.

NOTE *Think of your thesis as the one sentence you would keep if you could keep only one.*

Thesis as Framework. Consciously or unconsciously, readers look for a thesis, usually in the essay's early paragraphs. Even a single paragraph is hard to understand if the main point is missing. Read this paragraph once only—and then try answering the questions that follow.

A paragraph with its main point omitted

> His [or her] job is not to punish, but to heal. Most students are bad writers, but the more serious the injuries, the more confusing the symptoms, the greater the need for effective diagnostic work. When an accident victim is carried into the hospital emergency ward, the doctor does not start treating the patient at the top and slowly work down without a sense of priority, spending a great deal of time on the black eye before [getting] to the punctured lung. Yet that is exactly what the English teacher too often does. The doctor looks for the most vital problem; he [or she] wants to keep the patient alive, and . . . goes to work on the critical injury.
>
> —Donald Murray

Can you identify the paragraph's main idea? Probably not. Without the topic sentence, you have no framework for understanding this information in its larger meaning.

Now, insert the following sentence at the beginning and reread the paragraph.

The missing main idea

> The writing teacher must not be a judge, but a physician.

This orientation makes the message's exact meaning obvious.

In the basic essay framework, each body paragraph supports its own *topic statement,* which focuses on one aspect of the thesis. The thesis is the controlling idea; each topic statement treats one part of the controlling idea, as diagrammed here:

Introductory paragraph

Support paragraphs

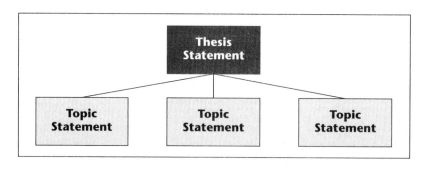

Some writers include in the thesis a preview of supporting points; some don't. For instance, an essay titled "Beef Cost and the Cattle Rancher" might have this thesis statement:

A thesis that includes a preview

> Because of rising costs, unpredictable weather, and long hours, many cattle ranchers have trouble staying in business.

Including a preview in their thesis helps some writers stay on track as they develop each support paragraph. With or without the preview, be sure that supporting points appear as topic statements in subsequent paragraphs, as in this next example:

Introductory
paragraph

_____

Thesis

_____ Starting university after age 30 hasn't been easy, but the good points definitely outweigh the bad.

Although the above thesis does not preview the main supporting points, each point is spelled out in respective topic statements:

First support para-
graph

My major obstacles were lack of self-confidence and fear of failure. [_topic statement_] _____

_____

Second support
paragraph

While struggling to overcome my panic, I worked at developing good study habits and sharpening my basic skills. [_topic statement_] _____

_____

Third support
paragraph

After realizing I could do the work, I began to relax and savour the "joy of learning." [_topic statement_] _____

_____

Evaluating Your Thesis. The first thing readers want to know is this:

What readers ask
about your thesis

What, exactly, is your point, and why is it worth reading about?

Always check to see that your thesis provides a sharp focus and a definite and significant viewpoint.

A. _Is the Topic Sharply Focused?_ In a short essay, avoid broad topics such as this one:

Too broad Some experiences can be unforgettable.

B. _Is a Definite and Informative Viewpoint Expressed?_ Preview your exact meaning. These next thesis statements offer no such preview:

No clear I will discuss my experience as a nontraditional student.
viewpoint I started university at age 35.
University can be a complex experience.

C. _Is the Viewpoint Significant?_ Whether your thesis is expressed as an opinion, attitude, observation, suggestion, or question, it should trigger some fresh insight or have some value or importance for readers. A thesis that contributes nothing new is worthless:

| **Insignificant viewpoints** | The university years can be traumatic. *[Everyone would agree, and so why discuss it?]* |
| | Every nontraditional student has a unique university experience. *[No big surprise here!]* |

Variations in Your Thesis. The thesis statement can appear in different forms and different locations:

How thesis form and location can vary

- The main supporting points are not always previewed.
- A thesis does not automatically call for only three supporting points. Three is a good minimum, but some topics call for more, others for less.
- The thesis usually is the final sentence in the introduction. In this position it "bridges" the introduction and the body. But for some purposes it can appear elsewhere in the introduction (as on page 46).
- The thesis need not be limited to one sentence.

How you phrase the thesis and where you place it depends on your purpose and audience.

When to Compose Your Thesis. In an ideal world, writers would be able to (1) settle on a topic, (2) compose a purpose statement, and (3) compose a thesis. But these steps rarely occur in such neat order. If you have trouble coming up with a thesis right away, go on to some other activity: list some ideas, work on an outline, do some freewriting, or take a walk. Writing, after all, is a way of discovering what you want to say.

Even if you do begin with a workable thesis, it might not be the one you end up with. As you work and discover new meanings, you might need to revise or start again.

Decide on Your Audience

"Who is my audience and what do they expect?"

Audiences you might encounter

Except for a diary or a journal, everything you write is for readers who will react to your information. You might write to a prospective employer who wants to know why you quit a recent job; or to a committee who wants to know why you deserve a scholarship; or to a classmate who wants to know you better; or to a professor who wants to know whether you understand the material. For any audience, your task is to deliver a message that makes a difference with readers, that helps them see things your way.

Out of school you will write for diverse audiences (customers, employers, politicians, and so on). But in school, you can envision a definite audience besides your instructor: your classmates. Like any audience, they expect your writing to be clear, informative, and persuasive. Whoever

What audiences expect

your readers are, they need enough material to understand your position and to react appropriately. Readers don't need repetition of material they already know. To put readers in your place, first put yourself in theirs. Anticipate their most probable questions.

Anticipating your readers' questions gives you a better chance of discovering and selecting material that really makes a difference—that offers readers what they need and expect.

CASE STUDY

ANALYZING YOUR WRITING SITUATION

Assume you are writing in response to this assignment:

> Illustrate some feature of our societal values or behaviour that you find humorous, depressing, contemptible, or admirable. Possible topics: our consumer or dress habits, the cars we drive, our ideas of entertainment, and so on.

First, you focus your topic:

Focusing your topic

societal values or behaviour
↓
the cars we drive
↓
our love affair with cars
↓
why we love our cars

This last topic seems focused enough for a short essay. But what in this topic do you wish to explore? What do you want readers to see and understand?

Your focused topic

How cars appeal to our sense of individualism

Now that you have a suitable topic, you're on your way. You might get stuck later and have to discard the whole thing, but for now you can decide on your purpose.

Because the essay examines "How," you organize a rough outline to lay out a sequence of examples:

Your rough outline

a. The car as individual statement
b. The car as political statement
c. The car as personal sanctuary

Now you can compose your statement of purpose:

Your purpose statement	My purpose is to poke fun at our obsession with cars by explaining to classmates how cars appeal to our sense of individuality. I'll discuss uses of the car as lifestyle statement, personal billboard, and private sanctuary.

This is your map for reaching your goal. (Keep in mind that the purpose statement is part of the discovery process, but the thesis is part of the finished essay.)

Based on the above purpose statement, assume you derive the following thesis:

Your thesis	Today's self-centred consumers demand cars that satisfy a craving for individuality.

As you consider your audience here (teacher and classmates), you anticipate the following general questions about your thesis:

General questions you can anticipate
- *Exactly what do you mean by "individualism"?*
- *What is the connection between cars and individualism?*
- *Can you give examples?*
- *Who cares?*

As this case continues, after the following section, you will identify more specific audience questions you need to answer.

DISCOVERING, SELECTING, AND ORGANIZING YOUR MATERIAL

Once you have analyzed your writing situation, you set out to answer these questions:

Questions for Exploring Your Assets

- *What do I know about the topic?*
- *How much of my material is useful in this situation?*
- *How will readers want this organized?*

Discover Useful Material

"What do I know about the topic?"

Discovering useful material is called *invention*. When you begin working with an idea or exploring a topic, you search for useful material, for content: insight, facts, statistics, opinions, examples, images that might help answer this question: *How can I find something worthwhile to say—something that will advance my meaning?*

Some people use invention as an early writing step, a way of getting started. Others save the invention stage until they've made other decisions. Regardless of the sequence, all writers use invention throughout the writing process.

The goal of invention is to get as much material as possible on paper, through the use of strategies like the following.

Keeping a Journal. A *journal* is an excellent way to build a personal inventory of ideas and topics. Here you can write for yourself only.

How to make a journal

To start, buy a hardcover notebook with a sewn binding (so that whatever you write becomes a permanent part of your journal). Record your reactions to something you've read or seen; ask questions or describe people, places, things, feelings; explore fantasies, daydreams, nightmares, fears, hopes; write conversations or letters that never will be heard or read; examine the things you hate or love. Write several times a day, once a week, or whenever you get the urge—or put aside some regular time to write. Every so often, go back and look over your entries—you might be surprised by the things you find.

Freewriting. *Freewriting* is a version of the "quickest-effort" approach discussed in Chapter 1. Shirley Haley's first attempt (page 11) is the product of freewriting. As the term suggests, when freewriting, you simply write whatever comes to mind, hoping that the very act of recording your thinking will generate some useful content.

How to freewrite

Try freewriting by exploring what makes you angry or happy or frightened or worried. Write about what surprises you or what you think is unfair or what you would like to see happen. Don't stop writing until you've filled a whole page or two, and don't worry about organization or correctness—just get it down. Although it will never produce a finished essay, freewriting can give you a good start by uncovering all kinds of buried ideas. It can be especially useful for curing "writer's block."

Using Journalists' Questions. To probe the many angles and dimensions of a topic, journalists ask these questions:

Questions Journalists Ask

- *Who was involved?*
- *What happened?*
- *When did it happen?*
- *Where did it happen?*
- *How did it happen?*
- *Why did it happen?*

Unlike freewriting, the journalists' questions offer a built-in organizing strategy—an array of different "perspectives" on your topic.

Asking Yourself Questions. If you can't seem to settle on a definite viewpoint, try answering any of these questions that apply to your topic.

Discovery Questions You Can Ask

- *What is my opinion of X?*
- *Am I for it or against it?*
- *Does it make me happy or sad?*
- *Is it good or bad?*
- *Will it work or fail?*
- *Does it make sense?*
- *What have I observed about X?*

- *What have I seen happen?*
- *What is special or unique about it?*
- *What strikes me about it?*
- *What can I suggest about X?*
- *What would I like to see happen?*
- *What should or should not be done?*

From your answers, you can zero in on the viewpoint that will provide the organizing insight for your essay.

Brainstorming. You can also try brainstorming—a sure bet for coming up with useful material. Here is how brainstorming works:

GUIDELINES FOR BRAINSTORMING

1. Find a quiet spot and bring an alarm clock, a pencil, and plenty of paper.

2. Set the alarm to ring in 30 minutes.

3. Try to protect yourself from interruptions: phones, music, or the like. Sit with your eyes closed for two minutes, thinking about absolutely nothing.

4. Now, concentrate on your writing situation. If you've already spelled out your purpose and your audience's questions, focus on these. Otherwise, repeat this question: *What can I say about my topic, at all?*

5. As ideas begin to flow, record every one. Don't stop to judge relevance or worth, and don't worry about complete sentences (or even correct spelling). Simply get everything on paper. Even the wildest idea might lead to some valuable insight.

6. Keep pushing and sweating until the alarm rings.

7. If the ideas are still flowing, reset the alarm and go on.

8. At the end of this session, you should have a chaotic mixture of junk, irrelevancies, and useful material.

9. Take a break.

10. Now confront your list. Strike out what is useless, and sort the remainder into categories. Include any other ideas that crop up. Your finished list should provide plenty of raw material.

NOTE *Try brainstorming at the computer. Try freewriting with the monitor turned off or covered, then, after 15 minutes, look at the screen and review your list.*

Reading and Researching. Some of our best ideas, insights, and questions often come from our reading (as discussed in Chapter 9). Or we might want to consider what others have said or discovered about our topic (as discussed in Chapter 19), before we reach our own conclusions. Reading and research are indispensable tools for any serious writer.

Select Your Best Material

"How much of my material is useful in this situation?"

Invention invariably produces more material than a writer needs. Select only the material that best advances your meaning (see Chapter 5, Revising the Content).

If you do find yourself trying to include everything you've discovered, you probably need to refocus on your purpose and audience.

Organize for Readers

"How will readers want this organized?"

When material is left in its original, unstructured form, readers waste time trying to understand it. With an outline, you move from a random listing of items as they occurred to you to a deliberate map that will guide readers from point to point.

All readers expect a definite beginning, middle, and ending that provide orientation, discussion, and review. But specific readers want these sections tailored to their expectations. Identify your readers' expectations by (1) anticipating their probable questions about your thesis, and (2) visualizing the sequence in which readers would want these questions answered.

Some writers can organize merely by working from a good thesis statement. Others prefer to begin with some type of outline. And some writers like to write a draft and then an outline to check their line of thinking. You might outline early or later. But you need to move from a random collection of ideas to an organized list that helps readers to follow your material.

NOTE *No single form of outline should be followed slavishly by any writer. The organization of any writing ultimately is determined by its audience's needs and expectations.*

CASE STUDY

EXPLORING AND ARRANGING ASSETS

For your essay on our obsession with cars, assume you've developed the brainstorming list that follows.

Your brainstorming list

1. to get us from point A to point B, junkers would suffice
2. we demand variety in our lives
3. we want cars that make us look cool
4. people seem to love their bumper stickers

5. with bumper stickers we exercise our right to free speech

6. nobody likes driving an old bomber

7. no matter what the sticker price we don't care

8. off-road vehicles are everywhere, but most of them never leave the pavement

9. "creativity is more important than knowledge"—what kind of bumper-sticker logic is that?

10. Henry Ford's Model Ts all looked exactly alike—they were basic transportation, not fashion statements!

11. today's cars are fibreglass and metal gods

12. today's automakers cater to our self-centred fantasies

13. we can run much of our lives without leaving the comfy car

14. the car is the ultimate personal space

15. a great way to escape the daily hassles

16. cars give us the freedom to go where we want when we want

17. we love to do our own thing—what Canada's all about

18. the car's popularity has led to the phenomenon of drive-through windows

19. people in other countries don't mind public transportation, but we seem to hate it

20. what about the bumper stickers that announce "I'm a tough guy" or "I'm an intellectual"?

21. we can even sing aloud in the car without seeming weird

With your raw material collected, you can now move into the selection phase—leaving open the possibility that new material may surface.

As you review your brainstorming list, you decide to cut items 11, 16, and 19.

Your selection of material to omit

- *Item 11 doesn't relate to the theme of individualism*
- *Item 16 is a cliché, and too general to have real meaning in this essay.*
- *Item 19 makes an unsupportable generalization*

(If you end up trying to include *all* your raw material, you probably need to refocus on your purpose and audience. Chapter 5 offers advice for selecting fresh and worthwhile material.)

Next you try to anticipate specific readers' questions about your essay, and you come up with this list of possibilities:

Specific reader questions you anticipate

- *Can you set the scene for us, and give us a context for your thesis?*
- *Why do we identify so strongly with our cars?*

- *Where do bumper stickers fit in?*
- *Why do we often hang out in the car?*
- *What does all this say about us as a culture?*

Your readers' expectations give you a basis for organizing your brainstorming material into categories:

Your general outline

    I. How Our Relationship to Cars Has Evolved

   II. How Cars Help Us Project an Ideal Self

 III. Why We Decorate Our Cars with Stickers

 IV. How Cars Provide a Private Space

  V. How Cars Serve as the Ultimate Mechanism for Achieving Individuality

Within each category, you arrange your brainstorming items, along with any other worthwhile material that occurs to you. Your final outline might resemble this one:

Your final outline

   I. Why do we love our cars so much?
     A. Cars originally were merely basic transportation.
     B. All Model Ts looked alike.
     C. Today's automakers cater to our urge to do our own thing.
     D. Consumers love this kind of attention.
     E. Thesis: Today's self-centred consumers demand cars that satisfy a craving for individualism.

  II. We want cars that make a unique lifestyle statement.
     A. If basic transportation was the issue, an old junker would do.
     B. But we want to project that special image.
     C. Roughly 50 percent of consumers buy some type of off-road vehicle.
     D. Most of these jeeps and SUVs never leave the pavement.
     E. Driving a sports car really makes us feel special.

 III. Stickers serve as our own personal billboard.
     A. They allow us to exercise our right to free speech.
     B. They announce exactly where we stand.
     C. They tell the world that we're animal lovers, intellectuals, tough guys, or whatever.
     D. Volvos often display political or intellectual statements.
     E. CUPE stickers remind me of summer-long strikes.

    IV. Public transportation is torture for individuals like us.

        A. Canada's cars are personal hideaways, places to escape other humans.

        B. Drive-through windows are one popular form of escape.

        C. We can transact business, order meals, and dine without ever leaving the car.

        D. We can sing along with the radio as we eat our Big Mac.

        E. If you try singing on a bus or subway, people look at you funny.

    V. Cars entice us because they provide the ultimate mechanism for achieving individuality.

        A. The cars we drive and the stickers we sport proclaim our prepackaged uniqueness.

        B. We can do what we want without seeming weird.

        C. We can avoid direct human contact.

        D. Our car is who we are.

This outline takes the form of short, kernel sentences that include key ideas for later expansion. Some writers use a less formal outline—a simple list of phrases without numerals or letters. (Use the form that works best for you.)

Later, during various drafts, you will discover more material and probably will delete some original material (as in the final draft, pages 52–53).

FINDING YOUR VOICE

Your planning inventory is nearly complete: you have a topic and a thesis, a clear sense of purpose and audience, a stock of material, and some sort of outline. In fact, if you were writing merely to get your message across, you could begin drafting the essay immediately. Except for diaries or some technical reports, however, we write not only to transmit information, but also to connect with readers.

Why voice matters

Whether your writing connects with readers depends on how it "sounds." The way your writing sounds depends on its *tone*, your personal mark—the voice readers hear between the lines. Readers who like the tone like the writer; they allow contact.

Consciously or unconsciously, readers ask three big questions about the writer:

Readers' questions in sizing up a writer

■ *What type of person is this (somebody businesslike, serious, silly, sincere, phony, boring, bored, intense, stuck-up, meek, confident, friendly, hostile)?*

■ *How is this person treating me (as a friend, acquaintance, stranger, enemy, nobody, superior, subordinate, bozo, somebody with a brain and feelings)?*

■ *What does this person really think about the topic (really involved or merely "going through the motions")?*

How readers answer these questions will depend on your voice.

Why fancy words don't always work

Some inexperienced writers mistakenly think that fancy words make them sound more intelligent and important. And sometimes, of course, only the complex word will convey your exact meaning. Instead of saying "Sexist language contributes to the ongoing existence of stereotypes," you could say more accurately and concisely, "Sexist language perpetuates stereotypes." (One "fancy" word effectively replaces six "simpler" words.) But when you use fancy words only to impress, your writing sounds stuffy and pretentious.

Find a Voice That Connects with Readers

Personal essays ordinarily employ a conversational tone: you write to your audience as if you were speaking to them. Look again at Shirley Haley's opening lines from page 13:

Conversational tone

> I'm probably the only person I know who still has the same two parents she was born with. We have a traditional Canadian family: we go to church and hockey games; we watch the Olympics on television and argue about politics; and we have Thanksgiving dinner at my grandmother Clancy's and Christmas dinner with my father's sister Jess, who used to let us kids put pitted olives on our fingertips when we were little.

Haley's tone is friendly and relaxed—the voice of a writer who seems at home with herself, her subject, and her readers. We are treated to comfortable images of family things. But the long list of "traditional" family activities also hints at the writer's restlessness and lets us share her mixed feelings of attraction and repulsion.

Suppose Haley had decided to sound more "academic":

Academic tone

> Among my friends and acquaintances, I am apparently the only individual with the good fortune to have parents who remain married. Our family activities are grounded in Canadian tradition: we attend church services and hockey games; we watch televised sporting events and engage in political debates; at Thanksgiving, we dine at Grandmother's, and at Christmas, with an aunt who has always been quite tolerant of children's behaviour.

Which is better? To see for yourself which version is more inviting, test each against the three big questions for readers on pages 34–35.

Avoid an Overly Informal Tone

How tone can be too informal

We generally do not write in the same way we would speak to friends at the local burger joint or street corner. Achieving a conversational tone does not mean lapsing into substandard usage, slang, profanity, or excessive colloquialisms. *Substandard usage* ("He ain't got none"; "I seen it today"; "She brang the book") ignores standards of educated expression. *Slang* ("hurling," "phat," "newbie") usually has specific meaning only for members of a particular in-group. *Profanity* ("Pissed off"; "This idea sucks"; "What the hell") not only displays contempt for the audience but often triggers contempt for the person using it. *Colloquialisms* ("O.K.," "a lot," "snooze," "in the bag") are understood more widely than slang, but tend to appear more in speaking than in writing.

How tone can offend

Tone is considered offensive when it violates the reader's expectations: when it seems disrespectful or tasteless, or distant and aloof, or too "chummy," or casual, or otherwise inappropriate for the topic, the reader, and the situation.

When to use an academic tone

A formal or academic tone, in fact, is perfectly appropriate in countless writing situations: a research paper, a job application, a report for the company president, and so on. In a history essay, for example, we would not refer to Pierre Elliott Trudeau and John Diefenbaker as "those dudes, Pete and John." Whenever we begin with freewriting or brainstorming, our tone might be overly informal and is likely to require some adjustment during subsequent drafts.

But while slang is usually inappropriate in school or workplace writing, some situations call for a measure of informality. The occasional colloquial expression helps soften the tone of any writing.

THE WRITER'S PLANNING GUIDE

Decisions and strategies covered in this chapter apply to almost any writing situation. You can make sure your own planning decisions are complete by following the Planning Guide whenever you write. Items in the Planning Guide are reminders of things to be done.

PLANNING GUIDE

Broad subject:

Limited topic:

Purpose statement:

Thesis statement:

Audience:

Probable audience questions:

Brainstorming list (with irrelevant items deleted):

Outline:

Appropriate tone for audience and purpose:

Your instructor might ask you to use the Planning Guide for early assignments and to submit your responses along with your essay. Remember that your decisions for completing the Planning Guide need not follow the strict order of the items listed—so long as you make all the necessary decisions.

This next Planning Guide has been completed to show a typical set of decisions for "Cars R Us."

THE COMPLETED PLANNING GUIDE

Broad topic: Societal values or behaviour

Limited topic: How cars appeal to our sense of individualism

Purpose statement (what you want to do): My purpose is to poke fun at our obsession with cars by explaining to my classmates how cars appeal to our sense of individualism. I'll discuss uses of the car as lifestyle statement, personal billboard, and private sanctuary.

Thesis statement (what you want to say): Today's self-centred consumers demand cars that satisfy our craving for individualism.

Audience: Classmates

Probable audience questions:
  Can you set the scene for us, and give us a context for your thesis?
  Why do we identify so strongly with our cars?
  Where do bumper stickers fit in?
  Why do we often hang out in the car?
  What does all this say about us as a culture?

Brainstorming list:
  1. to get us from point A to point B, junkers would suffice
  2. we demand variety in our lives
  3. we want cars that make us look cool . . . and so on

Outline:

  I. Why do we love our cars with such passion?
     A. Cars originally were merely basic transportation.
     B. Every Model T looked alike.
     C. Today's automakers cater to our urge to do our own thing
        . . . and so on.

Appropriate tone for audience and purpose: relaxed and humorous

---

Remember that your decisions for completing the Planning Guide need not follow the strict order of the items listed—so long as you make all the necessary decisions.

PLANNING FOR GROUP WORK

In the Introduction to Section One, you practised thinking ahead to the kinds of decisions groups must make if they are to benefit from all members' contributions. The following guidelines will enable your group to prepare for collaborative work.

GUIDELINES FOR WRITING COLLABORATIVELY

1. *Appoint a group manager.* The manager assigns tasks, enforces deadlines, conducts meetings, consults with the instructor, and generally "runs the show."

2. *Compose a purpose statement (pages 22–3, 37).* Spell out the project's goal and the group's plan for achieving the goal.

3. *Decide how the group will be organized.* Some possibilities:

   a. The group researches and plans together, but each person writes a different part of the document.

   b. Some members plan and research; one person writes a complete draft; others review, edit, revise, and produce the final version. Keep in mind that the final revision should display one consistent style throughout—as if written by one person only.

4. *Divide the task.* Who will be responsible for which parts of the essay or report or which phases of the project? Who is best at doing what (writing, editing, using a word processor, giving an oral presentation to the class)?

5. *Establish specific completion dates for each phase.* This will keep everyone focused on what is due and when.

6. *Decide on a meeting schedule and format.* How often will the group meet, and for how long? In or out of class? Who will take notes?

7. *Establish a procedure for responding to the work of other members.* Will reviewing and editing (pages 70–1) be done in writing, face-to-face, as a group, one-on-one, or online? Will this process be supervised by the project manager?

8. *Establish procedures for dealing with group problems.* How will gripes and disagreements be aired and resolved? How will irrelevant discussion be curtailed? Can inevitable conflict be used positively?

9. *Select a group decision-making style beforehand.* Will decisions be made alone by the group manager or be based on group input or majority vote?

10. *Appoint a different "observer" for each meeting.* This group member will make a list of what worked or didn't work during the meeting.

11. *Decide how to evaluate each member's contribution.* Will members evaluate each other? Criteria for evaluation might include dependability, cooperation, effort, quality of work, and the

GUIDELINES FOR WRITING COLLABORATIVELY (continued)

ability to meet deadlines. Figure 2.1 shows one possible form for a manager to evaluate members. Equivalent criteria for evaluating the manager include open-mindedness, fairness in assigning tasks, ability to organize the team, ability to resolve conflicts, and so on.

Note that any evaluation of strengths and weaknesses should be backed up by comments that explain the ratings (as in Figure 2.1). A group needs to decide beforehand what constitutes "effort," "cooperation," and so on.

12. *Prepare a project management plan.* Figure 2.2 shows a sample plan sheet. Distribute completed copies to members and the instructor.

FIGURE 2.1

Sample form for evaluating team members

> **Performance Appraisal for** _J. Fishkill_
>
> (Rate each element as *[superior]*, *[acceptable]*, or *[unacceptable]* and use the "Comment" section to explain each rating briefly)
>
> - *Cooperation:* [_superior_]
>   Comment: works extremely well with others; always willing to help out; responds positively to constructive criticism
>
> - *Dependability:* [_acceptable_]
>   Comment: arrives on time for meetings; completes all assigned work
>
> - *Effort:* [_acceptable_]
>   Comment: does fair share of work; needs no prodding
>
> - *Quality of work produced:* [_superior_]
>   Comment: produces work that is carefully researched, well documented and clearly written
>
> - *Ability to meet deadlines:* [_superior_]
>   Comment: delivers all assigned work on or before the deadline; helps other team members with last-minute tasks
>
> _R. P. Ketchum_
> Project manager's signature

Management Plan Sheet

Project title:
Audience:
Project manager:
Team members:
Purpose of the project:

Specific Assigments   **Due Dates**

    Research: Research due:
    Planning: Planning due:
    Drafting: First draft due:
    Revising: Reviews due:
    Preparing final document: Revisions due:
    Presenting oral briefing: Final document due:
                                             Progress report(s) due:

Specific Assigments

Group meetings:	*Date*	*Place*	*Time*	*Note taker*
#1				
#2				
#3				
etc.				
Mtgs. w/instructor				
#1				
#2				
etc.				

Miscellaneous

    How will disputes and grievances be resolved?
    How will performances be evaluated?
    Other matters (Internet searches, e-mail routing, computer conferences, etc.)?

FIGURE 2.2
Sample plan sheet for managing a collaborative project

APPLICATION **2-1**

Narrow two or three of the broad topics in this list to a topic suitable for a short essay. (Review page 22.)

EXAMPLE

social rituals

↓

high school grad formals

↓

how the romantic image of grad night has become a myth

↓

how today's typical grad night is based on competition and appearances and polluted by drugs, alcohol, and sex

TOPICS TO BE NARROWED

entertainment	careers	war	family
life	sports	crime	sex
social rituals	automobiles	fashion	music
marriage	alcohol	studying	drugs

APPLICATION **2-2**

Compose statements of purpose for essays on three or more of the topics in Application 2-1. (Review pages 22–23.)

EXAMPLE

Topic The problems with grad night

Purpose statement My purpose is to persuade past and present high school students that high school grad formals have become a waste of time. I will discuss four major problems with grad night: drugs and alcohol, sexual promiscuity, competition, and danger.

APPLICATION **2-3**

Convert your statements of purpose from Application 2-2 into thesis statements. (Review pages 23–26.)

EXAMPLE

Purpose statement My purpose is to persuade past and present high school students that grad formals have become a waste of time. I will discuss four major problems with grad night: drugs and alcohol, sexual promiscuity, competition, and danger.

Thesis statement   High school grad formals have lost their value as social events and have become expensive and exaggerated rituals that entrap students in situations they often despise.

APPLICATION **2-4**

For each thesis statement in Application 2-3, brainstorm and write three or four topic statements for individual supporting paragraphs. Arrange your topic statements in logical order. (Review pages 24–25.)

EXAMPLE

Thesis statement   High school grad formals have lost their value as social events and have become expensive and exaggerated rituals that entrap students in situations they often despise.

First topic statement   Parents, teachers, coaches, and other role models seem to merely accept the fact that students are going to drink or get high on grad night.

Second topic statement   It is almost an unspoken law that a couple (no matter how unacquainted) should have sex on grad night.

Third topic statement   Competition over who has the most expensive dress, the most unusual tux, the biggest limousine, or the cutest date also detracts from the evening.

Fourth topic statement   Not only do many feel obliged to attend the grad formal in order to fit in, but they also feel obliged to participate in often-dangerous after-grad events.

APPLICATION **2-5**

From Application 2-4, select the most promising set of materials, and write your best essay. Use selected items from your brainstorming list to develop each support paragraph. Outline as necessary. Provide an engaging introduction and a definite conclusion. Use the questions on page 18 as guidelines for revising your essay.

APPLICATION **2-6**

Collaborative Project: Organize into small groups. Choose a subject from the list at the end of this exercise. Then decide on a thesis statement and (not necessarily in this order) brainstorm. Identify a specific audience. Group similar items under the same major categories, and develop an outline. When each group completes this procedure, one representative can write the outline on the board for class suggestions about revision. (Review pages 30–31.)

a description of the ideal classroom

instructions for surviving the first semester of college or university

instructions for surviving a blind date

suggestions for improving one's college or university experience

causes of teenage suicide

arguments for or against a formal grading system

an argument for an improvement you think this college or university needs

the qualities of a good parent

what you expect the world to be like in ten years

young people's needs that parents often ignore

difficulties faced by nontraditional students

APPLICATION **2-7**

Collaborative Project: Exchange electronic copies of an essay you've written (or, in a lab, switch computers) and examine your partner's essay. Saving your edits in a new file, put the main topics in boldface and underline the supporting points. Assemble this material to form an outline of your partner's essay and then try out different arrangements of the headings or suggest new ones. Show your original and new outlines to your partner and discuss whether the essay achieved what she or he intended.

CHAPTER 3

Decisions in Drafting

Once you have a definite plan, you are ready to draft your essay. Here is where you decide on answers to some tough questions:

Decisions in Drafting Your Essay

- *How do I begin the essay?*
- *What does my reader need to know first?*
- *What comes after that?*
- *How much is enough?*
- *Am I forgetting anything?*
- *How do I end?*

As you work, remember that each writing sample in this book is the product of multiple drafts and revisions. None of these writers expected to get it right the first time—neither should you.

DRAFTING THE TITLE AND INTRODUCTION

Why titles are important

Titles—which are sometimes chosen after the essay is complete—should forecast an essay's subject and approach. Clear, attention-getting titles, such as "Let's Shorten the Baseball Season" or "Instead of Running, Try Walking," help readers plan how to interpret what they read.

Assume you are continuing your work from Chapter 2 where you planned your essay about Canada's obsession with cars. You have chosen the title, "Cars R Us."

The Introductory Paragraph

Introductions differ in shape and size and may consist of more than one paragraph; however, basic introductory paragraphs often have a funnel shape:

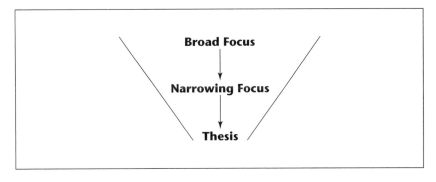

Now that you have decided on a title—"Cars R Us"—you can introduce your essay's final draft, using a funnel pattern:

Cars R Us

Broad focus (1–5)

[1]We Canadians love our automobiles, no question. [2]But why is next year's new model always front-page news? [3]Cars once were merely a way to get from point A to point B faster than by foot or horse and buggy. [4]Henry Ford's Model Ts all looked identical, like boxes on wheels, all painted black. [5]People bought Model Ts for basic transportation—and not to make a fashion statement. [6]As we leave the 20th century in the dust, however, automakers cater to our desire to "do our own thing." [7]We love their attention and they know it. [8]Today's self-centred consumers demand cars that satisfy our craving for individuality.

Narrowing Focus (6–7)

Thesis (8)

Why introductions are important

Introductory paragraphs do more than just lead into the essay; they invite readers in and set a tone. The first-person plural (we, us, our) invites us to look at ourselves. Amusing images (horse and buggy, boxes on wheels) and deliberate clichés (in the dust, do our own thing) signal the writer's intention to have fun with this essay. If your only aim were to lead into the main discussion, you might have given this introduction instead:

A lifeless opening

We love our cars because they enhance our sense of individuality.

But this version lacks the inviting tone and the images that engage our attention and make us want to read on.

Placing the Thesis

In a standard essay, the thesis often appears at the end of the introductory paragraph, as a bridge to the discussion. But sometimes readers want to know where you stand immediately, especially when the topic is controversial.

A controversial thesis as opener

Single-sex schools offer distinct advantages over coeducational schools. Coeducational classrooms inhibit student participation and tend to ignore gender-specific learning styles. Single-sex classrooms not only encourage participation but also allow for the kinds of gender-based teaching strategies that promote effective learning.

Sometimes, even personal writing can open directly with the thesis, especially when the viewpoint is unexpected.

A surprising thesis as opener

I hate summer beaches. Ocean swimming is impossible; upon conquering a wave, I simply lose to the next, getting pushed back onto the hard-packed, abrasive sand. Booby-traps of bottles, soda cans, toys, and rocks make walking hazardous. Heavy with the stench of suntan lotion, greasy French fries, dead fish, and sweat, the thick, searing air hangs motionless about the scorching sand. Blasting radios and growling hot rods cut the slap-swoosh of the green-grey surf to a weak hiss. People devour a summer beach, gouging the sand with umbrella spikes and gripping it with oiled limbs, leaving only trampled debris at summer's end.

In some essays, the thesis appears later, even near the end (as on page 234). A delayed thesis is especially useful in a story leading to some larger meaning (*Here is what happened*, and then, *Here is what it means*).

Selecting an Opening Strategy

"How do I begin?"

The specifics of your introduction are determined by what you know about your readers and your purpose.

Decisions in Analyzing Your Audience

- *Are my readers likely to be interested in this topic?*
- *How can I make them want to read on?*
- *Are they likely to react defensively?*

- *Is my purpose to describe something, to tell a story, to explain something, to change somebody's mind?*

The opening strategies that follow offer various possibilities for connecting with your audience.

Open with an Anecdote. An anecdote is a brief, personal story that makes a point.

> Last weekend, I gave a friend's younger brother a ride from the mall. As we drove, I asked him the same old questions about high school, marks, football, and girlfriends. He answered me in one-word sentences and then pulled out a cassette tape. "Wanna hear somethin' cool?" I shrugged and popped it into the tape player. What came pouring through my car speakers made me run a stop sign. The "rap" song spelled out, in elaborate detail, 101 ways to violate a woman's body. Needless to say, it was a long ride across town.
>
> I borrowed the tape and listened to every song, horrified by their recurrent theme of sexual violence and domination. But most horrifying is that a 15-year-old kid actually considers this music "cool."

Open with a Background Story. For example, in an essay that challenges a popular attitude, trace the development of that attitude.

> In 1945, a terrifying blast shook the New Mexico desert. Shortly afterward, the new, awesome force literally vaporized hundreds of thousands of lives, to end World War II. Thus began the atomic era. This horrid beginning, along with recent nuclear accidents and scandals, has caused increasing criticism. However, as we enter a new century the nuclear breeder reactor offers a promising energy alternative, but critics have drastically reduced its development and production. We need the breeder reactor, because it is one of our best long-range sources of energy.

This kind of opening is especially effective in persuasive writing, because it acknowledges opposing views, creating empathy (identification with the reader's attitude).

Open with a Question. An opening question can get readers thinking right away, especially when you write instructions, give advice, or argue for action.

> What do you do when you find yourself in the produce room cooler with your manager and he nonchalantly wraps his arm around your waist? Or how about when the guys you work with come out with a distasteful remark that makes you seem like a piece of meat? These are just a couple of problems you might face as the only female in a department. There are, however, ways of dealing with this kind of harassment.

Open with a Short Quotation. If a quotation can summarize your point, use it—and clarify its significance immediately.

> "The XL Roadster—anything else is just a car," unless the XL happens to be mine. In that case, it's just a piece of junk.

Open with a Direct Address. The second-person *you* can involve the readers and helps them pay attention—especially when you are giving instructions or advice or writing persuasively.

> Does the thought of artificially preserved, chemically treated food make you lose your appetite? Do limp, tasteless, frozen vegetables leave you cold? Then you should try your hand at organic gardening.

Use direct address in ads, popular articles, and brochures but not in academic reports or most business and technical documents.

Open with a Brief, Vivid Description. Instead of a thesis, some descriptive essays simply have an orienting sentence to set a scene or create a mood, to place readers at the centre of things.

> The raft bobs gently as the four divers help each other with scuba gear. We joke and laugh casually as we struggle in the cramped space; but a restlessness is in the air because we want to be on our way. Finally, everyone is ready, and we split into pairs. I steal a last glance over the blue ocean. I hear the waves slap the boat, the mournful cry of a seagull, and a steady murmur from the crowded beach a mile away. With three splashes my friends jump in. I follow. There is a splash and then silence. The water presses in, and all I hear is the sound of my regulator as I take my first breath. All I see is blue water, yellow light, and endless space. While the world rushes on, we feel suspended in time. Then my buddy taps me on the shoulder, and we begin a tour of a hidden world.

Description can also be a powerful way to make a point.

> They appear each workday morning from 7:00 to 9:00, role models for millions of career-minded women. Their crisp, clear diction and articulate reporting are second only to their appearance. Slender and lovely, the female co-hosts of morning news shows radiate that businesslike "chic" that networks consider essential in their newswomen. Such perfection is precisely why the networks hire these women as anchors. Network television rarely tolerates women commentators who are other than young, stylish, and attractive.

Notice how the businesslike tone parallels the topic itself.

Open with Examples. Examples enable readers to visualize the issue or problem. Consider the following (taken from a 1999 EAP/EFAP Newsletter), in which Dave Howard warns us of "Violence in the Workplace."

> In Ottawa, a public transit employee walks into his company's garage with a rifle and kills four fellow employees. . . . A nurse is threatened with a knife by a mentally ill woman in a hospital waiting room. . . . A secretary at her workstation is visited by her husband who pushes her against the wall, slaps her, and then leaves. All of these incidents are examples of the phenomenon of rising violence in the workplace.
>
> —*Dave Howard*

Open with a Definition. Clarify abstract terms for both writer and reader. In "Management of Breast Cancer Related Lymphedema" included in *Abreast in the Nineties* (Summer 98), Dr. Maria Hugi (BC Cancer Agency) starts by defining lymphedema:

> Lymphedema is a build-up of lymph fluid in your arm. Lymph fluid is a clear liquid that bathes all the tissues (muscles, tendons, ligaments, fat) of the arm to keep them clear and free of infection. The lymph fluid is filtered through lymph nodes (glands) in the armpit on its way to the blood stream. In breast cancer treatment, the lymph nodes in the armpit are often taken out by surgery (axillary dissection) to see if the cancer has spread there. You have developed lymphedema because lymph fluid can no longer leave your arm through its normal channels in your armpit. These channels have been disrupted by your treatment.

As you draft your introduction, consider the following suggestions:

Hints for an engaging introduction

■ The introduction can be the hardest part of an essay. Many writers complete it last. If you do write your introduction first, be sure to revise it later.

- In most college/university writing, avoid opening with personal qualifiers such as "it is my opinion that," "I believe that," and "in this paper I will."
- Let your introduction create suspense that is resolved by your thesis statement, usually at the end of the opening paragraph(s).
- If the opening is boring, vague, long-winded, or toneless, readers may give up. Don't waste their time.

DRAFTING THE BODY SECTION

"How much is enough, and how can I shape it?"

The body section delivers on the commitment made in your thesis. Readers don't want details that just get in the way, or a jigsaw puzzle they have to unscramble for themselves. To develop the body, therefore, answer these questions:

Decisions in Developing the Body of Your Essay

- *How much is enough?*
- *How much information or detail should I provide?*
- *How can I stay on track?*
- *What shape will reveal my line of thought?*

Decide about purpose and unity. Here you discard some material you thought you might keep, and maybe discover additional material. Look hard at everything you've discovered during freewriting, brainstorming, or questioning. Stand in the reader's place. Keep whatever belongs, and discard whatever doesn't.

Decide how many support paragraphs to include. College and university essays typically have three or more, but use as many as you need. Decide how to develop each support paragraph and how to order them. What paragraph order will make the most sense and provide the best emphasis?

Elements affecting the shape of your writing (unity, coherence, emphasis, and transition) are discussed fully in Chapter 6, "Revising the Paragraphs." Principles of developing the individual paragraph are principles as well of creating the whole essay—or of writing at any length.

DRAFTING THE CONCLUSION

Why conclusions are important

An essay's conclusion refocuses on the thesis and leaves a final—and lasting—impression on readers. Your conclusion might evaluate the meaning or significance of the body section, restate your position, predict an outcome, offer a solution, request an action, make a recommendation, or pave the way for more exploration. Avoid conclusions that repeat, apologize, or belabour the obvious:

Don't repeat		I have just discussed my views on the role cars play in our lives.
Don't apologize		Although some readers might disagree, this is how I see it.
Don't belabour the obvious		Now that you've read my essay, you should have a clear picture of the importance we place on our cars.

Selecting a Closing Strategy

"How do I end?"

Forgettable endings drain the life from any writing. This list of strategies samples ways of closing with meaning and emphasis.

Close with a Summary. A review of main points helps readers remember what is most important.

Close with a Question. A closing question provides readers something to think about.

> Overall, the advantages of the breeder reactor seem immeasurable. Because it can produce more fuel than it uses, it will theoretically be an infinite source of energy. And efficient use of the fuel it does burn makes it highly desirable in this energy-tight era. What other source promises so much for our long-range energy future?

Close with a Call to Action. Tell readers exactly what you want them to do.

> Just imagine yourself eating a salad of crisp green lettuce, juicy red tomato chunks, firm white slices of cucumber, and crunchy strips of green pepper—all picked fresh from your own garden. If this picture appeals to you, begin planning your summer garden now, and by July the picture of you eating that salad will become a reality. *Bon appetit!*

Close with a Quotation. This next writer quotes from journalist Ellen Goodman's essay, "Blame the Victim."

> I agree with Ellen Goodman's assertion that there is "something malignant about some of the extremists who make a public virtue of their health." The cancer is in the superior attitudes of the "healthy elite"—an attitude that actually discourages exercise and healthy habits by making average people feel too intimidated and inferior even to begin a fitness program.

Close with an Interpretation or Evaluation. Help readers understand the meaning of things.

> A growing array of so-called private information about Canadian citizens is collected daily. And few laws protect our right to be left alone. In the interest of pursuing criminals, government too often sacrifices the

privacy of innocent people, and new technology is making old laws obsolete. Huge collections of data are becoming available to your insurance company, to prospective employers, to companies doing mass mailings, and even to your neighbour. The invasion continues, and no one seems to know how to stop our world from fulfilling the prophecy in George Orwell's *1984*.

Whichever strategy or combination of strategies you select, make your conclusion refocus on your main point without repeating it.

CASE STUDY

DRAFTING THE ESSAY

As an illustration of how these drafting decisions produce a completed essay, consider "Cars R Us," reproduced below. (Chapter 4 traces the steps in revision that created the final version shown here.)

Notice that the thesis and each topic sentence appear in boldface and italics.

The finished essay
Introduction

CARS R US

We Canadians love our automobiles, no question. But why is next year's new model always front-page news? Cars once were merely a way to get from point A to point B faster than by foot or horse and buggy. Henry Ford's Model Ts all looked identical, like boxes on wheels, and were all painted black. People bought Model Ts for basic transportation—and not to make a fashion statement. As we enter the 21st century, however, automakers cater to our desire to "do our own thing." We love their attention and they know it. ***Today's self-centred consumers demand cars that satisfy our craving for individuality.***

First support
paragraph

We want automobiles that make a unique lifestyle statement about who we think we are. If today's cars were only a means to cruise to the grocery store, we'd all be willing to drive junkers. But most people hate rusty, old bombers. We want to be able to see our ideal (or idealized) images mirrored in our car's glossy paint job or our truck's chrome hubcaps. For example, roughly fifty percent of today's rugged individuals buy 4-wheel drive, off-road vehicles that never leave the pavement. Instead we navigate our urban and suburban wilderness in Hummers, Big Wheel trucks, and SUV land barges because these vehicles symbolize toughness and an uncompromising attitude. We buy sports cars not so much to impress others, but to impress ourselves: "Hey, I'm driving this red convertible Miata and I'm special."

Second support paragraph

Cars provide each individual with a personal billboard. As a way to exercise our right to free speech, bumper stickers announce exactly where we stand. They tell the world that we're intellectuals or tough guys or sensitive types. One of mine reads, "I love my humpback whale." Another promotes my favourite radio station. For some reason Volvos often carry political statements such as "Women, unite," or "Make love, not war," or profound observations such as Einstein's "creativity is more important than knowledge"—which might be fine for an individual like Einstein, but what about the rest of us mere mortals? Some individuals like to be more rugged than others. Pick-up trucks, for instance, often sport CUPE stickers that tell us to support unions.

Third support paragraph

Owning a car means not having to rely on—yikes—public transportation, torture for individuals like us. Our cars are personal sanctuaries, places to escape other humans. One popular form of escape is the drive-through window. Banks, doughnut shops, even dry cleaners enable us to transact business without leaving the car. Snug in our mobile dining rooms, we no longer have to budge from our orthopedically correct leather seat to order a meal. A simple adjustment of the tilt-steering allows laptop dining as we savour our grease-laden food in private, far from the noisy restaurant and screaming kids. We just stay in our cars. How convenient. We can even sing along to the stereo between bites or hum along as we chew. If you sing on a bus or subway, other commuters look at you strangely and hide their valuables.

Conclusion

Cars entice us because they offer the ultimate mechanism for achieving individuality. Through the kind of car we drive and how we adorn it, we can really "be somebody" and proclaim to strangers our singular selves. We can dine à-la-car and sing aloud without seeming weird. Isolated in our climate-controlled, stereophonic capsule, we can avoid direct human contact and concentrate full time on being individuals. At the beginning of *Mother Night,* novelist Kurt Vonnegut observes, "We are what we pretend to be"—a condition made increasingly possible by the cars we choose to drive.

—*Maureen Malloy*

Discussion

This essay presents a focused picture. And the picture is unified: nothing gets in the way; everything belongs.

But content alone cannot ensure contact. Thoughts need shaping to help us organize our understanding of the writer's way of seeing. Each paragraph helps detail the prepackaged identity offered by the automobile.

Finally, the concluding paragraph offers perspective on the whole essay, refocusing on the thesis, summing up the main points and leaving readers with a quotation that suggests a larger meaning for the essay. Readers remember last things best, and this essay's conclusion leaves us with something worth remembering.

DRAFTING ON THE COMPUTER

Word processing is especially useful as a drafting tool, enabling you to delete, move, or design text instantly. The following guidelines will help ensure that you capitalize on all the benefits a computer can offer.

GUIDELINES FOR DRAFTING ON THE COMPUTER

1. *Decide whether to draft on the computer or by hand for later transfer to the computer.* Experiment with each approach before deciding which works best for you.

2. *Beware of computer junk.* The ease of cranking out words on a computer can produce long, windy pieces that say nothing. Cut anything that fails to advance your meaning. (See pages 119–124 for ways to achieve conciseness.)

3. *Never confuse style with substance.* Laser printers and choices of typefaces, type sizes, and other design options can produce attractive documents. But not even the most attractive format can redeem worthless or inaccessible content.

4. *Save and print your work often.* Save each paragraph as you write it; print out each page as you complete it; and keep a copy of your document on a backup disk.

5. *Consider the benefits of revising from hard copy.* Nothing beats scribbling on the printed page with pen or pencil. The hard copy provides the whole text, right in front of you.

6. *Never depend only on automated "checkers."* Not even the most sophisticated writing aids can replace careful proofreading. A synonym found in an electronic thesaurus may distort your meaning. The spell checker cannot differentiate among correctly spelled words such as *their, they're,* or *there,* or *it's* versus *its.* And neither spell nor grammar checkers can evaluate *stylistic appropriateness* (the subtle choices of phrasing that determine tone and emphasis). Page 148 summarizes the limitations of computerized aids.

7. *Always print two final copies.* With all the paperwork that writing instructors (and their students) shuffle, papers sometimes get misplaced. Submit one copy and keep one for yourself—just in case!

APPLICATION 3-1

Plan and draft an essay based on one of the writing options on pages 19–20. Decide on an audience: your classmates, readers of the campus paper, or the like. Have a thesis and deliver on it.

Also, find a voice that will appeal to your readers. Create unity so that your writing sticks to the point; create order and use transitions so that it stands together. Use the questions on page 18 for guidance in improving your essay.

APPLICATION **3-2**

Collaborative Project: Locate a good introduction or a good conclusion to a short article in a popular magazine such as *Maclean's* or *Reader's Digest*. As a group, analyze the strategies that make the writing effective. (Review pages 45–50 and 50–52.)

APPLICATION **3-3**

Computer Application: Save three copies of your essay under different file names. Revise one of the copies, keeping in mind the ideas from this chapter. Take an overnight break and then revise a second copy of the original. Print the three versions and read them carefully. Then write a summary (pages 358–361) of your favourite version and explain why you think the changes improve the essay.

CHAPTER 4

Decisions in Revising

esides being a battle with impatience, writing is a battle with inertia: once we've written a draft, we are often too easily satisfied with what we've done. Good writers win the battle by revising often. For the sake of clarity, earlier chapters have presented a single sequence of steps for composing an essay. To review:

One sequence for composing an essay

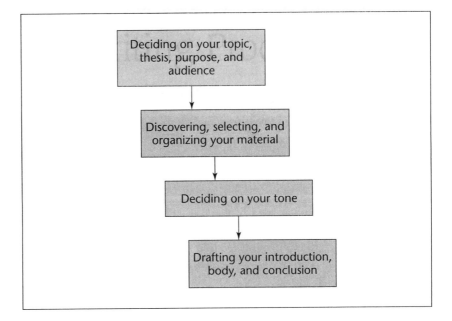

Deciding on your topic, thesis, purpose, and audience

Discovering, selecting, and organizing your material

Deciding on your tone

Drafting your introduction, body, and conclusion

We have seen that writers rarely follow this exact sequence. But no matter what the sequence, any effective writer depends on revision—the one constant in the writing process. When you finish a first draft, you really have only begun.

THE MEANING OF REVISION

Revision involves more than proofreading for spelling, punctuation, or other mechanical details (all covered in Appendix A). Mechanical correctness is essential, but what matters most are the essay's *rhetorical elements: worthwhile content, sensible organization,* and *readable style*. The rhetorical elements determine whether your writing connects with readers—and makes a difference. Your instructor might write suggestions on your first draft or have you revise on your own. In any case, revision never means merely recopying; it always means *rethinking*.

Why rhetorical elements are important

Useful revision happens only when you can evaluate accurately what you already have written. Use the Revision Checklist to pinpoint possible improvements in content, organization, and style. (Numbers in parentheses refer to the first page of discussion.)

REVISION CHECKLIST ☑

WORTHWHILE CONTENT

The essay's main point is clear and sharply focused.

- ☐ Does the title attract attention and provide a forecast? (45)
- ☐ Is the topic limited enough? (22)
- ☐ Do you get to your main point quickly? (46)
- ☐ Is the thesis definite, informative, and easy to find? (23)

The discussion delivers on the promise made in your thesis.

- ☐ Will your readers learn something new and useful? (80)
- ☐ Do you support every assertion with enough details? (79)
- ☐ Does everything belong, or can anything be cut? (84)
- ☐ Have you used only your best material? (31)

SENSIBLE ORGANIZATION

The essay has a definite introduction, body, and conclusion.

- ☐ Will your introduction make readers want to read on? (10)
- ☐ Does each body paragraph develop *one* supporting point? (90)
- ☐ Does the order of body paragraphs reveal a clear line of thought and emphasize what is most important? (10)
- ☐ Does the conclusion give a real sense of an ending? (10)

- ☐ Is everything connected? (15)
- ☐ If you varied this organization, was it for good reason? (155)

Except for paragraphs of transition or special emphasis, each body (or support) paragraph usually is a mini-essay.

- ☐ Does the paragraph have a topic (or orienting) statement? (92)
- ☐ Does the topic statement come at the beginning or end, depending on your desired emphasis? (92)
- ☐ Does everything stick to the point (unity), and stick together (coherence)? (94, 95)
- ☐ Is the paragraph developed enough to support the point? (83–4)

READABLE STYLE

Sentences are clear, concise, and fluent.

- ☐ Can each sentence be understood the first time it is read? (110)
- ☐ Are points made in the fewest words? (119)
- ☐ Are sentences put together with enough variety? (126)

Each word does its job.

- ☐ Is a real person speaking, and is the voice likable? (133)
- ☐ Is everything in plain English? (140)
- ☐ Is your meaning precise, concrete, and specific? (134)
- ☐ Is your tone appropriate for this situation and audience? (138)

USING THE CHECKLIST

As you use the Revision Checklist to rethink your essay, ask yourself questions such as these:

Questions for Critical Evaluation and Revision

- *Have I conveyed my exact point or feeling?*
- *Do vivid details from the event come to mind now that I've finished writing?*
- *What facts or figures or ideas do I now remember?*

- *Can I reorganize for greater emphasis or clarity?*
- *Can I find a better way of saying what I want to say?*
- *Does this draft sound as I wanted it to sound, or is it too corny or detached, or arrogant or humble?*

Eventually you will find that you can revise almost automatically, without following the checklist item by item.

CASE STUDY

REVISING THE DRAFT

Assume you've written this early draft of "Cars R Us" (whose final version appears on pages 52–53):

A draft to be revised

CAR CRAZY

We Canadians love our automobiles. No question. But why do we worship them? Nearly every country has access to cars but not every country has the freedom to use them as they please. Cars were once merely a way to get from point A to point B faster than by foot or horse and buggy. Now, cars are fibreglass and metal gods.

In the early 1900s when Henry Ford began producing Model Ts, they all had the same body style, sort of like rectangles on wheels. Black was a buyer's only choice of paint colour. People didn't purchase Model Ts because they were pretty; they were basic transportation, with no fancy options or "toys" like cars have now: tilt-steering, heated power seats, climate control, an eight-speaker stereo system with CD drive, and so on. We get sick of the same thing over and over. We demand variety in our lives and especially in our cars.

As we enter the 21st century automakers cater to us. We love their attention and they know it. Canadians are used to instant gratification. We want and get next year's new models NOW. Because they understand our "first person on the block to have it" mentality, the car manufacturers tantalize us with concept cars—you know: those weird, space-aged looking vehicles with gull's wings and rocket packs. To please our sense of beauty, each year the cars get more attractive. New cars are sleeker and shinier, and more pleasing to touch. With such beauty, though, comes higher sticker prices. But we don't care. We are willing to pay any price to practise the Automobile Religion.

Today, cars mean more to us than a way to cruise around town. If we saw them as only a means to get to the grocery store, then we'd all be willing to drive junkers. Instead, we see our cars as reflections of our personalities. Most people don't want to drive rusty, old bombers. We want to be able to see our ideal (or idealized) images mirrored in our car's glossy paint job. We want automobiles that make a statement about ourselves. People travel through the Canadian wilderness in jeeps and trucks because they symbolize toughness and an uncompromising attitude. We buy sports cars not so much to impress others, but to impress ourselves: "Hey, I'm driving this red convertible Miata and I feel like the master of the highway."

That's why we love our cars and decorate them as we do, to display a little of ourselves even while we drive. With bumper stickers, we exercise our constitutional rights to free speech. One of mine reads, "I love my humpback whale." Another promotes my favourite radio station. For some reason, I often see CUPE stickers on pick-up trucks. Again, drivers are making a statement to the rest of us motorists—"Honk to support those on picket lines." So I often honk as I pass by picketers walking the line.

The word *automobile* means "self-moving." Cars give us the freedom to go where we want, when we want, across town or across the country. There is plenty of wide-open space for our cars. Even owners of land barge SUVs usually find a place to park. Let's consider the Japanese for a moment. They, too, love their cars (with good reason) yet their autos are stuck on a tiny island, and parking laws are so strict that meter-readers write in chalk on the sidewalk how long a car has been parked in a certain spot. Too long, and it's towed. In Canada, we can usually park our cars illegally and get away with it (for at least as long as it takes to "run" into the bank or drugstore).

When we own a car, we don't have to rely on—yikes—public transportation, something people in other countries don't mind doing. Our cars are personal sanctuaries, places to escape other humans. The car's popularity has led to the phenomenon of drive-through windows. Banks, doughnut shops, even dry cleaners allow us to transact business without leaving the comfort and safety of our autos. Try getting a bus driver to stop at Tim Hortons because you have a sudden urge for a cruller. We no longer have to move from the driver's seat to order a meal. We no longer have to sit in a noisy McDonald's with screaming kids to eat our grease-laden food. We just stay in our cars. How convenient. We can even sing along to the stereo if we want. Other commuters look at you strangely and hide their valuables if you sing on a subway.

Cars entice us because they allow us to do the things that appeal to us: drive where we please, when we please, dine à-la-car, sing aloud in public and not be thought insane. And through the kind of car we drive and how we adorn them, we can share with strangers our personalities. Even though we may be isolated in our automobiles, we share with other motorists the camaraderie that comes with belonging to the Car Cult.

Discussion   This draft makes a good start but it needs substantial revision. First, there seems to be too much material. This lack of a clear focus leaves lots of reader questions unanswered:

- What and where is the thesis?
- Is this essay about cars and our love of freedom, of variety, of self-esteem, of free speech, of privacy, or what?
- What was the meaning of this whole observation for you?

Next, the organization of this draft hints at an introduction, body, and conclusion, but some paragraphs lack definite topic sentences and clear connections between ideas. And despite the colourful images, the conversational style (like a person talking), and the use of plain English, all this could be said in fewer words and with clearer emphasis.

The following pages will show how the checklist can help you revise to achieve the finished essay on pages 52–53. For reference, the paragraphs from the draft are labelled A through H. Specific needed improvements are explained on the facing page. Notice that the original, eight-paragraph draft has been reshaped into a five-paragraph revision.

NOTE   *This revision treats only the rhetorical features: content, organization, and style. See Appendix A for grammar, punctuation, and mechanics.*

Revision has created an essay with worthwhile content, sensible organization, and readable style. (For detailed advice on achieving these qualities in a final draft, see Chapters 5–8.)

Rewrite introduction to invite readers in

Cars R Us

~~Car Crazy~~

A

We Canadians love our automobiles. No question.
But why ~~do we worship them? Nearly every country has access to cars but not every country has the freedom to use them as they please.~~ *is next year's new model always front-page news?* Cars were once merely a way to get from point A to point B faster than by foot or horse and buggy. ~~Now, cars are fibreglass and metal gods.~~

Today's self-centred consumers demand cars that satisfy our craving for individuality. *Thesis*

B

Combine with introduction and edit for conciseness

~~In the early 1900s when~~ Henry Ford ~~began producing~~ Model Ts ~~they~~ all ~~had the same body style, sort of~~ *looked identical,* *boxes* *and were all painted* like ~~rectangles~~ on wheels. ~~Black~~ *was a buyer's only* choice of paint colour. People ~~didn't purchase~~ *bought* Model Ts ~~because they were pretty; they were~~ *for* basic transportation, ~~with no fancy options or "toys" like cars have now:~~ tilt-steering, heated power seats, climate control, an eight-speaker stereo system with CD drive, and so on. ~~We get sick of the same thing over and over. We demand variety in our lives and especially in our cars.~~

Save for final paragraph?

C

Combine with introduction

As we enter the 21st century auto makers cater to us. We love their attention and they know it. ~~Canadians are used to instant gratification. We want and get next year's new models NOW. Because they~~

FIGURE 4.1
A draft edited for revision

Paragraph A: The essay's title could be more specific about the theme here: namely, how we identify with our cars. The paragraph itself gives readers no clear sense of what to expect. Sentences 3 and 6 refer to car worship while sentence 4 (the thesis?) is about freedom. But the final draft will explore other themes such as self-esteem, free speech, and privacy—all elements of our craving for individuality.

Paragraph B: Much of this material could be trimmed and combined with the introductory paragraph, to focus on consumer attitudes toward the Model Ts versus today's cars. The two final sentences seem awfully general; they can be cut.

Paragraph C: The two opening sentences could be combined with the introductory paragraph, to focus again on the change in consumer attitudes. The rest of the paragraph, with its wordy and irrelevant details about instant gratification, concept cars, and high sticker prices, can be cut.

None of this material relates directly to the thesis

~~understand our "first person on the block to have it"~~ ~~mentality, the car manufacturers tantalize us with~~ ~~concept cars—you know: those weird, space-aged looking~~ ~~vehicles with gull's wings and rocket packs. To please~~ ~~our sense of beauty, each year the cars get more~~ ~~attractive. New cars are sleeker and shinier, and more~~ ~~pleasing to touch. With such beauty, though, comes~~ ~~higher sticker prices. But we don't care. We are~~ ~~willing to pay any price to practise the Automobile~~ ~~Religion.~~

Topic sentence — *We want automobiles that make a unique lifestyle statement about who we think we are.*

D

Say this more concisely

Today, cars mean more to us than a way to cruise around town. If we saw them as only as a means to get to the grocery store, then we'd all be willing to drive junkers. ~~Instead, we see our cars as reflections of our personalities.~~ Most people *hate* ~~don't want to drive~~ rusty, old bombers. We want to be able to see our ideal (or idealized) images mirrored in our car's glossy paint job *or in our truck's chrome hubcaps*. ~~We want automobiles that make a statement about ourselves.~~

Sharpen the images

People travel through the Canadian wilderness in jeeps and trucks because they symbolize toughness and an uncompromising attitude. We buy sports cars not so much to impress others, but to impress ourselves: "Hey, I'm driving this red convertible Miata and *I'm special* (*relates to theme of individuality*) ~~I feel like the master of the highway~~."

E

Topic sentence — *Cars provide each individual with a personal billboard.* ~~That's why we love our cars and decorate them as we do, to display a little of ourselves even while we~~

FIGURE 4.1
A draft edited for revision (continued)

Paragraph D: This paragraph provides informative details, but it lacks a topic sentence to frame readers' understanding of these details. Also, wordiness could be trimmed and images sharpened, to provide a more vivid picture. Otherwise the material here is definitely worthwhile.

Paragraph E: This paragraph, too, is generally strong, but it needs a more definite topic sentence and additional examples. The reference to pick-up trucks and CUPE stickers reminds us not to "mess with union guys"!

~~drive~~. With bumper stickers, we exercise our *They tell the world that we're intellectuals or tough guys or sensitive types.* constitutional rights to free speech. One of mine

reads, "I love my humpback whale." Another promotes my

Add more examples favourite radio station. ~~I~~~~xxxxxxxx~~ For some

reason, I often see CUPE stickers on pick-up trucks.

Again, the drivers are making a statement to the rest

of us motorists: ~~"I like to maim and kill~~! Honk to

support those on picket lines." So I often honk when

I pass by picketers walking the line. *Too aggressive— avoid name-calling*

F

None of this material relates to the thesis

~~The word "automobile" means self-moving. Cars give~~
~~us the freedom to go where we want, when we want,~~
~~across town or across the country. There is plenty of~~
~~wide open space for our cars. Even owners of land~~
~~barge SUVs usually find a place to park. Let's~~
~~consider the Japanese for a moment. They, too, love~~
~~their cars (with good reason) yet their autos are stuck~~
~~on a tiny island, and parking laws are so strict that~~
~~meter-readers write in chalk on the sidewalk how long a~~
~~car has been parked in a certain spot. Too long, and~~
~~it's towed. In Canada, we can usually park our cars~~
~~illegally and get away with it (for at least as long as~~
~~it takes to "run" into the bank or drugstore.)~~

Delete irrelevant comparison

G

When we own a car, we don't have to rely on--
torture for individuals like us.
yikes--public transportation, ~~something people in other~~
~~countries don't mind doing.~~ Our cars are personal

sanctuaries, places to escape other humans.

FIGURE 4.1
A draft edited for revision (continued)

Paragraph F: This entire paragraph strays from the essay's purpose: to explore our need to identify with our cars. It seems to belong to some other essay about cars and freedom, or some such.

Paragraph G: Another strong paragraph, with a basically solid topic sentence and vivid detail. The sweeping comparison with "other countries" and the "Tim Hortons" reference really add nothing and can be deleted. Some sharper images would intensify the picture, and a few style changes would improve emphasis and readability.

One popular form of escape is the
~~The car's popularity has led to the phenomenon of~~
drive-through windows. Banks, doughnut shops, even dry
cleaners allow us to transact business without leaving
the ~~comfort and safety of our autos.~~ *car* ~~Try getting a~~
~~bus driver to stop at Tim Hortons because you have a~~
Snug in our mobile dining rooms, we
~~sudden urge for a cruller.~~ We no longer have to move
our orthopedically correct leather
from ~~the driver's~~ seat to order a meal. We no longer
have to sit in a noisy McDonald's with screaming kids
to eat our grease-laden food. We just stay in our
cars. How convenient. We can even sing along to the
between bites or hum along as we chew.
stereo ~~if we want.~~ ~~[crossed out]~~ Other commuters look at
you strangely and hide their valuables if you sing on
a subway.

H

offer the ultimate mechanism
Cars entice us because they ~~allow us to do the~~
for achieving individuality.
~~things that appeal to us: drive where we please, when~~
We can *and* *without seeming weird.*
~~we please,~~ dine a-la-car, sing aloud ~~in public and~~
~~not be thought insane.~~ And through the kind of car we
it *really "be somebody" and proclaim*
drive and how we adorn ~~them,~~ we can ~~share with~~
singular selves
~~strangers~~ our ~~personalities.~~ Even though we may be
isolated in our automobiles, we share with other
motorists the camaraderie that comes with belonging to
the Car Cult.

Add more visual details like these

Rephrase for sentence variety

Invert for emphasis

Relate the ending directly to the thesis— without repeating it

Reverse these two sentences

Replace to focus on individuality

End with Kurt Vonnegut's observation that "we are what we pretend to be."

FIGURE 4.1
A draft edited for revision (continued)

Paragraph H: This conclusion needs a topic sentence that relates more explicitly to the thesis. The colourful images do a nice job of reflecting on the essay's main themes, but they should be followed by a closing statement that sums up the essay's larger meaning.

REVISING WITH PEERS

All writing can benefit from feedback. As part of the revision process, your writing course may include workshops for peer reviewing and editing. *Reviewing* means evaluating how well the writing connects with its intended audience:

Questions reviewers ask

- Is the content accurate, appropriate, and useful?
- Is the material organized for the reader's understanding?
- Is the style clear, easy to read, and engaging?

In reviewing you explain to the writer how you respond as a reader; you point out what works or doesn't work. This feedback helps a writer envision ways of revising. Criteria for reviewing an essay appear on page 58; for an argument, pages 273–274; and for a research paper, page 402.

Editing means actually "fixing" the piece by making it more precise and readable:

Some ways in which editors "fix" writing

- rephrasing or reorganizing sentences
- clarifying a thesis or topic sentence
- choosing a better word or phrase
- correcting spelling, usage, or punctuation, and so on.

Your task as editor is to help improve the writing—without altering the author's original meaning. Criteria for editing appear inside the rear cover.

GUIDELINES FOR REVIEWING AND EDITING THE WRITING OF PEERS

1. *Read the entire piece at least twice before you comment.* Develop a clear sense of the assignment's purpose and its intended audience.

2. *Remember that mere correctness offers no guarantee of effectiveness.* Poor usage, punctuation, or mechanics do distract readers and harm the writer's credibility. However, a "correct" piece of writing still might contain faulty rhetorical elements (inferior content, confusing organization, or unsuitable style).

3. *Understand the acceptable limits of editing.* In the workplace, "editing" can range from fine-tuning to an in-depth rewrite. In school, however, rewriting a piece to the extent that it ceases to belong to the writer may constitute plagiarism.

4. *Be honest but diplomatic.* Most of us are sensitive to criticism—even when it is constructive. Begin with something positive before moving to critique. Support rather than judge.

5. *Always explain "why" something doesn't work.* Instead of "this paragraph is confusing," say, "because this paragraph lacks a clear topic sentence, I had trouble discovering the main idea" (see pages 58, 273, 402).

GUIDELINES FOR REVIEWING AND EDITING THE WRITING OF PEERS (continued)

6. *Make specific recommendations for improvements.* Write out suggestions in enough detail for the writer to know what to do (see pages 63, 65, 67, 69).

7. *Be aware that not all feedback has equal value.* Even professional editors can disagree. If you receive conflicting opinions from different readers, seek your instructor's advice.

APPLICATION **4-1**

Using the Revision Checklist on page 58 as a guide, return to an essay you have written earlier, and revise it.

At this early stage, you are bound to feel a little confused about the finer points of content, organization, and style. But try your best.

In later chapters you will learn to improve your skill for diagnosing problems and prescribing cures.

Along with your revised essay, submit the original essay and an explanation of the improvements you've made.

APPLICATION **4-2**

Collaborative Project: Take an essay you have written earlier, and exchange it for a classmate's. Assume your classmate's essay has been written specifically for you as the audience. Write a detailed evaluation of your classmate's essay, making specific suggestions for revision. Using the Revision Checklist on page 58, evaluate all three rhetorical features: content, organization, and style. Use Appendix A to recommend improvements in grammar, punctuation, and mechanics. Do plenty of scribbling on the essay, and sign your evaluation.

APPLICATION **4-3**

Collaborative Project: E-mail a copy of your essay to a classmate and ask this reviewer to make specific comments using the Revision Checklist and then forward it to a second reviewer who repeats the exercise. Or, in a computer lab, after opening your essay file, everyone move one seat to the right and review the essay. Make comments, save the file, move again, and review the essay on the next screen.

APPLICATION **4-4**

Computer Project: Try out the "spell checker" supplied by the word processing program you're using. First, learn how to add words you use often (your name, for example) to the computer's dictionary, so the machine won't question you each time it encounters these words. Second, make a list of the words the computer lists as misspelled and the suggested corrections. Compare the computer's suggestions with the entries in a good dictionary. Do they match? Keep a log of the words you misspell.

Then proof your paper carefully, watching for the kinds of errors computers can't catch: *homonyms,* or words that sound alike but are spelled differently and have different meanings (*their* and *there, heel* and *heal*); and *transpositions* (*form* for *from*). Also note that the spell checker won't catch missing or extra words! How many of these corrections did you find?

APPLICATION **4-5**

Computer Project: Do a Web search to find dictionaries online and write a quick review of the sites you find most useful. (See also Application 16-5, page 262.)

SECTION TWO

Specific Revision Strategies

Introduction

Chapter 1 reminds us that only the rare piece of writing is ever "finished," in the strict sense. Most writing—even at later stages—is more of a work-in-progress, with considerable room for improvement. Even professional writers often revisit a "finished" work for further revision.

HOW GOOD IS "GOOD ENOUGH"?

Every writer eventually runs out of time or patience and decides that the piece is good enough. But exactly how good is "good enough"? The answer depends on your purpose and your audience's expectations. For example, a "good enough" note to a friend differs greatly from a "good enough" scholarship essay or job application. And so, to make real contact, everyone's writing at times must exceed mere adequacy and must approach excellence.

REVISING FROM THE TOP DOWN

What are some strategies for approaching excellence? One useful way to revise is to consider your essay from the top down. First, consider the actual content—your reason for writing in the first place; next, the shape and position of each paragraph; then, the flow of your sentences; and finally, the quality of your phrasing and word choice. Figure II.1 shows how essay revision can move from large matters to small.

FIGURE II.1
Top-down decisions in revising

Revising the Content
- Is the thesis clear, focused, and significant?
- Is the support credible, informative, and substantial?

Revising the Organization
- Is the essay's structure visible at a glance?
- Is each support paragraph basically its own mini-essay?

Revising the Sentences
- Is each sentence immediately understandable?
- Is rich information expressed in the fewest words possible?
- Are sentences constructed with enough variety?

Revising Word Choice
- Does each word clarify—rather than muddle—the meaning?
- Is the tone appropriate?

BEEFING UP THE CONTENT

Readers expect content that rewards their effort. To make it convincing, informative, and thorough, we provide plenty of *details:* facts, ideas, examples, numbers, names, events, dates, or reasons that help readers visualize what we mean. But we trim away needless details because excessive information causes readers to overlook or misinterpret the important material. Early drafts almost always need trimming.

HARNESSING PARAGRAPH POWER

Readers need structure to advance logically, so they look for shapes they can recognize. Instead of forcing readers to organize unstructured material for themselves, we shape it for their understanding. Our essential organizing tool is the paragraph: forming part of the essay's larger design while telling its own, self-contained story.

HONING THE SENTENCES

Readers have no patience with writing that's hard to interpret, takes too long to make the point, or reads like a Dick-and-Jane story from primary school. And so we work to produce razor-sharp sentences that are clear and forceful, waste no words, and make for easy reading.

FINDING THE PERFECT WORDING

Readers are turned off by wording that is poorly chosen, too fancy, or that sounds stuffy and impersonal. And so we fine-tune each word to convey precisely what we are seeing, thinking, and feeling.

> **NOTE**
>
> *Like other decisions about writing, the revising process is not always as systematic as outlined here. For example, you might revisit the content while working on the organization, or you might think of a better word while reshaping a paragraph. Once you learn the strategies in this section, how you decide to use them will be up to you.*

CHAPTER 5

Revising the Content: Writing Something Worthwhile

Readers hate to waste time. They expect an insightful thesis backed by solid content and support.

The first requirement of worthwhile content is *unity:* every word, every detail belongs. Three other qualities are also essential to worthwhile content: *credibility, informative value,* and *completeness.**

MAKE IT CREDIBLE

Anyone can assert opinions; *supporting* your assertion is the real challenge. We all have opinions about political candidates, cars, or controversial subjects such as abortion or nuclear energy. But *many* of our *opinions are uninformed;* instead of resting on facts, they lean mostly on a chaotic collection of beliefs repeated around us, notions we've inherited from advertising, things we've read but never checked, and so on.

UNINFORMED OPINIONS

Christopher Columbus was a hero.
Christopher Columbus was an oppressor.
Grindo toothpaste is best for making teeth whiter.
In a democracy, religion deserves a voice in government.

Informed opinion, in contrast, rests on fact or good sense. Any fact (*My hair is brown. Job prospects for today's college/university graduates are excellent. Canadians have more televisions than bathtubs.*) can be verified by anyone, either by observation (*I saw Felix murder his friend*); by research (*Wood smoke contains the deadly chemical dioxin*); by experience (*I was hugged this morning*); or by measurement (*less than 60 percent of our first-year students eventually earn a degree*).

INFORMED OPINIONS

Felix is guilty of murder.
Homes with woodstoves need good ventilation.
This has been a good day for me.
College or university clearly is not for everyone.

To *support an opinion,* you often must consider a variety of facts. You might be able to support with facts the claim that Grindo toothpaste makes teeth whiter, but a related fact may be that Grindo contains tiny silicone particles—an abrasive that "whitens" by scraping enamel from teeth. The second fact could change your opinion about Grindo.

---

*Adapted from James L. Kinneavy's assertion that discourse should be factual, unpredictable, and comprehensive. See James L. Kinneavy, *A Theory of Discourse* (Englewood Cliffs, NJ: Prentice, 1971).

The Grindo example illustrates that no two facts about anything are likely to have equal relevance. Assume you've asserted this opinion:

The Diablo Canyon nuclear plant is especially dangerous.

In deciding how to support this opinion, you compare the relevance of each of these facts:

1. The road system is inadequate for rapid evacuation of local residents.
2. Nuclear plants have found no suitable way to dispose of radioactive wastes.
3. The plant is only 150 kilometres from sizable population centres.
4. The plant is built near a major earthquake fault.

Although all these facts support the label "dangerous," the first three can apply to many nuclear plants. Only the fourth addresses the danger specific to the Diablo Canyon plant—and therefore has most relevance. Because readers can tolerate only so many details, you must decide which of your facts offer the best support.

Besides unifying your facts, arrange them for emphasis. Consider this opening passage:

PASSAGE A—AN OPINION SUPPORTED BY FACT

Child abuse has become our national disgrace. In the past decade, reported incidence has increased an average of 20 percent yearly. This year alone, more than 50 000 children (fewer than 20 percent of cases) will be the reported victims of physical, sexual, or emotional violence by one or both parents. And among the reported offenders, only 3 percent are ever convicted. Even more tragic, the pattern of violence is cyclical, with many abused children later becoming abusive parents themselves.

We move from the disquieting numbers to the tragically cyclical process.

Instead of relying on facts, certain moral or emotional opinions (mandatory gun registration, the existence of God, smoke-free work environments, children's rights) often rest on common sense and insight. The following passage supports the opinion that parents should limit their role in telling their children how to live.

PASSAGE B—AN OPINION SUPPORTED BY GOOD SENSE

The idea of the child as personal property has always bothered me, for personal reasons. . . . I lack the feeling that I own my children and have always scoffed at the idea that what they are and do is a continuation or rejection of my being. I like them, I sympathize with them, I acknowledge the obligation to support them for a term of years—but I am not so fond

> or foolish as to regard a biological tie as a lien on their loyalty or respect, nor to imagine that I am equipped with [special] powers of guidance as to their success and happiness. Beyond inculcating some of the obvious [manners] required in civilized life, who am I to pronounce on what makes for a happy or successful life? How many of us can say that we have successfully managed our own lives? Can we do better with our children?
>
> *—Anonymous*

The above passage offers no statistics, research data, or observable facts. However, the support is credible because of its insight into our shared reality as parents and children.

MAKE IT INFORMATIVE

Are you one of those writers who enter college or university as experts in the art of "stuffing"? The stuffing expert knows how to fill pages by cramming into the essay every thought that will pile up 500 words (or any required total) with minimal pain. But readers expect *something new and useful*. Writing has informative value when it does at least one of these things:

Elements of informative value

- Shares something new and significant
- Reminds us about something we know but ignore
- Offers fresh insight or perspective on something we already know

In short, informative writing gives readers exactly what they need.

Readers approach most topics with some prior knowledge (or old information). They might need reminding, but they don't need a rehash of old information; they can "fill in the blanks" for themselves. On the other hand, readers don't need every bit of new information you can think of, either.

As a reader of this book, for example, you expect to learn something worthwhile about writing, and our purpose is to help you do that. Which of these statements would you find useful?

a.   Writing is hard and frustrating work.
b.   Writing is a process of deliberate decisions.

Statement (a) offers no news to anyone who ever has picked up a pencil. But Statement (b) reminds you that producing good writing can be a lot more complex than we would like. Because Statement (b) offers new insight into a familiar process, then we can say it has informative value.

We see that Passages A and B (pages 79–80) satisfy our criteria for informative value. Passage A offers surprising evidence about child abuse; Passage B gives fresh insight into the familiar issue of parent–child relations. Sometimes we write for a mixed group of readers with varied needs. How, then, can our writing have informative value for each reader?

Imagine you are an ex-jogger and a convert to walking for aerobic exercise. You decide to write an essay for classmates on the advantages of walking over running. You can assume a few classmates are runners; others swim, cycle, or do other exercise; some don't do much, but are thinking of starting; and some have no interest in any exercise. Your problem is to address all these readers in one essay that each reader finds worthwhile. Specifically, you want to

- Persuade runners and other exercisers to consider walking as an alternative
- Encourage the interested nonexercisers to try walking
- Create at least a spark of interest among the die-hard nonexercisers—and maybe even inspire them to rise up out of their easy chairs and hit the bricks

First, you will need to answer questions shared by all readers:

Audience questions you can anticipate

- Why is walking better than running?
- How are they similar or different?
- What are the benefits in walking?
- Can you give examples?
- Why should I?

But some readers will have special questions. Nonexercisers might ask, *What exactly is aerobic exercise, anyway?* And the true couch potatoes might ask, *Who cares?* Your essay will have to answer all these questions.

Assume that many hours of planning, drafting, and revising have enabled you to produce this final draft:

AN ESSAY WITH INFORMATIVE VALUE

WALK BUT DON'T RUN

Our bodies gain aerobic benefits when we exercise at a fast enough pace for muscles to demand oxygen-rich blood from the heart and lungs. During effective aerobic exercise, the heart rate increases roughly 80 percent above normal. Besides strengthening muscle groups—especially the heart—aerobic exercise makes blood vessels stronger and larger.

Running, or jogging, has become a most popular form of aerobic exercise. But thousands of Canadians who began running to get in shape are now limping to their doctors for treatment of running injuries. To keep yourself in one piece as you keep yourself in shape, try walking instead of running.

All the aerobic benefits of running can be yours if you merely take brisk walks. Consider this comparison. For enough aerobic training to increase cardiovascular (heart, lungs, and blood vessels) efficiency, you need to run three times weekly for roughly 30 minutes. (Like any efficient system, an efficient cardiovascular system produces maximum work with minimum effort.) You can gain cardiovascular benefits equivalent to running, however, by taking a brisk walk three times weekly for roughly 60 minutes. Granted, walking takes up more time than running, but it carries fewer risks.

Because of its more controlled and deliberate pace, walking is safer than running. A walker stands far less chance of tripping, stepping in potholes, or slipping and falling. And the slower pace causes less physical trauma. Anyone who has ever run at all knows that a runner's foot strikes the ground with sizable impact. But the shock of this impact travels beyond the foot—to the shins, knees, hips, internal organs, and spine. Walking, of course, creates an impact of its own, but the walker's foot strikes the ground with only half as much force as the runner's foot.

Beyond its apparent physical dangers, running can provoke subtle stress for the devoted exerciser. Because running is generally seen as more competitive than just walking, we too easily can be tempted to push our bodies too far, too fast. Even though we might not compete in races or marathons, we often tend to compete against ourselves—maybe just to keep up with a jock neighbour or to break a personal record. And by ignoring the signals of overexertion and physical stress, we can easily run ourselves into an injury—if not the grave. Slowing to a walk instead is a safe way of leaving the "competition" behind.

—Jeff Leonard

Will this essay have informative value for all readers? Probably so. It seems to answer all the readers' questions we anticipated on page 81. Will all readers become converts? Probably not. But each should have something to think about. A worthwhile message makes some kind of a difference for its readers—even if it triggers only the slightest insight.

Now let's assume that you had written the walking essay by using the old high school strategy of filling up the page. Your opening paragraph might look like this:

AN OPENING WITHOUT INFORMATIVE VALUE

WALK BUT DON'T RUN

Medical science has made tremendous breakthroughs in the past few decades. Research has shown that exercise is a good way of staying healthy, beneficial for our bodies and our minds. More people of all ages are exercising today than ever before. Because of its benefits, one popular form of exercise for Canadians is aerobic exercise.

Your readers (in the situation described on page 81) already know all this. Even new material lacks informative value when it is irrelevant:

MATERIAL IRRELEVANT TO THE SITUATION

To avoid the perils of running, the Chinese attend sessions of T'ai-chi, a dancelike series of stretching routines designed to increase concentration and agility. Although T'ai-chi is less dangerous than running, it fails to provide a truly aerobic workout.

The above material might serve in an essay comparing certain aerobic and nonaerobic exercises, but not in this comparison between walking and running.

Nor would highly technical details have informative value here, as in this next example:

MATERIAL TOO TECHNICAL FOR THE SITUATION

Walking and jogging result in forward motion because you continually fall forward and catch yourself. With each stride, you lift your body, accelerate, and land. You go faster when running because you fall farther, but you also strike the ground harder, and for less time. Your increase in speed and distance fallen combine with the shorter contact period to cause an impact on your body that is more than double the impact from walking.

The above material would serve for students of biophysics, exercise physiology, or sports medicine, but seems too detailed for a mixed audience.

MAKE IT COMPLETE

All writers struggle with this question: *How much is enough?* (Or, *How long should it be?*) Again, anticipate readers' questions about your thesis.

Assume, for instance, that a friend now living in another province is thinking of taking a job similar to one you held last summer. Your friend has written to ask how you liked the job; your response will influence the friend's decision. Here is a passage from a first draft that tells but doesn't show:

NOT ENOUGH DETAIL

My job last summer as a flagger for a road construction company was boring, tiresome, dirty, and painful. All I did was stand in the road and flag cars. Every day I just stood there, getting sore feet. I was always covered with dirt and breathing it in. To make matters worse, the sun, wind, and bugs ruined my skin. By the end of summer, I vowed never to do this kind of work again.

The above passage has only limited informative value because it fails to make the experience vivid for readers. The sketchy details fail to answer our obvious questions.

- Can you show me what the job was like?
- What, exactly, made it boring, tiresome, dirty, and painful?

This next passage, on the other hand, is revised to include graphic details that make readers feel a part of it all:

ENOUGH DETAIL

> My job last summer as a flagger for a road construction company was boring, tiresome, dirty, and painful. All day I stood like a robot; waving a stupid red flag at oncoming traffic, my eardrums blasted by the racket of road machinery, each day dragging by more slowly than the last. My feet would swell, and my legs would ache from standing on the hard clay and gravel for up to fifteen hours a day. And the filth was disgusting. The fumes, oil, and grime from the road machinery and the exhaust from passing cars became like a second skin. Each breath sucked up more dust, clogging my sinuses, irritating my eyes. But worst of all was the weather. Blistering from sunburn, I was being sandblasted and rubbed raw by windstorms, pounded by hail, or chewed by mosquitoes and horseflies. By the end of summer, I was a freak: swollen feet and ankles, the skin of a water buffalo, and chronic sinusitis. I'd starve before taking that job again.

In the above situation, even more details (say, a day-by-day description of every event) probably would clutter the message. The reader here needed and *wanted* just enough information to make an informed decision.

Giving enough detail is not the same as merely adding more words. Whatever does nothing but fill the page is puffery:

HOT AIR

> My job last summer as a flagger for a road construction company was boring, tiresome, dirty, and painful. ~~Day in and day out~~, I stood ~~on that road~~ for endless hours getting ~~a severe case of~~ sore feet. My face and body were ~~always completely~~ covered with ~~the~~ dust blown up from the ~~passing cars and various other~~ vehicles, and I was forced to breathe in all ~~of~~ this ~~horrible~~ junk ~~day after day. To add to the problems of boredom, fatigue, and dirt~~, the weather murdered my skin. ~~Let me tell you that~~ by the time ~~the~~ summer ended, I ~~had made myself~~ a solemn promise never to ~~victimize myself by~~ taking this kind of awful job again.

Although the above passage is nearly twice as long as the original (page 83), it adds no meaning; hot air (shown crossed out) offers no real information.

| NOTE | *Don't worry about not having enough to say. Once you have begun the writing process (searching for details, rephrasing, making connections), you probably will find it harder to stay within the limit than to reach it. Your purpose is to make your point—not to show how smart you are. Instead of including every word, fact, and idea that crosses your mind, learn to select. Sometimes one single detail is enough. To make the point about a "boring" job, the passage at the top of this page describes the writer standing like a robot, waving a red flag.* |

The passages above show how you can measure the completeness of your own writing, *providing details that show,* by answering questions like the following:

Details answer
these questions

- *Who, what, when, where, and why?*
- *What did you see, feel, hear, taste, smell?*
- *What would a camera record?*
- *What are the dates, numbers, percentages?*
- *Can you compare it to something more familiar?*

APPLICATION 5-1

Each sentence below states either a fact or an opinion. Rewrite all statements of opinion as statements of fact. Remember that a fact can be verified. (Review pages 78–79.)

EXAMPLE

Opinion   My roommate isn't taking university work seriously.

Fact   My roommate never studies, sleeps through most classes, and has missed every exam.

1. Professor X grades unfairly.
2. My vacation was too short.
3. The salary for this position is $15 000 yearly.
4. This bicycle is reasonably priced.
5. We walked 10 kilometres last Saturday.
6. He drives recklessly.
7. My motorcycle gets great gas mileage.
8. This course has been very helpful.
9. German shepherds eat more than cocker spaniels do.
10. This apartment is much too small for our family.

APPLICATION 5-2

Return to Shirley Haley's essay on pages 13–15. Underline all statements of fact, and circle all statements of opinion. Are all the opinions supported by facts or by good sense? Now, perform the same evaluation on an essay you have written. (Review pages 78–80.)

APPLICATION 5-3

Assume you live in the Maritimes, and citizens in your province are voting on a solar energy referendum that would channel millions of tax dollars toward solar technology. The next paragraphs are designed to help you, as a voter, make an educated decision. Do both these versions of the same message have informative value? Explain. (Review pages 80–83.)

> Solar power offers a realistic solution to the Maritimes' energy problems. In recent years the cost of fossil fuels (oil, coal, and natural gas) has risen rapidly while the supply has continued to decline. High prices and short supply will continue to cause a worsening energy crisis. Because solar energy comes directly from the sun, it is an inexhaustible resource. By using this energy to heat and air-condition our buildings, as well as to provide electricity, we could decrease substantially our consumption of fossil fuels. In turn, we would be less dependent on the unstable Middle East for our oil supplies. Clearly, solar power is a good alternative to conventional energy sources.

> Solar power offers a realistic solution to the Maritimes' energy problems. To begin with, solar power is efficient. Solar collectors installed on fewer than 30 percent of roofs in the Maritime provinces would provide more than 70 percent of the area's heating and air-conditioning needs. Moreover, solar heat collectors are economical, operating for up to 20 years with little or no maintenance. These savings recoup the initial cost of installment within only ten years. Most important, solar power is safe. It can be transformed into electricity through photovoltaic cells (a type of storage battery) noiselessly and with no air pollution—unlike coal, oil, and wood combustion. In sharp contrast to its nuclear counterpart, solar power produces no toxic wastes and poses no catastrophic danger of meltdown. Thus, massive conversion to solar power would ensure abundant energy and a safe, clean environment for future generations.

APPLICATION 5-4

Collaborative Project: Review a classmate's essay and eliminate all statements that lack informative value (those that offer commonly known, irrelevant, or insignificant material). Be careful not to cut material the audience needs in order to understand the essay, such as

1. Details that help us see.
2. Details that help us feel.
3. Numerical details.
4. Vivid comparisons.

5. Details that a camera would record.

6. A detail that helps us hear.

Would some parts of your classmate's essay benefit from greater detail? Use the list above as a basis for making specific suggestions.

APPLICATION **5-5**

Computer Application: Make an electronic copy of a classmate's essay. Put the main topic in boldface and underline all supporting material that has informative value. Save the file. Copy it and cut anything not in bold or underlined. Working with your classmate, compare the two versions.

APPLICATION **5-6**

Return to one of your earlier essays. Study it carefully, and then brainstorm again to sharpen your details. Now write a revised version. (Review pages 78–85.)

APPLICATION **5-7**

Computer Application: Working from the joint computer file for your group, complete Application 5-4.

APPLICATION **5-8**

Computer Application: Select a paragraph you have written for an earlier assignment. Using the paragraph on page 83–4 as a guide, create and save at least two alternative versions of this paragraph by deleting different combinations of words and phrases. Print out all three versions. Then, from among the alternatives, choose what you think is the most effective version of *each sentence*. Recombine these sentences into a fourth version of the paragraph—one that achieves completeness without clutter.

APPLICATION **5-9**

Collaborative Project: Assume that your English teacher has just won $10 million in the provincial lottery. As a final grand gesture before retiring to a life of sailing, collecting fine wines, and breeding polo ponies, your soon-to-be ex-teacher makes this announcement to the class:

> After years of agonizing over ways to motivate my writing audience, I've discovered what could be the ultimate solution. I'm going to hold a contest offering $1 million to the student who writes the best essay on this topic: How I Would Spend $1 Million. Essays will be evaluated on the basis of originality, credibility, richness of detail, and clarity of explanation. The whole class will pick the winner from among the five finalists I select.

Write your essay, revising as often as needed to make it a winner.

CHAPTER 6

Revising the Paragraphs: Shaping for Readers' Access

An essay's basic design makes its content accessible for readers. But this larger design (introduction, body, conclusion) depends on the smaller design of each paragraph. A paragraph is a place for things that belong together.

SUPPORT PARAGRAPHS AS MINI-ESSAYS

Paragraphs in an essay have various shapes and purposes. Introductory paragraphs draw us into the writer's reality; concluding paragraphs ease us out; transitional paragraphs help hold things together. But here the subject is *support paragraphs*—those middle blocks of thought, each often a mini-shape of the whole essay. Just as the thesis is sustained by its supporting points, each major supporting point is sustained by its paragraph:

FIGURE 6.1
Support paragraphs
in the basic essay

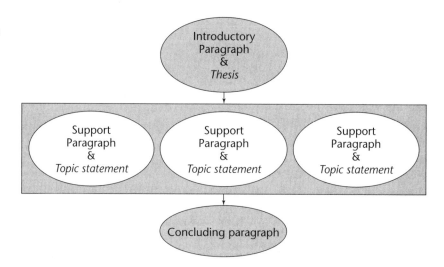

Although part of the essay's larger design, each support paragraph usually can stand alone in meaning and emphasis. In her article on "Measuring Excellence" in *Maclean's* (10th Annual Ranking of Universities issue, November 2000), Ann Dowsett Johnston reports on the competition students face when applying to specific programs:

A TYPICAL SUPPORT PARAGRAPH

Introduction (topic statement, 1)

Body (2–8)

[1]In the most elite programs, entry grades have ratcheted up in the process. [2]What did you need to get into Queen's high-profile commerce program this year? [3]Ninety per cent. [4]Computer engineering or electrical engineering at Waterloo? [5]Low to mid-90s. [6]Fourteen hundred students applied for 80 spots in McMaster University's new bachelor of health sciences program. [7]Of those offered admission, three-quarters had

averages of 92 per cent or higher. [8]And at McGill, it was easier to get into medicine than to win a spot in electrical engineering. [9]"The standards of admission are becoming extraordinary," says Bernard Shapiro, principal of McGill. [10]George Granger, registrar at McMaster, points out that universities have begun installing more sophisticated selection procedures and mandatory supplementary applications to aid in "choosing elites from elites."

Conclusion (9–10)

Dowsett Johnston's paragraph is part of a much longer essay, but its shape is familiar enough: the opening sentence asserts her definite viewpoint, the body walks us through her reasoning to support her viewpoint, and the last sentence provides a perspective on what universities are doing to cope with the situation.

¶ PARAGRAPH FUNCTION

Writers need definite paragraph divisions for control; readers need them for access.

Paragraphs *increase your writing control*. Each support paragraph is an idea unit, one distinct space for developing one supporting point. If Dowsett Johnston begins her paragraph with the point that entry grades have increased in elite university programs, she can tailor everything in her paragraph to advance her meaning.

Paragraphs also *give readers orientation*. Readers need to know where they are and where they're going. By dividing a long piece of writing, paragraphs allow readers to focus on each point. The paragraph indent (five spaces) gives a breathing space, a signal that the geography is changing and that it's time to look ahead.

¶lgth PARAGRAPH LENGTH

Paragraph length depends on *the writer's purpose* and the reader's capacity for understanding. Writing that carries highly technical information or complex instructions may use short paragraphs or perhaps a list. In a newspaper article, paragraphs of only one or two sentences keep the reader's attention. In writing that explains concepts, attitudes, or viewpoints (as in college essays), support paragraphs generally run from 100 to 300 words.

But word count really means very little. What matters is *how thoroughly the paragraph makes your point*. A flabby paragraph buries readers in needless words and details; but just skin-and-bones leaves readers looking for the meat. Each paragraph requires new decisions. Try to avoid too much of anything. A clump of short paragraphs can make some writing seem choppy and poorly organized, but a stretch of long ones is tiring. A well-placed short paragraph—sometimes just one sentence—can supply special emphasis:

> More than 30 percent of our province's municipal water supplies have been under "boil-water" advisories.

For real impact, you can even use just one word:

> Exactly.

¶ts

THE TOPIC STATEMENT

A college essay needs a thesis that asserts the main point, and each support paragraph needs a *topic statement* that asserts a supporting point. Sometimes the topic statement comes at the end of the paragraph; sometimes in the middle; but usually it comes first. The paragraph's first sentence should focus and forecast.

The Topic Statement as Readers' Framework

Most paragraphs in university or college writing begin by *telling readers what to look for.* Don't write

No focus

> Some jobs are less stressful than others.

when you mean

Better

> Mortuary management is an ideal major for anyone craving a stress-free job.

The first topic statement above doesn't give a very clear forecast; the second helps us focus.
    Don't write

No forecast

> Summers in Goonville are awful.

when you mean

Better

> I hate Goonville summers because of the blackflies, horseflies, mosquitoes, and no-see-ums.

The Topic Statement as Writer's Framework

Without a topic statement, writers struggle to make their paragraphs more than a collection of stuff. Always *take a definite stand; assert something significant.*
    Imagine you are a member of city council, about to vote on spending $200 000 to re-establish holiday bus service. One of your constituents has responded to your request for citizens' viewpoints with a letter that begins like this:

No focus or
forecast

> *Running transit buses on holidays like Christmas is a complex issue.* Many people are for it, many people are against it, and many people don't care. This is another one of those budget issues that is debated every year and nothing ever seems to be resolved.

Because this writer never identified his purpose, never discovered his own exact meaning, the above paragraph merely parrots a number of unrelated thoughts that are all common knowledge. If, instead, our writer had refined his meaning by asserting a definite viewpoint, he might have written a worthwhile paragraph. Depending on his purpose, he might have begun with, say:

Better

> *Cancelling municipal bus service on holidays, such as Christmas, discriminates against the poor.*

or

> *Not allowing the poor to visit family and friends or to get to work on holidays such as Christmas demonstrates council's lack of concern for the poor.*

Before you can explain yourself, you have to figure out exactly what you mean.

STRUCTURAL VARIATIONS IN SUPPORT PARAGRAPHS

Your main idea might have several distinct parts, which would result in an excessively long paragraph. You might then break up the paragraph, making your topic statement a brief introductory paragraph that forecasts various subparts, which are set off as independent paragraphs.

A TOPIC STATEMENT THAT SERVES SEVERAL PARAGRAPHS

> *Trees that provide most of the raw material produced and used in Canada are grouped into two general classifications: conifers and broadleaves, or coniferous and deciduous.*
>
> Conifers, or softwoods, are evergreens that do not normally lose their leaves in the winter. The most common species include white pine, red pine, jack pine, black spruce, white spruce, Douglas fir, cedar, and redwood. Characterized by their needle-shaped leaves, conifers survive well in harsh climates where soil conditions are generally poor. Conifers are used commercially for pulp and paper, furniture, and construction.
>
> Broadleaves, or hardwoods, normally lose or drop their leaves in the fall, particularly in the temperate zones. The most common species in the temperate zones are maple, oak, elm, birch, ash, beech, poplar, and alder. The majority of the species grow well in moderate climates where soil

conditions are good. Broadleaves are used to make furniture, flooring, and panelling.

As you can see, each paragraph begins with a clear statement of the subtopic discussed in it.

NOTE   *Remember that you won't always be able to think first of the right topic statement, and then of your support. Your actual framework might not appear until you've done some freewriting or brainstorming. The sequence is unimportant—as long as the finished paragraph offers a definite framework and solid support.*

¶un

PARAGRAPH UNITY

Each paragraph in an essay requires *external unity* and *internal unity*. A paragraph has external unity when (as on pages 52–53) it belongs with all the other paragraphs in an essay. But each paragraph requires internal unity as well: everything in the paragraph should belong there.

Imagine that you're composing a paragraph beginning with this topic statement:

Chemical pesticides and herbicides are both ineffective and hazardous.

The words that signal the meaning here are **ineffective** and **hazardous;** everything in the paragraph should directly advance that meaning. Here is the unified paragraph:

A UNIFIED PARAGRAPH

Chemical pesticides and herbicides are both ineffective and hazardous. Because none of these chemicals has permanent effects, pest populations invariably recover and need to be resprayed. Repeated applications cause pests to develop immunity to the chemicals. Furthermore, most pesticides and herbicides attack species other than the intended pest, killing off its natural predators, thus actually increasing the pest population. Above all, chemical residues survive in the environment (and in living tissue) for years and often are carried hundreds of kilometres by wind and water. This toxic legacy includes such biological effects as birth deformities, reproductive failures, brain damage, and cancer. Although intended to control pest populations, these chemicals ironically threaten to make the human population their ultimate victims.

One way to destroy unity in the paragraph above would be to veer from the focus on **ineffective** and **hazardous** to material about the cost of the chemicals or their unpleasant odour or the number of people who oppose their use.

Every topic statement has a *signal term*, a key word or phrase that announces the viewpoint. In the paragraph below, the signal term is **intelligent,** causing readers to expect material about whale intelligence. But the shift to food problems fails to advance the meaning of intelligence, throwing the paragraph—and the reader—off track:

A DISUNIFIED PARAGRAPH

> *Whales are among the most intelligent of all mammals.* Scientists rank whale intelligence with that of higher primates because of whales' sophisticated group behaviour. These impressive mammals have been seen teaching and disciplining their young, helping their wounded comrades, engaging in elaborate courtship rituals, and playing in definite gamelike patterns. Whales continually need to search for food in order to survive. Their search for krill and other sea organisms can cause them to migrate thousands of kilometres yearly.

¶coh

PARAGRAPH COHERENCE

In a coherent paragraph, everything not only belongs but also sticks together: topic statement and support form *a connected line of thought*, like links in a chain.

This next paragraph (written by a track team veteran addressing new runners) is both unified and coherent: everything relates to the topic in a continuous line of thinking.

A COHERENT PARAGRAPH

> [1]*To be among the first out of the starting blocks in any race, follow these instructions.* [2]First, when the starter says, "Into your blocks," make sure you are the last runner down. [3]Take your sweet time; make all the others wait for you. [4]You take your time for three good reasons: one, you get a little more stretching than your competitors do; two, they are down in the blocks getting cold and nervous while you're still warm and relaxed from stretching; and three, your deliberate manner tends to weaken other runners' confidence. [5]The second step is to lean forward over your shoulders, in the "set" position. [6]This way, you will come out of the blocks forward and low, meeting less wind resistance. [7]The third and final step is to pump your arms as fast as you can when you come off the blocks. [8]The faster your arms pump, the faster your legs will move. [9]By concentrating on each of these steps, you can expect your quickest possible start.

The material in this paragraph seems easy enough to follow:

1. The topic statement sets a clear direction.

2. The first step is introduced.

3–4. The importance of "taking your time" is emphasized and explained.

5–6. The second step is introduced and its importance explained.

7–8. The third step is introduced and its importance explained.

9. The conclusion sums up.

Because the material follows a logical order (in this case, chronological), readers know exactly where they are at any place in the paragraph. Let's now examine specific ways of achieving coherence.

Ordering Ideas for Coherence

The mind works in structured ways to arrange and make sense of its many perceptions. If you decide you like a class (a general observation), you then identify your particular reasons (friendly atmosphere, interesting subject, dynamic teacher, and so on); your thinking has followed a *general-to-specific order*. Or, if you tell a friend about your terrific weekend, you follow the order of events, how things happened over the weekend; your thinking has followed a *chronological order*. These are just two of several ordering patterns the mind uses to create a sensible sequence of information. Here are the most common ordering patterns:

Common ways
of arranging
information

- general-to-specific order
- specific-to-general order
- emphatic order
- spatial order
- chronological order

These ordering patterns can help you answer the following questions:

- What comes first?
- What comes next?
- Does the subject have any features that suggest an order?

Answers will be based on your subject and purpose. In a letter describing your new car (subject) to a friend, you might decide to move from outside to inside in a spatial order, as one would when first examining the car. Or, if you decided to concentrate on the car's computerized dashboard (subject), you might move from left to right (as one would view it from the driver's seat). If, instead, you were trying to persuade someone to stay in school or to quit smoking, you probably would present your reasons in an emphatic order, from least to most important or vice versa.

As we will see, some kinds of order call for your topic statement to come last instead of first. Even then, your opening sentence should tell readers what to expect. Before considering those variations, however, let's begin with the standard ordering pattern: general to specific.

General-to-Specific Order. The most usual way of arranging a paragraph is from general to specific: *a general topic statement supported by specific* *details.* Most sample paragraphs we've seen so far follow a general-to-specific order, as this next one does:

STARTING WITH THE BIG PICTURE

General assertion
(topic statement, 1)
Specific support
(2–8)

Conclusion (9)

¹*Canadians everywhere are obsessed with speed.* ²The airlines think it's so important that they've developed jets that can cross the ocean in a few hours. ³Despite energy shortages, Oshawa often makes the speed of a car and the power of its engine a focal point of its advertising campaign. ⁴Ads for oil companies boast of ten-minute oil changes at their gas stations. ⁵Even pedestrians aren't spared: some shoemakers will put soles and heels on shoes "while you wait." ⁶Fast-food restaurants prosper as increasing millions gobble increasing billions of "all-beef" hamburgers and guzzle their Cokes in seconds flat. ⁷And the Day of Rest, too, has given way to the stopwatch as more and more churches offer brief evening services or customize their offerings to suit "people on the go." ⁸Some churches even offer drive-in ceremonies—pay your money, spit out your prayer, and hit the road, streaking toward salvation with Ronald McDonald. ⁹These days, even the road to eternity has a fast lane.

Paragraphs of general-to-specific order are the workhorses of virtually all nonfiction writing.

Specific-to-General Order. For some purposes, instead of narrowing and restricting your meaning, you will generalize and extend it. Thus, your *support will come first, and your topic statement last.* A specific-to-general order is especially useful for showing how pieces of evidence add up to a convincing conclusion, as in this next paragraph.

STARTING WITH THE SUPPORTING DETAILS

Orienting
statements (1–2)
Specific details
(3–7)

General conclusion
(topic statement,
8–9)

¹I've been thinking about seeing. ²There are lots of things to see, unwrapped gifts and free surprises. ³The world is fairly studded and strewn with pennies cast broadside from a generous hand. ⁴But—and this is the point—who gets excited by a mere penny? ⁵If you follow one arrow, if you crouch motionless on a bank to watch a tremulous ripple thrill on the water and are rewarded by the sight of a muskrat paddling from its den, will you count that sight a chip of copper only, and go your rueful way? ⁶It is dire poverty indeed when a man is so malnourished and fatigued that he won't stoop to pick up a penny. ⁷But if you cultivate a healthy poverty and simplicity, so that finding a penny will literally make your day, then, since the world is in fact planted in pennies, you have with your poverty bought a lifetime of days. ⁸*It is that simple.* ⁹*What you see is what you get.*
—Annie Dillard

But even though the topic statement appears last, the opening statements forecast the paragraph. Whenever you decide to delay your topic sentence, be sure the paragraph's opening sentence gives readers enough orientation for them to know what's going on.

A specific-to-general order works best for supporting a position that some readers might disagree with, as in this next example:

SAVING THE BIG PICTURE FOR LAST

Specific observation in orienting statement (1)
Specific arguments (2–7)

[1]Strange that so few ever come to the woods to see how the pine lives and grows and spires, lifting its evergreen arms to the light—to see its perfect success; but most are content to behold it in the shape of many broad boards brought to market, and deem *that* its true success! [2]But the pine is no more lumber than [the person] is, and to be made into boards and houses is no more its true and highest use than the truest use of a [person] is to be cut down and made into manure. [3]There is a higher law affecting our relations to pine as well as to [people]. [4]A pine cut down, a dead pine, is no more a pine than a dead human carcass is a [person]. [5]Can [one] who has discovered only some of the values of whalebone and whale oil be said to have discovered the true use of the whale? [6]Can [one] who slays the elephant for [its] ivory be said to have "seen the elephant"? [7]These are petty and accidental uses; just as if a stronger race were to kill us in order to make buttons and flutes of our bones; for everything may serve a lower as well as a higher use. [8]*Every creature is better alive than dead, [people] and moose and pine trees, and [one] who understands it correctly will rather preserve its life than destroy it.*

General conclusion (topic statement, 8)

—*Henry David Thoreau*

Some readers (especially those in the paper and lumber industry, as well as hunters) would find Thoreau's main point harder to accept if it were placed at the beginning. By moving from the specific to the general, Thoreau presents his evidence before drawing his conclusion. Also, things that come last (last word in a sentence, last sentence in a paragraph, last paragraph in an essay) are the things readers remember best.

Emphatic Order. In earlier chapters, we've seen how emphasis can make important ideas stand out, become easier to remember. Writers *achieve emphasis within paragraphs by positioning material* in two common ways: (1) *from least to most important* or *serious* or *dramatic*, and (2) *vice versa*. The next paragraph is from an essay analyzing television advertisements for toys of violence. Joe Bolton offers dramatic support for his opening assertion by saving his strongest example for last.

HELPING READERS FOCUS

Topic statement (1–2)

[1]*Too many toys advertised during television programs for children are of what I call the "death and destruction" variety: toys that simulate the killing of humans by humans.* [2]Such toys make children's "war games" seem far too real. [3]During the pre-Christmas season, children are

Examples in increasing order of importance (3–5)

bombarded with ads promoting all the new weapons: guns, tanks, boats, subs, helicopters, lasers, and more. [4]One new warplane is described as "the wickedest weapon yet," and a new mobile weapon resembles an old "Nike" missile, designed to be moved around on railroad tracks to avoid an enemy strike. [5]One of the enemy dolls is even dubbed a "paranoid schizophrenic killer" and advertised as such on the side of the box.

Spatial Order. Sometimes, you create a word picture by treating the parts of your subject in the same order that readers would follow if they actually were looking at it. In this next paragraph, the writer describes someone who is to be picked up at a busy airport.

HELPING READERS VISUALIZE

Topic statement

A gradually narrowing focus

Roger should be easy to recognize. When I last saw him, he was wearing dark blue jeans, a pair of dark brown hunting boots with red laces, and a light blue cableknit sweater with a turtleneck; he was carrying a red daypack with black trim filled with books. He stands about 200 cm, has broad, slouching shoulders, and carries roughly 85 kg on a medium frame. He walks in excessively long strides, like a cowboy. His hair is sunstreaked, sandy blond, cut just below his ears and feathered back on the sides. He has deep purple eyes framed by dark brown eyelashes and brows set into a clear, tanned complexion. The bridge of his nose carries a 2 cm scar in the shape of an inverted crescent. His right front tooth has a small chip in the left corner.

The above sequence follows the order of features readers would recognize in approaching Roger: first, from a distance, by his clothing, size, posture, and stride; next, from a closer view—the hair, eye colour, and so on; and, finally, from right up close—the scar on his nose and the chip on his tooth. The earlier details, visible from a distance, would alert readers, and the later ones would confirm their impression as they moved nearer. The writer decided to take the angle of a movie camera gradually closing in.

Chronological Order. A chronological order follows the *actual sequence of events.* Writers use chronological order to give instructions (how to be first out of the starting blocks), to explain how something works (how the heart pumps blood), or to show how something happened. This paragraph from George Orwell's essay "Shooting an Elephant" shows how something brutal happened. As with many paragraphs that tell a story, this one has no topic statement. Instead, the opening sentence places us in the middle of the action.

HELPING READERS EXPERIENCE

Orienting statement (1–2)

[1]When I pulled the trigger I did not hear the bang or feel the kick— one never does when a shot goes home—but I heard the devilish roar of glee that went up from the crowd. [2]In that instant, in too short a time,

one would have thought, even for the bullet to get there, a mysterious, terrible change had come over the elephant. [3]He neither stirred nor fell, but every line on his body had altered. [4]He looked suddenly stricken, shrunken, immensely old, as though the frightful impact of the bullet had paralyzed him without knocking him down. [5]At last, after what seemed like a long time—it might have been five seconds, I dare say—he sagged flabbily to his knees. [6]His mouth slobbered. [7]An enormous senility seemed to have settled upon him. [8]One could have imagined him thousands of years old. [9]I fired again into the same spot. [10]At the second shot he did not collapse but climbed with desperate slowness to his feet and stood weakly upright, with legs sagging and head drooping. [11]I fired a third time. [12]That was the shot that did it for him. [13]You could see the agony of it jolt his whole body and knock the last remnant of strength from his legs. [14]But in falling he seemed for a moment to rise, for as his hind legs collapsed beneath him he seemed to tower upwards like a huge rock toppling, his trunk reaching skywards like a tree. [15]He trumpeted, for the first and only time. [16]And then down he came, his belly towards me, with a crash that seemed to shake the ground even where I lay.

—George Orwell

The actual chronology in Orwell's paragraph is simple:

a. With the first shot, the elephant falls to its knees.

b. With the second shot, instead of collapsing, the elephant drags itself up.

c. With the third shot, the elephant falls, rises, and then falls for good.

But note that if narrating these events in order were the writer's only purpose, the paragraph might look like this:

TRACING THE EVENT

When I pulled the trigger, a change came over the elephant. He neither stirred nor fell, but every line on his body had altered as if the impact of the bullet had paralyzed him without knocking him down. At last, he sagged to his knees. His mouth slobbered. I fired again into the same spot. At the second shot, he did not collapse but climbed slowly to his feet and stood with legs sagging and head drooping. I fired a third time. That was the shot that did it for him. But in falling he seemed for a moment to rise. And then, down he came, with his belly towards me, with a crash that shook the ground.

The above paragraph presents the kinds of details a camera might record.

Compare the first and second version of Orwell's paragraph. Which has the greatest impact? Why?

Notice that this chapter asks you to practise specific strategies, but remember: when you write on your own, you won't begin by saying, "I've decided to write a spatial paragraph, and so now I need to find a subject that will fit that order." Instead, you will say, "I want to discuss X; therefore, I need to select the ordering pattern that best reveals my thinking. Much of your writing will, in fact, call for a combination of these ordering patterns.

Parallelism

Several other devices enhance coherence. The first is *parallelism*—similar grammatical structures and word order for similar items, or for items of equal importance. Note how parallelism is employed in this next paragraph:

EXPRESSING EQUAL ITEMS EQUALLY

[1]*What does Thunder Bay have to offer?* [2]Thunder Bay, first and foremost, is the recreationist's paradise. [3]*It offers the sailor* and the sea kayaker Lake Superior; *the white-water kayaker* Current River; *the canoeist* the Kaministiquia River. [4]*It offers the fisher* salmon, pickerel, trout, and the great northern pike; *the camper* Sleeping Giant, Kakabeka Falls, and Quetico Provincial Parks; *the hiker* trails throughout the rugged Pre-Cambrian Shield. [5]*It offers the cross-country skier* Sibley, Kamview, and Lappe; *the downhill skier* Mount Baldy, Loch Lomond, and Candy Mountain. [6]*Living in Thunder Bay allows one to sit* at the Marina, watching the sun rise over the Sleeping Giant; *to walk* the paths around Boulevard Lake; *to enjoy* the beautiful flowers in the Sunken Gardens and Friendship Gardens; and *to explore* the Cascades, Centennial Park and Trowbridge Falls, and Mount McKay.

The above paragraph displays parallelism between and within sentences. Sentences 3, 4, and 5 open with identical structures ("It offers") to signal that they treat the same subject. Inside these sentences are additional parallel structures ("the sailor Lake Superior ... the fisher salmon ... the downhill skier Mount Baldy.") These structures provide balance and unity. Sentence 6 features a series of infinitive phrases ("to sit at the Marina ..., to walk the paths ..., to enjoy the flowers ..., and to explore the Cascades) that are set in parallel.

Repetition, Restatement, and Variation

To help link ideas, repeat key words or phrases or rephrase them in different ways, as in this next paragraph (emphasis added):

FORWARDING THE MAIN IDEA

[1]*Whales are among the most intelligent of all mammals.* [2]Scientists rank whale *intelligence* with that of higher primates because of whales' *sophisticated* group behaviour. [3]These *bright* creatures have been seen teaching and disciplining their young, helping their wounded comrades, engaging in elaborate courtship rituals, and playing in definite gamelike

patterns. [4]They are able to coordinate such *complex cognitive activities* through their highly effective communication system of sonar clicks and pings. [5]Such *remarkable social organization* apparently stems from the *humanlike* devotion that whales seem to display toward one another.

The signal word **intelligent** in the topic statement reappears as **intelligence** in sentence 2. Synonyms (different words with similar meaning) describing intelligent behaviour (**sophisticated, bright, humanlike**) reinforce and advance the main idea throughout.

NOTE   *Keep in mind that needless repetition makes writing tedious and annoying to read. For a clear distinction between effective and ineffective repetition, see page 120.*

Pronouns for Coherence

Instead of repeating certain nouns, it is sometimes more natural to use pronouns that refer to an earlier key noun. Pronouns improve coherence by relating sentences, clauses, and phrases to each other. This next paragraph uses pronouns to avoid repeating **the bull fighters** (emphasis added):

USING PRONOUNS AS CONNECTORS

The *bull fighters* march in across the sand to the president's box. *They* march with easy professional stride, swinging along, not in the least theatrical except for *their* clothes. *They* all have the easy grace and slight slouch of the professional athlete. From *their* faces *they* might be major league ball players. *They* salute the president's box then spread out along the barrera, exchanging *their* heavy brocaded capes for the fighting capes that have been laid along the red fence by the attendants.

—*Ernest Hemingway*

Be sure each pronoun refers clearly to the appropriate noun. The pronouns in Hemingway's paragraph, for example, clearly refer to the **bull fighters.** See page 112 for a full discussion of pronoun-antecedent agreement.

Consistency for Coherence

Coherence always relies on consistent tense, point of view, and number. In general, do not shift from past to present tense, from third- to first-person point of view, or from singular to plural nouns or pronouns. See Appendix A for a discussion of shifts that destroy coherence.

Transitions

The above devices for achieving coherence (order, parallelism, repetition and restatement, pronouns) *suggest* specific relations between ideas. Transitional expressions, on the other hand, *announce* those relations.

Words or phrases such as **for example, meanwhile, however,** and **moreover** work like bridges between thoughts. Each has a definite meaning—even without a specific context—as shown below.

TRANSITION	RELATION
X; furthermore, Y	Y is in addition to X.
X; on the other hand, Y	Y is different from X.
X; yet, Y	Y is in contrast to X.
X; therefore, Y	Y is a result of X.

Here is a paragraph in which these transitions are used to clarify the writer's line of thinking (emphasis added):

USING TRANSITIONS TO BRIDGE IDEAS

Conversations with first-year students living in residence indicate that they thoroughly enjoy their new-found freedom from parental control and cherish the new friends from around the world they have made. *Furthermore,* they love the fact that they can roll out of bed mere minutes before their 8:30 classes, grab a muffin and coffee from Tim Hortons, and make it to class on time. *On the other hand*, they are often confronted with distractions, such as parties and football games that can take them away from their studies and disrupt their schedules. *Yet,* given the choice of living off campus, most would choose residence. *Therefore,* perhaps all first-year out-of-town students should experience residence life, at least for one year.

NOTE *Transitional expressions should be a limited option for achieving coherence. Use them sparingly, and only when a relationship is not already made clear by the devices discussed earlier.*

Whole sentences can serve as transitions between paragraphs and a whole paragraph can serve as a transition between sections of writing. Assume, for instance, that you work as a marketing intern for a stereo manufacturer. You have just completed a section of a memo on the advantages of the new AKS amplifier and are now moving to a section on selling the idea to consumers. This next paragraph might link the two sections:

A TRANSITIONAL PARAGRAPH

Because the AKS amplifier increases bass range by 15 percent, it should be installed as a standard item in all our stereo speakers. Tooling and installation adjustments, however, will add roughly $50 to the list price of each model. We must, therefore, explain the cartridge's long-range advantages to consumers. Let's consider ways of explaining these advantages.

Notice that this transitional paragraph *contains* transitional expressions as well.

COMMON TRANSITIONS AND THE RELATIONS THEY INDICATE

An addition: *moreover, in addition, and, also*

> I am majoring in naval architecture; *also,* I spent three years crewing on a racing yawl.

Results: *thus, hence, therefore, accordingly, thereupon, as a result, and so, as a consequence*

> Mary enjoyed all her courses; *therefore,* she worked especially hard last semester.

An example or illustration: *for instance, to illustrate, for example, namely, specifically*

> Competition for part-time jobs is fierce; *for example,* 80 students applied for the clerk's job at Sears.

An explanation: *in other words, simply stated, in fact*

> Louise had a terrible semester; *in fact,* she flunked three courses.

A summary or conclusion: *in closing, to conclude, to summarize, in brief, in short, in summary, to sum up, all in all, on the whole, in retrospect, in conclusion*

> Our credit is destroyed, our bank account is overdrawn, and our debts are piling up; *in short,* we are bankrupt.

Time: *first, next, second, then, meanwhile, at length, later, now, the next day, in the meantime, in turn, subsequently*

> Mow the ball field this morning; *afterward,* clean the dugouts.

A comparison: *likewise, in the same way, in comparison, similarly*

> Our reservoir is drying up because of the drought; *similarly,* water supplies in neighbouring towns are dangerously low.

A contrast or alternative: *however, nevertheless, yet, still, in contrast, otherwise, but, on the other hand, to the contrary, notwithstanding, conversely*

> Felix worked hard; *however,* his marks remained poor.

APPLICATION 6-1

This next essay is shown without appropriate paragraph divisions. Mark the spot where each new paragraph should begin. *Hint:* Here is a rough (six-paragraph) outline: (1) introduction, (2) description of the plant, (3) a typical night shift, (4) the writer's specific job, (5) overview, (6) concluding story. Material that belongs together—and not length—should dictate specific paragraph divisions. (Review pages 91–92.)

SWING SHIFT

> Have you ever worked in a factory? Have you ever worked swing shift? Can you stand to function like a machine in 35-degree heat or more? Let alone stand it—can you work in it for eight hours of endless repetition and mindless labour? I did, for more than eight years. The Acme Tire and Rubber Company, about 10 kilometres east of our campus, resembles a

prison. (Look for a massive and forbidding three-storey building occupying two city blocks on Orchard Street.) The plant was built 50 years ago, and its windows, coated by the soot and grit of a half-century, admit no light, no hope of seeing in or out. Add to this dismal picture the drab red bricks and the stench of burned rubber. This is what I faced five nights a week at 10:00 p.m. when I reported for work. A worker's life inside the plant is arranged so as not to tax the mind. At exactly 10:00 p.m. a loud bell rings. Get to work. The bell has to be loud in order to be heard over the roar of machinery and hissing steam escaping from the high-pressure lines. In time you don't even notice the noise. It took me about two weeks. At midnight the bell rings again: a ten-minute break. At 2:00 a.m. it rings again: lunch, 20 minutes. Two hours later, it rings for the last break of the night. At 6:00 a.m. the final bell announces that the long night is over; it's time to go home. My dreary job was stocking tires. (I say "was" because I quit the job last year.) I had to load push trucks, the kind you see in railway stations. I picked the tires up from the curing presses. A curing press is a 3-metre-high by 2-metre-wide by 2-metre-deep pressure cooker. There are 18 curing presses all in a row, and the temperature around them is over 35 degrees. Clouds of steam hang just below the 6-metre ceiling. By the time I had worked for ten minutes, my clothes were drenched with sweat and reeked with the acrid stench of steamed rubber. Once the truck was full, I'd push it to the shipping department on the other side of the plant. It's quiet there; they ship only during the day. And it's cooler. I'd feel chilled even though the temperature was around 25 degrees. Here I would leave the full truck, look for an empty one, push it back, and start again. It was the same routine every night: endless truckloads of tires, five nights a week—every week. Nothing ever changed except the workers; they got older and worn out. I wasn't surprised to hear that a worker had hanged himself there a few weeks ago. He was a friend of mine. Another friend told me that the work went on anyway. The police said to leave the body hanging until the medical examiner could clear it—like so much meat hanging on a hook. Someone put a blanket around the hanging body. They had to move around it. The work went on.

—*Glenn Silverberg*

APPLICATION **6-2**

Most paragraphs employ a combination of devices for achieving coherence; not every paragraph employs them all. The next paragraph contains a variety of such devices. How many can you identify?

   [1]*In a society based on self-reliance and free will, the institutionalization of life scares me.* [2]Today, Canada has government-funded programs to treat all society's ills. [3]We have day-care centres for the young, nursing

homes for the old, psychologists in schools who use mental health as an instrument of discipline, and mental hospitals for those whose behaviour does not conform to the norm. [4]We have drug-abuse programs, methadone-maintenance programs, alcohol programs, vocational programs, rehabilitation programs, learning-how-to-cope-with-death-for-the-terminally-ill programs, make-friends-with-your-neighbourhood-police officer programs, helping-emotionally-disturbed-children programs, and how-to-accept-divorce programs. [5]Unemployment benefits and welfare are programs designed to institutionalize a growing body of citizens whose purpose in life is the avoidance of work. [6]They are dependent on the state for their livelihood. [7]We can't even let people die in peace. [8]We put them in hospitals for the dying, so that they can be programmed into dying correctly. [9]They don't need to be hospitalized; they would be better off with their families, dying with dignity instead of in these macabre halfway houses. [10]All this is a displacement of confidence from the individual to the program. [11]We can't rely on people to take care of themselves anymore so we have to funnel them into programs. [12]This is a self-perpetuating thing, for the more programs we make available, the more people will become accustomed to seeking help from the government. [emphasis added]

—Ted Morgan

APPLICATION 6-3

Identify the subject and the signal term in each of these sentences. (Review pages 94–95.)

EXAMPLE

The pressures of the sexual revolution are everywhere.

—Joyce Maynard

Subject	pressures of the sexual revolution
Signal term	everywhere

1. High voltage from utility transmission lines can cause bizarre human and animal behaviour.

2. Nuclear power plants need stricter supervision.

3. Producers of television commercials have created a loathsome gallery of men and women patterned, presumably, on Mr. and Mrs. America.

—Marya Mannes

4. From the very beginning of school, we make books and reading a constant source of possible failure and possible humiliation.

—John Holt

5. High interest rates cripple the auto and housing industries.

APPLICATION **6-4**

Collaborative Project and Computer Application: The paragraph below is unified but not coherent, because the sentences are not in logical order. On computer disks, each member of your group should individually rearrange the sentences so that the line of thinking is clear, and then print a hard copy. As a group, compare your different versions, with each member explaining the order he or she chose. Then agree on a final version, which one group member will create by rearranging the sentences on his or her disk. Print this final version for the entire class, justifying your group's decisions.

> [1]The U.S. Supreme Court's ruling against sex discrimination has touched all parts of daily life—even the doll industry. [2]For example, Mattel, a large manufacturer of dolls, decided to change its ways—and make a little profit as well. [3]Now, little girl mommies might not have realized the significance of this arrival had it not been for the television announcement that "No family is complete without a tender Baby Brother." [4]Where would they find that little boy before Christmas? [5]In short, the doll was one small step for Mattel, but one giant leap for man. [6]Thus sexism died, and a new doll was born: Mattel's Baby Brother Tender Love, a soft, lovable doll complete with boy parts. [7]Not only did it give children a dose of sex education, but it also made men grin with satisfaction upon having invaded the doll industry. [8]As a consequence, parents quivered with anxiety that they would be unable to meet the demand of little mothers. [9]Yes, Baby Brother Tender Love was Mattel's gift to society that year.

APPLICATION **6-5**

Select one of these assignments and write a paragraph organized from the general to the specific.

- Picture the ideal summer job. Explain to an employer why you would like the job.
- Assume that it's time for end-of-semester student course evaluations. Write a one-paragraph evaluation of your favourite course to be read by your professor's department chairperson.
- Explain your views on video games. Write for your classmates.
- Describe the job outlook in your chosen field. Write for a high school senior interested in your major.

APPLICATION **6-6**

Identify a problem in a group to which you belong (such as family, club, sorority). Or select a topic from the following list or make up one of your own. After reviewing pages 98–99, write two emphatic paragraphs, one featuring the emphatic material at the beginning and the other positioning it at the end. Be prepared to explain which version works best for you and why.

- Advice to a first-year student about surviving in university
- Your life goal to your academic advisor, who is recommending you for a scholarship
- Your reasons for wanting to live off campus to the dean of students

APPLICATION **6-7**

Select the best paragraph or essay you have written thus far (or one that your instructor suggests). Using the strategies in this chapter, revise the paragraph or essay for improved coherence. After revising, list the specific strategies you employed (logical order, parallelism, repetition of key terms, restatement, pronouns, transitions).

CHAPTER 7

Revising the Sentences: Writing with Style

No matter how vital your content and how sensible your organization, your writing will mean little unless it is easy to understand—in a word, readable. A readable sentence requires no more than a single reading.

One requirement for readable sentences, of course, is correct grammar, punctuation, and mechanics. But "correctness" alone is no guarantee of readability. Readers also are distracted when writing is hard to interpret, slow to make the point, or choppy. Sentences that are clear, concise, and fluent emphasize relationships, make every word count, and flow smoothly.

Before working with this section, you may wish to review some basic grammatical elements in Appendix A.

AIM FOR CLARITY

These guidelines will help you write clear sentences that convey your meaning on the first reading.

Avoid Faulty Modifiers

Modifiers explain, define, or add detail to other words or ideas. Prepositional phrases, for example, usually define or limit adjacent words as do other types of phrases and clauses.

Prepositional phrases:

> the foundation **with the cracked wall**
>
> the journey **to the moon**

Phrases with "-ing" verbs:

> the student **painting the portrait**
>
> **Opening the door,** we entered quietly.

Phrases with "to + verb" forms:

> **To succeed,** one must work hard.

Clauses:

> the person **who came to dinner**
>
> the job **that I recently accepted**

If a modifier is too far from the words it modifies, the message can be ambiguous.

> **Misplaced**   At our campsite, **devouring the bacon,** I saw a
> **modifier**   huge bear.

Was it *I* who was devouring the bacon? Moving the modifier next to bear clarifies the sentence:

> **Revised**   At our campsite, I saw a huge bear **devouring the bacon.**

The order of adjectives and adverbs also affects the meaning of sentences:

> **I often** remind myself to balance my chequebook.
>
> I remind myself to balance my chequebook **often.**

Position modifiers to reflect your meaning:

> **Misplaced modifier**   Jeanette read a report on using nonchemical pesticides **in our conference room.** [*Are the pesticides to be used in the conference room?*]
>
> **Revised**   In our conference room, Jeanette read a report on using nonchemical pesticides.
>
> **Misplaced modifier**   **Only** press the red button in an emergency. [*Does "only" modify "press" or "emergency"?*]
>
> **Revised**   Press **only** the red button in an emergency
> *or*
> Press the red button in an emergency **only.**

Another problem with ambiguity occurs when a modifying phrase has no word to modify.

> **Dangling modifier**   **Answering the telephone,** the cat ran out the door.

The cat obviously did not answer the telephone. But because the modifier **Answering the telephone** has no word to modify, the noun beginning the main clause (**cat**) seems to name the one who answered the phone. Without any word to connect to, the *modifier dangles*. Inserting a subject repairs this absurd message.

> **Revised**   **As Mary answered the telephone,** the cat ran out the door.

A dangling modifier also can obscure your meaning.

> **Dangling modifier**   **After completing the student financial aid application form,** the Financial Aid Office will forward it to the appropriate provincial agency.

Who completes the form—the student or the financial aid office?
Here are other dangling modifiers:

Dangling modifier	**By planting different varieties of crops,** the pests were unable to adapt.
Revised	By planting different varieties of crops, **farmers** prevented the pests from adapting.
Dangling modifier	**As an expert in this field,** I'm sure your advice will help.
Revised	**Because of your expertise in this field,** I'm sure your advice will help.

ref   Keep Your Pronoun References Clear

Pronouns (**she, it, his, their,** and so on) must clearly refer to the noun they replace.

Ambiguous referent	Our patients enjoy the warm days while **they** last. [*Are the patients or the warm days on the way out?*]

Depending on whether the referent (or antecedent) for *they* is *patients* or *warm days,* the sentence can be clarified.

Clear referent	While these warm days last, our patients enjoy them.
	or
	Our terminal patients enjoy these warm days.
Ambiguous	Sally told Sarah that **she** was obsessed with **her** job.
Revised	Sally told Sarah, "I'm obsessed with my job." Sally told Sarah, "I'm obsessed with your job."

What other interpretations are possible for the ambiguous sentence above?
    Avoid using **this, that,** or **it**—especially to begin a sentence—unless the pronoun refers to a specific antecedent (referent).

Vague	As Pierre drove away from his menial job, boring lifestyle, and damp apartment, he was happy to be leaving **it** behind.
Revised	As Pierre drove away, he was happy to be leaving his menial job, boring lifestyle, and damp apartment behind.
Vague	The problem with our defective machinery is only compounded by the new operator's incompetence. **This** annoys me!
Revised	I am annoyed by the problem with our defective machinery as well as by the new operator's incompetence.

Avoid Cramming

A sentence crammed with ideas makes details hard to remember and relationships hard to identify.

Crammed   A smoke-filled room causes not only teary eyes and runny noses but also can alter people's hearing and vision, as well as creating dangerous levels of carbon monoxide, especially for people with heart and lung ailments, whose health is particularly threatened by "second-hand" smoke.

Clear things up by sorting out the relationships:

Revised   Besides causing teary eyes and runny noses, a smoke-filled room can alter people's hearing and vision. One of "second-hand" smoke's biggest dangers, however, is high levels of carbon monoxide, a particular health threat for people with heart and lung ailments.

Keep Equal Items Parallel

To reflect relationships among items of equal importance, express them in identical grammatical form (see also page 101).

For example, if you begin the series with a noun, use nouns throughout the series; likewise for adjectives, adverbs, and specific types of clauses and phrases.

Faulty   The new tutor is **enthusiastic, skilled,** and **you can depend on her.**

Revised   The new tutor is **enthusiastic, skilled,** and **dependable.** [*all subjective complements*]

Faulty   In his new job Ramon felt **lonely** and **without a friend.**

Revised   In his new job Ramon felt **lonely** and **friendless.** [*both adjectives*]

Faulty   Lulu plans **to study** all this month and **on scoring** well in her licensing examination.

Revised   Lulu plans **to study** all this month and **to score** well in her licensing examination. [*both infinitive phrases*]

Arrange Word Order for Coherence and Emphasis

In coherent writing, everything sticks together; each sentence builds on the preceding sentence and looks ahead to the following sentence.

Sentences generally work best when the beginning looks back at familiar information and the end provides the new (or unfamiliar) information.

Effective word order

FAMILIAR		UNFAMILIAR
My dog	has	fleas.
Our boss	just won	the lottery.
This company	is planning	a merger.

Besides helping a message stick together, the familiar-to-unfamiliar structure emphasizes the new information. Just as every paragraph has a key sentence, every sentence has a key word or phrase that sums up the new information. That key word or phrase usually is emphasized best at the end of the sentence.

Faulty emphasis	We expect a **refund** because of your error in our shipment.
Correct	Because of your error in our shipment, we expect a **refund.**
Faulty emphasis	After your awful behaviour, an apology is something I expect. But I'll probably get an excuse.
Correct	After your awful behaviour, I expect an **apology.** But I'll probably get an excuse.

One exception to placing key words last occurs with an imperative statement (a command, an order, an instruction) with the subject [*you*] understood. For instance, each step in a list of instructions should contain an action verb (**insert, open, close, turn, remove, press**). To give readers a forecast, place the verb in that instruction at the beginning.

Correct	**Insert** the diskette before activating the system.
	Remove the protective seal.

With the key word at the beginning of the instruction, readers know immediately the action they need to take.

Use Proper Coordination

Give equal emphasis to ideas of equal importance by joining them, within simple or compound sentences, with coordinating conjunctions: **and, but, or, nor, for, so,** and **yet.**

Correct	This course is difficult, **but** it is worthwhile.
	My horse is old **and** grey.
	We must decide to support **or** reject the dean's plan.

But too much coordination can confound your meaning. Below, notice how the meaning becomes clear when the less important ideas (**nearly floating, arms and legs still moving, my mind no longer having**) are shown as dependent on, rather than equal to, the most important idea (**jogging almost by reflex**).

Excessive coordination	The climax in jogging comes after a few kilometres **and** I can no longer feel stride after stride **and** it seems as if I am floating **and** jogging becomes almost a reflex **and** my arms and legs continue to move **and** my mind no longer has to control their actions.
Revised	The climax in jogging comes after a few kilometres, when I can no longer feel stride after stride. By then I am jogging almost by reflex, nearly floating, my arms and legs still moving, my mind no longer having to control their actions.

Avoid coordinating ideas that cannot be sensibly connected:

Faulty	I was late for work **and** wrecked my car.
Revised	Late for work, I backed out of the driveway too quickly, hit a truck, and wrecked my car.

sub   Use Proper Subordination

Proper subordination shows that a less important idea is dependent on a more important idea. A dependent (or subordinate) clause in a complex sentence is signalled by a subordinating conjunction: **because, so that, if, unless, after, until, since, while, as,** and **although.** Consider these complete ideas:

> Joe studies hard. He has severe math anxiety.

Because these ideas are expressed as simple sentences, they appear coordinate (equal in importance). But if you wanted to indicate your opinion of Joe's chances of succeeding, you would need a third sentence: **His handicap probably will prevent him from succeeding** or **His willpower will help him succeed** or some such. To communicate the intended meaning concisely, combine the two ideas. Subordinate the one that deserves less emphasis and place the idea you want emphasized in the independent (main) clause.

> Despite his severe math anxiety [*subordinate idea*], Joe studies hard [*independent idea*].

Below, the subordination suggests the opposite meaning:

> Despite his diligent study [*subordinate idea*], Joe is unlikely to overcome his learning disability [*independent idea*].

Do not coordinate when you should subordinate:

Faulty Television viewers can relate to a person they idolize, and they feel obliged to buy the product endorsed by their hero.

Of the two ideas in the sentence above, one is the cause, the other the effect. Emphasize this relationship through subordination.

Revised Because television viewers can relate to a person they idolize, they feel obliged to buy the product endorsed by their hero.

av Use Active Voice Often

A verb's voice signals whether a sentence's subject acts or is acted upon. The active voice (**I did it**) is more direct, concise, and persuasive than the passive voice (**It was done by me**). In the active voice, the agent performing the action serves as subject:

	AGENT	ACTION	RECIPIENT
Active	Leslie	lost	your report.
	SUBJECT	VERB	OBJECT

The passive voice reverses the pattern, making the recipient of an action serve as subject:

	RECIPIENT	ACTION	AGENT
Passive	YOUR REPORT	WAS LOST	BY LESLIE.
	SUBJECT	VERB	PREPOSITIONAL PHRASE

Sometimes the passive eliminates the agent altogether:

Passive Your report was lost. [*Who lost it?*]

Some writers mistakenly rely on the passive voice because they think it sounds more objective and important. But the passive voice often makes writing seem merely wordy or evasive:

Concise and direct (active) **I underestimated** expenses for this semester. [*7 words*]

Wordy and indirect (passive) Expenses for this semester **were underestimated by me.** [*9 words*]

Evasive (passive) Expenses for this semester **were underestimated.**

Do not evade responsibility by hiding behind the passive voice:

Passive	A mistake was made in your shipment. [*By whom?*]
"irresponsibles"	It was decided not to hire you. [*Who decided?*]

Use the active voice when you want action. Otherwise, your statement will have no power:

Weak passive	If my claim is not settled by May 15, the Better Business Bureau will be contacted, and their advice on legal action will be taken.
Strong active	If you do not settle my claim by May 15, I will contact the Better Business Bureau for advice on legal action.

Ordinarily, use the active voice for giving instructions:

Faulty passive	The door to the cobra's cage should be locked. Care should be taken with the dynamite.
Correct active	Lock the door to the cobra's cage. Be careful with the dynamite.

pv

Use Passive Voice Selectively

Passive voice is appropriate in lab reports and other documents in which the agent's identity is immaterial to the message.

Use the passive voice if the person behind the action needs to be protected.

Correct passive	The criminal **was identified.** The victim **was asked** to testify.

Similarly, use the passive when the agent is unknown, unapparent, or unimportant:

Correct passive	Mr. Wong **was brought** to the emergency room. The bank failure **was publicized** nationwide. Amir's article **was published** last week.

Prefer the passive when you want to be indirect or inoffensive:

Active but offensive	**You have not paid** your bill. **You need to overhaul** our filing system.
Inoffensive passive	This bill **has not been paid.** Our filing system **needs to be overhauled.**

APPLICATION **7-1**

These sentences are unclear because of faulty modification, unclear pronoun reference, cramming, faulty parallelism, or key words buried in mid-sentence. Revise them so that their meaning is clear. For sentences suggesting two meanings, write separate versions—one for each meaning intended. (Review pages 110–114.)

1. Bill told Fred that he was mistaken.
2. In all writing, revision is required.
3. Only use this elevator in a fire.
4. Making the shelves look neater was another of my tasks at X-Mart that is very important to a store's business because if the merchandise is not always neatly arranged, customers will not have a good impression, whereas if it is neat they probably will return.
5. Wearing high boots, the snake could not hurt me.
6. When my ninth-grade teacher caught daydreamers, she would jab them in the shoulder with gritted teeth and a fierce eye.
7. While they eat dead fish, our students enjoy watching the alligators.
8. Education enables us to recognize excellence and to achieve it.
9. Student nurses are required to identify diseases and how to treat them.
10. My car needs an oil change, a grease job, and the carburetor should be adjusted.

APPLICATION **7-2**

Use coordination or subordination to clarify relationships in these sentences. (Review pages 114–116.)

1. Inga loves Mario. She also loves Bruno.
2. You will succeed. Work hard.
3. I worked hard in calculus and flunked the course.
4. Now I have no privacy. My cousin moved into my room.
5. The instructor entered the classroom. Some students were asleep.

APPLICATION **7-3**

Convert these passive voice sentences to concise, forceful, and direct expressions in the active voice. (Review pages 116–117.)

1. The evaluation was performed by us.
2. The essay was written by me.

3. Unless you pay me within three days, my lawyer will be contacted.

4. Hard hats should be worn at all times.

5. It was decided to decline your invitation.

APPLICATION 7-4

The sentences below lack appropriate emphasis because of improper use of the active voice. Convert each to passive voice. (Review page 117.)

1. Joe's company fired him.

2. You are paying inadequate attention to student safety.

3. A power surge destroyed more than 2000 lines of our new computer program.

4. You did a poor job editing this report.

5. The selection committee awarded Anna a Silver Jubilee Scholarship.

TRIM THE FAT

Concise writing conveys the most meaning in the fewest words. But it does not omit the details necessary for clarity. Use fewer words whenever fewer will do.

> **Cluttered**   At this point in time I must say that I need a vacation.
>
> **Concise**   I need a vacation now.

First drafts rarely are concise. Trim the fat:

Avoid Wordy Phrases

Each needless phrase here can be reduced to one word.

Revising wordy phrases

at this point in time	=	now
has the ability to	=	can
aware of the fact that	=	know
due to the fact that	=	because
dislike very much	=	hate
athletic person	=	athlete
the majority of	=	most
being in good health	=	healthy
on a daily basis	=	daily
in close proximity	=	near

red   ## Eliminate Redundancy

A redundant expression says the same thing twice in different words, as in **fellow classmates.**

Spotting redundant phrases

a [dead] corpse	enter [into]
the reason [why]	[totally] monopolize
the [final] conclusion	[totally] oblivious
[utmost] perfection	[very] vital
[mental] awareness	[past] experience
[the month of] August	correct [amount of] change
[mutual] cooperation	[future] prospects
mix [together]	[valuable] asset
[viable] alternative	[free] gift

rep   ## Avoid Needless Repetition

Unnecessary repetition clutters writing and dilutes meaning.

Repetitious   In trauma victims, breathing is restored by **artificial respiration.** Techniques of **artificial respiration** include mouth-to-mouth **respiration** and mouth-to-nose **respiration.**

Repetition in the above passage disappears when sentences are combined.

Concise   In trauma victims, breathing is restored by artificial respiration, either mouth-to-mouth or mouth-to-nose.

NOTE   *Don't hesitate to repeat, or at least rephrase, if you feel that readers need reminders. Effective repetition helps avoid cross-references like these: "See page 3" or "Review page 1."*

Th   ## Avoid *There* and *It* Sentence Openers

Many **there is, there are,** and **it** sentence openers can be eliminated.

Faulty   There are several good reasons why Boris dropped out of school.

Concise   Boris dropped out of school for several good reasons.

Of course, in some contexts, proper emphasis would call for a *there* opener:

Correct   People often have wondered about the rationale behind Boris's sudden decision. Actually, there are several good reasons for his dropping out of school.

Most often, however, *there* openers are best dropped.

Faulty	There is a serious fire danger created by your smoking in bed.
Concise	Your smoking in bed creates danger of fire.
Wordy	[It was] his negative attitude [that] caused him to fail.
Wordy	It gives me great pleasure to introduce our speaker.
Concise	I am pleased to introduce our speaker.

Avoid Needless Phrases

To be, as well as **that** and **which** phrases, can often be cut.

Wordy	She seems [to be] upset.
Wordy	I find some of my classmates [to be] brilliant.
Wordy	The Batmobile is a car [that is] worth buying.
Wordy	This [is a] math problem [that] is impossible to solve.
Wordy	The book [,which is] about Stanfield [,] is fascinating.

Avoid Weak Verbs

Prefer verbs that express a definite action: **open, close, move, continue, begin.** Avoid verbs that express no specific action: **is, was, are, has, give, make, come, take.** All forms of the verb **to be** are weak. Substitute a strong verb for conciseness:

Weak and wordy	Please **take into consideration** my application.
Concise	Please **consider** my application.

Here are some weak verbs converted to strong:

Revising weak verbs

give a summary of	=	summarize
make an assumption	=	assume
come to the conclusion	=	conclude
take action	=	act
make a decision	=	decide
come to the realization	=	realize

Avoid Excessive Prepositions

Wordy	Some **of** the members **of** the committee made these recommendations.

Concise   Some committee members made these
recommendations.

Wordy   I gave the money **to** Marta.

Concise   I gave Marta the money.

nom   Avoid Nominalizations

Nouns manufactured from verbs (nominalizations) often accompany
weak verbs and needless prepositions.

**Weak and
wordy**   We ask for the **cooperation** of all students.

**Strong and
concise**   We ask that all students **cooperate.**

**Weak and
wordy**   Give **consideration** to the possibility of a career
change.

**Strong and
concise**   **Consider** a career change.

Besides causing wordiness, nominalizations can be vague—by hiding the
agent of an action.

**Wordy and
vague**   A need for immediate action exists. [*Who should
take the action? We can't tell.*]

Precise   We must act immediately.

Nominalizations drain the life from your style. In cheering for your
favourite team, you wouldn't say:

| Blocking of that kick is a necessity!

instead of

| Block that kick!

Here are nominalizations restored to their action verb forms:

*Trading nouns for
verbs*

conduct an investigation of	=	investigate
provide a description of	=	describe
conduct a test of	=	test
engage in the preparation of	=	prepare
make a discovery of	=	discover

neg ## Make Negatives Positive

A positive expression is easier to understand than a negative one.

Indirect and wordy	I did **not** gain anything from this course.
Direct and concise	I gained nothing from this course.
Confusing and wordy	Do **not** distribute this memo to employees who have **not** received security clearance.
Clear and concise	Distribute this memo only to employees who have received security clearance.

Besides the directly negative words (**no, not, never**), some indirectly negative words (**except, forget, mistake, lose, uncooperative**) also force readers to translate.

Confusing and wordy	Do **not neglect** to activate the alarm system. My conclusion was **not inaccurate.**
Clear and concise	Be sure to activate the alarm system. My conclusion was **accurate.**

Some negative expressions, of course, are perfectly correct, as in expressing disagreement.

Correct negatives	This is **not** the best plan. Your offer is **unacceptable.** This project **never** will succeed.

Here are other negative expressions translated into positive versions:

Trading negatives for positives

did not succeed	=	failed
does not have	=	lacks
did not prevent	=	allowed
not unless	=	only if
not until	=	only when
not absent	=	present

cl ## Clear Out Clutter Words

Clutter words stretch a message without adding meaning. Here are some of the commonest: **very, definitely, quite, extremely, rather, somewhat, really, actually, situation, aspect, factor.**

Cluttered	**Actually,** one **aspect** of a relationship **situation** that could **definitely** make me **very** happy would be to have a **somewhat** adventurous partner who **really** shared my **extreme** love of travelling.
Concise	I'd like to meet an adventurous person who loves travelling.

Delete Needless Prefaces

Instead of delaying the new information in your sentence, get right to the point.

Wordy	[I am writing this letter because] I wish to apply for the position of residence counsellor.
Wordy	[The conclusion we can draw is that] writing is hard work.

Delete Needless Qualifiers

Qualifiers such as **I feel, it would seem, I believe, in my opinion,** and **I think** express uncertainty or soften the tone and impact of a statement.

Appropriate qualifiers	Despite Frank's poor academic performance last semester, he will, **I think,** do well in college. Your product **seems to be** what I need.

But when you are certain, eliminate the qualifier so as not to seem tentative or evasive.

Needless qualifiers	[It seems that] I've wrecked the family car. [It would appear that] I've lost your credit card. [In my opinion,] you've done a good job.

NOTE   *In communicating across cultures, keep in mind that a direct, forceful style might be considered offensive (page 145).*

APPLICATION 7-5

Make these sentences more concise by eliminating redundancies and needless repetition. (Review pages 119–120.)

1. She is a woman who works hard.
2. I am aware of the fact that Pierre is a trustworthy person.
3. Clarence completed his assignment in a short period of time.

4. Bruno has a stocky build.

5. Sally is a close friend of mine.

6. I've been able to rely on my parents in the past.

APPLICATION 7-6

Make these sentences more concise by eliminating **There is** and **There are** sentence openers, and the needless use of **it, to be, is, of, that,** and **which.** (Review pages 120–121.)

1. I consider Ahmed to be a good friend.
2. Our summer house, which is located on Lake of the Woods, is for sale.
3. The static electricity that is generated by the human body is measurable.
4. Writing must be practised in order for it to become effective.
5. Another reason the job is attractive is because the salary is excellent.
6. There are many activities and sports that I enjoy very much, but the one that stands out in my mind is the sport of jogging.
7. Friendship is something that people should be honest about.
8. Smoking of cigarettes is considered by many people to be the worst habit of all habits of human beings.
9. There are many students who are immature.
10. It is necessary for me to leave immediately.

APPLICATION 7-7

Make these sentences more concise by replacing weak verbs with strong ones and nouns with verbs, by changing negatives to positives, and by clearing out clutter words, needless prefatory expressions, and needless qualifiers. (Review pages 121–124.)

1. I have a preference for Ferraris.
2. Your conclusion is in agreement with mine.
3. We request the formation of a committee of students for the review of grading discrepancies.
4. I am not unappreciative of your help.
5. Actually, I am very definitely in love with you.
6. I find Nhieu to be an industrious and competent employee.
7. It seems that I've made a mistake in your order.
8. Igor does not have any friends at this school.

9. In my opinion, winter is an awful season.

10. As this academic year comes upon us, I realize that I will have trouble commuting to school this semester.

11. There is an undergraduate student attrition causes study needed at our school.

12. A need for your caution exists.

13. Never fail to attend classes.

14. Our acceptance of the offer is a necessity.

HELP SENTENCES FLOW

Fluent sentences are easy to read because of clear connections, variety, and emphasis. Their varied length and word order eliminate choppiness and monotony. Fluent sentences enhance *clarity* by emphasizing the most important idea. Fluent sentences enhance *conciseness*, often replacing several short, repetitious sentences with one longer, more economical sentence. To write fluently, use the following strategies:

Combine Related Ideas

Disconnected	Jogging can be healthful. You need the right equipment. Most necessary are well-fitting shoes. Without this equipment you take the chance of injuring your legs. Your knees are especially prone to injury. [*5 sentences*]
Clear, concise, and fluent	Jogging can be healthful if you have the right equipment. Shoes that fit well are most necessary because they prevent injury to your legs, especially your knees. [*2 sentences*]

Most sets of information can be combined to form different relationships, depending on what you want to emphasize. Imagine that this set of facts describes an applicant for a ski instructor's position:

- Sarah James has been skiing since age three.
- She has no experience teaching skiing.
- She has won several slalom competitions.

Assume that you are Snow Mountain Ski Area's head instructor, conveying your impression of this candidate to the manager. To convey a negative impression, you might combine the facts in this way:

Strongly negative emphasis	Although Sarah James has been skiing since age three and has won several slalom competitions, **she has no experience teaching skiing.**

The *independent idea* (in boldface) receives the emphasis (also see page 115 on subordination). But if you are undecided, yet leaning in a negative direction, you might write:

> **Slightly** Sarah James has been skiing since age three and
> **negative** has won several slalom competitions, **but** she has
> **emphasis** no experience teaching skiing.

In this sentence, the ideas before and after **but** are both independent. Joining them with the coordinating word **but** suggests that both sides of the issue are equally important (or "coordinate"). Placing the negative idea last, however, gives it slight emphasis.

Finally, to emphasize strong support for the candidate, you could say:

> **Positive** Although Sarah James has no experience teaching
> **emphasis** skiing, **she has been skiing since age three and
> has won several slalom competitions.**

Here, the earlier idea is subordinated by **although,** leaving the two final ideas independent.

Combine sentences only to simplify the reader's task. Crammed or overstuffed sentences with too much information and too many connections can be hard for readers to sort out. Notice how many times you have to read the following overstuffed instruction in order to understand what to do:

> **Overcombined** In developing less than a tankful of film, be sure to
> put in enough empty reels to fill all the space in the
> tank so that the film-loaded reels won't slide
> around when the tank is agitated.

var   Vary Sentence Construction and Length

Related ideas often need to be linked in one sentence so that readers can grasp the connections.

> **Disconnected** The nuclear core reached critical temperature. The
> loss-of-coolant alarm was triggered. The operator
> shut down the reactor.

> **Connected** As the nuclear core reached critical temperature,
> triggering the loss-of-coolant alarm, the operator
> shut down the reactor.

But an idea that should stand alone for emphasis needs a whole sentence of its own:

> **Correct** Core meltdown seemed inevitable.

However, an unbroken string of long or short sentences can bore and confuse readers, as can a series with identical openings:

Dreary   There are some drawbacks about diesel engines. They are difficult to start in cold weather. They cause vibration. They also give off an unpleasant odour. They cause sulfur dioxide pollution.

Varied   Diesel engines have some drawbacks. Most obvious are their noisiness, cold-weather starting difficulties, vibration, odour, and sulfur dioxide emission.

Similarly, when you write in the first person, overusing **I** makes you appear self-centred. Do not, however, avoid personal pronouns if they make the writing more readable (say, by eliminating passive constructions).

 ## Use Short Sentences for Special Emphasis

All this talk about combining ideas might suggest that short sentences have no place in good writing. Wrong. Short sentences (even one-word sentences) provide vivid emphasis. They stick in a reader's mind. Consider a student pilot's description of taking off:

> Our airspeed increases. The plane vibrates. We reach the point where the battle begins.

Instead, the student might have written:

> As our airspeed increases, the plane vibrates, and we reach the point where the battle begins.

However, she wanted to emphasize three discrete phases here: (1) the acceleration, (2) the vibration, and (3) the critical point of lifting off the ground.

APPLICATION **7-8**

The sentence sets below lack fluency because they are disconnected, have no variety, or have no emphasis. Combine each set into one or two fluent sentences.

Choppy   Last summer, Lynn Schooler was walking along the shores of the Tatshenshini River. The river is located in a remote northwest corner of British Columbia. He could literally smell the grizzly bear in the prints he was tracking. The prints were along the shore. The water was at its lowest level in recent history. The normally narrow strip was an expansive sand dune. The dune stretched for miles.

Revised Walking along the shores of the Tatshenshini River in a remote northwest corner of British Columbia last summer, Lynn Schooler could literally smell the grizzly bear in the prints he was tracking along the shore. With the water at its lowest level in recent history, the normally narrow strip was an expansive sand dune that stretched for miles.

—*Equinox* June/July 1997

1. The world's population is growing.
   It has grown from 4 billion in 1975.
   It has reached 6.5 billion in 2000.
   This is an increase of more than 50 percent.

2. In sheer numbers, population is growing.
   It is growing faster than in 1975.
   It adds 100 million people each year.
   This figure compares with 75 million in 1975.

3. Energy prices are expected to increase.
   Many less-developed countries will have increasing difficulty.
   Their difficulty will be in meeting energy needs.

4. One-quarter of humanity depends primarily on wood.
   They depend on wood for fuel.
   For them, the outlook is bleak.

5. The world has finite fuel resources.
   These include coal, oil, gas, oil shale, and uranium.
   These resources, theoretically, are sufficient for centuries.
   These resources are not evenly distributed.

APPLICATION **7-9**

Combine each set of sentences below into one or two fluent sentences that provide the requested emphasis.

Sentence set Bea is a loyal employee.
Bea is a motivated employee.
Bea is short-tempered with her colleagues.

Combined for positive emphasis Even though Bea is short-tempered with her colleagues, she is a loyal and motivated employee.

Sentence set This word processor has many excellent features.
It includes a spelling checker.
It includes a thesaurus.
It includes a grammar checker.

Combined to emphasize the thesaurus	Among its many excellent features, such as spelling and grammar checkers, this word processor includes a thesaurus.

1. The job offers an attractive salary.
   It demands long work hours.
   Promotions are rapid.
   (*Combine for negative emphasis.*)

2. The job offers an attractive salary.
   It demands long work hours.
   Promotions are rapid.
   (*Combine for positive emphasis.*)

3. Company X gave us the lowest bid.
   Company Y has an excellent reputation.
   (*Combine to emphasize Company Y.*)

4. Superinsulated homes are energy efficient.
   Superinsulated homes can promote indoor air pollution.
   The toxins include radon gas and urea formaldehyde.
   (*Combine for negative emphasis.*)

5. Computers cannot think for the writer.
   Computers eliminate many mechanical writing tasks.
   They speed the flow of information.
   (*Combine to emphasize the first assertion.*)

APPLICATION 7-10

Collaborative Project and Computer Application: Have each group member revise this next passage to improve fluency by combining related ideas; by varying sentence structure, openings, and length; and by using short sentences for special emphasis. (*Note:* When rephrasing to achieve conciseness, be sure to preserve the meaning of the original.) Then compare your versions and collaborate on an effective revision to present to the class.

> Heart's Content is just down from Heart's Delight and Heart's Desire. It clings to a windswept cove. Hardly a tree is in sight. It is as rugged as many other Newfoundland fishing villages. It's bigger than some. It was blessed with a more diverse economy. It served as the North American terminus of a trans-Atlantic telephone cable until 1966. Like so many others, the town suffered a regrettable brain drain. Young people sought their fortunes elsewhere. But some of the native sons and daughters are growing older. They are returning. They are lured by the vistas of the bay. To "come-from-aways," living in a place like Heart's Content might seem akin to living in a fishbowl. That's the wrong attitude. Newfoundland

villages are famous for their genuine neighbourliness. They are also famous for their pervasive sense of community. You can buy a decent house for $40 000. Some pundits think the fishing villages may yet be revived. They will be revived by the retirement crowd. Some of these people have never set foot on the Rock. It has quaint old houses and a harbour setting. Heart's Delight would be an excellent choice.

—Tom Cruikshank

APPLICATION **7-11**

Computer Application: Try the grammar function of your word processing program. First, look for problems with clarity, conciseness, and fluency yourself. Then compare your changes with those the computer suggests. If the computer contradicts your own judgment, ask a classmate or your peer group for feedback. If the computer suggests changes that seem ungrammatical or incorrect, consult a good handbook for confirmation. Try to assess when and how the grammar function can be useful and when you can revise best on your own.

For class discussion, prepare a list of the advantages and disadvantages of your automated grammar checker: Use your grammar checker on the first two sentences from Applications 7-1 through 7-6. Are the suggested changes correct? Which of the topics covered in this chapter does the checker miss?

APPLICATION **7-12**

Computer Application: Do a Web search to find some online style and grammar source and write a one-page evaluation of the site's usefulness.

SAMPLE SITES:

McMaster University Communications Site
www.humanities.mcmaster.ca/~hcomm/centre/commwww.htm

Tutorial for using Web search engines, from Okanagan University College
www.sci.ouc.bc.ca/libr/connect96/search.htm

Discussion of forms and classes of sentences, from the University of Ottawa
www.uottawa.ca/academic/arts/writcent/hypergrammar/bldsent.html

CHAPTER 8

Revising the Words and Phrases: Fine-Tuning

The quality of our contact with an audience ultimately depends on the wording we choose and the tone we convey.

SAY SOMETHING GENUINE

Readers look between the lines for a real person; don't disappoint them.

Avoid Triteness

Writers who rely on tired old phrases (clichés) such as the following come across as too lazy or too careless to find exact, unique ways to say what they mean:

Worn-out phrases

first and foremost	tough as nails
in the final analysis	holding the bag
needless to say	up the creek
work like a dog	over the hill
last but not least	bite the bullet
dry as a bone	fly off the handle
victim of circumstance	get on the stick

If it sounds like a "catchy phrase" you've heard before, don't use it.

Avoid Overstatement

Exaggeration sounds phony. Be cautious when using words such as **best, biggest, brightest, most,** and **worst.** Recognize the differences among **always, usually, often, sometimes,** and **rarely** or among **all, most, many, some,** and **few.**

Overstated You never listen to my ideas.

Everything you say is obnoxious.

This is the worst essay I've ever read.

How would you rephrase the above examples to make them more reasonable?

Avoid Misleading Euphemisms

A form of understatement, euphemisms are expressions aimed at politeness or at making unpleasant subjects seem less offensive. Thus, **we powder our noses** or **use the boy's room** instead of **using the washroom;** we **pass away** or **meet our Maker** instead of **dying.**

When a euphemism is deceptive

When euphemisms avoid offending or embarrassing people, they are perfectly legitimate. But they are unethical if they understate the truth when only the truth will serve:

- Instead of being **laid off** or **fired,** employees are **surplused** or **deselected,** or the company is **downsized.**
- Instead of **lying** to the public, the government engages in a **policy of disinformation.**
- Instead of **wars** and **civilian casualties,** we have **conflicts** and **collateral damage.**

APPLICATION 8-1

Revise these sentences to eliminate triteness, overstatements, and euphemisms.

1. This course gives me a pain in the neck.
2. There is never a dull moment in my residence.
3. Television is rotting everyone's brain.
4. I was less than candid.
5. This student is poorly motivated.
6. You are the world's most beautiful person.
7. Marriage in Canada is a dying institution.
8. I love you more than life itself.
9. We have decided to terminate your employment.
10. People of our generation are all selfish.

AIM FOR PRECISION

Even words listed as synonyms can carry different shades of meaning. Do you mean to say, "I'm slender; you're slim; he's lean; and she's scrawny"? The wrong choice could be disastrous. A single, wrong word can be offensive, as in this statement by a university applicant:

Another attractive feature of the university is its adequate track program.

While **adequate** might convey honestly the writer's intended meaning, the word seems inappropriate in this context (an applicant expressing a judgment about a program). Although the program may not have been highly ranked, the writer could have used any of several alternatives (**solid, promising, growing**—or no modifier at all).

Be especially aware of similar words with dissimilar meanings, as in these examples:

Words often confused	affect/effect	fewer/less
	all ready/already	healthy/healthful
	among/between	imply/infer
	continual/continuous	uninterested/disinterested
	eager/anxious	worse/worst
	farther/further	than/then

Does your professor expect **fewer** or **less** technical details in your essay? Do not write **Skiing is healthy** when you mean that skiing promotes good health (is healthful). **Healthy** means to be in a state of health. **Healthful** things help keep us healthy.

Be on the lookout for imprecisely phrased (and therefore illogical) comparisons:

Faulty	Your bank's interest rate is higher than BusyBank. [*Can a rate be higher than a bank?*]
Revised	Your bank's interest rate is higher than BusyBank's.

Imprecision can create ambiguity. For instance, is **send us more personal information** a request for more information that is personal or for information that is more personal? Precision ultimately enhances conciseness, when one exact word replaces multiple inexact words.

Wordy and less exact	I have **put together** all the financial information. **Keep doing** this exercise for ten seconds.
Concise and more exact	I have **assembled** all the financial information. **Continue** this exercise for ten seconds.

APPLICATION 8-2

Revise these sentences to make them precise.

1. Our outlet does more business than Saskatoon.
2. Low-fat foods are healthy.
3. Marie's licence is for driving a passenger vehicle only.
4. This is the worse course I've taken.
5. Unlike many other children, her home life was good.
6. Provincial law requires that restaurant personnel serve food with a sanitation certificate.

spec

SHARPEN THE VISUAL DETAILS

General words name broad classes of things, such as **job, car,** or **person.** Such terms usually need to be clarified by more *specific* ones:

General terms traded for specific terms

> job = senior accountant for Rockford Press
>
> car = red, four-door, Ford Escort station wagon
>
> person = male Caucasian, with red hair, blue eyes (and so on)

The more specific your words, the sharper your meaning:

How the level of generality affects writing's visual quality

General	1. structure	1. animal
	2. dwelling	2. pet
	3. vacation home	3. dog
	4. log cabin	4. Doberman
	5. log cabin in New Brunswick	5. my Doberman, Fang
Specific	6. a three-room log cabin on the banks of the Miramichi River in New Brunswick	6. my 40-kilogram, black and tan Doberman, Fang

Notice how the picture becomes more vivid as we move to lower levels of generality. To visualize your way of seeing and your exact meaning, readers need specifics.

Abstract words name qualities, concepts, or feelings (**beauty, luxury, depression**) whose exact meaning has to be nailed down by *concrete* words—words that name things we can visualize:

Abstract terms traded for concrete terms

> a beautiful view = snowcapped mountains, a wilderness lake, pink granite ledge, 30-metre blue spruce trees
>
> a luxury condominium = redwood hot tub, hand-painted Mexican tile counters, floor-to-ceiling glass walls, oriental rugs
>
> a depressed person = suicidal urge, feelings of worthlessness, no hope for improvement, insomnia

Your discussion must be concrete and specific enough to provide clear and convincing support. Let's say that your topic statement is this one:

> Pedestrians crossing the street in front of my house place their lives in danger.

In supporting your main point you need to **show** with concrete and specific examples.

| **Abstract** | For example, a person was injured there by a vehicle recently. |
| **Concrete** | My Uncle Omar was hit by a speeding garbage truck last Tuesday and had his leg broken. |

Similarly, don't write **thing** when you mean **problem, pencil,** or **gift.** Instead of evaluating a co-worker as **nice, great,** or **terrific,** use terms that are more concrete and verifiable, such as **reliable, skillful,** and **competent** or **dishonest, irritable,** and **awkward**—further clarified by examples (**never late for work**).

NOTE *In some instances, of course, you may wish to generalize. Instead of writing* **Bill, Mary, and Sam have been tying up the office phones with personal calls,** *you might prefer* **Some employees have been tying up. . . .** *The second version gets your message across without pointing the finger.*

Most good writing offers both general and specific information. The more general material is in the topic statement and sometimes in the conclusion because these parts, respectively, set the paragraph's direction and summarize its content. Informative writing invariably has a balance of *telling* and *showing.* Abstract and general expressions tell, and concrete and specific expressions show.

| **Meaningless abstraction** | Professor Able's office is a sight to behold. [*What does "a sight to behold" mean?*] |
| **Informative abstraction** | Professor Able's office looks like a dump. |

Now, the telling needs clarification through concrete and specific showing:

| **Concrete showing** | The office has a floor strewn with books, a desk buried beneath a mountain of uncorrected papers, and ashtrays overflowing with ripe cigar butts. |

APPLICATION 8-3

In each set of terms, identify the most abstract or general and the most concrete or specific. Give reasons for your choices.

1. a prime ministerial candidate, a Canadian Member of Parliament, Sheila Copps, a politician
2. a favourite spot, a beautiful place, an island in the Bahamas, a hideaway
3. woman, surgeon, person, professional individual
4. an awful person, a cruel and dishonest person, a nasty person
5. a competitor, a downhill racer, an athlete, a skier, a talented amateur
6. violence, assassination, terrorism, political action

tone

ADD SOME PERSONALITY

How tone is created

Your tone is your personal stamp—the personality that takes shape between the lines. The tone you create depends on (1) the distance you impose between yourself and the reader, and (2) the attitude you show toward the subject.

Assume, for example, that a friend is going to take over a job you've held. You're writing your friend instructions for parts of the job. Here is your first sentence:

Informal

> Now that you've arrived in the glamorous world of office work, put on your track shoes; this is no ordinary clerical job.

This sentence imposes little distance between you and the reader (it uses the direct address, **you,** and the humorous suggestion to **put on your track shoes**). The ironic use of **glamorous** suggests just the opposite, that the job holds little glamour.

For a different reader (say, the recipient of a company training manual) you would have chosen some other opening:

Semiformal

> As an office assistant with Acme Explosives Corporation, you will spend little of your day seated at your desk.

The tone now is serious, no longer intimate, and you express no distinct attitude toward the job. For yet another audience (say, clients or investors who will read an annual report) you might alter the tone again:

Formal

> Office assistants at Acme Explosives are responsible for duties that extend far beyond desk work.

Here, the businesslike shift from second- to third-person address makes the tone too impersonal for any writing addressed to the assistants themselves.

Similarly, letters to your professor, your grandmother, and your friend, each about a disputed grade, would have a different tone:

Formal

> Dear Professor Snapjaws:
>   I am convinced that my failing grade in calculus did not reflect a fair evaluation of my work over the semester.

Semiformal

> Dear Granny,
>   Thanks for your letter. I'm doing well in school, except for my unfair grade in calculus.

Informal

> Dear Carol,
>   Have I been shafted or what? That old turkey, Snapjaws, gave me an F in calculus.

Establish an Appropriate Distance

We already know how tone works in speaking. When you meet someone new, for example, you respond in a tone that defines your relationship.

Tone announces
interpersonal
distance

> Honoured to make your acquaintance. [*formal tone—greatest distance*]
>
> How do you do? [*formal*]
>
> Nice to meet you. [*semiformal—medium distance*]
>
> Hi. [*informal—least distance*]
>
> What's happening? [*informal*]

Each of these responses is appropriate in some situations, inappropriate in others:

GUIDELINES FOR DECIDING ABOUT TONE

1. Use a formal or semiformal tone in writing for superiors, professionals, or academics (depending on what you think the reader expects).

2. Use a semiformal or informal tone in essays and letters (depending on how close you feel to your reader).

3. Use an informal tone when you want your writing to be conversational, or when you want it to sound like a person talking.

4. Above all, find out what tone your particular readers prefer.

Whichever tone you decide on, be consistent throughout your message:

Inconsistent tone   My residence room isn't fit for a pig: it is ungraciously unattractive.

Revised   My dilapidated residence room is unfit to live in.

In general, lean toward an informal tone without falling into slang. Make your writing conversational by following these suggestions:

GUIDELINES FOR ACHIEVING A CONVERSATIONAL TONE

1. Use simple and familiar words.
2. Use an occasional contraction.
3. Address readers directly when appropriate.
4. Use **I** and **We** when appropriate.
5. Prefer active to passive voice.

Use Simple and Familiar Wording. Don't write like the author of a report on the benefits of leisure activity who argued that "**leisure has been shown to be an effective medium for the social experimentation and the acquisition of developmental capabilities and it enables the youth to cope more effectively with psychological pressures and crises in adult life**" (36 words, 70 syllables). Here is a plain English translation: **Youth involved in leisure activities usually mature socially, physically, and psychologically** (11 words, 31 syllables).

Inflated	Upgrade your present employment situation. [*5 words, 12 syllables*]
Revised	Get a better job. [*4 words, 5 syllables*]
Inflated	I am thoroughly convinced that Sam is a trustworthy individual.
Revised	I trust Sam.

Whenever possible, trade for less and simpler:

Multiple syllables traded for fewer

utilize	=	use
to be cognizant	=	to know
to endeavour	=	to try
endeavour	=	effort
to secure employment	=	to find a job
concur	=	agree
effectuate	=	do
terminate	=	end
deem	=	think

Of course, now and then the complex or more elaborate word best expresses your meaning if it replaces a handful of simpler words.

Weak	Six loops around **the outside edges** of the dome tent **are needed for** the pegs **to fit into.**
Informative and precise	Six loops around the dome tent's **perimeter accommodate** the pegs.
Weak	We need a **one-to-one exchange of ideas and opinions.**
Informative and precise	We need a **dialogue.**

Use an Occasional Contraction. Unless you have reason to be formal, use (but do not overuse) contractions. Balance an **I am** with an **I'm,** a **you are** with a **you're,** an **it is** with an **it's.** Generally, use contractions only with pronouns—not with nouns or proper nouns (names).

Awkward contractions	Lisa'll be here soon. Health's important. Love'll make you happy.
Ambiguous contractions	The dog's barking. The baby's crying.

These ambiguous contractions could be confused with possessive constructions.

Address Readers Directly. Use the personal pronouns **you** and **your** to connect with readers.

Impersonal tone	Students at our university will find the faculty always willing to help.
Personal tone	As a student at our university, **you** will find the faculty always willing to help.

Readers relate better to something addressed to them directly.

NOTE

*Use **you** and **your** only to correspond directly with the reader, as in a letter, instructions, or some form of advice, encouragement, or persuasion. By using **you** and **your** in a situation that calls for first or third person, you might write something like this:*

Wordy and awkward	When **you** are in northern Ontario, **you** can see wilderness lakes everywhere around **you.**
Appropriate	Wilderness lakes are everywhere in northern Ontario.

Use "I" and "We" When Appropriate. Instead of disappearing behind your writing, use **I** or **we** when referring to yourself or your group.

Distant	This writer would like a refund.
Revised	I would like a refund.
Distant	The fear was awful until the police arrived.
Revised	We were terrified until the police arrived.

Prefer the Active Voice. Because the active voice is more direct and economical than the passive voice, it generally creates a less formal tone. Review pages 116–117 for use of active and passive voice.

Express a Clear and Appropriate Attitude

In addition to setting the distance between writer and reader, your tone implies your attitude toward the subject and the reader:

Tone announces
attitude

> We dine at seven.
>
> Dinner is at seven.
>
> We eat at seven.
>
> We chow down at seven.
>
> We strap on the feedbag at seven.
>
> We pig out at seven.

The words you choose tell readers a great deal about where you stand.

One problem with tone occurs when your attitude is unclear. Say **I enjoyed the course** instead of **My attitude toward the course was one of high approval.** Try to convey an attitude that reflects your relationship with the reader. For instance, in an upcoming conference about a late paper, does the professor expect to **discuss the situation, talk it over, have a chat,** or **chew the fat?** Decide how casual or serous your attitude should be.

Don't be afraid to inject personal commentary when it's called for. Consider how the message below increases in force and effectiveness with the boldfaced commentary:

> Student demand for a university education is expected to increase by 40 percent over the course of the next decade. To date, Ontario has lost 2000 full-time equivalent faculty, representing more than 15 percent of the total complement. In addition, a third of current faculty members are between the ages of 55 and 64, suggesting that a further 5500 professors—**who are the heart and soul of their institutions**—will leave their universities by 2010.

If, however, your job is to report objectively, try to suppress any bias you might have; do not volunteer your attitude.

Avoid Personal Bias

If people expect an impartial report, try to keep your own biases out of it. Imagine, for instance, that you are a campus newspaper reporter, investigating a confrontation between part-time faculty and the administration. Your initial report, written for tomorrow's edition, is intended simply to describe what happened. Here is how an unbiased description might read:

A factual account

> At 10:00 a.m. on Wednesday, October 24, 80 sessional faculty members set up picket lines around the university's administration building, bringing business to a halt. The group issued a formal protest, claiming that their salary scale was unfair, their fringe benefits [health insurance, and so on] inadequate, and their job security nonexistent. The group insisted that the university's wage scales and employment policies be revised. The demonstration ended when Glenn Tarullo, vice-president in charge of personnel, promised to appoint a committee to investigate the group's claims and to correct any inequities.

Notice the absence of implied judgments. A less impartial version of the event, from a protester's point of view, might read like this:

A biased version

Last Wednesday, sessional faculty struck another blow against exploitation when 80 members paralyzed the university's repressive administration for more than six hours. The timely and articulate protest was aimed against unfair salary scales, inadequate fringe benefits, and lack of job security. Stunned administrators watched helplessly as the group organized their picket lines, determined to continue their protest until their demands for fair treatment were met. An embarrassed vice-president quickly agreed to study the group's demands and to revise the university's discriminatory policies. The success of this long-overdue confrontation serves as an inspiration to oppressed sessional faculty everywhere.

NOTE

Writing teacher Marshall Kremers reminds us that being unbiased, of course, doesn't mean remaining "neutral" about something you know to be wrong or dangerous.* If, for instance, you conclude that the university protest was clearly justified, say so.

INVITE EVERYONE IN

Not only do the words you choose reveal your way of seeing, but they also influence your reader's way of seeing. Insensitive language carries built-in judgments, and as the renowned linguist S. I. Hayakawa reminds us: Judgment stops thought. Writing that makes human contact is writing that excludes no one.

Avoid Sexist Language

The way we as a culture use language reflects the way we think about ourselves. Usage that gives people in general a male identity allows no room for females. In fact, females become virtually invisible in a world of **policemen, firemen, foremen, businessmen,** and **aldermen.**

Sexist usage refers to doctors, lawyers, and other professionals as **he** or **him** while referring to nurses, secretaries, and homemakers as **she** or **her.** In this traditional stereotype, males do the jobs that really matter and that pay higher wages, whereas females serve only as support and decoration. And when females do invade traditional "male" roles, we might express our surprise at their boldness by calling them **female executives, female sportscasters, female surgeons,** or **female hockey players.** Likewise, to demean males who have taken "female" roles, we sometimes refer to **male secretaries, male nurses, male flight attendants,** or **male models.**

*See *IEEE Transactions on Professional Communication* 32.2 (1989): 58–61.

GUIDELINES FOR NONSEXIST USAGE

1. Use neutral expressions:

chair, or chairperson	rather than	**chairman**
supervisor	rather than	**foreman**
police officer	rather than	**policeman**
letter carrier	rather than	**mailman**
homemaker	rather than	**housewife**
humanity	rather than	**mankind**
actor	rather than	**actor vs. actress**

2. Rephrase to eliminate the pronoun, if you can do so without altering your original meaning.

Sexist	A writer will succeed if he revises.
Revised	A writer who revises succeeds.

3. Use plural forms.

Sexist	A writer will succeed if **he** revises.
Revised	Writers will succeed if **they** revise. (But *not a writer will succeed if* **they** *revise.*)

   When using a plural form, don't create an error in pronoun-referent agreement by having the plural pronoun **they** or **their** refer to a singular referent:

   Each writer should do **their** best.

4. When possible (as in direct address) use you:

Direct address	You will succeed if you revise.

   But use this form only when addressing someone directly. (See page 141.)

Avoid Offensive Usage of All Types

Enlightened communication respects all people in reference to their specific cultural, racial, ethnic, and national background; sexual and religious orientation; age or physical condition. References to individuals and groups should be as neutral as possible; no matter how inadvertent, any expression that seems condescending or judgmental or that violates the reader's sense of appropriateness is offensive. Detailed guidelines for reducing biased usage appear in these two works:

Schwartz, Marilyn et al. *Guidelines for Bias-Free Writing.* Bloomington: Indiana UP, 1995.

Publication Manual of the American Psychological Association, 5th ed. Washington: American Psychological Association, 2001.

Below is a sampling of suggestions adapted from the above works.

5. Use occasional pairings (**him or her, she or he, his or hers, he/she**):

Effective pairing   A writer will succeed if she or he revises.

But note that overuse of such pairings can be awkward:

Awkward pairing   A writer should do his or her best to make sure that he or she connects with his or her readers.

6. Use feminine and masculine pronouns alternately:

Alternating pronouns   An effective writer always focuses on her audience.

The writer strives to connect with all his readers.

7. Drop condescending diminutive endings such as **-ess** and **-ette** used to denote females (**poetess, drum majorette, actress**, etc.).

8. Use **Ms.** instead of **Mrs.** or **Miss,** unless you know that the person prefers one of the traditional titles. Or omit titles completely: **Jane Kelly** and **Roger Smith; Kelly and Smith.**

9. In quoting sources that have ignored present standards for nonsexist usage, consider these options:

   - Insert [*sic*] (for **thus** or **so**) following the first instance of sexist terminology in a particular passage.
   - Use ellipses to omit sexist phrasing.
   - Paraphrase instead of quoting directly.

Consider the Cultural Context

Cultures differ in their style preferences

The style guidelines throughout Chapters 7 and 8 apply specifically to standard English in North America. But practices and preferences differ widely in various cultural contexts.

Certain cultures might prefer complicated sentences and elaborate language to convey an idea's full complexity. Other cultures value expressions of politeness, praise, and gratitude more than mere clarity or directness (Hein 125–26; Mackin 349–50).

Writing in non-English languages tends to be more formal than in English, and some relies heavily on the passive voice (Weymouth 144). French readers, for example, may prefer an elaborate style that reflects sophisticated and complex modes of thinking. In contrast, our "plain English," conversational style might connote simple-mindedness, disrespect, or incompetence (Thrush 277).

GUIDELINES FOR INOFFENSIVE USAGE

1. When referring to members of a particular culture, be as specific as possible about that culture's identity: Instead of **Latin American** or **Asian** or **Hispanic,** for instance, prefer **Cuban American** or **Korean** or **Nicaraguan.** Instead of **American students,** specify **U.S. students** when referring to the United States.

   Avoid judgmental expressions: Instead of **third-world** or **undeveloped nations** or the **Far East,** prefer **developing** or **newly industrialized nations** or **East Asia.** Instead of **non-whites,** refer to **people of colour.**

2. When referring to someone who has a disability, avoid terms that could be considered pitying or overly euphemistic, such as **victims, unfortunates, special** or **challenged** or **differently abled.** Focus on the individual instead of the disability: instead of **blind person** or **amputee** refer to a **person who is blind** or a **person who has lost an arm.**

   In general usage, avoid expressions that demean those who have medical conditions: **retard, mental midget, insane idea, lame excuse, the blind leading the blind, able-bodied workers,** and so on.

3. When referring to members of a particular age group, prefer **girl** or **boy** for people of age 14 or under; **young person, young adult, young man** or **young woman** for those of high school age; and **woman** or **man** for those of college age. (**Teenager or juvenile** carries certain negative connotations.) Instead of **the elderly,** prefer **older persons.**

In translation or in a different cultural context, certain words carry offensive or unfavourable connotations. For example, certain cultures use "male" and "female" in referring only to animals (Coe 17). Other notable disasters (Gesteland 20; Victor 44):

- The Chevrolet *Nova*—meaning "don't go" in Spanish
- The Finnish beer *Koff*—for an English-speaking market ("cough")
- Colgate's *Cue* toothpaste—an obscenity in French
- A bicycle brand named *Flying Pigeon*—imported for a U.S. market

Idioms ("strike out," "over the top") hold no logical meaning for other cultures. Slang ("bogus," "phat") and colloquialisms ("You bet," "Gotcha") can strike readers as being too informal and crude.

Offensive writing can alienate audiences—toward you *and* your culture (Sturges 32).

APPLICATION **8-4**

Rewrite these statements in plain and precise English, with special attention to tone.

1. This writer desires to be considered for a position with your company.
2. My attitude toward your behaviour is one of disapproval.
3. A good writer is cognizant of how to utilize grammar in correct fashion.
4. Replacement of the weak battery should be effectuated.
5. Sexist language contributes to the ongoing prevalence of gender stereotypes.
6. Make an improvement in your studying situation.
7. We should inject some rejuvenation into our lifeless and dull relationship.

APPLICATION **8-5**

Find examples of overly euphemistic language (such as "chronologically challenged") or of insensitive language—possibly on the Internet or in a newsgroup. Discuss your examples in class.

APPLICATION **8-6**

Collaborative Project and Computer Application: A version of this next letter was published in a local newspaper. Working on the computer, each group member should rewrite the letter in plain English and then e-mail your version to group members. Discuss the changes electronically, and agree on a final version that one group member will compose. Print this final version for the whole class, justifying your group's revision.

> In the absence of definitive studies regarding the optimum length of the school day, I can only state my personal opinion based upon observations made by me and upon teacher observations that have been conveyed to me. Considering the length of the present school day, it is my opinion that the school day is excessive lengthwise for most elementary pupils, certainly for almost all of the primary children.
>
> To find the answer to the problem requires consideration of two ways in which the problem may be viewed. One way focuses upon the needs of the children, while the other focuses upon logistics, scheduling, transportation, and other limits imposed by the educational system. If it is necessary to prioritize these two ideas, it would seem most reasonable to

give the first consideration to the primary and fundamental reason for the very existence of the system itself, i.e., to meet the educational needs of the children the system is trying to serve.

APPLICATION **8-7**

Rewrite these statements to eliminate sexist and other offensive expressions—without altering the meaning.

1. An employee in our organization can be sure he will be treated fairly.
2. Almost every child dreams of being a fireman.
3. The average man is a good citizen.
4. The future of mankind is uncertain.
5. Being a stewardess is not as glamorous as it may seem.
6. Everyone has the right to his opinion.
7. Every married surgeon depends on his spouse for emotional support.
8. Dr. Marcia White is not only a female professor, but also chairman of the English department.
9. The accident left me blind as a bat for nearly an hour.
10. What a dumb idea!

AVOID RELIANCE ON AUTOMATED TOOLS

The limits of automation

Many of the strategies in Chapters 7 and 8 could be executed rapidly with word processing software. By using the global *Search-and-replace function* in some programs, you can command the computer to search for ambiguous pronoun references, overuse of passive voice, **to be** verbs, **There** and **It** sentence openers, negative constructions, clutter words, needless prefatory expressions and qualifiers, sexist language, and so on. With an online dictionary or thesaurus, you can check definitions or see a list of synonyms for a word you have used in your writing.

But these editing aids can be extremely imprecise. They can't eliminate the writer's burden of choice. None of the "rules" offered in Chapters 7 and 8 applies universally. Ultimately the informed writer's sensitivity to meaning, emphasis, and tone—the human contact—determines the effectiveness of any message.

APPLICATION **8-8**

Computer Application: Explore the thesaurus function on your word processing program. Remember that a thesaurus never can provide an exact synonym. Check the computer's suggestions against the dictionary definitions of the words. Compare the computer's suggestions with a good traditional thesaurus and with *Roget's Thesaurus* online **www.thesaurus.com**. Assess the advantages and disadvantages of each.

Works Cited

Coe, Marlana. "Writing for Other Cultures." *Intercom* Jan. 1997: 17–19.

Gesteland, Richard R. "Cross-Cultural Compromises." *Sky* May 1993: 20+.

Hein, Robert G. "Culture and Communication." *Technical Communication* 38.1 (1991): 125–26.

Mackin, John. "Surmounting the Barrier between Japanese and English Technical Documents." *Technical Communication* 36.4 (1989): 346–51.

Sturges, David L. "Internationalizing the Business Communication Curriculum." *Bulletin of the Association for Business Communication* 55.1 (1992): 30–39.

Thrush, Emily A. "Bridging the Gap: Technical Communication in an Intercultural and Multicultural Society." *Technical Communication Quarterly* 2.3 (1993): 271–83.

Victor, David A. *International Business Communication.* New York: Harper, 1992.

Weymouth, L. C. "Establishing Quality Standards and Trade Regulations for Technical Writing in World Trade." *Technical Communication* 37.2 (1990): 143–47.

SECTION THREE

Essays for Various Goals

Introduction

arlier chapters have stressed the importance of deciding on a goal and of refining the goal into a purpose (goal plus plan). This section shows you how to focus on your purpose in order to achieve a variety of writing goals.

THREE MAJOR GOALS OF WRITING

Most writing can be categorized according to three major goals: expressive, referential, and persuasive.

Expressive writing is mostly about you, the writer (your feelings, experiences, impressions, personality). This personal form of writing helps readers understand something about you or your way of seeing.

Expressive writing situations

- You write to cheer up a sick friend with a tale about your latest blind date.
- You write a Dear John (or Jane) letter.
- You write to your parents, explaining why you've been feeling down-in-the-dumps.

Examples of expressive writing appear in the sample essays in Section One on pages 13 and 16. Many students find expressive writing easiest because it is a kind of storytelling.

Instead of focusing on the writer, *referential (or explanatory) writing* refers to some outside subject. Your goal might be (a) to inform readers about something they need to know or (b) to explain something they need to understand. Referential writing doesn't focus on your feelings and experiences but on the subject at hand.

Referential writing situations

- You write to describe the exterior of your new residence room so that your parents can find it next weekend.
- You define *condominium* for your business law class.
- You report on the effects of budget cuts at your university for the campus newspaper.
- You write to advise a younger sibling about how to prepare for university-level work.

An example of referential writing appears on page 52.

Persuasive writing is mostly about your audience. Beyond merely imparting information or making something understandable, your goal is to win readers' support, to influence their thinking, or motivate them in some way. Persuasive writing appeals both to the audience's reason and emotions.

Persuasive writing situations

- You write an editorial for the campus newspaper, calling for a stricter alcohol policy in the residences.
- You write a diplomatic note to your obnoxious neighbour, asking him to keep his dogs quiet.

- You write to ask a professor on sabbatical to reconsider the low grade you received in history.
- You write to persuade citizens in your county to vote against a proposal for a toxic-waste dump.

These three goals (expressive, referential or explanatory, and persuasive) often overlap. For example, persuading the dean to beef up campus security might mean discussing your personal fears (expressive goal) and explaining how some students have been attacked (referential goal). But most writing situations have one primary goal. Keeping that goal in focus can help you choose the best strategies for getting the job done.

Traditionally, the strategies for writing are considered to be *description, narration, exposition* (informing or explaining), and *argument.* But description, narration, and exposition can be used for expressive, referential, or persuasive goals. While Chapter 1 focuses on expressive writing, Section Three is mostly about communication between readers and writers on subjects of interest to both. Therefore, it focuses primarily on referential and persuasive uses of these strategies—that is, writing to inform, explain, or make a point. Persuasive writing, however, raises special concerns that we will cover in Chapters 17 and 18.

NOTE
Keep in mind that none of these development strategies is an end in itself. In other words, we don't write merely for the sake of contrasting or discussing causes and effects, and so on. Instead, we use a particular strategy because it provides the best framework for organizing our information and clarifying our thinking on a particular topic. Each strategy is merely one way of looking at something—another option for gaining control of the countless writing situations we face throughout our lives and careers.

MAJOR DEVELOPMENT STRATEGIES

A *development strategy* is simply a plan for coming up with the details, events, examples, explanations, and reasons that convey your exact meaning—a way of answering readers' questions. *Description* paints a word picture, while *narration* tells a story or depicts a series of related events, usually in chronological order. Narration relies on descriptive details to make the events vivid. *Exposition,* meanwhile, relies on description and narration, but it does more than paint a picture or tell a story: this strategy explains the writer's viewpoint. Strategies of exposition include *illustration, classification, process analysis, cause-effect analysis, comparison-contrast,* and *definition,* all of which are explored in the following chapters. Essays often employ some combination of these strategies but usually have one primary strategy.

Finally, *argument* strives to win readers to our point of view. Whereas the main point in exposition can usually be shown to be true or valid, the main point in an argument is debatable—capable of being argued by reasonable people on either side. The stronger argument, then, would be the one that makes the more convincing case.

NOTE *Although argument follows its own specified patterns of reasoning, it also relies on the strategies of description, narration, and exposition.*

USING THIS SECTION

This section begins with a chapter on methods for reading and responding to essays written by others. The following chapters then introduce a particular strategy and show how the strategy can support referential and persuasive writing.

Next, the chapters provide guidelines for using the strategy yourself, along with a sample essay for your analysis and response. When you read these sample essays, refer to the Chapter 9 questions as well as to the more specific questions provided in each chapter. Then examine the case study that shows one student's response to the sample essay.

A WORD ABOUT STRUCTURAL VARIATIONS

Most sample essays in earlier chapters have a basic introduction-body-conclusion structure: a one-paragraph introduction that leads into the thesis; several support paragraphs, each developed around a topic statement that treats one part of the thesis; and a one-paragraph conclusion that relates to the main point. But a quick glance at published writing shows much variation from this formula: Some topics call for several introductory paragraphs; some supporting points require that one topic statement serve two or more body paragraphs; some paragraphs may be interrupted by digressions like personal remarks or flashbacks that are linked to the main point; some conclusions take up more than one paragraph. Single-sentence paragraphs will open, support, or close an essay.

Instead of the final sentence in the introduction, the thesis might be the first sentence of the essay, or it may be saved for the conclusion or not stated at all—although a definite thesis almost always is unmistakably implied.

Still other essays have neither introductory nor concluding paragraphs. Instead, the opening or closing is incorporated into the main discussion. Such *structural variations are a part of a writer's deliberate decisions*—decisions that determine the ultimate quality of an essay. Many of the essays in the following chapters embody one or more of these variations. Use them as inspiration for your own writing, but remember that *effective writing always reveals a distinct beginning, middle, and ending*—and a clear line of thought.

CHAPTER 9

Decisions about Reading for Writing

This book asks you to read other people's writing (students and professionals) in order to consider their ideas and trace their decision making. Reading also provides raw material that helps you craft your own writing. But not all reading is equal in terms of the level of interaction it requires.

DIFFERENT LEVELS OF READING

Reading to be entertained

Different reasons for reading call for different levels of interacting with a piece of writing. In reading something like a Stephen King novel, for instance, we tend to skim the surface, flipping pages to find the juicy scenes and basically enjoying the ride.

Reading to get information

In reading a textbook in psychology or some other discipline, we work to grasp important facts and main ideas. Later, we often write to demonstrate our knowledge or understanding.

Reading to make a critical judgment

For this course, we go beyond merely retrieving and absorbing information. In *critical reading,* we dig beneath the surface and examine the writing itself—its content, organization, and style. Instead of accepting the ideas at face value, we weigh the evidence, the assumptions, and the reasoning behind them.

Questions for Critical Reading

ABOUT PURPOSE

- *What is the author asking us to think or do?*
- *In what ways does this piece succeed or fail in its purpose?*

ABOUT CONTENT

- *Is the title effective? Why?*
- *What is the thesis? Is it stated, or is it implicit? Where does it appear?*
- *Does this placement contribute to the main point?*
- *Does the piece offer something new and useful?*
- *Does the reasoning make sense?*
- *Is the essay convincing? What kinds of support does the writer offer for the main points?*
- *Are other conclusions or interpretations possible?*

ABOUT ORGANIZATION

- *Is the discussion easy to follow?*
- *How is the introduction structured? Are the writer's decisions effective? Why?*
- *Does the essay vary the standard introduction-body-conclusion format (page 155)? If so, how? Do the writer's decisions help promote the purpose?*
- *How is the conclusion structured? Is it effective? Why?*

ABOUT STYLE

- *What is the outstanding style feature of this essay? Give examples.*
- *How effective is the tone? Give examples of word choice and sentence structure that contribute to the tone.*

Reading to discover personal meaning

This critical evaluation provides essential groundwork for writing about reading. But much of the energy for *any* writing comes from our personal response to something we read.

In reading for personal meaning, we join a "conversation": reacting to something that was said, we offer something of our own. We read to explore and inspire our own thinking or to make up our minds or to discover buried feelings or ideas. Then we reinvent that material with a force and passion that will make a difference to our own readers.

Questions for Personal Responses to Reading

- *What special meaning does this piece have for me?*
- *What grabs my attention?*
- *Does this piece make me angry, defensive, supportive, or what?*
- *Why do I feel this way?*
- *With which statement do I agree or disagree?*
- *Has the piece reminded me of something, taught me something, changed my mind, or what?*
- *How do I want to reply?*

DIFFERENT READERS, DIFFERENT MEANINGS

The connection that writing creates is both public and private. On the one hand, a piece of writing connects publicly with its entire audience; on the other hand, the writing connects privately with each of its readers. Consider, for example, "Confessions of a Food Addict" (pages 16–18): Most readers of this essay feel the writer's anxiety and sense of failure. Beyond our common reaction, however, each of us has a unique and personal reaction as well—special feelings or memories or thoughts.

You as the reader interpret and complete the "private" meaning of anything you read. And, like you, other readers come away from the same piece with a personal meaning of their own. It is this personal meaning that ultimately inspires your own writing.

READING STRATEGIES FOR WRITERS

A worthwhile critical and personal response to writing calls for a good strategy. Instead of just a single reading, you need to really "get into" the piece. And you do this by rereading and by writing *while* you read: First you take notes, underline, scribble questions and comments in the margins, and summarize the main ideas. Then you examine the author's technique, evaluate the ideas, and discover what the piece means to you personally. Once you have a genuine grasp of the piece, you can decide exactly how you want to respond.

The following case study shows how student writer Jacqueline LeBlanc employs each of these strategies in preparing her response to a reading.

RESPONDING TO READING

Judy Brady's "Why I Want a Wife" was published in the very first issue of *Ms.* magazine in spring 1972. Even though Brady seems to write for married readers in particular, her essay speaks to anyone familiar with married people in general. Please read the essay carefully.

Essay for analysis and response

WHY I WANT A WIFE

I belong to that classification of people known as wives. I am A Wife. And, not altogether incidentally, I am a mother.

Not too long ago a male friend of mine appeared on the scene fresh from a recent divorce. He had one child, who is, of course, with his ex-wife. He is looking for another wife. As I thought about him while I was ironing one evening, it suddenly occurred to me that I, too, would like to have a wife. Why do I want a wife?

I would like to go back to school so that I can become economically independent, support myself, and, if need be, support those dependent upon me. I want a wife who will work and send me to school. And while I am going to school I want a wife to take care of my children. I want a wife to keep track of the children's doctor and dentist appointments. And to keep track of mine, too. I want a wife to make sure my children eat properly and are kept clean. I want a wife who will wash the children's clothes and keep them mended. I want a wife who is a good nurturant attendant to my children, who arranges for their schooling, makes sure that they have an adequate social life with their peers, takes them to the park, the zoo, etc. I want a wife who takes care of the children when they are sick, a wife who arranges to be around when the children need special care, because, of course, I cannot miss classes at school. My wife must arrange to lose time at work and not lose the job. It may mean a small cut in my wife's income from time to time, but I guess I can tolerate that. Needless to say, my wife will arrange and pay for the care of the children while my wife is working.

I want a wife who will take care of my physical needs. I want a wife who will keep my house clean. A wife who will pick up after my children, a wife who will pick up after me. I want a wife who will keep my clothes clean, ironed, mended, replaced when need be, and who will see to it that my personal things are kept in their proper place so that I can find what I need the minute I need it. I want a wife who cooks the meals, a wife who is a good cook. I want a wife who will plan the menus, do the necessary grocery shopping, prepare the meals, serve them pleasantly, and then do the cleaning up while I do my studying. I want a wife who will care for me when I am sick and sympathize with my pain and loss of time from school.

I want a wife to go along when our family takes a vacation so that someone can continue to care for me and my children when I need a rest and change of scene.

I want a wife who will not bother me with rambling complaints about a wife's duties. But I want a wife who will listen to me when I feel the need to explain a rather difficult point I have come across in my course of studies. And I want a wife who will type my papers for me when I have written them.

I want a wife who will take care of the details of my social life. When my wife and I are invited out by my friends, I want a wife who will take care of the babysitting arrangements. When I meet people at school that I like and want to entertain, I want a wife who will have the house clean, will prepare a special meal, serve it to me and my friends, and not interrupt when I talk about things that interest me and my friends. I want a wife who will have arranged that the children are fed and ready for bed before my guests arrive so that the children do not bother us. I want a wife who takes care of the needs of my guests so that they feel comfortable, who makes sure that they have an ashtray, that they are passed the hors d'oeuvres, that they are offered a second helping of the food, that their wine glasses are replenished when necessary, that their coffee is served to them as they like it. And I want a wife who knows that sometimes I need a night out by myself.

I want a wife who is sensitive to my sexual needs, a wife who makes love passionately and eagerly when I feel like it, a wife who makes sure that I am satisfied. And, of course, I want a wife who will not demand sexual attention when I am not in the mood for it. I want a wife who assumes the complete responsibility for birth control, because I do not want more children. I want a wife who will remain sexually faithful to me so that I do not have to clutter up my intellectual life with jealousies. And I want a wife who understands that my sexual needs may entail more than strict adherence to monogamy. I must, after all, be able to relate to people as fully as possible.

If, by chance, I find another person more suitable as a wife than the wife I already have, I want the liberty to replace my present wife with another one. Naturally, I will expect a fresh, new life; my wife will take the children and be solely responsible for them so that I am left free. When I am through with school and have a job, I want my wife to quit working and remain at home so that my wife can more fully and completely take care of a wife's duties.

My God, who *wouldn't* want a wife?

—*Judy Brady*

Discussion

Now let's examine our critical and personal opinions of "Why I Want A Wife." Is this bleak view of the "housewife's" destiny basically accurate, in your view? What particular meaning does this essay have for you?

Maybe Brady's essay leaves you feeling irate toward (1) men, (2) the writer, (3) yourself, or (4) someone else. Or maybe you feel threatened or offended. Or maybe you feel amused or confused about your own attitudes toward gender roles. The questions on pages 157 and 158 will help you explore your reactions.

Before you decide on a response to Brady's essay, see how another student responded. Here are some of the notes Jacqueline LeBlanc wrote in her journal after first reading the essay:

One of Jackie's journal entries

> This essay is annoying because it reminds me too much of some women in my own generation who seem to want nothing more than a wifely role for themselves. For all we hear about "equal rights," women still feel the pressure to conform to old-fashioned notions. I can really take this essay personally.

After rereading the essay and reviewing her journal entries, Jackie highlighted and annotated key passages. Here is what she jots on one paragraph of the Brady essay:

Jackie's highlighting and annotations of one paragraph

extremely self-centred

(I) want a wife who will take care of (my) physical needs. (I) want a wife who will keep (my) house clean. A wife who will pick up after (my) children, a wife who will pick up after (me) (I) want a wife who will keep my clothes clean, ironed, mended, replaced when need be, and who will see to it that (my) personal things are kept in their proper place so that (I) can find what (I) need the minute (I) need it. (I)

a maid/ house-keeper

not just any old cook!

want a wife who cooks the meals, a wife who is a (good) cook. (I) want a wife who will plan the menus, do the necessary grocery shopping,

a cook

service with a smile!

prepare the meals, serve them (pleasantly,) and then do the cleaning up while (I) do (my) studying. (I) want

wants to be pampered too!

a wife who will care for (me) when (I) am sick and (sympathize) with (my) pain and loss of time from

a nurse

How common is all this in today's marriages?

school. (I) want a wife to go along when our family takes a vacation so that someone can continue to care for (me) and my children when (I) need a rest and change of scene.

a nanny

What about women's view of "husbandly" duties? How are they similar or different?

To ensure her grasp of Brady's position, Jackie follows page 360 guidelines to summarize the essay in her own words:

Jackie's summary of the essay

> In "Why I Want a Wife," Judy Brady offers a graphic view of the lowly status of women in marriage. The typical wife is expected to serve as financial provider, nanny, nurse, maid, cook, secretary, and sex slave. And no matter how well she performs these and other oppressive duties, this wife is ultimately disposable in the event that the husband finds someone "more suitable" for the role.

Sometimes a direct quotation is necessary to preserve a special meaning or emphasis (page 356–357). Notice that Jackie is careful to place Brady's exact wording in quotation marks.

Next, Jackie uses the critical-reading questions on page 157 to evaluate Brady's case. She measures the piece's strengths and weaknesses in terms of its purpose, thesis, support, line of reasoning, accuracy, and style. Here is part of her analysis:

Jackie's partial analysis

> Brady sets out here to shock women (as well as men) out of traditional attitudes by defining her concept of "wife." Even though she offers no explicit thesis, her main point might be stated like this: *Women in the traditional "wifely" role are exploited and unappreciated.*
>
> Her many vivid examples are extremely depressing and somewhat exaggerated, but most of them should be familiar to anyone who has experienced the "traditional" family—and they really don't seem all that outdated, either.
>
> Brady's tone certainly is sarcastic, but, given the situation, her sarcasm seems justified and it adds to the essay's shock value.

She continues her critical evaluation using the Revision Checklist facing the inside front cover.

Now that she has a solid handle on the essay, Jackie uses the personal-response questions on page 158 to explore the special meaning she finds here. Finally, she decides on the viewpoint that will guide her own response:

Jackie's own view-point as a basis for responding

> The stereotypical role condemned by Brady almost three decades ago continues to be disturbingly evident.

Jackie expresses her viewpoint in a definite thesis statement:

Jackie's thesis

> Although today's "equality-minded" generation presumably sees marriage as more than just an occupation, the wifely stereotype persists.

Here, after several revisions, is the essay that explains Jackie's viewpoint:

A LONG WAY TO GO

Judy Brady's portrait of a servile wife might appear somewhat dated—until we examine some of today's views about marriage. Brady defines a wife by the work she does for her husband: she is a secretary, housemaid, babysitter, and sex object. She is, in a word, her husband's employee. Although today's "equality-minded" generation presumably sees marriage as more than an occupation, the wifely stereotype persists.

Among my women friends, I continue to encounter surprisingly traditional attitudes. Last week, for instance, I was discussing my career possibilities with my roommate, who added to the list of my choices by saying, "You can always get married." In her view, becoming a wife seems no different from becoming a teacher or journalist. She implied that marriage is merely another way of making a living. But where do I apply for the position of wife? The notion struck me as absurd. I thought to myself, "Surely, this person is an isolated case. We are, after all, in the twenty-first century. Women no longer get married as a substitute for a job—do they?"

Of course many women do have both job and marriage, but as I look closely at others' attitudes, I find that my roommate's view is not so rare. Before the recent wedding of a female friend, my conversations with the future bride revolved around her meal plans and laundry schedule. To her vows "to love, honour, and cherish" she could have added, "to cook, serve, and clean up." She had been anticipating the first meal she would prepare for her husband. Granted, nothing is wrong with wanting to serve and provide for the one you love—but she spoke of this meal as if it were a pass-or-fail exam given by her employer on her first day on the job. Following the big day of judgment, she was elated to have passed with flying colours.

I couldn't help wondering what would have happened if her meal had been a flop. Would she have lost her marriage as an employee loses a job? As long as my friend retains such a narrow and materialistic view of wifely duties, her marriage is not likely to be anything more than a job.

Not all my friends are obsessed with wifely duties, but some do have a definite sense of husbandly duties. A potential husband must measure up to the qualifications of the position, foremost of which is wealth. One of the first questions about any male is, "What does he do?" Engineering majors or pre-med students usually get highest ranking, and humanities or music majors end up at the bottom. University women are by no means opposed to marriage based on true love, but, as we grow older, the fantasy of a Prince Charming gives way to the reality of an affluent provider. Some women look for high-paying marriages just as they look for high-paying jobs.

Some of my peers may see marriage as one of many career choices, but my parents see it as the only choice. To my parents, my not finding a husband is a much more terrifying fate than my not finding a job. In their view, being a wife is no mere occupation, but a natural vocation for all women. But not just any man will do as a husband. My parents have a built-in screening procedure for each man I date. Appearance, money, and general background are the highest qualifications. They ignore domestic traits because they assume that his parents will be screening me for such qualifications.

I have always tried to avoid considering male friends simply as prospective husbands; likewise, I never think of myself as filling the stereotypical position of wife. But sometimes I fall into my parents' way of thinking. When I invite a friend to dinner at my house, I suddenly find myself fretting about his hair, his religion, or his job. Will he pass the screening test? Is he the right man for the role of husband? In some ways my attitudes seem no°more liberated than those of my peers or parents.

Today's women have made a good deal of progress, but apparently not enough. Allowing the practical implications of marriage to overshadow its emotional implications, a surprising number of us seem to feel that we still have to fit the stereotype that Brady condemns.

Our second respondent, David Galuski, discovers in Brady's essay the possibility for humour, summed up in this thesis:

Instead of a wife, I need an assistant.

Dave pokes fun at his own inability to cope with an impossibly busy schedule. Also, he discovers that (like all of us, at times) he is merely looking for a little sympathy.

Dave's response to
Brady's essay

I NEED AN ASSISTANT

I am much too busy. Being eighteen takes a lot out of a person—especially one who attends college full time, works two part-time jobs, plays sports, and tries to have a social life. I need someone to help me get through the day. Instead of a wife, I need an assistant.

For one thing, my assistant would help with school chores. Although I usually find time to do homework, it is never without a lot of pain. My assistant could ease the pain by doing some of my reading, which he could then summarize and explain to me. Maybe she could do some of my research and type my papers. Fluent in all subjects, my assistant would be able to transfer his knowledge to me.

Studying is easy—when I have enough time. But keeping up my grades while holding down two part-time jobs is another story. I spend twenty hours weekly at Max's, a gourmet restaurant, where I am expected to cater to my customers. But when I'm exhausted from studying, I'm likely to be forgetful and irritable. My assistant would stand by me at all times, to help with the work and cover for any lapses in my patience or attention.

My work as timekeeper for hockey games consumes five hours weekly. I need an assistant to cover games I miss because of the restaurant job or homework and to take over when I fall asleep during the late hours at which these games are scheduled.

Even though I need these jobs to pay college expenses, my life isn't all work and study. I save at least one hour daily to run, cycle, or swim. No matter what my other commitments, without daily exercise, I feel useless. I need an assistant to encourage me to run that extra step or swim that extra lap. She would push me out the door to exercise in the cold and rain. He would compete alongside me in the six triathlons I do each year. She would be a good hockey player, who would attend practices in my place, leaving the team happy and giving me time to finish homework or earn money.

I try—without much success—to maintain an active social life. I need an assistant to keep me informed about my friends and girlfriend. I never have time to call them and hardly ever see them. My assistant would make my phone calls and arrange my dates at times when I can squeeze them in.

Dates are something I can't really make with my parents, but I try to see them as much as possible. I try to help out at home, but that could be a job for my assistant. He could do my household chores, wash the cars, and mow the lawn. My assistant would make my bed and wash my clothes while I hurry off to some pressing engagement.

Finally, I need an assistant who will give me emotional support. I want an assistant to whisper in my ear, to say that everything will turn out all right—one who will sing me to sleep and hold me when I cry. Maybe all I'm looking for after all is a little pity.

These two student writers reached deep into their reading and into themselves to discover a real connection. Their writing, in turn, makes us part of that connection.

The possible responses to Brady's essay are almost infinite. What are some possibilities for your own response?

SUGGESTIONS FOR READING AND WRITING

Some of the readings in later chapters are professionally written, others student written. Besides triggering your own writing, each reading provides a model of worthwhile content, sensible organization, and readable style.

Here are suggestions for reading to respond to the selections assigned throughout the semester:

GUIDELINES FOR READING TO RESPOND

1. Read the piece at least three times: first, to get a sense of the geography; next, to explore your reactions; finally, to see what you find most striking or important or outrageous.

2. Record initial impressions, ideas, or other reactions to the piece, using a journal (page 161).

3. Highlight and annotate passages, underlining the statements that strike you or set you off, and jot questions and comments in the margins.

4. Summarize the entire piece, to be sure you understand the author's purpose, meaning, and main ideas. (See the guidelines on page 360–361.)

5. Using the critical questions on page 157, evaluate the content, organization, and style to see exactly how well the author connects with readers.

6. Answer the personal questions on page 158.

7. Once you see what makes the piece tick, settle on the main thing you want to say in reply—your viewpoint.

8. Express your viewpoint in a thesis statement. (See page 23.)

APPLICATION 9-1

Respond to Brady's essay with an essay of your own. Share with us a new way of seeing. Imagine you are conversing with the writer: How would you reply if someone had just spoken what you have read? The above guidelines will help you reach deep into your reading experience. Record your responses in a hard-copy or an electronic reading journal. Compose your essay based on your responses.

APPLICATION 9-2

Collaborative Project: Share or e-mail your essay from Application 9-1 with others in your group who have responded to the same essay. Can you pinpoint any places where your responses were very similar or where they were radically different? As a group, discuss the possible reasons for the differences. Have one group member record the reasons for discussion with the entire class.

APPLICATION 9-3

Computer Application: Using your group's *listserv* or e-mail network, conduct Application 9-2 electronically. Transmit and exchange your documents as e-mail attachments.

CHAPTER 10

Helping Others See and Share an Experience: Description and Narration

Description creates a word picture; it tells about things as they appear in space. Because it helps readers *visualize,* description is a common denominator in all writing.

What readers expect to learn from a description

- *What is it?*
- *What does it look like?*
- *How could I recognize it?*
- *What is it made of?*
- *What does it do?*
- *How does it work?*
- *What is your impression of it?*
- *How does it make you feel?*

Narration also creates a word picture, telling how events occur in time. It relies on the showing power of descriptive details to make the story vivid, but its main goal is to help readers follow events.

What readers expect to learn from a narrative

- *What happened?*
- *Who was involved?*
- *When did it happen?*
- *Where did it happen?*
- *Why did it happen?*

Because any topic or event can be viewed in countless ways, your decisions about descriptive and narrative details depend on your purpose and the reader's needs. Both strategies can serve either *objective (referential) goals*—that is, they can merely report—or they can be selected and used differently by different writers. They then fill *subjective (and often persuasive) goals*—they make a point.

USING OBJECTIVE DESCRIPTION TO INFORM

Objective description filters out—as much as appropriate—personal impressions, focusing on observable details. It provides factual information about something for someone who will use it, buy it, or assemble it, or who needs to know more about it for some good reason. Objective description records exactly what is seen from the writer's vantage point. If your CD player has been stolen, the police need a description that includes the brand name, serial number, model, colour, size, shape, and identifying marks or scratches. For this audience, a subjective description (that the item was a handsome addition to your car; that its sound quality was superb; that it made driving a pleasure) would be useless.

AN OBJECTIVE DESCRIPTION

Orienting sentence
(1)

[1]The 5-hectare building lot for my proposed log cabin sits on the northern shore of Moosehead Lake, roughly 300 metres east of the Seboomook

View from water
(2–5)

View from shore-
line (6–7)

Point camping area. ²The site is marked by a granite ledge, 10 metres long and 5 metres high. ³The ledge faces due south and slopes gradually east. ⁴A rock shoal along the westerly frontage extends about 10 metres from the shoreline. ⁵On the easterly end of the frontage is a landing area on a small gravel beach immediately to the right of the ledge. ⁶Lot boundaries are marked by yellow stakes a few feet from the shoreline. ⁷Lot numbers are carved on yellow-marked trees adjacent to the yellow stakes.

The above paragraph, written to help a soil engineer locate the property by boat, follows a spatial order, moving from whole to parts—the same order in which we would actually view the property. Instead of a standard topic statement, the paragraph begins with a simple description, which nonetheless gives us a definite sense of what to expect.

Because the goal above is referential, only factual information appears: a brief but specific catalogue of the lot's major features. Other situations might call for more specifics. For instance, the soil engineer's evaluation of the Moosehead site, written for officials who approve building permits, might look like this:

Hand-dug test holes revealed a well-draining, granular material, with a depth of at least 120 centimetres to bedrock.

The quantity of detail in a description is keyed to the writer's purpose and the audience's needs.

NOTE *Pure objectivity is, of course, humanly impossible. Each writer has a unique perspective on the facts and their meaning, and chooses what to put in and what to leave out.*

USING SUBJECTIVE DESCRIPTION TO MAKE A POINT

No useful description can be strictly subjective; to get the picture, readers need some observable details. Subjective description colours objective details with personal impressions and metaphors. It usually strives to draw readers into the writer's view of the world, often by creating a mood or sharing a feeling, as shown in the italicized expressions below.

A SUBJECTIVE DESCRIPTION

OFF-SEASON

Thesis

I hate summer beaches. Ocean swimming is impossible; upon conquering a wave, I simply lose to the next, getting pushed back onto the hard-packed, abrasive sand. *Booby-traps* of bottles, soda cans, toys, and rocks make walking hazardous. *Heavy with the stench* of suntan lotion, greasy French fries, dead fish, and sweat, *the thick, searing air hangs motionless about the scorching sand.* Blasting radios and growling dune buggies cut the *slap-swoosh* of the green-grey surf to a *weak hiss. People devour a summer beach, gouging the sand with umbrella spikes and gripping it with oiled limbs, leaving only trampled debris at summer's end.*

My interest in beaches begins, then, after the summer people leave. Gone are the trash and trappings. The winter wind is bitter but clean, *fresh with the damp, earthy scent* of cold seaweed. Only broken shells litter the sand, and nearer the water, ice-grey, surf-worn rocks rise like *smooth serpents' backs.* Wave upon wave, the *bruise-coloured* sea thunders in, each rolling arc pouring ahead of the next, breaking into smaller and smaller waves, crawling up the beach.

Things endure but things change. Constant waves wash the face of the shore into roundness. Dunes fuse and slide apart, transformed into new mounds by the *coarse* wind. Erosion fences *whistle and ripple and clack, protesting* the sand shifting between the slats. No longer covered by sprawling sun worshipers, the beach forms *a smooth slide of continent into ocean.*

Waves naturally push and pull and wear things down. In time, the ocean will claim as its own the snack shack and the parking lots, the sea walls and the cottages. *Walking the ocean's edge awakens a small fear that the waves might slither around my ankles and draw me into that icy foam. Paralyzed with cold, I will be worn and washed by the surf until I become just another part of the ever-shrinking beach.*

So far, at least, I've been lucky: I walk winter beaches often and see nothing more sinister than gulls cracking crabs on the rocks. But I still avoid the water's edge—*beaches ravaged in summer might harbour a winter impulse for revenge.*

—Pam Herbert

Pam's essay blends objective and subjective description (in italics) to help us visualize the contrast between the summer beach, with its "stench" of various offensive odours, and the "clean, fresh" winter beach. The writer's impressions give us a real feel for the place and a new way of seeing.

Beyond creating a mood or sharing a feeling, description can serve practical purposes. The following selection conveys personal impressions to make a persuasive point.

SUBJECTIVE DESCRIPTION IN PERSUASIVE WRITING

Close your eyes for a moment, and picture a professional baseball game. You probably see something like this: a hot summer afternoon, complete with sizzling bats, fans clad in the reds and yellows and pastels of summer, and short-sleeved vendors yelling "ICE CREAM HEEERE!" If you recall some recent World Series, though, you might envision a scene more like this: a c-c-cold starlit night highlighted by players in Thinsulate gloves and turtlenecks, fans in ski hats instead of baseball caps, and vendors hurriedly hawking coffee. This "football-like" image suggests that baseball season is just plain too long!

—Mike Cabral

Similarly, a colourful description of your messy residence room or apartment might encourage roommates to clean up their act. Or a nauseating catalogue of greasy food served in the university dining hall might prompt school officials to improve the menu. Subjective writing can move readers to see things your way.

USING DESCRIPTION BEYOND THE WRITING CLASSROOM

- **In other courses:** Whether you are describing a lab experiment, a field trip, or a fire hazard in the residence, you would focus on the observable details, not on your feelings. What specific types of objective description have you written in other courses?
- **In the workplace:** Your descriptions might inform customers about a new product or service. Banks require applicants for loans to describe the property or venture. Architects and engineers would describe their proposed building on paper before construction begins. Medical professionals write detailed records of a patient's condition and treatment. Whenever readers need to visualize the item itself, objective description is essential. What specific types of objective description do you expect to write in your career?
- **In the community:** You might describe the problems with discipline or drugs or violence or overcrowding at the local junior high in an attempt to increase community awareness.

Can you think of other situations in which objective description could make a difference?

USING OBJECTIVE NARRATION TO EXPLAIN

To see how narration, like description, can serve both referential and persuasive purposes, let's look first at narration that informs, reports, or explains. These narratives simply give a picture of what happened, without stating—or even implying—any particular viewpoint. Newspaper stories or courtroom testimonies often provide only the bare facts. This next paragraph simply describes events without inserting personal impressions.

A NARRATIVE THAT MERELY REPORTS

Introduction (1–2)

Details of accidents (3–6)

[1]The city experienced its first major snowstorm of the year, a blizzard that roared in from the West during the night. [2]Thirty centimetres of snow and 100 kilometre-per-hour wind gusts created nearly impassible driving and walking conditions. [3]Yet hundreds of motorists decided to test their driving skills and challenge Mother Nature. [4]Between 6:00 a.m. and 10:00 a.m., regional police and the Ontario Provincial Police reported 86 minor motor-vehicle collisions and 35 cars in ditches and against hydro poles. [5]Most of these accidents were caused by drivers who lost control of

Conclusion (7)

their vehicles because they didn't adapt their driving habits to the road conditions. [6]That same morning, a tractor-trailer driver lost control on a curve and hit a van head-on, killing six occupants; a 19-year-old driving an SUV hit a pedestrian crossing on a green light, sending her to the hospital with a broken leg; and a 67-year-old grandmother driving a 1972 Buick rolled her car over an embankment on her cottage road, dislocating her left shoulder and elbow in the process. [7]Drivers, even experienced ones, tend to ignore the weather and drive as if the roads were dry and bare.

GUIDELINES FOR DESCRIPTION

1. *Always begin with some type of orienting statement.* Objective descriptions rarely call for a standard topic or thesis statement, because their goal merely is to catalogue the details that readers can visualize. Any description, however, should begin by telling readers what to look for.

2. *Choose descriptive details to suit your purpose and the reader's needs.* Brainstorming yields more details than a writer can use. Select only those details that advance your meaning. Use objective details to provide a picture of something exactly as a camera would record it. Use subjective details to convey your impressions—to give us a new way of seeing or appreciating something, as in "Off-Season."

3. *Select details that are concrete and specific enough to convey an unmistakable picture.* Most often description works best at the lowest levels of abstraction and generality.

Vague	Exact
at high speed	120 kilometres per hour
a tiny office	a 3-by-4-metre office
some workers	the accounting staff

4. *Use plenty of sensory details.* Allow readers to *see* "gulls cracking crabs on the rocks," *hear* "the slap-swoosh of the . . . surf," *smell* "the stench of suntan lotion and greasy French fries," *feel* "the hard-packed, abrasive sand." Let readers touch and taste. Use vivid *comparisons* such as "surf-worn rocks rise like smooth serpents' backs" or "bruise-coloured sea," to make the picture come to life. Rely on *action verbs* to convey the energy of movement, to show how the erosion fences "whistle and ripple and clack." Sensory details bring a description to life.

5. *Order details in a clear sequence.* Descriptions generally follow a spatial or general-to-specific order—whichever parallels the angle of vision readers would have if viewing the item. Or the details are arranged according to the dominant impression desired.

The paragraph on page 171–172 implies no main point. The writer simply reports on the details of a major snowstorm.

Note, however, that the first two sentences describe the changing weather conditions to attract our interest. Then, the rest of the paragraph details the sequence of events that happened that morning to demonstrate how poor driving caused so much devastation. Consistent use of past tense and third-person point of view help us follow the story.

Using Narrative Reports Beyond the Writing Classroom

- **In other courses:** You might report on experiments or investigations in chemistry, biology, or psychology. Or you might retrace the events leading up to the Russian Revolution or the 1929 stock market crash. What specific types of narrative reports have you written in other courses?
- **On the job:** You might report on the events that led up to an accident on the assembly line or provide daily accounts of your crew's progress on a construction project. Whenever readers need to understand *what happened*, narrative reporting is essential. What specific types of narrative reports might you write in your career?
- **In the community:** As a witness to an accident, a crime, or some other incident, you might report what took place.

In what other situations might a narrative report make a difference?

USING SUBJECTIVE NARRATION TO MAKE A POINT

Narration can be an excellent strategy for advancing some definite viewpoint or thesis because a well-told story is easy to remember. When you recount last night's date, your purpose usually is to suggest a particular viewpoint: say, that some people can be fickle, or that first dates can be disastrous. The following brief story shares a special moment in the author's favourite activity—flying a small plane.

A NARRATIVE THAT MAKES A POINT

Orienting sentence

Rolling down Runway Alpha, I feel so intensely alone that I become part human, part machine—everything working together. My mind's eye is locked on the runway's centre line while my eyes flash from windshield to instruments, reading, calculating, missing nothing. Meanwhile, feet and hands make delicate adjustments on the pedals and control yoke, gently . . . gently . . . . Relaxed, yet poised, I concentrate so intensely that I and the plane are one. Our airspeed increases. The plane vibrates. We reach the point where the battle begins. Time stops as *83 Bigdog* and I wage silent war with gravity. It pulls at us, insisting that we are bound to the earth, slaves of its laws, this vibrating second seeming like an eternity.

Main point

> But in the end we win. The wheels leave the ground and we climb, that empty-stomach feeling one gets in an elevator intensified threefold. As the ground recedes, we glide above the stress of life down below. *This burst of sensations, these physical and emotional responses to each takeoff, draw me back to the cockpit, again and again.*
>
> —*Phoebe Brown*

Notice how the entire event is filtered through the author's impressions. The subjective details make the author's sensations real and vivid to readers and support her point about the thrill of taking off. Telling a story can be an effective way of *showing*.

The present tense and first-person point of view give the paragraph a consistent sense of direction (the author tells of her experience). An alternative point of view for narration is the third person (telling of someone else's experience).

Like description, narratives also can move readers to change their attitudes or take action. For instance, you might tell about a boating accident to elicit voter support for tougher boating laws. You might recount the details of a conflict among employees to persuade your boss to institute a stress-management program. By telling the story, you can help readers see things your way.

SUBJECTIVE NARRATION IN PERSUASIVE WRITING

> I entered community college at 17 and began taking classes with some 25- and 30-year-old students. Such an age difference made me feel much luckier than these older people. What were they doing in a first year class, anyway? Compared to them, I had unlimited time to succeed—or so I thought. Soon after my eighteenth birthday, the horrid piece of lung tissue I coughed into the sink gave a whole new meaning to my notion of "youth." Five years of inhaling hot smoke, carbon monoxide, nicotine, and tobacco pesticides finally had produced enough coughing and sickness to terrify me. "Oh, my god, I'm going to die young; I'm going to die before all those 30-year-olds." For years, I had heard my mother tell me that I was committing suicide on the installment plan. Now I seemed to be running out of installments.
>
> —*Chris Adey*

By letting the story make the point, Chris's narrative seems more persuasive than the usual sermons: "Smoking is bad for you," and so on.

The main point in a narrative might be expressed as a topic or thesis statement at the beginning or end of the story. Or, as in the two narratives above, the main point might not be stated at all, but only implied by the story. But even when its point is saved for last or just implied, the story often opens with some statement that orients readers to the events.

The most powerful narratives often are those that combine objective and subjective details to reveal their point. In the following essay, a university English professor explores how an overcrowded curriculum affects the learning experiences of many university students. As you read, think about how the writer's analysis compels his audience to examine their points of view.

THESE HOURS HAVE 50 MINUTES

We begin in September. The registration line snakes slowly toward the gym in the afternoon sunshine, but the students don't seem to mind. They are dancing to ghetto blasters, comparing notes about courses, throwing footballs, catching up with each other on the summer. When they get inside, my colleagues and I hand them computerized course stickers that look like they belong on cans in a supermarket.

On the first day of classes, I make my little professorial jokes. Students laugh. My syllabus promises a feast for the intellect: Emily Dickinson, *The Scarlet Letter*, Walt Whitman, Thoreau's *Walden*, Whittier's *Snowbound* and *Uncle Tom's Cabin*. I explain about papers and tests and tell how to score a 90. "Are there any questions?" I ask. There are, and they are intelligent. It promises to be a great year.

In November, males stop shaving. Women forsake makeup. Faces become pallid. Even the pre-meds in the front row wander to my 8:15 class through the morning darkness with their shoes untied. December tests confirm what students feared. It is a war of attrition and they have been assigned to a chickens—t outfit.

In January, my suffering troops are passing around viruses they brought back from Christmas vacation. I wonder how they hear me above the sound of their coughing. "I don't know whether to lecture you or conduct you," my colleague across the hall told his Shakespeare class.

In February, the room smells of disinfectant, fumes from the oil furnace, disappointment and paranoia. Student papers show signs of haste, critical re-hash, sometimes of outright plagiarism.

By March, my ragged platoon is pasted against the back wall. I ask a question. The two pairs of eyes that were on my face drop to the floor. I answer the question myself. It was a stupid question anyway.

During office hours, the chaplain hears confessions. A paper on *Bartleby the Scrivener* is late because the student's father left her mother, who is having a nervous breakdown. Another student's girlfriend broke up with him the night before the paper was due and he has been walking around in a fog ever since. But he can have the paper in by Friday. Someone's grandmother died; a paper was lost; a notebook was stolen.

One student told me that she was carrying her paper on Walt Whitman from the annex when the wind came up and blew it from her hand. She chased it across the parking lot and saw it sailing over the football field toward the Trans-Canada highway. I gave her the extension she requested. I lost a hat to that wind once. Others report confrontations with the dean, harassment by the business office, conflicts with other professors.

King Solomon himself could not determine which of these stories are true. Try to judge them and your office will be like tryout night for an amateur play. Word goes out the professor wants to be convinced. If your boyfriend dropped you and you want your deadline extended, he wants tears. If you have a severe cold and cannot take the test, he wants to hear a cough from deep in your lungs. If your grandfather died and you're on your way to the funeral, he wants to see a stoic look of acceptance in your face and you in your Sunday best.

A colleague, riding in the elevator, overheard one student tell another how to get his professor, a priest, to extend a deadline for a theology paper: "Tell him you think you are losing your faith."

But cynicism is corroding, and unworthy of one's high calling to the life of the mind. Another student read Thoreau's *Walden* and realized that a university town in the rural Maritimes is exactly the right place to replicate Thoreau's experiment. He found an abandoned shack overlooking the Atlantic on the Harbour Road. Now he hitch-hikes to classes, burns wood in a small stove, and feels the salt wind through his un-puttied windows as he reads his assignments. I suspect he knows more about the real cost of enlightenment than most of his professors.

My students write papers totalling 50 pages or more. If they carry five arts classes, they will write 200 pages of papers in an academic year. I write words like "pretentious" and "awkward" in the margins. I circle misspellings. I would be insulted if my friends were as candid when they detected my intellectual pretensions. I could not write well under the pressures I put on my students.

"They are 20, not 45-year-olds," a younger colleague replied to my late Friday afternoon rant on this subject in the faculty bar." Besides, students could accomplish more than they do if they didn't spend so much time on other things."

She is right. Studying for my test on Whitman's *Song of Myself* while researching a philosophy paper on Plato's concept of the beautiful, and memorizing the valence table for Chemistry 101 is only part of what they must do for tomorrow. They also help the chaplain organize retreats, drink beer, go to games and concerts, attend dances, line up dates for Friday night. They operate a student government that has as much energy, betrayal, and confusion as the one in Ottawa. They put out a student newspaper that is surprisingly professional, though university administrators and student government types tend to be as thin-skinned and vindictive as Haitian dictators. Students wedge the overcrowded academic year inside their overcrowded extra-curricular year.

An academic year has eight months. A week has five days. An hour has 50 minutes. All learning—from the Plays of Shakespeare to a course on playing saxophone in a jazz band—is crammed into 50-minute or 75-minute slots (with time for questions at the end).

Each tick of the clock is measured, dissected, and pretended to be something larger than it is. Could anyone except a baffle of university administrators have created such a calendar? We faculty and administrators deserve the misshapen fruit—Coles Notes and BS Unlimited Term Paper Co. are representative examples—that the system we operate has spawned.

In early May, the last students load their ghetto blasters, books, posters, and clothing into cars and head home to Glace Bay, West Bay, New Glasgow, Toronto, Calgary or North Adams, Mass.

After they leave, I put in my garden. I turn the cold earth with my shovel, then roto-till it, sprinkle on some of my neighbour's horse manure, decide what goes where, and plant the seeds. In northern Nova Scotia, where the winter lets go grudgingly, I cannot put my tomatoes out until the middle of June. If I put them out before that, the frost kills them. The growing season has its own cycle. Days have 24 hours, weeks seven days. You can't rush things in a garden.

It is pleasant work, and it leaves me time to ask my question. Why did my own and my students' clear-eyed best dry up sometime in November?

—*Philip Milner*

Milner analyzes the mental and physical decline of his students as they progress through the academic year. He attributes the decline to an academic curriculum and a social calendar that does not allow students the opportunity to benefit from either.

What are Milner's most enjoyable objective and subjective details in his narrative?

GUIDELINES FOR NARRATION

1. *Set the scene immediately.* Place readers right at the centre of the action. If you open with some sort of background explanation (as in "Hawk among the Chickens," page 179), keep it short and sweet.

2. *Convey your main point, whether stated or implied, through the narrative details.* A narrative that simply reports, of course, has no main point. But if your narrative does make a point, consider delaying that point until the end; use an earlier orienting statement to let us know what's going on.

3. *Choose details to serve specifically your purpose and the reader's needs.* Select only those details that directly advance your meaning. Focus on the important details, but don't leave out lesser details that hold the story

together. Decide when to describe events objectively and when to filter events through your own impressions.

4. *Choose details that are concrete and specific enough to show clearly what happened.* Narration is most effective at the lowest levels of abstraction and generality. Use plenty of visual details—the details of real life. Try to show people "doing," and let us hear them talking.

5. *Order details in a clear sequence.* Chronological ordering often works best in a narrative, because it enables readers to follow events as they occurred. But for special emphasis, you might use a *flashback* or a *flashforward* to present certain events out of sequence.

GUIDELINES FOR NARRATION (continued)

6. *Control your tenses and transitions.* To keep readers on track, indicate a clear time frame for each event: present, past, past perfect ("had been"), or even future tense (as in paragraph 5, page 182). If you move from one time frame to another, be sure to keep the tense consistent within each frame (as in "The Old Guy," page 181). To create a sense of immediacy, use the present tense.

   Use transitions to mark time and sequence. Review pages 102–104 for use of transitions.

7. *Keep the point of view straight.* Decide whether you are describing an event from the perspective of a participant (first-person point of view) or an observer (third person). Narratives designed to make a point (as in "Hawk among the Chickens," page 179) often blend both perspectives. If you move from one perspective to another, be sure to maintain a consistent point of view for each perspective.

8. *Explore the larger meaning of the events.* Help readers process the story; tell us what all this means and what we should remember about it.

APPLICATION **10-1**

PARAGRAPH WARM-UP: DESCRIPTION THAT INFORMS

Assume that a close friend has been missing for two days. The police have been called in. Because you know this person well, the police have asked you for a written description. Write an objective description that would help the police identify this person. To create a clear picture, stick to details any observer could recognize. If possible, include one or more unique identifying features (scar, mannerisms, and so on). Leave out personal comments, and give only objective details. Refer to the Guidelines for Description, page 172. Use the paragraph on page 99 as a model.

APPLICATION **10-2**

PARAGRAPH WARM-UP: DESCRIPTION THAT MAKES A POINT

Assume that your university newspaper runs a weekly column titled "Memorable Characters." You have been asked to submit a brief sketch of a person you find striking in some way. Create a word portrait of this person in one paragraph. Your description should focus on a dominant impression, blending objective details and subjective commentary. Be sure to focus on personal characteristics that support your dominant impression. Develop your description according to the Guidelines for Description on page 172.

APPLICATION 10-3

PARAGRAPH WARM-UP: NARRATION THAT INFORMS

Assume that you have recently witnessed an event or accident in which someone has been accused of an offence. Because you are an objective witness, the authorities have asked you to write a short report, telling them exactly what you saw. Your report will be used as evidence. Tell what happened without injecting personal impressions or interpretations. Refer to the Guidelines for Narration on page 177.

APPLICATION 10-4

PARAGRAPH WARM-UP: NARRATION THAT MAKES A POINT

Tell about a recent experience or incident you witnessed that left a strong impression on you. Write for your classmates, and be sure to include the facts of the incident as well as your emotional reaction to it. In other words, give your audience enough details so that they will understand and ideally share your reaction. Use Chris Adey's paragraph as a model, letting the details of the story imply your main point. Refer to the Guidelines for Narration on page 177.

APPLICATION 10-5

ESSAY PRACTICE

The following essay "Hawk among the Chickens" by Dan Needles (from *Harrowsmith Country Life*, February 2000) recalls a moral dilemma the author faced when deciding the fate of the hawk killing his chickens.

ESSAY FOR ANALYSIS AND RESPONSE

HAWK AMONG THE CHICKENS

In the days when I worked in the city and rode the subway to work, my observations about the outdoors were limited to whether or not I needed to wear a coat. Today, in the short walk from the house to the barn, I absorb enough information to carry the conversation over morning coffee.

I check the thermometer on the verandah, sniff the air and glance over to Blue Mountain, which brings us all our weather. I note automatically whether the wind is up or down, what direction it is coming from and the height of the clouds. I watch as a deer strolls along the fence line in the winter wheat, and a red-tailed hawk screams in the distance, circling over the bush at the back of the farm.

Country people watch the natural world as closely as market analysts track consumer spending and trade statistics. Today, I take special note of that hawk. My hens have been confined to barracks for three months now because of him. He made off with four hens in September before I noticed something was amiss. Every couple of days I'd find a few loose feathers wafting about in the orchard and the count would be short another hen at bedtime. One afternoon, I caught him red-handed, tearing apart a buff-coloured hen named Sophie that I had raised from a chick in a box two years ago. The hawk departed in haste and flew up to the top branch of a dead elm tree. There, he waited for me to return to the house.

I have never shot a hawk because they are such graceful, wild creatures but this one had murdered an old pal and my Old Testament instincts surged through my veins. I buried Sophie and searched out the other hens, one by one, from their hiding places in the tall grass along the rail fence and returned them to the safety of the henhouse. In the reflective calm of the verandah swing chair, nursing a gin and tonic, I decided to keep the hens indoors until the hawk flew south. But the snow came and stayed and so did the hawk.

I called my friend, Dr. George Peck of Thornbury, who is a respected authority on the nesting birds of Ontario, and explained the situation. George said that this was unusual behaviour for the slow-moving red-tail. "Are you sure it wasn't a goshawk," he asked.

"No," I said." We've got him on videotape."

George then informed me solemnly that red-tails don't fly south. I said, "So what am I supposed to do."

I already knew the answer. George is an ardent conservationist and his advice is always of the uncompromising New Testament variety. Forgive the hawk and keep the hens in protective custody. In time, he'll have to return to his regular diet of mice. My children suggested we fit him for cement shoes and drop him in the pond. My wife doesn't like brown eggs and was hoping the hawk would clear out space for some nice white Leghorns. It appeared that I was alone with a difficult moral dilemma, until Kenny Jardine came by with the mail.

"That hawk has been killing chickens all the way up the sideroad," said Kenny. "People have been blasting at him for weeks."

"But hawks are a protected species," I protested.

"Yep, and chickens are pretty well protected too," said Kenny." I give him another week, at the most."

It appears the moral problem has been taken out of my hand.

—*Dan Needles*

QUESTIONS ABOUT THE READING

Refer to the general questions on page 157 as well as these specific questions:

PURPOSE

- In your view, what does Dan Needles want the audience to be thinking or feeling after reading the piece?
- Does the essay succeed in making a difference with readers? If so, how?

CONTENT

- Does this essay merely inform or does it make a point, and if so, what is the point?
- Can you identify any new insights or unusual perspectives?

ORGANIZATION

- What major devices lend coherence to this narrative? Give examples of each.

STYLE

- What about the short sentences and paragraphs? Are they effective? Explain.
- What is the writer's attitude toward his subject, toward his audience? How do we know? What are the signals?
- Which images here most help us visualize?

RESPONDING TO YOUR READING

"Hawk among the Chickens" is a personal account of how rural folks have to deal with moral dilemmas that city folks don't normally concern themselves with. Explore your personal reactions to this essay by using the personal response questions on page 158. Then respond with your own narrative about an event that challenged your ability to make a tough decision. Work to recapture for us the event and its impact on you. Tell us what happened, but be sure to let us know what meaning the event ultimately had for you.

CASE STUDY

RESPONDING TO READING

Al Andrade decided to write about a different type of personal dilemma, one that forces him to think about other types of decisions that face people every day. To produce his final draft, Al combines the Reading Guidelines on page 166 with the questions about the readings and relies on the Narration Guidelines on page 177 and the Revision Checklist on page 58.

THE OLD GUY

Alternates first- and third-person points of view throughout Paragraph 1 sets the scene Begins in past tense

[1]The workout was progressing as it usually does. My father and I took turns grunting the weights up and down off our chests. Our pectorals, shoulders, and arms were shaking. Throughout the one-hour session, we encouraged and coached one another. Fortunately, weight lifting demands short breaks after each set. Without these breaks our workouts might last only two minutes. The time spent preparing for the next set (or recovering from the last one) is important, not because I'm lazy but because it gives

Uses present tense to give background

Paragraph 2 leads into orienting statement
Returns to past tense for main events
Events throughout follow chronological order
Paragraphs 1–4 offer a participant's perspective
Shows someone talking
Orienting statement previews the main point
Transitions throughout mark time and sequence
Shows someone "doing"

Paragraphs 4–5 focus on the author's impressions

Paragraphs 5–6 offer an observer's perspective
Uses future tense for flashforward

Uses present tense to explore the larger meaning of these events

me a chance to catch up on things with Dad. Since we don't get to see each other very often, the latest news, gossip, and philosophies get aired in the weight room.

²While I was changing the weight on the barbell for our next set, Dad was hanging around the exercise room. We'd been talking about the possibility of building an apartment on the lot next door. This discussion led to real estate, which led to the stock market, which led to his retirement. Lately Dad has been complaining a lot about his company's lousy retirement plan. I figured he was just a practical guy planning for more comfortable retirement. Then he looked up from behind the squat rack and said, "You know, Al, if I'm lucky, I have only twenty or twenty-five years left, and I don't want to be eating dog food when I retire." I snickered at the dog food remark. He's always overstating things for emphasis. The other part of his remark—the part about having only twenty or twenty-five years left—seemed a bit melodramatic. At first, Dad's comment rolled off me like a bead of sweat, until I began doing some personal arithmetic of my own.

³Our workout moved from the bench press to the chinning bar. I went first. Then I watched while Dad strained to pull himself up for the tenth repetition. "Not bad for an old guy," he said after he jumped down off the bar. I looked at him and thought he really wasn't bad. Aside from a minor middle-aged belly, he is more powerful now than ever. He routinely dead lifts 450 pounds. And even with a bad shoulder, Dad can still bench press over 250 pounds. Not bad for an old guy is right—or a young guy, for that matter. This time, however, the reference to his age wasn't as easy for me to shrug off.

⁴No longer concentrating on the weights, I thought about aging. The thought of Dad aging didn't overly distress me. I mean, the man was healthy, strong, and sweating just a few feet away. But then I pictured myself getting old, considered what I'd be doing and saying in twenty-five years. Would I be grousing about retirement plans? Would I be working out twice as hard with the notion that I might live a little longer?

⁵Most likely I'll be doing the same things Dad is doing now. A 50-year-old family man counting the years he has left. I'll be a man too busy making a living to ever make enough money. Instead of counting up the years, I'll be counting them down: five years until my retirement, ten years until I can withdraw money from my RRSP without penalty, and two years before my son's twenty-fifth birthday. The cycle will be complete. I will replace my father and a son will replace me.

⁶I understand how "life goes on" and how "we're not getting any younger." But I now worried about the inevitability of middle age. I couldn't help putting myself in the Old Guy's place—of retirement worries and declining chin-ups. Twenty-three-year-old people aren't supposed to worry about retirement, or even middle age. Brilliant careers and healthy, productive lives lie ahead for us, right? We've got everything to look forward to. We think about raising families, achieving goals, and becoming

successful—not about our own mortality. But we all eventually reach a time when thoughts of our own old age and death become an everyday reality.

[7]Dad wrapped his hands around the chinning bar for his last set. This time he struggled to get six repetitions. I jabbed him and jokingly scolded, "What's the matter with you." He turned and grinned and shook his finger at me and said, "We'll see what you can do at fifty years old." I told him I could wait.

—Al Andrade

Returns to participant's perspective and past tense Ends with implied thesis (main point)

OPTIONS FOR ESSAY WRITING

1. Explore your reactions to "Off-Season" (page 169) by using the personal response questions on page 158. Then respond with an essay of your own. If you describe a place that is special, give a picture of the place as well as your feelings about it.

2. Explore your reactions to "These Hours Have 50 Minutes" by using the questions on pages 157, 158, and those below.

   - For whom does Milner seem to be writing?
   - What assumptions does he make about the audience's knowledge and attitudes? Are these assumptions accurate? Why or why not?
   - What are the main issues here? How has this essay affected your thinking about these issues?
   - What point is Milner making about university students?
   - What is the writer's attitude toward his subject? Toward his primary audience? How do we know? What are his signals?
   - How would you characterize the tone of this essay? Is it appropriate for this writer's audience and purpose?

   Those of us who have experienced the Canadian university/college systems understand what it takes to survive and do well. Based on your own post-secondary experiences, relate an event that has affected your outlook on university life.

3. Do you have a hero or know a villain? Describe this person in an essay for your classmates. Provide enough descriptive details for your audience to understand why you admire or despise this person. Supply at least three characteristics to support your dominant impression.

4. Assume that you are applying for your first professional job after university. Respond to the following request from the job application:

Each of us has been confronted by an "impossible situation"—a job that appeared too big to complete, a situation that seemed too awkward to handle, or a problem that felt too complex to deal with. Describe such a situation and how you dealt with it. Your narrative should make a point about the situation, problem solving, or yourself.

5. Tell an audience about the event that has caused you the greatest guilt, anger, joy, or other strong emotion, and how you reacted.

CHAPTER 11

Illustrating for Readers: Examples

The backbone of explanation, *examples* are concrete and specific instances of a writer's main point.

What readers
expect to learn
from examples

- What makes you think so?
- Can you show me?

Examples provide the evidence that enables readers to understand your meaning and accept your viewpoint. The best way to illustrate what you mean by an "inspiring teacher" is to use one of your professors as an example. You might illustrate this professor's qualities by describing several of her teaching strategies. Or you might give an extended example (say, how she helped you develop confidence). Either way, you have made the abstract notion "inspiring teacher" concrete and thus understandable. (Notice how this paragraph's main point is clarified by the professor example.)

Using Illustration Beyond the Writing Classroom

- **In other courses:** For a psychology course, you might give examples of paranoid behaviour among world leaders; for an ecology course, an example of tree species threatened by acid rain.
- **On the job:** You might give examples of how the software developed by your company can be used in medical diagnosis, or examples of how certain investments have performed in the recent decade.
- **In the community:** You might give examples of how your town can provide a favourable economic climate for new industry, or examples of how other towns have coped with cutbacks in school funding.

What other specific uses of examples can you envision in any of the above three areas?

USING EXAMPLES TO EXPLAIN

In referential writing, *examples help readers grasp an abstract term or a complex principle.* You could explain what grunge music is by pointing out examples of well-known bands that have incorporated its influence. Or suppose you wanted to explain how the *liberal arts* have practical value in one's career; for this purpose, the paragraph below would not be very understandable:

A PASSAGE NEEDING EXAMPLES

The irony of the emphasis being placed on careers is that nothing is more valuable for anyone who has had a professional or vocational education than to be able to deal with abstractions or complexities, or to feel comfortable with subtleties of thought or language, or to think sequentially. People who have such skills will have a major advantage in just about any career. In all these respects, the liberal arts have much to offer. Just in terms of career preparation, therefore, a student is shortchanging himself or herself by shortcutting the humanities.

Because this paragraph tells, but doesn't show, it fails to make a convincing case for a liberal arts education. Any reader will have unanswered questions:

- What do you mean by "abstractions or complexities," "subtleties of thought or language," or "to think sequentially"?
- How, exactly, do students "shortchange" themselves by shortcutting the humanities?
- Can you show me how a liberal arts education is useful in one's career?

Now consider the revised version of the same paragraph:

A REVISION THAT INCLUDES EXAMPLES

Main point (1)

Examples (2–5)

Summary (6)
Conclusion
explains how the
examples fit the
main point (7)

[1]*The irony of the emphasis being placed on careers is that nothing is more valuable for anyone who has had a professional or vocational education than to be able to deal with abstractions or complexities, or to feel comfortable with subtleties of thought or language, or to think sequentially.* [2]*The doctor* who knows only disease is at a disadvantage alongside the doctor who knows at least as much about people as [he or she] does about pathological organisms. [3]*The lawyer* who argues in court from a narrow legal base is no match for the lawyer who can connect legal precedents to historical experience and who employs wide-ranging intellectual resources. [4]*The business executive* whose competence in general management is bolstered by an artistic ability to deal with people is of prime value to [her] company. [5]*For the technologist,* the engineering of consent can be just as important as the engineering of moving parts. [6]In all these respects, the liberal arts have much to offer. [7]Just in terms of career preparation, therefore, a student is shortchanging himself by shortcutting the humanities. [*emphasis added*]

—*Norman Cousins*

The examples (in italics) help convince us that the author has a valid point.

USING EXAMPLES TO MAKE A POINT

Because examples so often provide the evidence to back up assertions, they have great persuasive power. For one thing, they can make writing more convincing simply by making it more interesting. In "Thin Edge of the Wedge," published in *Canadian Geographic*, Lesley Choyce uses descriptive examples to illustrate the desolate landscape of Wedge Island, Nova Scotia.

EXAMPLES THAT MAKE A POINT

THIN EDGE OF THE WEDGE

[1]Wedge Island is barely discernible on a road map of Nova Scotia because there are no roads leading there. Although it is not truly an island, its tether to the eastern shore is so tenuous that it remains remote and seemingly adrift. Eroded by the forces of the North Atlantic, it is a mere fragment of what was once a formidable headland. Within a lifetime, it will most likely be reduced to a rubble of stone, an insignificant reef at high tide. But for now, the Wedge exists, a reminder that nothing is permanent on this shore. Geologists define it as a "drowned coast" because the sea is gradually engulfing it. It has been for a long time.

[2]Something like a dinosaur's bony spine of boulders leads a wary hiker from the salt-bleached fish shacks on the mainland to the Wedge. If it's a fine July day—blue skies, big and bold above—the hiker might slide his hand along the silky beards of sea oats as he leaves solid land, then dance from rock to rock. Low tide is the best bet to make it there in one piece. Still, waves will spank the rocks from both sides, slap cold saltwater on his shoes, and spit clean, frothy Atlantic into his face.

[3]Wedge Island is a defeated drumlin, a dagger-shaped remnant of land stretching a good kilometre out to sea. Smashed lobster traps, shreds of polypropylene rope as well as bones of birds and beasts litter the rocks near the shore. Thirty metres up the red dirt cliff sits a parliament of herring gulls peering down at a rare visitor with suspicion. If the visitor scurries up the side of crumbling dirt, the gulls will complain loudly at this intrusion, then take to the sky and let him pass.

[4]At the top is a grassy peninsula a mere 60 centimetres wide where both sides have been sculpted away by rains and pounding seas. It's a place of vertigo and lost history. The island widens as it extends seaward onto this near-island of bull thistles, raspberry bushes, and grass that seems cropped short as a putting green.

[5]Farther out, at the very tip of the island, bare ribs of bedrock protrude into the sea. This is the same rock you'd find if you could make one giant leap from here across the Atlantic and step ashore on the edge of the Sahara. It is the very rock that was once part of the super-continent that drifted north to crash into this coast, and then drag itself away to form Africa.

[6]The island is a forgotten domain on the edge of the continent. It is easy to imagine that no man has ever been here before. But on the way back to the mainland, the truth reveals itself on the western shore.

Not three metres from the edge of a cliff eight stories high is a circle of lichen-covered rocks in the grass. A man-made well. The water is deep and long-legged insects skim along its obsidian surface. The well is full, nearly to the brim—it seems impossible given its elevation on this narrow wedge of land.

[7]Nearby are two dents in the ground, as if some giant had punched down into a massive surface of dough. Those two dents were once the foundations of a farm house and barn. Nearby fields sprouted cabbage and turnips. A family lived on vegetables from the stony soil, cod and mackerel from the sea. There were no roads, no cars, nothing but boats for commerce with Halifax. A way of life long gone.

[8]The rains and seas will continue to conspire to undo the ribbon of land left between the well's fresh water and the sky. The well's stone walls will collapse. The drumlin's cliff will be pried by ice, and pocked by pelting rain. The sea will slip out stones from beneath the hill, the turf up above will tumble, and eventually the water of the farmer's well will gush out of the heart of the headland and race down to meet the sea.

—Lesley Choyce

In what order (chronological, spatial, general-to-specific) are the above examples presented? Is this order effective? Explain.

In contrast to the previous writing sample, with its series of brief examples, this next persuasive paragraph presents one, single extended example:

EXTENDED EXAMPLE

Main point (1)

[1]*From the very beginning of school, we make books and reading a constant source of possible failure and public humiliation.* [2]When children are little, we make them read aloud, before the teacher and other children, so that we can be sure they "know" all the words they are reading. [3]This means that when they don't know a word, they are going to make a mistake, right in front of everyone. [4]Instantly they are made to realize that they have done something wrong. [5]Perhaps some of the other children will begin to wave their hands and say "Oooooh!-ooo-oh!" [6]Perhaps they will just giggle, or nudge each other, or make a face. [7]Perhaps the teacher will say, "Are you sure?" or ask someone else what [she] thinks. [8]Or, perhaps, if the teacher is kindly, she will just smile a sweet, sad smile—often one of the most painful punishments a child can suffer in school. [9]In any case, the child who has made the mistake knows he has made it, and feels foolish, stupid, and ashamed, just as any of us would in his shoes.

Conclusion explains how the example fits the main point (9)

—John Holt

To support his point about the unintentional humiliation of children, this author offers a vivid example of how the process occurs.

GUIDELINES FOR ILLUSTRATING WITH EXAMPLES

1. *Fit the examples to your purpose and the readers' needs.* An effective example fits the point it is designed to illustrate. Also, the example is familiar and forceful enough for readers to recognize and remember.

2. *Use brief or extended examples.* Some examples need more explanation than others. For example, John Holt (page 189) spells out the details of a subtle process whereas Lesley Choyce (page 188) describes the stages of a violent natural process.

3. *Make the example more specific and concrete than the point it illustrates.* Vivid examples usually occupy the lowest level of generality and abstraction. They enable readers to *visualize*.

4. *Arrange examples in a series in an accessible order.* If your illustration is a narrative or some historical catalogue, order your examples chronologically. Otherwise, try a "least-to-most" (least-to-most-dramatic or important or useful) order. Placing the most striking example last ensures greatest effect.

5. *Know "how much is enough."* Overexplaining insults a reader's intelligence.

6. *Explain how the example fits the point.* Close by refocusing on the larger meaning of your examples.

APPLICATION 11-1

PARAGRAPH WARM-UP: USING EXAMPLES TO EXPLAIN

Pierre, a French student who plans to attend a Canadian university, has asked what the typical Canadian university student is like. He has inquired about interests, activities, attitudes, and tastes. Selecting one or more characteristics *you* think typify Canadian university students, write a response to Pierre.

APPLICATION 11-2

PARAGRAPH WARM-UP: USING EXAMPLES TO MAKE A POINT

Assume your campus newspaper is inviting contributions for a new section called "Insights," a weekly collection of one-paragraph essays by students. Student contributors should focus on examples gained by close observation of campus life and Canadian values or habits to offer some fresh insight on a problem facing our culture. Using the paragraph by Holt as a model, write such a paragraph for the newspaper. Choose examples to convince your audience that the problem you discuss really exists.

APPLICATION **11-3**

ESSAY PRACTICE

The following essay was written by a 44-year-old mature student who decided he wanted to earn his university degree after being away from school for nearly 30 years.

ESSAY FOR ANALYSIS AND RESPONSE

BEING A MATURE STUDENT

I found that being a mature student in university presents some challenges that can be overcome with a little planning and a sense of humour. Returning to school, after I had been absent for nearly 30 years, I was quickly reminded that my body had gone through some changes since I was a teenager. These changes became conspicuously apparent on registration day, which was an experience that tested my resolve to return to school. There was no place to hide or to sit and rest as I inched forward in line with my fellow students. I felt out of place, as if I were an intruder amongst this youthful crowd who seemed to be enjoying themselves, for the most part, as my legs screamed out for a chair.

As the line moved slowly forward, I saw some of my younger peers sitting on the floor in positions that would make most yoga masters proud. The thought temporarily crossed my mind to join them. However, I knew that with my mid-life girth my descent to the floor would be less than graceful and my return to the vertical doubtful. So, I remained standing.

Finally reaching the first stop in the registration process, I was rewarded by being directed to the next line, which snaked its way throughout the room, and subsequently to three more queues. When I finally reached the end of the last line, I received my student card and limped out of the university. While I walked home, physically and mentally bushed, I had some unsettling thoughts. This was only the first day, and I was already exhausted. I began to wonder what other challenges lay ahead of me at university. I did not have to wonder for long.

Indeed, after I was at school for only a few days, the realities of being a mature student began to make themselves known. One would think that the library, computer labs, classrooms, and the student lounge would be the most important locations that first-year students would search out, but as a mature student, I quickly learned that the washrooms were the most important. As I generally visit the washroom before each class, their locations in each of the academic buildings soon became part of my expanding knowledge base.

My next major concern was my position within the lecture theatre and classroom. As I had to sit close enough so I could hear the professor and read the notes on the board or on the overhead, I didn't have the luxury of hiding in the back row. As well, I realized that I would have to wear those dreaded bifocals, or I would have no readable notes to rely on when I was studying for tests and exams.

After visiting the washroom and finding a seat in the front row of the classroom, I soon realized that my years of sitting in comfortable, padded chairs behind my office desks had not prepared me for sitting for up to three hours on wooden or plastic seats designed for someone with the circulation of a 20-year-old Olympian. Now, I knew that I would have to avoid three-hour classes as much as possible as I would probably fall out of my chair when the class was over.

I also had to remember to keep a little food in my stomach, because the sound emitted from the gastrointestinal tract of a hungry mature student can cause fits of laughter or looks of concern from my younger peers. I once had two students who were sitting beside me look curiously under their seats and then at each other with a look that bordered on shock after my body emitted a sound that even surprised me. My professor, who was writing on the board, stopped in mid chalk stroke, cocked his head, and turned slightly to see where the sound had come from. The students seemed to think that something was under their seat, as I looked straight ahead without blinking and made a mental note to make sure I ate something before each class.

Being a mature student, then, comes with its own set of challenges, but they are all manageable with a little planning, courage to be different, and a sense of humour. But then, these traits are the hallmarks of any good university student, regardless of age.

—*John K. Anthony*

Questions about the Reading

PURPOSE

- Does the essay succeed in making a difference with readers? If so, how?

CONTENT

- What are Anthony's assumptions about his audience's knowledge and attitudes?
- Discuss the series of examples Anthony selects to describe his experiences as a mature student.
- Are the examples specific enough?

ORGANIZATION

- Is the ordering of the examples effective? Explain.

STYLE

- Is the tone appropriate for this writer's audience and purpose? Explain.
- What is the writer's attitude toward his subject? Toward his audience? How do we know? What are the signals?

RESPONDING TO YOUR READING

Explore your personal reactions to "Being a Mature Student" by using the questions on pages 157 and 158. Then respond with an essay of your own, using powerful examples to make your point.

Perhaps someone has misjudged or stereotyped you or a group to which you belong. If so, set the record straight in a forceful essay to a specified audience. Or perhaps you can think of other types of media messages that seem to present a distorted or inaccurate view (say, certain commercials or sports reporting or war movies, and so on). For instance, do certain movies or TV programs send the wrong message? Give your readers examples they can recognize and remember.

Or you might challenge readers' assumptions by asserting a surprising or unorthodox viewpoint: that some natural foods can be hazardous, that exercise can be bad for health, or that so-called advances in electronics or medical science leave us worse off. Or maybe you want to talk about examples of things we take for granted or what makes a good friend. Whatever the topic, be sure your examples illustrate and explain a definite viewpoint.

CASE STUDY

RESPONDING TO READING

After reading John K. Anthony's "Being a Mature Student," Gina Ciofli settles on a similar light-hearted goal for her own essay: She decides to challenge our assumptions about the value of junk-filled purses by giving us colourful examples of her own buried treasures. To analyze Anthony's techniques, Gina combines the reading guidelines on page 166 with questions about the essay on page 192.

MY TIME CAPSULE

Opening paragraph invites us in and sets the tone

I always seem to be searching for the right change at checkout counters, rummaging through junk in my little brown change purse for those few extra pennies and usually coming up red-faced and empty-handed. But despite repeated frustrations, I just can't bring myself to clean that purse. I guess I hang onto things I don't need because some of my worst junk holds vivid memories. If someone were to find the purse, they would have a record of my recent life—a kind of time capsule.

Thesis

One extended example
Gives vivid and visual examples throughout

Whenever I dig for coins, I encounter an old car key. It belonged to my '91 Chevy, a car that rarely started on cold mornings. I still remember the hours spent huddled on that frosty front seat, flicking the ignition on and off, pumping the accelerator, and muttering various profanities every time the engine sputtered and died. Even though I junked the car last year, the key survives in my so-called change purse.

A second extended example

Also in there is a torn half-ticket to the Broadway musical, *Cats,* which I've saved for years. The show is outstanding. Unfortunately, though, I had to miss a good part of it simply because I needed to use the bathroom at the same time as half the audience. And much of what I did see was obscured by the green, porcupine hairdo of the guy in front of me. From my view behind Mr. Porcupine, the actors looked like they were in the woods. But I still keep my ticket stub—in my purse, of course.

A third extended example

Somewhere near the key and the ticket sits another artifact; the coat button that came undone earlier this year. (The same button I always initially mistake for a coin.) The button helps me remember the day I wore not only a turtleneck sweater but also two scarves for one of last winter's coldest days. Like a fool, I tried tying my coat collar around what had now become a 50-centimetre neck. Naturally the button popped off, and naturally, it got thrown into my purse.

Saves strongest extended example for last

For months I've been buying "micro-rays of hope" toward millionaire-hood in the province's 6/49 lottery. I can't resist playing my usual six numbers on Wednesdays and Saturdays—even though I always lose. *Not winning* poses no real problem for me, but kissing my obsolete ticket good-bye does. Somehow the act of throwing away even a losing ticket symbolizes admitting defeat. It means the province's racket has caught another sucker. It means my latest tangible flash of financial hope must sit among the soggy potato skins in my garbage pail. So I "temporarily" save my defunct tickets by folding them neatly away in my purse. Every time I see them, I'm reminded of the many times I COULD have become a millionaire.

Concludes with a series of brief but visual examples

The passage of time seems directly related to the bloatedness of my change purse because it's forever expanding. In fact, if I opened it right now, I'd find many more memories than the few just mentioned. I'd see the semi-wrapped sourball I almost ate, until I realized it was lime green. I'd find the three unmated earrings, each with its own life history. I'd rediscover the safety pin that once saved me from awful embarrassment. And my old pen cap (minus the pen), a golf tee, a matchbook, a packet of sugar, and a few expired coupons would all be in there, all with legends of their own.

Avoids overexplaining Explains how the examples illustrate the main point Facetiously suggests other meanings to be explored

Even though I'm a slow learner, I know now that metal money belongs not in a purse but in a piggy bank. I'll never have to worry about a coin in my time capsule again—unless, of course, it's my old 1948 quarter. But that's another story.

—*Gina Ciolfi*

APPLICATION 11-4

Collaborative Project and Computer Application: Use e-mail or your *listserv* to brainstorm collectively for examples to support one or more claims your group has generated in response to one of the readings or essay options in this chapter.

APPLICATION **11-5**

Computer Application: Look up the homepage for a business and, pretending you're the public-relations manager for that company, write an essay to convince a new client to use the business's services or products. Use the Web to find specific examples to support your claim.

OPTIONS FOR ESSAY WRITING

1. Write a human-interest essay for your campus newspaper in which you illustrate some feature of our society that you find humorous, depressing, contemptible, or admirable. Possible subjects: our eating, consumer, or dress habits; our idea of a vacation or a good time; the cars we drive, and so on. Provide at least three well-developed examples to make your point. Lesley Choyce's passage, page 188, offers one example of how you might approach this assignment.

2. What pleases, disappoints, or surprises you most about university life? Illustrate this topic for your parents (or some other specific audience) with at least three examples.

3. Assume you've been assigned a faculty advisor who likes to know as much as possible about each advisee. The advisor asks each student to write an essay on this topic:

   Is your hometown (city, neighbourhood) a good or a bad place for a child to grow up?

   Notice that you are not asked to write about yourself directly (as in a personal narrative). Support your response with specific examples that will convince the reader of your sound judgment.

CHAPTER 12

Explaining Parts and Categories: Division and Classification

Division and classification are both strategies for sorting things out, but each serves a distinct purpose. *Division* deals with *one thing only*. It separates that thing into parts, pieces, sections, or categories—for closer examination (say, an essay divided into introduction, body, and conclusion).

What readers
expect to learn
from a division

- *What are its parts?*
- *What is it made of?*

Classification deals with *an assortment of things* that share certain similarities. It groups these things systematically (say, a record collection into categories—jazz, rock, country and western, classical, and pop).

What readers
expect to learn from
a classification

- *What relates to what?*
- *In what categories do X, Y, and Z belong?*

We use division and classification in many aspects of our lives. Say you are shopping for a refrigerator. If you are mechanically inclined, you could begin by thinking about the major parts that make up a refrigerator: storage compartment, cooling element, motor, insulation, and exterior casing. You can now ask questions about these individual parts to determine the efficiency or quality of each part in different kinds of refrigerators. You have *divided* the refrigerator into its components.

After shopping, you come home with a list of 20 refrigerators that seem to be built from high-quality parts. You make sense of your list by grouping items according to selected characteristics. First, you divide your list into three *classes* according to size in cubic feet of capacity: small, middle-sized, and large refrigerators. But you want economy, too, so you group the refrigerators according to cost. Or you might *classify* them according to colour, weight, or energy efficiency. Here is how division and classification are related:

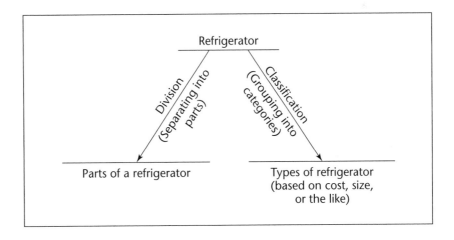

Whether you choose to apply division or classification depends on your purpose. An architect designing a library will think almost entirely of *division*. Once she has defined the large enclosed area that is needed, she must identify the parts into which that space must be divided: the reference area, reading areas, storage areas, checkout facilities, and office space. She might consider providing space for special groups of users (such as reading areas for children). In very large libraries she might need to divide further into specialized kinds of space (such as highly secure areas for rare manuscripts or special collections, or areas with special acoustic provisions for listening to recorded materials). But however simple or complex her problem, she is thinking now only about the appropriate division of space. She is not worrying about how the library will classify its books and other material.

But *classification* is one of the library staff's main problems. The purpose of a library is not only to store books and other forms of information, but above all to make the information retrievable. In order for us to find a book or item, the thousands or millions of books stored in the library must be arranged in logical categories. That arrangement becomes possible only if the books are carefully classified.

USING DIVISION TO EXPLAIN

We encounter referential uses of division every day. Division is used in manuals to help us understand how a computer or a car engine, for example, works. Division allows readers to tackle one aspect of a complex task at a time, as in the following instructions for campers.

A DIVISION THAT EXPLAINS

Before pitching your tent, take the time to prepare the area that will be under the tent. Not only does this step prevent damage to the tent floor, but it also helps you get a good night's sleep. Begin by removing all stones, branches, and other debris. Use your camping shovel for anything too large or deep to remove by hand. Next, fill in any holes with dirt or leaves. Finally, make a few light sweeps with the shovel or a leafy branch to smooth the area.

To increase readability, the steps or substeps in a complex task often appear in list form.

USING DIVISION TO MAKE A POINT

In the following paragraph, Watts uses division to explain his view of the ideal education. If we accept his divisions, we are more likely to agree that his opinion makes sense.

DIVISION THAT MAKES A POINT

Lead-in to main
point (1–3)
Main point (4)
Parts of the "ideal
education" (5)
Most important
part (6)

[1]It is perhaps idle to wonder what, from my present point of view, would have been an ideal education. [2]If I could provide such a curriculum for my children they, in their turn, might find it all a bore. [3]But the fantasy of what I would have liked to learn as a child may be revealing, since I feel unequipped by education for problems that lie outside the cloistered, literary domain in which I am competent and at home. [4]Looking back, then, I would have arranged for myself to be taught survival techniques for both natural and urban wildernesses. [5]I would want to have been instructed in self-hypnosis, in aikido (the esoteric and purely self-defensive style of judo), in elementary medicine, in sexual hygiene, in vegetable gardening, in astronomy, navigation, and sailing; in cookery and clothesmaking, in metalwork and carpentry, in drawing and painting, in printing and typography, in botany and biology, in optics and acoustics, in semantics and psychology, in mysticism and yoga, in electronics and mathematical fantasy, in drama and dancing, in singing and in playing an instrument by ear; in wandering, in advanced daydreaming, in prestidigitation, in techniques of escape from bondage, in disguise, in conversation with birds and beasts, in ventriloquism, in French and German conversation, in planetary history, in morphology,* and in Classical Chinese. [6]Actually, the main thing left out of my education was a proper love for my own body, because one feared to cherish anything so obviously mortal and prone to sickness.

—*Alan Watts*

The topic statement *tells;* the rest *shows* by dividing the ideal education into specific kinds of instruction. This writer knew the guidelines on page 200.

USING CLASSIFICATION TO EXPLAIN

Like division, classifying as a referential or informative strategy is a part of our lives. Your biology textbook shows you how scientists have classified life forms into plants, animals, bacteria, and other categories; scientists examining fossils write up their discoveries by assigning them to one of these classes. A city planner might write a report classifying plans for conserving water on the basis of cost, efficiency, or some other basis. The following classification explains major career specialties in computer science on the basis of their central tasks.

CLASSIFICATION THAT EXPLAINS

Specialties in computer science can be grouped into three major categories. First, systems programmers write programs that run the computer equipment itself. Next, applications programmers develop

*The structure of organisms.

programs that put the computer to work on specific jobs (such as keeping track of bank accounts). Finally, systems analysts troubleshoot, debug, and update both systems and applications programs and they develop specifications for new computer systems. All three specialties involve analyzing a problem and then reducing it to a sequence of small, deliberate steps that a computer can carry out.

GUIDELINES FOR DIVISION

1. *Apply the division to a singular item.* Only one item at a time can be divided (*ideal education;* not *ideal education* and *ideal career*).

2. *Make the division consistent with your purpose.* Watts could have divided education into primary, secondary, and higher education; into social sciences, humanities, sciences, and mathematics—and so on. But his purpose was to explain a view that goes beyond traditional categories. We are given "parts" of an education that we may not yet have considered.

3. *Make your division complete.* Only 100 percent of something can be divided, and the parts, in turn, should add up to 100 percent. If a part is omitted, the writer should say so ("some of the parts of an ideal education").

4. *Subdivide the subject as needed to make the point.* Watts's first division is into survival techniques for (a) natural and (b) urban wildernesses. He then subdivides each of these into the specific parts listed in sentences 5 and 6. If he had stopped after the first division, he would not have made his point.

5. *Follow a logical order.* In sentence 5 the parts of an ideal education range from practical to recreational to intellectual skills. In sentence 6 the most important part appears last—for emphasis.

USING CLASSIFICATION TO MAKE A POINT

Like division, classification also can be persuasive. This next paragraph uses classification to explain the opportunities to be physically active at the university level.

CLASSIFICATION THAT MAKES A POINT

Canadian universities encourage their students to be physically active by providing opportunities for them—male and female—to play sports at three levels. An elite few play at the fully funded varsity level (basketball, football, hockey) where they play home and away games competing for conference and national championships. Those who play not-so-popular sports compete at the club level (cross-country running, Nordic skiing, indoor track and field), where the funding and the competition are less and the conference championships are fewer than at the varsity level. However, some club teams do travel to compete for conference championships, but may have to fund-raise to cover costs and pay for equipment. Those who still like to compete for the exercise and enjoyment participate at the intramural level (curling, bowling, co-ed volleyball) where they normally play on campus, using their own equipment, and sometimes paying a fee.

—Bill Reid

In developing his message, Reid used the following guidelines.

GUIDELINES FOR CLASSIFICATION

1. *Apply the classification to a plural subject.* In Reid's paragraph, the subject is levels of university athletic programs.

2. *Make the basis of the classification consistent with your purpose.* To make his point, Reid classifies the three levels by popularity and funding.

3. *Make the classifications complete.* All three levels of competition are covered.

4. *Arrange the categories in logical order.* The categories Reid uses move from highest level to lowest level.

5. *Don't let categories overlap.* Had Reid added the category competitiveness, his classification would overlap because being competitive is not regulated by levels of competition.

APPLICATION **12-1**

PARAGRAPH WARM-UP: DIVIDING TO EXPLAIN

Addressing a prospective new member, use division to explain either the organization or the function of committees in a social or service group you belong to.

APPLICATION **12-2**

PARAGRAPH WARM-UP: DIVIDING TO MAKE A POINT

Using the paragraph on page 199 as a model, write a paragraph for the university curriculum committee, explaining your idea of an ideal education.

APPLICATION **12-3**

PARAGRAPH WARM-UP: CLASSIFYING TO EXPLAIN

You are helping prepare the orientation for next year's incoming students. Your supervisor asks you to write a paragraph outlining the jobs available to graduates in your major by organizing the jobs into major categories. Your piece will be published in a career pamphlet for new students. (You may need to do some library research, say in *The Occupational Outlook Handbook*.)

APPLICATION **12-4**

PARAGRAPH WARM-UP: CLASSIFYING TO MAKE A POINT

Identify a group you find in some way interesting. Sort the members of that group into at least three categories. Your basis for sorting (say, driving habits, attitudes toward marriage, hairstyles) will depend on the particular point you want to make about the group.

APPLICATION **12-5**

Computer Application: A World Wide Web homepage is an excellent example of classification and division at work. Browse your institution's homepage. Explore the arrangement of the page, deciding to what extent the divisions and classifications follow the guidelines in this chapter.

- Do all the arrangements make sense?
- How do the divisions and classifications made by the creators of the page affect the way visitors to the page see the school?
- Could the page have been arranged differently for different effects? Your instructor may ask that your analysis/critique be submitted in writing.

APPLICATION **12-6**

ESSAY PRACTICE

Read this essay, and answer the questions that follow it. Then select one of the essay assignments.

FRIENDS, GOOD FRIENDS—AND SUCH GOOD FRIENDS

Women are friends, I once would have said, when they totally love and support and trust each other, and bare to each other the secrets of their souls, and run—no questions asked—to help each   1 other, and tell harsh truths to each other (no, you can't wear that dress unless you lose ten pounds first) when harsh truths must be told.

Women are friends, I once would have said, when they share the same affection for Ingmar Bergman, plus train rides, cats, warm rain, charades, Camus, and hate with equal ardor Newark and Brussels sprouts and Lawrence Welk and camping.   2

In other words, I once would have said that a friend is a friend all the way, but now I believe that's a narrow point of view. For the friendships I have and the friendships I see are conducted at many levels of intensity, serve many different functions, meet different needs and range from those as all-the-way as the friendship of the soul sisters mentioned above to that of the most nonchalant and casual playmates.   3

Consider these varieties of friendship: 4

1. Convenience friends. These are the women with whom, if our paths weren't crossing all the time, we'd have no particular reason to be friends: a next-door neighbor, a woman in our car pool, the mother of one of our children's closest friends or maybe some mommy with whom we serve juice and cookies each week at the Glenwood Co-op Nursery.   5

Convenience friends are convenient indeed. They'll lend us their cups and silverware for a party. They'll drive our kids to soccer when we're sick. They'll take us to pick up our car when we need a lift to the garage. They'll even take our cats when we go on vacation. As we will for them.   6

But we don't, with convenience friends, ever come too close or tell too much; we maintain our public face and emotional distance. "Which means," says Elaine, "that I'll talk about being overweight but not about being depressed. Which means I'll admit being mad but not blind with rage. Which means I might say that we're pinched this month but never that I'm worried sick over money."   7

But which doesn't mean that there isn't sufficient value to be found in these friendships of mutual aid, in convenience friends.   8

2. Special-interest friends. These friendships aren't intimate, and they needn't involve kids or silverware or cats. Their value lies in some interest jointly shared. And so we may have an office friend or a yoga friend or a tennis friend or a friend from the Women's Democratic Club.   9

"I've got one woman friend," says Joyce, "who likes, as I do, to take psychology courses. Which makes it nice for me—and nice for her. It's fun to go with someone you know and it's fun to discuss what you've learned, driving back from the classes." And for the most part, she says, that's all they discuss.   10

"I'd say that what we're doing is *doing* together, not being together," Suzanne says of her Tuesday-doubles friends. "It's mainly a tennis relationship, but we play together well. And I guess we all need to have a couple of playmates."   11

I agree.   12

My playmate is a shopping friend, a woman of marvelous taste, a woman who knows exactly *where* to buy *what,* and furthermore is   13 a woman who always knows beyond a doubt what one ought to be buying. I don't have the time to keep up with what's new in eyeshadow, hemlines and shoes and whether the smock look is in or finished already. But since (oh, shame!) I care a lot about eyeshadow, hemlines and shoes, and since I don't *want* to wear smocks if the smock look is finished, I'm very glad to have a shopping friend.

3. Historical friends. We all have a friend who knew us when . . . maybe way back in Miss Meltzer's second grade, when our family lived in that three-room flat in Brooklyn, when our dad was out of work for seven months, when our brother Allie got in that fight where they had to call the police, when our sister married the endodontist from Yonkers and when, the morning after we lost our virginity, she was the first, the only, friend we told.   14

The years have gone by and we've gone separate ways and we've little in common now, but we're still an intimate part of each other's past. And so whenever we go to Detroit we always go to visit this friend of our girlhood. Who knows how we looked before our teeth were straightened. Who knows how we talked before our voice got un-Brooklyned. Who knows what we ate before we learned about artichokes. And who, by her presence, puts us in touch with an earlier part of ourself, a part of ourself it's important never to lose.   15

"What this friend means to me and what I mean to her," says Grace, "is having a sister without sibling rivalry. We know the texture of each other's lives. She remembers my grandmother's cabbage soup. I remember the way her uncle played the piano. There's simply no other friend who remembers those things."   16

4. Crossroads friends. Like historical friends, our crossroads friends are important for *what was*—for the friendship we shared at a crucial, now past, time of life. A time, perhaps, when we roomed in college together; or worked as eager young singles in the Big City together; or went together, as my friend Elizabeth and I did through pregnancy, birth and that scary first year of new motherhood.   17

Crossroads friends forge powerful links, links strong enough to endure with not much more contact than once-a-year letters at Christmas. And out of respect for those crossroads years, for those dramas and dreams we once shared, we will always be friends.   18

5. Cross-generational friends. Historical friends and crossroads friends seem to maintain a special kind of intimacy—dormant but always ready to be revived—and though we may rarely meet, whenever we do connect, it's personal and intense. Another kind of intimacy exists in the friendships that form across generations in what one woman calls her daughter-mother and her mother-daughter relationships.   19

Evelyn's friend is her mother's age—"but I share so much more than I ever could with my mother"—a woman she talks to of music, of books and of life. "What I get from her is the benefit of her experience. What she gets—and enjoys—from me is a youthful perspective. It's a pleasure for both of us."   20

I have in my own life a precious friend, a woman of 65 who has 21
lived very hard, who is wise, who listens well; who has been where I am
and can help me understand it; and who represents not only an ultimate
ideal mother to me but also the person I'd like to be when I grow up.

In our daughter role we tend to do more than our share of self- 22
revelation; in our mother role we tend to receive what's revealed. It's
another kind of pleasure—playing wise mother to a questing younger
person. It's another very lovely kind of friendship.

6. Part-of-a-couple friends. Some of the women we call our 23
friends we never see alone—we see them as part of a couple at
couples' parties. And though we share interests in many things and
respect each other's views, we aren't moved to deepen the relationship.
Whatever the reason, a lack of time or—and this is more likely—a
lack of chemistry, our friendship remains in the context of a group.
But the fact that our feeling on seeing each other is always, "I'm *so*
glad she's here" and the fact that we spend half the evening talking
together says that this too, in its own way, counts as a friendship.

(Other part-of-a-couple friends are the friends that came with the 24
marriage, and some of these are friends we could live without. But sometimes, alas, she married our husband's best friend; and sometimes, alas,
she *is* our husband's best friend. And so we find ourself dealing with her,
somewhat against our will, in a spirit of what I'll call *reluctant* friendship.)

7. Men who are friends. I wanted to write just of women friends, 25
but the women I've talked to won't let me—they say I must mention
man-woman friendships too. For these friendships can be just as close
and as dear as those that we form with women. Listen to Lucy's
description of one such friendship:

"We've found we have things to talk about that are different 26
from what he talks about with my husband and different from what
I talk about with his wife. So sometimes we call on the phone or meet
for lunch. There are similar intellectual interests—we always pass on
to each other the books that we love—but there's also something
tender and caring too."

In a couple of crises, Lucy says, "he offered himself, for talking 27
and for helping. And when someone died in his family he wanted
me there. The sexual, flirty part of our friendship is very small, but
some—just enough to make it fun and different." She thinks—and I
agree—that the sexual part, though small is always *some,* is always
there when a man and a woman are friends.

It's only in the past few years that I've made friends with men, 28
in the sense of a friendship that's *mine,* not just part of two couples.
And achieving with them the ease and the trust I've found with
women friends has value indeed. Under the dryer at home last week,
putting on mascara and rouge, I comfortably sat and talked with a
fellow named Peter. Peter, I finally decided, could handle the shock of
me minus mascara under the dryer. Because we care for each other.
Because we're friends.

8. There are medium friends, and pretty good friends, and very   29
good friends indeed, and these friendships are defined by their level
of intimacy. And what we'll reveal at each of these levels of intimacy
is calibrated with care. We might tell a medium friend, for example,
that yesterday we had a fight with our husband. And we might tell a
pretty good friend that this fight with our husband made us so mad
that we slept on the couch. And we might tell a very good friend that
the reason we got so mad in that fight that we slept on the couch
had something to do with that girl who works in his office. But it's
only to our very best friends that we're willing to tell all, to tell what's
going on with that girl in his office.

The best of friends, I still believe, totally love and support and   30
trust each other, and bare to each other the secrets of their souls, and
run—no questions asked—to help each other, and tell harsh truths to
each other when they must be told.

But we needn't agree about everything (only 12-year-old girl   31
friends agree about *everything*) to tolerate each other's point of view.
To accept without judgment. To give and to take without ever keeping
score. And to *be* there, as I am for them and as they are for me, to
comfort our sorrows, to celebrate our joys.

—*Judith Viorst*

QUESTIONS ABOUT THE READING

Refer to the general questions on page 157 as well as these specific questions.

PURPOSE

■ How many bases can you identify in the above classification? Are
these bases consistent with the writer's purpose? Explain.

CONTENT

■ Is the classification offered here complete? Explain.

ORGANIZATION

■ How many paragraphs make up the introduction? Is the introduction
effective? Explain.
■ Does the arrangement of supporting paragraphs provide the best
emphasis for the thesis? Explain.
■ Are the many short paragraphs appropriate to the writer's purpose?
Explain.

STYLE

■ What is the writer's attitude toward her subject? Toward her audience?
How do we know? Where are the signals?
■ Is the tone appropriate for this writer's audience and purpose?
Explain.
■ Are the sentence fragments acceptable and effective here? (See page 456.)

RESPONDING TO YOUR READING

Explore your reactions to Viorst's "Friends, Good Friends—And Such Good Friends" by using the personal response questions on page 158. Then respond with an essay of your own that uses classification (and division, as needed) to support some particular point about different types of friends. Or you might write about different types of dates you've had, different types of people in your life, different places you've lived or schools you've attended, and so on.

Whether your approach is humorous or serious, be sure your classification supports a clear and definite viewpoint.

CASE STUDY

RESPONDING TO READING

After reading and analyzing Viorst's essay and answering the questions on page 158, Anne McCourt decides to examine her neighbourhood on the basis of the characteristics that it had when she decided to move there. To sort out the elements of this complex subject, Anne focused on Prospect School, the heart of her neighbourhood. She settled on four main categories: the description of the school, the description of the school ground, the importance of the school to the neighbourhood, and the importance of the school to her.

In drafting and revising her essay, Anne relies on the Division and Classification Guidelines and the Revision Checklist on pages 200, 201, and 58.

NOTE

Even though classification is the dominant strategy in Anne's essay, note how she also relies on the strategies of description, narration, and examples to get her point across.

Title gives a clear forecast

Paragraph 1 defines a neighbourhood

Paragraph 2 narrows definition to her favourite neighbourhood

THE HEART OF MY NEIGHBOURHOOD

Every great neighbourhood has a heart. It can be a park, a doughnut shop or a pub; a community centre, a cafe, or a church; a plaza or somebody's home. The heart of a neighbourhood is where people meet, talk, share information, and share their lives. It's what makes a neighbourhood a neighbourhood and not just a collection of buildings.

The best neighbourhood I have ever lived in was in Thunder Bay. It didn't have a name, but everyone knew where it was. It went from Red River Road north to River and from Pine Street east to Algoma. The heart of the neighbourhood was Prospect School.

Prospect was an elementary school. It was built in 1912, a beautiful example of the kind of building you don't see anymore: solid and imposing with high ceilings, tall windows, wide halls and airy rooms; a building that said school is important. It stood on a full block of land said to have been the site of a 19th-century mine—amethyst or maybe silver. Every few years a kid would find some pyrite in the schoolyard and start another gold rush that was usually over by afternoon recess.

Paragraphs 3–7 divide the school into four categories: description of the school, the school ground, the importance of the school to the community, and the importance of the school to her

Over the years, a tennis court, a baseball diamond, a basketball court, and playground equipment were added to the land around the school. The northwest corner was flat enough for soccer and football. But the best part was the northeast hill with its toboggan runs in the winter and dozens of outcrops and hiding places and bike jumps in the summer. The kids said it was the greatest playground in the city, and they played there seven days a week, all year round, well before they were old enough to attend school and long after they graduated from grade 8.

My children went to Prospect for 10 years. They thought it was their school, but I knew it was ours—theirs, mine, and the neighbourhood's. It was a school that opened its doors not just to students, but to the whole community. The children and their families, and many of the teachers, were also our friends and neighbours. Older neighbours had attended Prospect long ago, or had sent their children there. And younger families who moved into the area were drawn in part by the solid, welcoming presence of the school that stood at its centre.

Prospect School was the reason I moved into the neighbourhood and the reason I stayed.

It was where I made lifelong friends, watched my children grow and learn, got to know my adopted city of Thunder Bay, learned to make tea for 500 people, painted faces, edited a book of kindergarten stories, coached public speaking, sewed costumes, laughed, cried, and fought city hall.

Paragraph 8 shifts the focus to the thesis
Paragraph 9 ends with the thesis

Two years ago, the school was closed.

Today, the windows are boarded up and the playground equipment is gone. I still live in the same part of town. But it's not a neighbourhood anymore since its heart was taken away.

—*Anne McCourt*

OPTIONS FOR ESSAY WRITING

1. Television seems to invade every part of our lives. It can influence our buying habits, political views, attitudes about sex, marriage, family, and violence. Identify a group of commercials, sitcoms, talk shows, sports shows, or the like that have a bad (or good) influence on viewers. Sort the group according to a clear basis, using at least three categories, and be sure your essay supports a definite thesis.

2. Reread the passage by Alan Watts (page 199), and respond with an essay that lays out as specifically as possible the types of knowledge that you hope to acquire in university or the types you think everyone should acquire in higher education.

CHAPTER 13

Explaining Steps and Stages: Process Analysis

A *process* is a sequence of actions or changes leading to a product or result (say, in producing maple syrup). A *procedure* is a way of carrying out a process (say, in swinging a golf club). A *process analysis* explains these various steps and stages to instruct or inform readers.

USING PROCESS ANALYSIS BEYOND THE WRITING CLASSROOM

- **In other courses:** You might instruct a classmate in dissecting a frog or in using the school's e-mail network. You might answer an essay question about how economic inflation occurs or how hikers and campers can succumb to hypothermia.
- **On the job:** You might instruct a colleague or customer in accessing a database or shipping radioactive waste. You might explain to co-workers how the budget for various departments is determined or how the voice-mail system works.
- **In the community:** You might instruct a friend in casting for large-mouth bass or preparing for a job interview. You might explain to parents the selection process for new teachers followed by your PTA.

What additional audiences and uses for process analysis can you think of?

USING PROCESS ANALYSIS TO EXPLAIN

The most common referential uses of process analysis are to give instructions and to explain how something happens.

Explaining How to Do Something

As the above examples show, anyone might need to write instructions. And everyone reads some sort of instructions. The new employee needs instructions for operating the office machines; the employee going on vacation writes instructions for the person filling in. A car owner reads the manual for service and operating instructions.

What readers want to know about a procedure

- *How do I do it?*
- *Why do I do it?*
- *What materials or equipment will I need?*
- *Where do I begin?*
- *What do I do next?*
- *Are there any precautions?*

Instructions emphasize the reader's role, explaining each step in enough detail for the reader to complete the task safely and efficiently. This next passage is aimed at inexperienced joggers:

EXPLAINING HOW TO DO SOMETHING

Main point (1)
First step (2)
Supporting detail (3)
Second step (4)
Supporting detail (5)
Transitional sentence (6)
Third step (7–8)

Precaution (9–10)
Supporting details (11–15)

[1]Instead of breaking into a jog too quickly and risking injury, take a relaxed and deliberate approach. [2]Before taking a step, spend at least ten minutes stretching and warming up, using any exercises you find comfortable. [3](After your first week, consult a jogging book for specialized exercises.) [4]When you've completed your warm-up, set a brisk pace walking. [5]Exaggerate the distance between steps, taking long strides and swinging your arms briskly and loosely. [6]After roughly 100 yards at this brisk pace, you should feel ready to jog. [7]Immediately break into a very slow trot: lean your torso forward and let one foot fall in front of the other (one foot barely leaving the ground while the other is on the pavement). [8]Maintain the slowest pace possible, just above a walk. [9]Do not bolt like a sprinter! [10]The biggest mistake is to start fast and injure yourself. [11]While jogging, relax your body. [12]Keep your shoulders straight and your head up, and enjoy the scenery—after all, it is one of the joys of jogging. [13]Keep your arms low and slightly bent at your sides. [14]Move your legs freely from the hips in an action that is easy, not forced. [15]Make your feet perform a heel-to-toe action: land on the heel; rock forward; take off from the toe.

GUIDELINES FOR GIVING INSTRUCTIONS

1. *Know the process.* Unless you have performed the task, do not try to write instructions for it.

2. *Explain the purpose of the procedure.* Give users enough background to understand why they need your instructions.

3. *Make instructions complete but not excessive.* Don't assume that people know more than they really do, especially when you can perform the task almost automatically. (Think about when someone taught you to drive a car—or perhaps you have tried to teach someone else.) As in the previous jogging instructions, include enough detail for users to understand what to do, but omit general information that users probably know. Excessive details get in the way.

4. *Show users what to do.* Give them enough examples to visualize the procedure clearly.

5. *Divide the procedure into simple steps and substeps.* Allow readers to focus on one task at a time.

6. *Organize for the user's understanding.* Instructions almost always are arranged in chronological order, with notes and precautions inserted for specific steps.

7. *Make instructions immediately readable.* Instructions must be understood upon first reading, because users usually take immediate action. Because they emphasize the user's role, write instructions in the second person, as direct address.

   Begin all steps and substeps with action verbs by using the *active voice*

GUIDELINES FOR GIVING INSTRUCTIONS (continued)

(**move your legs** versus **your legs should be moved**) and the *imperative mood* (**rock forward** versus **you should rock forward**), giving an immediate signal about the specific action to be taken.

Use shorter sentences than usual: use one sentence for one step, so users can perform one action at a time.

Finally, use transitional expressions (**while, after, next**) to show how the steps are connected.

8. *Maintain a user-friendly tone.* Be encouraging instead of bossy.

9. *Include troubleshooting advice.* Explain what to do when things go wrong.

NOTE: *If X doesn't work, first check Y and then do Z.*

Place this near the end of your instructions.

Note that these instructions do not explain terms such as *long stride*, *torso*, and *sprinter* because these should be clear to the general reader. But a *slow trot* is explained in detail; different readers might have differing interpretations of this term.

Explaining How Something Happens

Besides showing how to do something, you often have to explain how things occur: how sunlight helps plants make chlorophyll; how a digital computer works; how your town decided on its zoning laws. *Process explanation* emphasizes the process itself—instead of the reader's or writer's role.

What readers want to know about a process

- *How does it happen? Or, how is it made?*
- *When and where does it happen?*
- *What happens first, next, and so on?*
- *What is the result?*

USING PROCESS ANALYSIS TO MAKE A POINT

Although many process explanations are referential, others are closely related to cause and effect (see Chapter 14). In these cases, providing complete explanations and clear connections between steps helps convince readers that the process you're describing really does happen as you say. These kinds of causal chains often support larger arguments. In the next example, Julia Schoonover uses a process analysis to support her claim that credit cards and students create a dangerous combination.

PROCESS ANALYSIS THAT MAKES A POINT

Orienting statement (1)
Details of the process and its results (2–8)

Main point (9)

[1]Granted, the temptation is hard to refuse. [2]Credit card companies marketing on campus offer free cards and sign-up gifts "with no obligation." [3]The "gifts" might include candy, coffee mugs, T-shirts, sports squeeze bottles, hip bags, and other paraphernalia. [4]The process seems harmless enough: Just fill in your social insurance number and other personal information, take your pick from the array of gifts, and cancel the card when it arrives. [5]But these companies know exactly what they're doing. [6]They know that misusing the card is often easier than cancelling it. [7]They know that many of us work part time and are paid little. [8]They know that most of us will be unable to pay more than the minimum balance each month—meaning big-time interest for years. [9]Don't be seduced by instant credit.

—*Julia Schoonover*

APPLICATION 13-1

PARAGRAPH WARM-UP: GIVING INSTRUCTIONS

Choose some activity you perform well. Think of a situation requiring you to write instructions for that activity. Single out a major step within the process (such as pitching a baseball or adjusting ski bindings for safe release). Provide enough details so that the reader can perform that step safely and efficiently.

APPLICATION 13-2

PARAGRAPH WARM-UP: EXPLAINING HOW SOMETHING HAPPENS

Select some process in your university—admissions, registration, changing majors, finding a parking place. Write a process analysis that could anchor an argument for changes in the procedure.

APPLICATION 13-3

ESSAY PRACTICE: GIVING INSTRUCTIONS

Read Scott Earl Smith's essay and answer the questions following it. Then select one of the essay assignments.

Scott Smith is a freelance writer on hunting and fly fishing who publishes regularly in Canada and the United States. These instructions are part of a longer essay that also teaches dog owners how to teach their dogs to sit, to come, to change direction, and to quarter, based first on word commands but ultimately on hand and/or whistle commands.

ESSAY FOR ANALYSIS AND RESPONSE

TEACHING YOUR GUN DOG TO RETRIEVE

[1] Most experts suggest that serious training for a gun dog should begin at about eight months of age, although some dogs will be capable at six months. At this point, the dog is at the stage where he will respond best to a progressive training regimen without being over-stressed.

[2] Conduct retrieving sessions in a small confined area, such as a dead-end hallway devoid of items (and other persons) that will only serve to distract your dog, until he is retrieving consistently in this environment. From the outset, use the command "fetch" every time you throw the retrieving dummy, as this will play a big part in future training.

[3] Once the dog is performing well in a small, confined indoor setting, begin experimenting with conducting the retrieving sessions in a larger room. If your dog still performs satisfactorily, introduce him to outside retrieving sessions, but only if they can be conducted in a fenced-in yard. The fence provides containment for the dog and a level of control by the owner. The backyard in the owner's home will also be familiar to the dog and will also be fairly sterile as far as other animal scents are concerned.

[4] If the dog doesn't retrieve properly in the yard environment, try returning to the hallway routine or having the dog retrieve while on a lightweight cord. That way, if he doesn't return properly, you can call him back and pull him towards you to reinforce the requirements for him to return after the retrieve.

[5] From here, shift the natural progression for retrieving sessions from your own fenced-in back yard, to a grassed parkland (where unleashed dogs are allowed—don't forget to scoop the poop!), to a field with tall grasses and shrubs, and finally to a wooded area where you could conceivably encounter game birds.

[6] But this progression will take months and months of careful and plan-ful training. One of the key things to remember in retrieving is that the more open and wild the training environment, the more distractions there will be and the less control you will have on his movements. Subsequently, you must ensure that your dog is disciplined enough for the next level before you change the training arena.

—Scott Earl Smith

QUESTIONS ABOUT THE READING

CONTENT

- What opening strategy is used to create interest?
- Is the information adequate and appropriate for the stated audience and purpose? Explain.
- What specific readers' questions are answered here?

ORGANIZATION

- What is the order of the body paragraphs? Is this the most effective order? Explain.
- Is the conclusion adequate and appropriate? Explain.

STYLE

- Are these instructions immediately readable? Explain.
- Is the tone of these instructions too "bossy"? Explain.

RESPONDING TO YOUR READING

Assume a specific situation and audience (like those for training a gun dog), and write instructions for a specialized procedure, or for anything that you can do well (no recipes, please). Be sure you know the process down to the smallest detail. Narrow your subject (perhaps to one complex activity within a longer procedure) so you can cover it fully. Avoid day-to-day procedures that university readers would already know (brushing teeth, washing hair, and other such elementary activities).

APPLICATION 13-4

Computer Application: Write instructions for conducting a Web search using one of the popular Internet search engines. (Hint: Consult the sites' Help, FAQ, or Search Tips page for raw material. Be sure to cite the exact source of any material you quote or paraphrase (see pages 356–359.)

SAMPLE SEARCH ENGINES:

Alta Vista **www.altavista.com**

The Argus Clearinghouse **www.clearinghouse.net**

Ask Jeeves **www.askjeeves.com**

Excite **www.excite.com**

Google **www.google.ca**

HotBot **www.hotbot.com**

Lycos **www.lycos.com**

Savvy Search **www.savvysearch.com**

CASE STUDY

RESPONDING TO READING

After reading and analyzing Scott Earl Smith's essay and answering the questions on pages 157 and 214, Cathy Nichols recalls her own experience as a new commuter student, and decides to write a basic "survival guide" for commuters during their first week of school. To keep her instructions brief and straightforward, Cathy divides the procedure into four basic steps: getting essential items, checking out the library, meeting one's advisor, and establishing a support network.

In drafting and revising her essay, Cathy follows the Instruction Guidelines and Revision Checklist on pages 211 and 58.

NOTE

Even though process analysis is the dominant rhetorical strategy in Cathy's essay, she also relies on other strategies such as description, illustration, division, and classification.

Title gives a forecast
Uses encouraging tone
Establishes writer's knowledge on this topic
Explains the procedure's purpose, in a friendly tone
First major step (classifies "essential items")
Transitions throughout mark time and sequence
Gives example
Uses chronological order for steps and substeps

Uses note to emphasize vital information
Second major step
Divides each major step into simple substeps
Addresses the readers directly throughout

Third major step

Gives just enough detail for this audience

Fourth major step

Uses a short sentence for each substep

A First-Week Survival Guide for Commuters

Welcome, first-year students! You've probably read most of the "official" literature provided by this university. But as a recent first-year commuter who spent most of her first week lost, I'd like to offer some "unofficial" advice! If, like many commuters, you've managed to avoid freshman orientation, I hope you'll consider this a crash course for avoiding needless stress and dodging some common headaches.

Begin by getting the essential items: campus map, ID card, books, and a parking sticker. First, pick up a campus map at the Registrar's office. Next, find the Campus Centre, and go to the Student Services office to pick up your student ID. Adjacent to Student Services is your next stop, the bookstore. Bring your class schedule so that you buy the right books for your class "section." If your schedule says "ENL 101–09," that means the subject is English, the class name is Reading and Writing I, and at least nine separate classes of that course exist. (Different teachers assign different texts.) Finally, head for the Campus Police office to pick up your parking sticker. Bring your student ID and car registration. *Note:* Try to do these things *before* classes begin.

As a commuter, your best bet for studying on campus is the school library, so get to know it right away. Jot down the library hours, usually posted by the entrance. (The library closes for national holidays and has some quirky weekend hours.) Library seating is ample, but noisy groups tend to collect at the larger tables. Look for a quiet corner on one of the upper floors. English 101 classes usually take a group library tour during the semester. If your class doesn't, or if you miss it, make an appointment with one of the librarians. No one graduates without producing research papers, and acquainting yourself with the computers and research materials ahead of time will save valuable study hours.

As soon as classes begin, get to know your advisor—the person you see for choosing or adding and dropping courses, and for any kind of advice. Offices are usually on the third floor of academic buildings, organized by departments. Each department has a main office and a secretary. If you don't know who your advisor is, the secretary can tell you. The department office can also provide you with a course "checklist." This will tell you which courses you need to complete your degree. Unlike high school teachers, university professors are not required to be on campus all day. Jot down your advisor's office hours (posted outside individual offices or in the department), office phone number, and e-mail address.

Commuters don't have the luxury of always being on campus, so establish a support network during your first week of classes. As corny as it sounds, find a buddy in each class. Or better yet, find someone who shares more than one class with you. Exchange phone numbers (and e-mail addresses if possible). This way, if you do have to miss a class you will be able to keep up with the assignments. Also, check out the Tutoring Centre (Blake Hall, second floor)—in case you ever need help. Paid for by your basic tuition, tutors are available for most subjects. They are fellow students who are not only familiar with the university but with the specific courses and professors as well. Tutoring is available on a walk-in basis or by regular appointment.

Includes detail as needed

You're being asked to adjust to many different expectations, all at the same time. A little confusion and anxiety are understandable. But the entire university community is committed to helping its new students.

Maintains an encouraging tone throughout

Note: If you have any questions about these steps—or about anything else—*ask someone!* Chances are other people have asked the same question or experienced the same problem. Best of luck.

Includes trouble-shooting advice

—*Catherine Nichols*

APPLICATION **13-5**

ESSAY PRACTICE: EXPLAINING HOW SOMETHING HAPPENS

The next essay was written by Bill Kelly, a biologist, for a pamphlet on environmental pollution. It is aimed at an uninformed audience.

ESSAY FOR ANALYSIS AND RESPONSE

HOW ACID RAIN DEVELOPS, SPREADS, AND DESTROYS

[1]Acid rain is environmentally damaging rainfall that occurs after fossil fuels burn, releasing nitrogen and sulfur oxides into the atmosphere. Acid rain, simply stated, increases the acidity level of waterways, because these nitrogen and sulfur oxides combine with the air's normal moisture. The resulting rainfall is far more acidic than normal rainfall. Acid rain is a silent threat because its effects, although slow, are cumulative. This analysis explains the cause, the distribution cycle, and the effects of acid rain.

[2]Most research shows that power plants burning oil or coal are the primary cause of acid rain. Fossil fuels contain a number of elements that are released during combustion. Two of these, sulfur oxide and nitrogen oxide, combine with normal moisture to produce sulfuric acid and nitric acid. The released gases undergo a chemical change as they combine with atmospheric ozone and water vapour. The resulting rain or snowfall is more acid than normal precipitation.

[3]Acid level is measured by pH readings. The pH scale runs from 0 through 14; a pH of 7 is considered neutral. (Distilled water has a pH of 7.) Numbers above 7 indicate increasing degrees of alkalinity. (Household ammonia has a pH of 11.) Numbers below 7 indicate increasing acidity. Movement in either direction on the pH scale, however, means multiplying by 10. Lemon juice, which has a pH value of 2, is 10 times more acidic

than apples, which have a pH of 3, and 1000 times more acidic than carrots, which have a pH of 5.

[4]Because of carbon dioxide (an acid substance) normally present in air, unaffected rainfall has a pH of 5.6. At this time, the pH of precipitation in the northeastern United States and Canada is between 4.5 and 4. In Massachusetts, rain and snowfall have an average pH reading of 4.1. A pH reading below 5 is considered to be abnormally acidic, and therefore a threat to aquatic populations.

[5]Although it might seem that areas containing power plants would be most severely affected, acid rain can in fact travel thousands of kilometres from its source. Stack gases escape and drift with the wind currents. The sulfur and nitrogen oxides thus are able to travel great distances before they return to earth as acid rain.

[6]For an average of two to five days after emission, the gases follow the prevailing winds far from the point of origin. Estimates show that about 50 percent of the acid rain that affects Canada originates in the United States; at the same time, 15 to 25 percent of the U.S. acid rain problem originates in Canada.

[7]The tendency of stack gases to drift makes acid rain a widespread menace. More than 200 lakes in the Adirondacks, hundreds of kilometres from any industrial centre, are unable to support life because their water has become so acidic.

[8]Acid rain causes damage wherever it falls. It erodes various types of building rock, such as limestone, marble, and mortar, which are gradually eaten away by the constant bathing in acid. Damage to buildings, houses, monuments, statues, and cars is widespread. Some priceless monuments and carvings already have been destroyed, and even trees of some varieties are dying in large numbers.

[9]More important, however, is acid rain damage to waterways in the affected areas. Because of its high acidity, acid rain dramatically lowers the pH in lakes and streams. Although its effect is not immediate, acid rain eventually can make a waterway so acidic it dies. In areas with natural acid-buffering elements such as limestone, the dilute acid has less effect. The northeastern United States and Canada, however, lack this natural protection, and so are continually vulnerable.

[10]The pH level in an affected waterway drops so low that some species cease to reproduce. In fact, a pH level of 5.1 to 5.4 means that fisheries are threatened; once a waterway reaches a pH level of 4.5, no fish reproduction occurs. Because each creature is part of the overall food chain, loss of one element in the chain disrupts the whole cycle.

[11]In the northeastern United States and Canada, the acidity problem is compounded by the runoff from acid snow. During the cold winter months, acid snow sits with little melting, so that by spring thaw, the acid released is greatly concentrated. Aluminum and other heavy metals normally present in soil also are released by acid rain and runoff. These toxic substances leach into waterways in heavy concentrations, affecting fish in all stages of development.

—*Bill Kelly*

QUESTIONS ABOUT THE READING

CONTENT

- Is the information appropriate for the intended audience (uninformed readers)? Explain.
- What specific readers' questions are answered in the body?

ORGANIZATION

- Are the body paragraphs arranged in the best order for readers to follow the process? Explain.
- Why does this essay have no specific conclusion?

STYLE

- Is the discussion easy to follow? If so, what style features help? If not, what might be changed?
- Give one example of each of the following sentence constructions, and explain briefly how each reinforces the writer's meaning: passive construction, subordination, short sentence.

RESPONDING TO YOUR READING

Select a specialized process that you understand well (from your major or from an area of interest) and explain that process to uninformed readers. Choose a process that has several distinct steps, and write so that your composition classmates gain detailed understanding. Do not merely generalize. Get down to specifics.

APPLICATION 13-6

ESSAY PRACTICE: USING PROCESS ANALYSIS TO MAKE A POINT

Processes occur in our personal experiences as well—for example, our stages of maturation, of emotional growth and development, of intellectual awareness. The following essay traces a personal process some readers might consider horrifying: the stages of learning to live by scavenging through garbage. As you read, think about how the factual and "objective" style paints a gruesome portrait of survival beyond the margin of North American affluence.

ESSAY FOR ANALYSIS AND RESPONSE

DUMPSTER DIVING

[1] I began Dumpster diving about a year before I became homeless.

[2] I prefer the term scavenging. I have heard people, evidently meaning to be polite, use the word foraging, but I prefer to reserve that word for gathering nuts and berries and such, which I also do, according to the season and opportunity.

[3]I like the frankness of the word scavenging. I live from the refuse of others. I am a scavenger. I think it a sound and honorable niche, although if I could I would naturally prefer to live the comfortable consumer life, perhaps—and only perhaps—as a slightly less wasteful consumer owing to what I have learned as a scavenger.

[4]Except for jeans, all my clothes come from Dumpsters. Boom boxes, candles, bedding, toilet paper, medicine, books, a typewriter, a virgin male love doll, coins sometimes amounting to many dollars: all came from Dumpsters. And, yes, I eat from Dumpsters, too.

[5]There is a predictable series of stages that a person goes through in learning to scavenge. At first the new scavenger is filled with disgust and self-loathing. He [or she] is ashamed of being seen.

[6]This stage passes with experience. The scavenger finds a pair of running shoes that fit and look and smell brand-new. He finds a pocket calculator in perfect working order. He finds pristine ice cream, still frozen, more than he can eat or keep. He begins to understand: people do throw away perfectly good stuff, a lot of perfectly good stuff.

[7]At this stage he may become lost and never recover. All the Dumpster divers I have known come to the point of trying to acquire everything they touch. Why not take it, they reason; it is all free. This is, of course, hopeless, and most divers come to realize that they must restrict themselves to items of relatively immediate utility.

[8]The finding of objects is becoming something of an urban art. Even respectable, employed people will sometimes find something tempting sticking out of a Dumpster or standing beside one. Quite a number of people, not all of them of the bohemian type, are willing to brag that they found this or that piece in the trash.

[9]But eating from Dumpsters is the thing that separates the dilettanti from the professionals. Eating safely involves three principles: using the senses and common sense to evaluate the condition of the found materials; knowing the Dumpsters of a given area and checking them regularly; and seeking always to answer the question "Why was this discarded?"

[10]Yet perfectly good food can be found in Dumpsters. Canned goods, for example, turn up fairly often in the Dumpsters I frequent. I also have few qualms about dry foods such as crackers, cookies, cereal, chips, and pasta if they are free of visible contaminants and still dry and crisp. Raw fruits and vegetables with intact skins seem perfectly safe to me, excluding, of course, the obviously rotten. Many are discarded for minor imperfections that can be pared away.

[11]A typical discard is a half jar of peanut butter—though nonorganic peanut butter does not require refrigeration and is unlikely to spoil in any reasonable time. One of my favorite finds is yogurt—often discarded, still sealed, when the expiration has passed—because it will keep for several days, even in warm weather.

[12]No matter how careful I am I still get dysentery at least once a month, oftener in warm weather. I do not want to paint too romantic a picture. Dumpster diving has serious drawbacks as a way of life.

¹³I find from the experience of scavenging two rather deep lessons. The first is to take what I can use and let the rest go. I have come to think that there is no value in the abstract. A thing I cannot use or make useful, perhaps by trading, has no value, however fine or rare it may be. The second lesson is the transience of material being. I do not suppose that ideas are immortal, but certainly they are longer-lived than material objects.

¹⁴The things I find in Dumpsters, the love letters and rag dolls of so many lives, remind me of this lesson. Now I hardly pick up a thing without envisioning the time I will cast it away. This, I think, is a healthy state of mind. Almost everything I have now has already been cast out at least once, proving that what I own is valueless to someone.

¹⁵I find that my desire to grab for the gaudy bauble has been largely sated. I think this is an attitude I share with the very wealthy—we both know there is plenty more wherever we have come from. Between us are the rat-race millions who have confounded their selves with the objects they grasp and who nightly scavenge the cable channels for they know not what.

¹⁶I am sorry for them.

—*Lars Eighner*

Questions about the Reading

CONTENT

- What are Eighner's assumptions about his audience's knowledge and attitudes? Are these assumptions accurate? Why or why not?
- Point out some of the referential details Eighner selects to make his point. How selective do you think he has been? Explain.

ORGANIZATION

- How does Eighner "frame" his process analysis through his introduction and conclusion? Do these framing elements make the depiction of the process itself more or less convincing? Explain.

STYLE

- What is the writer's attitude toward his subject? Toward his audience? How do we know? Where are the signals?
- Is the tone appropriate for this writer's audience and purpose? Explain.

Responding to Your Reading

Explore your reactions to "Dumpster Diving" (pages 219–221) by using the questions on page 158. What is Eighner's point about values? What are the main issues here? How has this essay affected your thinking about these issues? As you reread the essay, try to recall some process that has played a role for you personally or for someone close to you. Perhaps you want to focus on the process of achievement (say, preparing for academic or athletic or career competition). Perhaps you have experienced or witnessed the process of giving in to human frailty (say, addiction to drugs, tobacco, alcohol, or food). Perhaps you know something about the process of enduring and recovering from personal loss or misfortune or disappointment. Identify your audience, and decide what you want these readers to do, think, or feel after reading your essay. Should they appreciate this process, try it themselves, avoid it, or what?

Whatever you write about—university or college or high school or family life or city streets—make a definite point about the larger meaning beyond the details of the process, about the values involved.

CHAPTER 14

Explaining Why It Happened or What Will Happen: Cause-and-Effect Analysis

A nalysis of reasons (causes) or consequences (effects) explains why something happened or what happens as a result of some event or incident.

- *Why did it happen?*
- *What caused it?*
- *What are its effects?*
- *What will happen if it is done?*

For example, if you awoke this morning with a sore shoulder (effect), you might recall exerting yourself yesterday at the college Frisbee Olympics (cause). You take aspirin, hoping for relief (effect). If the aspirin works, it will have *caused* you to feel better. But some causes and effects are harder to identify:

        [CAUSE]   [EFFECT]
1. I tripped over a chair and broke my nose.

    [EFFECT]   [CAUSE]
2. I never studied because I slept too much.

Other causes or effects could be identified for each of the above statements.

    [EFFECT]   [CAUSE]
I tripped over the chair because my apartment lights were out.

      [EFFECT]   [CAUSE]
The lights were out because the power had been shut off.

        [EFFECT]   [CAUSE]
The power was off because my roommate forgot to pay the hydro bill.
or
     [EFFECT]   [CAUSE]
Because I slept too much, my marks were awful.

       [EFFECT]   [CAUSE]
Because my marks were awful, I hated college.

      [EFFECT]   [CAUSE]
Because I hated college, I dropped out.

     [EFFECT]   [CAUSE]
Because I dropped out of college, I lost my scholarship.

In the examples above, the causes or effects become more distant. The *immediate* cause of example 1, however—the one most closely related to the effect—is that the writer tripped over the chair. Likewise, the *immediate* effect of example 2 is that the writer did no studying. Thus, the challenge is often to distinguish between immediate causes or effects and distant ones. Otherwise, we might generate illogical statements like these:

[CAUSE]   [EFFECT]
Because my roommate forgot to pay the hydro bill, I broke my nose.

[EFFECT]   [CAUSE]
I lost my scholarship because I slept too much.

USING CAUSAL ANALYSIS TO EXPLAIN: DEFINITE CAUSES

As in process analysis (Chapter 13), writing that connects definite causes to their effects clarifies the relations among events in a causal chain. A *definite cause is apparent* ("The engine's overheating is caused by a faulty radiator cap"). You write about definite causes when you explain why the combustion in a car engine causes the wheels to move, or why the moon's orbit makes the tides rise and fall.

USING CAUSAL ANALYSIS BEYOND THE WRITING CLASSROOM

- **In other courses:** A research paper might explore the causes of the Israeli-Palestinian conflict or the effects of stress on university students. A report for the Dean of Students might explain students' disinterest in campus activities or the effect of a ban on smoking in public buildings.
- **On the job:** In workplace problem solving, you might analyze the high absenteeism among company employees or the malfunction of equipment.
- **In the community:** Perhaps local citizens need to know how air quality will be affected if your power plant changes from coal to oil or how increasing enrollment has affected education quality at your local high school.

In what other situations might causal analysis make a difference?

EXPLAINING A DEFINITE CAUSE

Topic sentence (1)
Causal chain (2–3)

Effects (4)
Conclusion (5)

¹Some of the most serious accidents involving gas water heaters occur when a flammable liquid is used in the vicinity. ²The heavier-than-air vapors of a flammable liquid such as gasoline can flow along the floor—even the length of a basement—and be explosively ignited by the flame of the water heater's pilot light or burner. ³Because the victim's clothing often ignites, the resulting burn injuries are commonly serious and extremely painful. ⁴They may require long hospitalization, and can result in disfigurement or death. ⁵Never, under any circumstances, use a flammable liquid near a gas heater or burner.

—*U.S. Consumer Product Safety Commission*

USING CAUSAL ANALYSIS TO MAKE A POINT: POSSIBLE OR PROBABLE CAUSES

Causal writing often explores *possible or probable causes—causes that are not apparent*. In these cases, much searching, thought, and effort usually are needed to argue for a specific cause.

Suppose you ask: "Why are there no children's day-care facilities on our campus?" Brainstorming yields these possible causes:

lack of need among students

lack of interest among students, faculty, and staff

high cost of liability insurance

lack of space and facilities on campus

lack of trained personnel

prohibition by provincial law

lack of government funding for such a project

Say you proceed with interviews, questionnaires, and research into provincial laws, insurance rates, and availability of personnel. You begin to rule out some items, and others appear as probable causes. Specifically, you find a need among students, high campus interest, an abundance of qualified people for staffing, and no provincial laws prohibiting such a project. Three probable causes remain: lack of funding, high insurance rates, and lack of space. Further inquiry shows that lack of funding and high insurance rates are issues. You think, however, that these causes could be eliminated through new sources of revenue: charging a fee for each child, soliciting donations, or diverting funds from other campus organizations. Finally, after examining available campus space and speaking with school officials, you conclude that the one definite cause is lack of space and facilities.

The persuasiveness of your causal argument will depend on the quality of research and evidence you bring to bear, as well as your ability to explain the links in the chain clearly. You must also convince audiences that you haven't overlooked important alternative causes.

Any complex effect is likely to have more than one cause; you have to make the case that the one you have isolated is the real issue.* You must also demonstrate sound reasoning. For example, the fact that one event occurs just before another is no proof that the first caused the second. You might have walked under a ladder in the hallway an hour before flunking your chemistry exam—but you would be hard-pressed to argue convincingly that the one event had caused the other.

---

*For example, one could argue that the lack of space and facilities somehow is related to funding. And the university's inability to find funds or space may be related to student need, which is not sufficiently acute or interest sufficiently high to exert real pressure.

REASONING FROM EFFECT TO CAUSE

In reasoning from effect to cause we examine a particular result, *consequence,* or outcome and we try to determine the circumstances that may produce such a result.

AN EFFECT-TO-CAUSE ANALYSIS

Effect (main point)
(1–2)

Distant and immediate causes (3–6)

[1]For over 100 years, the Muskoka region was renowned for its pristine beauty and serenity. [2]However, that once pristine and peaceful wilderness is being rapidly transformed into a sprawling playground for the rich sun worshippers at the expense of both the native Muskokans and the environment. [3]The influx of money from wealthy Americans and Europeans has driven up property prices to the point where locals cannot afford to pay rent, so more and more residents have joined the ranks of the homeless. [4]As well, locals are being denied access to the shorelines as hundreds of large private cottages have eliminated the once accessible public beaches, cliffs, and lakeshore trails. [5]In addition, lakes have suffered from massive sedimentation caused by the construction of 18-hole golf courses and the serenity has been shattered by the swarm of high-powered ski boats that have invaded the waterways. [6]The land no longer belongs to those who enjoyed it for its simplicity.

—*Brian Yantha*

GUIDELINES FOR EFFECT-TO-CAUSE ANALYSIS

1. *Be sure the cause fits the effect.* Brian Yantha, a Muskoka resident, provides examples of the reasons why the residents and the environment are being affected by the recreational development of Muskoka.

2. *Make the links between effect and cause clear.* Yantha's reasoning follows:

   [DISTANT CAUSE]   [IMMEDIATE CAUSE]
   wealthy people ⟶ invading
   looking for   Muskoka
   recreational properties

          [EFFECT]
   ⟶ harm to residents
      and environment

The influx of money is discussed first so that the immediate causes of harm to residents and the environment makes sense.

3. *Distinguish clearly between possible, probable, and definite causes.* Unless the cause is obvious, limit your assertions by using *perhaps, probably, maybe, most likely, could, seems to, appears to,* or similar qualifiers that prevent you from making an unsupportable claim.

NOTE *Keep in mind that faulty causal reasoning is extremely common, especially when we ignore other possible causes or we confuse mere coincidence with causation. (See page 302, for examples and discussion.)*

REASONING FROM CAUSE TO EFFECT

In reasoning from cause to effect, we examine a given set of circumstances and we try to ascertain the outcome of these circumstances.

A CAUSE-TO-EFFECT ANALYSIS

[1]What has the telephone done to us, or for us, in the hundred years of its existence? [2]A few effects suggest themselves at once. [3]It has saved lives by getting rapid word of illness, injury, or famine from remote places. [4]By joining with the elevator to make possible the multistory residence or office building, it has made possible—for better or worse—the modern city. [5]By bringing about a quantum leap in the speed and ease with which information moves from place to place, it has greatly accelerated the rate of scientific and technological change and growth in industry. [6]Beyond doubt it has crippled if not killed the ancient art of letter writing. [7]It has made living alone possible for persons with normal social impulses; by so doing, it has played a role in one of the greatest social changes of this century, the breakup of the multigenerational household. [8]It has made the waging of war chillingly more efficient than formerly. [9]Perhaps (though not probably) it has prevented wars that might have arisen out of international misunderstanding caused by written communications. [10]Or perhaps—again not probably—by magnifying and extending irrational personal conflicts based on voice contact, it has caused wars. [11]Certainly it has extended the scope of human conflicts, since it impartially disseminates the useful knowledge of scientists and the babble of bores, the affection of the affectionate and the malice of the malicious.

—*John Brooks*

GUIDELINES FOR CAUSE-TO-EFFECT ANALYSIS

1. *Show that the effects fit the cause.* To clarify and support his point, the author John Brooks shows the telephone's effects on familiar aspects of modern life. Because his purpose is to discuss effects in general (not only positive effects), the author balances his development with both positive and negative effects.

2. *Make links between cause and effects clear.* The reasoning goes like this:

   [CAUSE]   [IMMEDIATE EFFECT]
   telephone ⟶ created rapid communication

   [ULTIMATE EFFECTS]
   ⟶ saved lives, led to the modern city, and so on

GUIDELINES FOR CAUSE-TO-EFFECT ANALYSIS (continued)

[CAUSE]   [IMMEDIATE EFFECT]
telephone→ enabled people to live alone

[ULTIMATE EFFECT]
→ led to breakup of multigenerational household

Without the link provided by the immediate effects, the ultimate effects would make no sense:

The telephone has saved lives. [*Why?*]

It has made possible the modern city. [*Why?*]

It perhaps has caused wars. [*Why?*]

For further linking, the paragraph groups definite effects (3–8), then possible effects (9–10), with a conclusion that ties the discussion together.

3. *Consider "confounding factors" (alternate explanations for a particular effect).* For instance, studies indicating that regular exercise improves health might be overlooking the fact that healthy people tend to exercise more often than those who are unhealthy.

APPLICATION 14-1

PARAGRAPH WARM-UP: USING CAUSAL ANALYSIS TO EXPLAIN

Ordinary life in the modern world depends on technology, but technology often frustrates us by letting us down when we most need it. Think of the last time you found yourself screaming at a machine. Using library research if necessary, explain the immediate and distant causes of the problem you experienced, limiting your discussion to definite causes as much as possible. Think of your paragraph as the heart of a letter to a friend explaining how to avoid the problem in the future.

APPLICATION 14-2

PARAGRAPH WARM-UP: USING CAUSAL ANALYSIS TO MAKE A POINT

Identify a problem that affects you, your community, family, school, residence, or other group ("The library is an awful place to study because ———"). In a paragraph, analyze the causes of this problem as a prelude to an argument for change. Choose a subject you know about or one you can research to get the facts. Identify clearly the situation, the audience, and your purpose.

APPLICATION **14-3**

Computer Application and Collaborative Project: Application 14-1 suggested investigating the causes of common technological glitches. Using your *listserv* or e-mail, interview the group members to discover the problems they most commonly encounter when they use computers. Choose a glitch that seems to cause widespread frustration. Investigate the usual or probable causes of the glitch and write a report for one group member to present to the class. Note whether you are discovering definite, probable, or possible causes. How might the type of cause you find affect the way your readers should deal with the problem in the future?

APPLICATION **14-4**

ESSAY PRACTICE: ANALYZING CAUSES

In the following essay from *Explore* (January/February 2000), the author examines the reasons why Banff has been sacrificed and why the further development of the area should be supported.

ESSAY FOR ANALYSIS AND RESPONSE

BANFF: THE SACRIFICIAL LAMB

[1]Parks Canada's vision for the Town of Banff is finally emerging from a series of superficial confusing *pronunciamentos:* in favour of hotel extensions, but against ski hill expansions; in support of fishing for winter-stressed trout, but opposed to summertime gondola rides over browsing bears.

[2]The objective is to mollify environmentalists by pruning back development outside the town boundaries, while increasing the flow of free-spending tourists through the town itself. The model for the Town of Banff now is clear: it is Carmel, California.

[3]Carmel is a cute, compact town tucked profitably between the Pebble Beach golf resort and Big Sur. Fishing charters, but no gondola rides. Luxury hotels, but no ski hills. Carmel is a commercial magnet for hundreds of thousands of Asian and American tourists on their way to Yosemite Park to photograph each other against a backdrop of waterfalls.

[4]Carmel's civic authorities don't allow T-shirt shops or fast-food drive-throughs, just elegant international boutiques and bowered patios serving chilled Chardonnay in the warm rays of mesquite logs smouldering in clay firepots. Clint Eastwood and his Hog's Breath Cafe serve as celebrity tourist bait.

[5]To increase its tourist throughput, Banff needs its own celebrity cachet. With nobody important actually living there, Ottawa has decided to mount a series of life-sized statues, starting with one of Wayne Gretzky. A Gretzky statue would be every bit at home in Carmel as in Banff. Gretzky,

after all, made all his big money playing in California and is now the figurehead of San Diego's Wayne Gretzky Hockey Roller Centres.

[6]Banff's mayor called the whole idea "tacky" and inconsistent with "park values." He just didn't get it. As far as Banff is concerned, park values are counted in dollars, marks, and, above all, yen.

[7]Why else raise next to Gretzky's a statue of Lucy Maud Montgomery, a worthy Victorian author of pastoral children's stories about faraway Prince Edward Island? The answer is simple: Montgomery's *Anne of Green Gables* is a cultural icon in Japan, far more than at home where she is outclassed by Japan's own contribution to childhood imaginings, Pokémon.

[8]There is almost nothing for sale or to eat in Banff that has the slightest affinity to the Rocky Mountains, or even to Canada. Banff has shops purveying cigars rolled in Cuba, models of CPR trains made in China, and stateless fashions labelled Polo Ralph Lauren and LaCache. Visitors can eat and drink in a pseudo Irish pub, a fake southwestern grill, phony tavernas, trattorias, and bodegas, or any of several mock sukiyaki houses, and noodle shops.

[9]To be fair, Banff's Saitoh furrier does cater, in Japanese, to visitors who want to take home authentic Canadiana in the form of a few dozen dead mammals. Some Banff merchants don't even bother with signage in English or French. They advertise in Japanese only.

[10]Opponents of commercialism in the parks might be surprised to learn that some year-round residents want Carmelification to continue in Banff. They understand that Banff is like a spiral of flypaper, keeping the pests away from mountain towns that are still authentic communities.

[11]They applaud ski mogul Charlie Locke for urging his season pass holders to express support for expansion of Locke's resorts at Banff and Lake Louise. "For years now the federal government has listened more to small vocal groups, some of which have a stated mission to end downhill skiing in our national parks, than to people who believe in balancing sustainable conservation and human enjoyment." Hear! Hear!

[12]They support Locke's designs on the park because they hope he will turn his attentions away from the rest of the Rockies. He is threatening, for instance, to build a "New Whistler" in southeastern British Columbia. Locke easily convinced the city of Cranbrook to extend the runways of its municipal airport to accept ski charters directly from Europe. He has the enthusiastic support of the British Columbia government and, if he succeeds, a region very pleasant to live in and visit will be converted into another luxury camp for wealthy transients, and swathes of still-healthy human and animal habitats will be sacrificed.

[13]Already, the slopes of the Columbia Valley are sprouting country clubs likely built according to blueprints picked up second-hand in Santa Barbara. Lego-style condominiums are ranged like prison blockhouses on the floodplain of the Elk River. In brawny working towns like Canal Flats and Crowsnest Pass, fears that sushi bars will displace honest saloons are as palpable as raw squid.

[14]Banff is done for. There is no sense in a rearguard action that will just disperse the war. The government has wisely chosen to sacrifice Banff altogether, in order to save the rest of the Rockies from the barbarians. I say let's stop whining about bad taste and cynical greed and erect between Wayne and Lucy Maud a statue of Sheila Copps, saviour of the Canadian Rockies.

—*David Thomas*

QUESTIONS ABOUT THE READING

Refer to the general questions on page 157 as well as these specific questions.

PURPOSE

- In your view, what does Thomas want the audience to be thinking or feeling after reading this piece?
- Does the essay succeed in making a difference with readers? If so, how?

CONTENT

- Are the causes presented here definite, probable, or possible? Explain.
- Has the author explored distant or alternative causes adequately? Explain.
- What assumptions does the author make about his audience's attitudes and awareness? Are these assumptions accurate? Explain.
- What are the main issues here? How has this essay affected your thinking about these issues?

ORGANIZATION

- What combination of opening strategies is used in the introduction?
- Are the body paragraphs arranged in an order (such as general-to-specific) that emphasizes the thesis? If so, what is that order?

STYLE

- What is the author's attitude toward his subject? Toward his audience? How do we know? What are the signals?
- Is the tone appropriate for the intended audience and purpose? Explain.

RESPONDING TO YOUR READING

Explore your reactions to Thomas's essay by using the questions on page 158. Think about how this essay has made a difference in the way you think about the status of Canada's national parks and then respond with an essay of your own that examines the causes of something that you feel strongly about.

CASE STUDY

RESPONDING TO READING

After reading Thomas's essay on the reasons why Banff has "been lost to the barbarians," and ultimately why he doesn't like Banff anymore, Sarah Lannon thinks about how much she loves paintings and decides to examine why. Because she is analyzing her intense personal experience, Sarah, like Thomas, is able to identify causes that seem definite.

In drafting and revising her essay, Sarah relies on the Guidelines for Effect-to-Cause Analysis and the Revision Checklist (pages 227 and 58.)

NOTE

Even though causal analysis is the dominant rhetorical strategy in Sarah's essay, she also relies on other strategies such as vivid narration and description, colourful illustration, and process analysis.

Title announces the topic
Opens directly with the "effect": her love of paintings.
Gives immediate cause: visual pleasure.
Gives first related cause: freedom and surprise.
Shows people talking
Vivid examples throughout help readers "visualize"
Gives second related cause: family history.
"Probably" qualifies Sarah's assertion about this probable cause
Provides clear links between effect and causes throughout
Gives extended example of her family's influence
Uses narration and description
Uses process analysis

IN LOVE WITH PAINTINGS

One of my favourite things in the world is a good piece of art work, but in particular I love paintings. I love how in some paintings the paint brush dances lightly on the canvas, spreading pinks and blues with tones of swift brush marks. And in other paintings I love how there's harsh movement with blacks and dark reds eyeing you from across the room.

In doing a painting you can let yourself free and give in to pure enjoyment. No one can tell you, "Oh, this belongs there" or "That's a terrible colour." You do what you please and hope it will turn out as you expected. Then again, you never know what to really expect when you're painting at your will. You might start painting a simple green bush and then, all of a sudden, the next thing you know it's a lavish garden with blues and greens, roses and daffodils.

Going back many many years, my family has always been in love with paintings. I probably inherited my passion from them. In my grandparents' house there are tons of paintings with sailboats in dark seas and old, foreign art. There are paintings of naked ladies and ones dating back hundreds of years. My father especially loves art work.

Just last week my parents went out and bought two paintings. The first is a rather large one, dark and rust coloured, with odd-looking brick buildings and a grey road running vertically up the middle toward a fabulous sunset. Then there are random, tiny, antique portraits of people's heads stuck here and there. At first, it seemed depressing. I took one look at it and was utterly surprised my parents had picked such a piece; it seemed so not like them. "It will grow on you," my mother assured. I, on the other hand, was skeptical. Sure enough, the more I studied it, the more I grew to appreciate its mysteries. The other, smaller painting depicts a lovely, naked woman. This one was less of a surprise; at least it suited my parents better, I thought. My house is filled with art and it's great because I can stare at the paintings and just let myself get lost in them.

<table>
<tr><td>

Thesis presents the larger meaning of this causal analysis Sarah delays this controversial thesis until she has a chance to make a persuasive case Conclusion re-emphasizes the main point

</td><td>

Paintings are essential to life because whether you're the painter or the onlooker, it's one place you can put your troubles far behind. Some paintings have deep, hidden meanings; some have light, sunny afternoons; and then there are thousands of different other types. One of my personal favourites is Degas' *Dancers,* not only because I love to dance but also because his dancers are so real I get the idea I'm standing right there with them.

I wish every house could be filled with wonderful paintings everywhere; I think this would add more smiles to people's faces.

—Sarah Lannon

</td></tr>
</table>

APPLICATION **14-5**

ESSAY PRACTICE: ANALYZING EFFECTS

In this next selection, from *Professionally Speaking* (June 2001), Phillipa Davies analyzes the effects of homework or too much homework on students and their families.

ESSAY FOR ANALYSIS AND RESPONSE

THE HOMEWORK DEBATE: WHEN IS IT JUST TOO MUCH?

[1] It's 11:40 in the morning and Jane and her mother are barricaded in their cosy kitchen for the duration. Eight-year-old Jane, seated at the table, collapses over a pile of books and papers. The math workbook, open at page 21, reads, "You have 36 sides altogether, made up of an equal number of squares and . . ."

[2] Jane lets out a sob; her shoulders heave up and down. Her mother, Sara, barely pauses as she lifts the next cookie from the baking tray to the cooling rack. They've been at it since 9:00 and Jane hasn't finished the first page.

[3] Sara and Jane wonder if they're the only ones doing homework this Saturday morning. Most kids get homework, and many fret over it. We all had homework to do as kids. But now, some educators, researchers, and parents are questioning whether some students are getting too much homework.

[4] Jane's older sister, now in Grade 5 at the same central Toronto school, is bringing home two to three hours of homework a night. "We wonder if we're just not being efficient," Sara confides, "but I finally broke down and spoke to other parents, and they are facing a similar situation. It's hard when both parents are working, and we also want to give the girls the opportunity to explore other extracurricular interests, like music or Guides. You start to wonder, where is the down time?"

[5]Jack, a seven-year-old just starting Grade 1, shares an apple fruit roll-up with his father, Mark, as they hunch over the purple and gold covered storybook. "And . . . I'll . . . puff . . . and . . . I'll . . . puff . . . and . . . I'll . . . b . . . b . . . b . . . bl . . . ." Mark deliberately bites his tongue. "Blow!" shouts Jack triumphantly. Father and son laugh happily. "I enjoy this time with Jack," says Mark, a father of three who works from home. "But sometimes it is a strain, when I have a deadline, and my wife is away on a business trip and the two older boys have projects to do. There's a lot of stress, a lot of nerves."

[6]Back in Sara's kitchen, Jane has five more pages to go. So far the family has done no groceries; the dog is wearing a track across the carpet as she paces back and forth. "I would love it if the children could be outside all day, but this just isn't possible." Sara smiles hesitantly.

GROWING ATTENTION

[7]Sara is not alone in her feeling that perhaps there are better ways for young children to spend their free time than doing homework. Over the past two years, articles in the *National Post*, *The New York Times*, and *Time Magazine* have expressed a wave of concern over homework. The *Times* reported on the Piscaway school district in New Jersey, which last fall limited the amount of homework to be sent home to 30 minutes a night for elementary school and formally discouraged the assignment of homework on weekends.

[8]No similar measures have been taken by any of the large Ontario school boards, although several have homework policies, among them, the Toronto District School Board (TDSB) and Durham District School Board. Durham's advice on homework encourages parents to have a positive attitude toward homework. "Homework is time with your child. Make it part of every day."

[9]Individual schools will often have homework policies, even if their boards do not. The Near North District School Board has nothing at board level, but many schools may have their own guidelines. The Lakehead Board of Education does not actively promote a homework policy, but among the schools in the region, Nor'wester View and Five Mile schools propose their own policies which call for no extra assigned school work to be given to students below Grade 5.

[10]Similarly, the Conseil des ecoles publiques de l'Est de l'Ontario (CEPEO) has no clear guidelines, but individual schools have in some cases strict rules regarding the completion of homework. This French board commented, however, that the issue is currently under review at the board level and new policies may apply to all schools in the board in the near future.

FOCAL POINT

[11]*The End of Homework*, published in August 2000 by Beacon Press, has become a focal point in the debate over homework. Authors John

Buell and Etta Kralovec—both teacher educators at the College of the Atlantic—captured media and popular attention, and stimulated discussion in the press by questioning the legitimacy of traditionally held views on the value of homework.

[12]As Suzanne Ziegler pointed out in her 1986 research report on homework for the Toronto Board of Education, "parental involvement in their children's schooling is strongly associated with children's achievement." But a significant amount of recent research shows no conclusive evidence that homework itself contributes to academic success at the elementary school level.

[13]Harris Cooper, professor of psychology at the University of Missouri-Columbia and one of the leading authorities in the field in North America, says that recent research confirms earlier findings. "In the upper-level elementary school grades, there was no relation between time on homework and achievement." Yet surveys show that teachers are giving more and more homework. A University of Michigan study published last year shows that while six- to nine-year olds spent 44 minutes per week on homework in 1981, in 1997, they spent over two hours.

[14]The Toronto District School Board recommends 10 to 30 minutes of homework per day most evenings for K–3. But Jane's weekly assignments, handed out on Friday, are taking her up to six hours to complete. Jack, in Grade 1, is spending at least half an hour per night reading. Clearly, not all Toronto teachers are following the TDSB guidelines.

[15]By one o'clock, Jane has brightened up a little. She pushes the blue notebook labelled "math" aside and pulls a red folder marked "spelling" from a tottering pile of books and papers. Her mother sighs quietly with relief.

Too Much to Do

[16]Some teachers say it is getting harder to stick to the recommended number of homework hours. They say they have not yet had time to adjust to the new material they are required to cover following the implementation of the new curriculum in September 1999.

[17]For Jane and other Grade 3s, new province-wide testing has added to the challenges facing teachers. Many say they are sending more work home, either to help cover the curriculum or to meet higher demands for student output under the new curriculum.

[18]Beverly Conner, a teacher at Arlington Middle School, also in Toronto, has noticed that she has been giving more homework lately. "Increased pressure and increased accountability in the school system mean that I need more product from students," she says.

[19]David Booth, a professor in the Curriculum, Teaching and Learning department at the Ontario Institute for Studies in Education at the University of Toronto (OISE/UT), also finds that the new curriculum is putting strains on the system that can result in more homework, and more importantly, homework which is not well thought out.

[20]Harris Cooper notes that parents' demands also figure in this equation. He warns that some of the concern over the increased amount of homework may be exaggerated. A U.S. poll in October 2000 showed that only 10 per cent of parents thought their kids were getting too much homework.

PARENTAL BACKLASH

[21]Cooper sees these parents as part of a vocal minority who have demanded high standards and challenges for their children to meet their own high social and economic goals. Ironically, these are often the same parents who were pushing for more homework in the past.

[22]"There is now a backlash amongst these parents who feel resentful about the amount of time that has to be spent helping children with their homework," he says.

[23]At the same time, Cooper does not dismiss the concerns over homework, especially for children who cannot get much help at home. "For disadvantaged children, (homework may) create frustrating situations that are detrimental to learning."

[24]In *The End of Homework*, Kralovec and Buell argue that homework can in fact foster social inequities. The authors stress that children do not all go home to the same environment. Some kids are greeted by enthusiastic parents with books on hand to research or enhance the topic under discussion; others go home to a negative or at best distracting situation.

DO IT AT SCHOOL

[25]Even parents with strong academic backgrounds themselves are feeling the strain when demanding jobs for both parents outside the home run up against increased demands from the school in the form of more and more homework. Buell and Kralovec have a solution. "If we all need a quiet well-lit place to study, far away from the TV, we would like to suggest that we know a perfect spot that precisely meets those requirements: the schoolhouse."

[26]Jane's 10-year-old sister, legs curled under her in the wide brown plush armchair, looks up from her book expectantly as the grandmother clock chimes 2:00. The little Border collie sets up a low persistent whine. Sara has the grilled cheese and tomato sandwiches on plates on the counter, but the kitchen table needs to be cleared. There sits Jane, her elbows on her books, pushing her fist across her face and smearing it with tear-marks.

[27]Otto Weininger, professor emeritus in the Early Childhood Education Department at OISE/UT, is concerned about the demands on children beginning earlier and earlier. "I am seeing considerable resentment amongst parents, starting with children at the Kindergarten level, over homework. This resentment can lead to conflict between parent and child, with deleterious effects on the child's long-term academic progress."

[28]David Booth also doesn't like to see the increase in the amount of homework without any clear philosophy behind it. He wants to see

homework used more effectively. Often teachers simply send home the work that has not been completed in class. "I would like to see homework be a curriculum course in schools, with clear, thoughtful objectives."

[29]He has proposed a course on homework at OISE/UT. But he warns that progress is slow. "In any of the care-giving professions, change is a delicate process." In the meantime, poorly thought-out or inappropriate homework can add to the frustrations and negative feelings that many children and their families have expressed.

[30]"Repetitive, unmeaningful practice results in nothing but negative attitudes to schools and learning. I hate homework," says Booth.

[31]At 5:00 o'clock, the homework is finished, at least for today. Jane is lying flat out on the floor rubbing her head into the dog's beige and white silken fur. The battle over homework is over. But who has won? Sara sounds carefully ambivalent. "Of course homework comes first, but we do feel as a family a little bit cheated if the weekend goes by and all we've done is clean the house and do homework," she says with a small smile. Jane looks up from the carpet; her smile mirrors her mother's. After all, tomorrow is Sunday.

—*Phillipa Davies*

Questions about the Reading

Refer to the general questions on page 157 as well as these specific questions.

CONTENT

- What assumptions does the author seem to make about her audience's attitudes and awareness? Are these assumptions accurate? Explain.
- What are the main issues here? How has this essay affected your thinking about these issues? Explain.
- Is Davies's essay credible? Are you convinced this writer knows what she is talking about? Explain.
- Is the writer arguing for definite, probable, or possible effects? Support your answer with specific examples.
- Does the essay have informative value? Explain.

ORGANIZATION

- Trace the line of reasoning from paragraph to paragraph. Is this arrangement effective in supporting Davies's causal claims? Explain.
- Identify four devices that increase coherence in this essay, and give examples of each.

STYLE

- What attitude does Davies have toward her subject? Toward her audience? How do we know? What are the signals?
- Is the tone appropriate for the audience and purpose? Explain.

RESPONDING TO YOUR READING

Explore your reactions to "The Homework Debate: When Is It Just Too Much?" by using the questions on page 158. Then respond with an essay about your own views on the homework issue.

As an alternative project, analyze the effects of a place, an event, or a relationship. You might trace the effects in your life from having a specific friend or belonging to a specific family or group. Or you might explain the effects on your family, school, or community of a tragic event (such as a suicide) or a fortunate one (say, a financial windfall). Or you might want to show how the socioeconomic atmosphere of your hometown or neighbourhood or family has affected the person you have become. Or you might explain how the weather, landscape, or geography of your area affects people's values, behaviour, and lifestyle. Or you might speculate about the effects that today's racial or gender socioeconomic divisions will have on the next generation.

Whatever the topic, be sure your discussion supports a definite viewpoint about the effects of something.

CHAPTER 15

Explaining Similarities or Differences: Comparison and Contrast

omparison examines similarities; contrast examines differences. Comparison and contrast (sometimes just called comparison) help us evaluate things or shed light on their relationship; they help us to visualize the Big Picture.

What readers of comparison and contrast want to know

- *In what significant ways are X and Y similar or alike?*
- *In what significant ways are X and Y different?*
- *Can something about X help us understand Y?*
- *In what significant ways is one preferable to the other?*

DEVELOPING A COMPARISON

Comparison offers perspective on one thing by pointing out its similarities with something else. The two items compared are of the same class: two cars, two countries, two professors. The next paragraph compares drug habits among people of all times and places to those among people of modern times:

A COMPARISON

Main point (1)

Historical similarity to modern habits (2–3)

Religious similarity to modern habits (4–5)

Modern continuation of habit (6–7)

Concluding point (8)

[1]All the natural narcotics, stimulants, relaxants, and hallucinants known to the modern botanist and pharmacologist were discovered by primitive [people] and have been in use from time immemorial. [2]One of the first things that *Homo sapiens* did with his newly developed rationality and self-consciousness was to set them to work finding out ways to bypass analytical thinking and to transcend or, in extreme cases, temporarily obliterate the isolating awareness of the self. [3]Trying all things that grew in the field or forest, they held fast to that which, in this context, seemed good—everything, that is to say, that would change the quality of consciousness, would make it different, no matter how, from everyday feeling, perceiving, and thinking. [4]Among the Hindus, rhythmic breathing and mental concentration have, to some extent, taken the place of mind-transforming drugs used elsewhere. [5]But even in the land of yoga, even among the religious and even for specifically religious purposes, *Cannabis indica* (marijuana) has been freely used to supplement the effects of spiritual exercises. [6]The habit of taking vacations from the more-or-less purgatorial world, which we have created for ourselves, is universal. [7]Moralists may denounce it; but, in the teeth of disapproving talk and repressive legislation, the habit persists, and mind-transforming drugs are everywhere available. [8]The Marxian formula, "Religion is the opium of the people," is reversible, and one can say, with even more truth, that "Opium is the religion of the people."

—Aldous Huxley

DEVELOPING A CONTRAST

A contrast is designed to point out differences between one thing and another. This next paragraph contrasts the beliefs of Satanism with those of Christianity:

A CONTRAST

Main point (1)
First difference
(2–3)

Second difference
(4)
Third difference
(5–8)

Final—and
major—difference
(9–10)

[1]The Satanic belief system, not surprisingly, is the antithesis of Christianity. [2]Their theory of the universe, their cosmology, is based upon the notion that the desired end state is a return to a pagan awareness of their humanity. [3]This is in sharp contrast to the transcendental goals of traditional Christianity. [4]The power associated with the pantheon of gods is also reversed: Satan's power is waxing (increasing); God's, if he still lives, waning. [5]The myths of the Satanic church purport to tell the true story of the rise of Christianity and the fall of paganism, and there is a reversal here too. [6]Christ is depicted as an early "con man" who tricked an anxious and powerless group of individuals into believing a lie. [7]He is typified as "pallid incompetence hanging on a tree." [8]Satanic novices are taught that early church fathers deliberately picked on those aspects of human desire that were most natural and made them sins, in order to use the inevitable transgressions as a means of controlling the populace, promising them salvation in return for obedience. [9]And finally, their substantive belief, the very delimitation of what is sacred and what is profane, is the antithesis of Christian belief. [10]The Satanist is taught to "be natural; to revel in pleasure and in self-gratification; to emphasize indulgence and power in this life."

—Edward J. Moody

DEVELOPING A COMBINED COMPARISON AND CONTRAST

A combined comparison and contrast examines similarities and differences displayed by two or more things. This next paragraph first contrasts education with training and, second, compares how each serves important needs of society:

A COMBINED COMPARISON/CONTRAST

Main point (1)

Difference of purpose (2)
How "trained"
people serve society (3–5)

Similarity of effects
(6)

[1]To understand the nature of the liberal arts college and its function in our society, it is important to understand the difference between education and training. [2]Training is intended primarily for the service of society; education is primarily for the individual. [3]Society needs doctors, lawyers, engineers, teachers to perform specific tasks necessary to its operation, just as it needs carpenters and plumbers and stenographers. [4]Training supplies the immediate and specific needs of society so that the work of the world may continue. [5]And these needs, our training centers— the professional and trade schools—fill. [6]But although education is for the improvement of the individual, it also serves society by providing a

How "educated" people serve society (7–11)

leavening of men and women of understanding, of perception and wisdom. [7]They are our intellectual leaders, the critics of our culture, the defenders of our free traditions, the instigators of our progress. [8]They serve society by examining its function, appraising its needs, and criticizing its direction. [9]They may be earning their livings by practicing one of the professions, or in pursuing a trade, or by engaging in business enterprise. [10]They may be rich or poor. [11]They may occupy positions of power and prestige, or they may be engaged in some humble employment. [12]Without them, however, society either disintegrates or else becomes an anthill.

Conclusion (12)

—*Harry Kemelman*

USING COMPARISON/CONTRAST BEYOND THE WRITING CLASSROOM

- **In other courses:** In sociology, you might assess the economic progress made by minority groups by comparing income figures from earlier decades with today's figures.

- **On the job:** You might compare the qualifications of various job applicants or the performance of various stock and bond portfolios.

- **In the community:** You might compare the voting records of two politicians or the literacy scores of local students compared to the national average.

In what other situations might comparison and contrast make a difference?

USING COMPARISON AND CONTRAST TO EXPLAIN

Referential comparison usually helps readers understand one thing in terms of another. For example, we could explain the effects of high-fat diets on heart disease and cancer by comparing disease rates in Japan (with its low-fat diet) with those in North America. To explain how new knowledge of earthquakes has affected the way engineers design buildings, we can contrast modern buildings with buildings constructed years ago.

Referential comparison also often permits us to explain a complex or abstract idea in terms of another. For example, it's easier to understand how earlier civilizations understood a term like "honour" if we contrast their concept with our own today.

USING COMPARISON AND CONTRAST TO MAKE A POINT

Like other development strategies, comparison and contrast can also support persuasion. For example, it is often used in evaluation, in which we judge the merits of something by measuring it in relationship to something else.

We might compare two (or more) cars, computers, political candidates, college courses, or careers to argue that one is better. In Chapter 1 (pages 13–15), Shirley Haley contrasts her parents' lifestyle with the one she prefers for herself.

Comparisons can support other kinds of arguments as well. Huxley's comparison of past and present drug habits, for example (page 241), supports the thesis that any habit so long entrenched will be hard to eliminate. Kemelman's analysis of the differences and similarities between training and education (page 242) supports his claim that the liberal arts university has an important function in our society.

Do you think that Moody's contrast of Christians and Satanists (page 242) also supports an implied argument, or is it mainly referential? Explain.

As always, the evidence with which you support your content, your organizational skills, and your command of style are what make your argumentative comparisons persuasive.

A SPECIAL KIND OF COMPARISON: ANALOGY

Ordinary comparison shows similarities between two things of the same class (two teachers, two styles of dress, two political philosophies). *Analogy,* on the other hand, shows similarities between two things of *different classes* (writing and skiing, university registration and a merry-go-round, a residence room and a junkyard). Analogy answers the reader's question:

Can you explain X by comparing it to something I already know?

Analogies are useful in explaining something abstract, complex, or unfamiliar, as long as the easier subject is broadly familiar to readers. This next analogy helps clarify a complex subject (taking care of one's body) by comparing it to something more familiar (farming).

ANALOGY

If you want your farm to flourish, you've got to keep it irrigated; the same goes for skin. Nothing looks good when it's dull and cracked. First, shower (you don't want to smell like a barnyard), then to keep that water level up, moisturize, moisturize, moisturize.

—*Jen Nessel*

APPLICATION 15-1

PARAGRAPH WARM-UP: COMPARISON/CONTRAST

Using comparison or contrast (or both), write a paragraph discussing the likenesses or differences between two people, animals, attitudes, activities, places, or things. Identify clearly the situation, the audience, and your purpose. Then classify your paragraph: does it primarily inform, or does it make a point? Here are some possible subjects:

two places I know well
two memorable teaching styles (good or bad)
two similar consumer items
two pets I've had
the benefits of two kinds of exercise

GUIDELINES FOR COMPARISON AND CONTRAST

1. *Compare or contrast items in the same class.* Compare dogs and cats, but not dogs and trees; men and women, but not women and bicycles. Otherwise you have no logical basis for comparison. If one item is less familiar than the other, define it immediately, as Moody does with Satanism.

2. *Rest the comparison on a clear and definite basis: costs, uses, benefits/ drawbacks, appearance, results.* Huxley compares people of all times for their drug habits; Moody compares Satanism and Christianity for their primary beliefs; Kemelman compares education and training by their function in our society. In evaluating the merits of competing items, identify your specific criteria and rank them in order of importance. For example, Kemelman asserts that training supplies society's "immediate needs," but education supplies "the instigators of our progress" and the leadership required for cultural survival.

3. *Establish your credibility for evaluating items.* Instead of merely pointing out similarities and differences (as in Moody), comparisons often evaluate competing items. (See pages 251–253.)

Answer the reader's implied question "How do you know X is better than Y?" by briefly describing your experience with this issue.

4. *Give both items balanced treatment.* Both Moody and Kemelman give roughly equal space to each item. In Huxley's paragraph, the other item in the comparison, modern drug use habits, is only briefly mentioned, but readers can infer its place in the discussion from their own general knowledge. Huxley, then, offers an implied comparison. Points discussed for one item also are discussed (or implied) for the other, generally in the same order.

5. *Support and clarify the comparison or contrast through credible examples.* Use research if necessary, for examples that readers can visualize.

6. *Follow either a block pattern or a point-by-point pattern.* In the block pattern, first one item is discussed fully, then the next, as in Kemelman: "trained" people in the first block; "educated" people in the second. Choose a block pattern when the overall picture is more important than the individual points.

GUIDELINES FOR COMPARISON AND CONTRAST (continued)

In the point-by-point pattern, one point about both items is discussed, then the next point, and so on, as in Moody: the first difference between Satanism and Christianity is in their respective cosmologies; the second is in their view of God's power; the third, in their myths about the rise of Christianity, and so on. Choose a point-by-point pattern when specific points might be hard to remember unless placed side by side.

Block pattern	Point-by-point pattern

Item A
  first point
  second point
  third point, etc.
	First point of A/first
	point of B, etc.

Block pattern	Point-by-point pattern

Item B
  first point
  second point
  third point, etc.
	Second point of A/
	second point of B, etc.

7. *Order your points for greatest emphasis.* Try ordering your points from least-to-most important, dramatic, useful, or reasonable. Placing the most striking point last gives it greatest emphasis.

8. *In an evaluative comparison, offer your final judgment.* Base your judgment squarely on the evidence presented.

APPLICATION 15-2

PARAGRAPH WARM-UP: ANALOGY

Develop a paragraph explaining something abstract, complex, or unfamiliar by comparing it to something concrete, simple, or familiar. ("Writing is like . . . "; "Love is like . . . "; "Osmosis works like . . . "). Identify a specific purpose or audience. Do you have an informative or a persuasive goal?

APPLICATION 15-3

Computer Application: Many schools now have writing centres online. These centres often have exercises or tip sheets you can browse or download. Some even have opportunities for collaboration and consultation via e-mail or "chat rooms." Do a Web search and compare and contrast two online writing centres, assessing the quality of the services and the information provided.

APPLICATION 15-4

Computer Application: Compare three popular Internet search engines on the basis of specific criteria such as the following:

- search page (interface) is easy to use
- searches rapidly
- categories are well organized and easy to browse
- offers customizable features for finding of information
- offers good navigational aids
- offers good Help, FAQ, and Search Tips pages
- lists a large index of sites
- ratings system identifies quality sites
- site listings are up-to-date
- searches are easy to limit by topic or user
- images are easy to download and waste no screen space
- supports advanced searches using Boolean operators (see page 342)

Be sure to specify the criteria you have chosen.

SAMPLE SEARCH ENGINES:

Alta Vista **www.altavista.com**

The Argus Clearinghouse **www.clearinghouse.net**

Ask Jeeves **www.askjeeves.com**

Excite **www.excite.com**

Google **www.google.ca**

HotBot **www.hotbot.com**

Lycos **www.lycos.com**

Savvy Search **www.savvysearch.com**

APPLICATION 15-5

GENDER DIFFERENCES

Collaborative Project: Recent research on ways men and women communicate in meetings indicates a definite gender gap. Communication specialist Kathleen Kelley-Reardon offers this assessment of gender differences in group communication:

> Women and men operate according to communication rules for their gender, what experts call "gender codes." They learn, for example, to show gratitude, ask for help, take control, and express emotion, deference, and commitment in different ways. (88–89)

Professor Kelley-Reardon describes specific elements of a female gender code: Women are more likely than men to take as much time as needed to explore an issue, build consensus and relationships among members, use tact in expressing views, use care in choosing their words, consider the listener's feelings, speak softly, allow interruptions, make requests instead of giving commands ("Could I have the report by Friday?" versus "Have this ready by Friday"), preface assertions in ways that avoid offending ("I don't want to seem disagreeable here, but . . . ").

Divide into small groups of mixed genders and complete the following tasks to test the hypothesis that women and men communicate differently.

Each group member prepares the following brief messages—without consulting with other members.

- A thank you note to a friend who has done you a favour.
- A note asking a friend for help with a problem or project.
- A note asking a collaborative peer to be more cooperative or to stop interrupting or complaining.
- A note expressing impatience, frustration, confusion, or satisfaction to members of your group.
- A note offering support to a good friend who is depressed.
- A note to a new student, welcoming this person to the residence.
- A request for a higher mark, based on your hard work.
- The collaborative meeting is out of hand, so you decide to take control. Write out what you would say.
- Some members of your group are dragging their feet on a project. Write out what you would say.

As a group, compare messages, draw conclusions, and appoint one member to present the findings to the class.

APPLICATION 15-6

ESSAY PRACTICE

The writer in this next selection reflects on her search for a rational conclusion about a volatile issue: she measures her personal reasons for supporting abortion rights against her reasons for opposing them. As you read, think about the types of comparisons presented and how you might respond with comparisons of your own.

ESSAY FOR ANALYSIS AND RESPONSE

ABORTION IS TOO COMPLEX TO FEEL ALL ONE WAY ABOUT

It was always the look on their faces that told me first. I was the freshman dormitory counselor and they were the freshmen at a women's college where everyone was smart. One of them could come into my room, a golden girl, a valedictorian, an 800 verbal score on the SATs, and her eyes would be empty, seeing only a busted future, the devastation of her life as she knew it. She had failed biology, messed up the math; she was pregnant.

That was when I became pro-choice.

It was the look in his eyes that I will always remember, too. They were as black as the bottom of a well, and in them for a few minutes I thought I saw myself the way I had always wished to be—clear, simple, elemental, at peace. My child looked at me and I looked back at him in the delivery room, and I realized that out of a sea of infinite possibilities it had come down to this: a specific person born on the hottest day of the year, conceived on a Christmas Eve, made by his father and me miraculously from scratch.

Once I believed that there was a little blob of formless protoplasm in there and a gynecologist went after it with a surgical instrument, and that was that. Then I got pregnant myself—eagerly, intentionally, by the right man, at the right time—and I began to doubt. My abdomen still flat, my stomach roiling with morning sickness, I felt not that I had protoplasm inside but instead a complete human being in miniature to whom I could talk, sing, make promises. Neither of these views was accurate; instead, I think, the reality is something in the middle. And there is where I find myself now, in the middle, hating the idea of abortions, hating the idea of having them outlawed.

For I know it is the right thing in some times and places. I remember sitting in a shabby clinic far uptown with one of those freshmen, only three months after the Supreme Court had made what we were doing possible, and watching with wonder as the lovely first love she had had with a nice boy unraveled over the space of an hour as they waited for her to be called, degenerated into sniping and silences. I remember a year or two later seeing them pass on campus and not even acknowledge one another because their conjoining had caused them so much pain, and I shuddered to think of them married, with a small psyche in their unready and unwilling hands.

I've met fourteen-year-olds who were pregnant and said they could not have abortions because of their religion, and I see in their eyes the shadows of twenty-two-year-olds I've talked to who lost their kids to foster care because they hit them or used drugs or simply had no money for food and shelter. I read not long ago about a teenager who said she meant to have an abortion but she spent the money on clothes instead; now she has a baby who turns out to be a lot more trouble than a toy. The people who hand out those execrable little pictures of dismembered fetuses at abortion clinics seem to forget the extraordinary pain children may endure after they are born when they are unwanted, even hated or simply tolerated.

I believe that in a contest between the living and the almost living, the latter must, if necessary, give way to the will of the former. That is what the fetus is to me, the almost living. Yet these questions began to plague me—and, I've discovered, a good many other women—after I became pregnant. But they became even more acute after I had my second child, mainly because he is so different from his brother. On two random nights eighteen months apart the same two people managed to conceive, and on one occasion the tumult within turned itself into a curly-haired brunet with merry black eyes who walked and talked late and loved the whole world, and on another it became a blond with hazel Asian eyes and a pug nose who tried to conquer the world almost as soon as he entered it.

If we were to have an abortion next time for some reason or another, which infinite possibility becomes, not a reality, but a nullity? The girl with the blue eyes? The improbable redhead? The natural athlete? The thinker? My husband, ever at the heart of the matter, put it another way. Knowing that he is finding two children somewhat more overwhelming than he expected, I asked if he would want me to have an abortion if I accidentally became pregnant again right away. "And waste a perfectly good human being?" he said.

Coming to this quandary has been difficult for me. In fact, I believe the issue of abortion is difficult for all thoughtful people. I don't know anyone who has had an abortion who has not been haunted by it. If there is one thing I find intolerable about most of the so-called right-to-lifers, it is that they try to portray abortion rights as something that feminists thought up on a slow Saturday over a light lunch. That is nonsense. I also know that some people who support abortion rights are most comfortable with a monolithic position because it seems the strongest front against the smug and sometimes violent opposition.

But I don't feel all one way about abortion anymore, and I don't think it serves a just cause to pretend that many of us do. For years I believed that a woman's right to choose was absolute, but now I wonder. Do I, with a stable home and marriage and sufficient stamina and money, have the right to choose abortion because a pregnancy is inconvenient right now? Legally I do have the right; legally I want always to have that right. It is the morality of exercising it under those circumstances that makes me wonder.

Technology has foiled us. The second trimester has become a time of resurrection: a fetus at six months can be one woman's late abortion, another's premature, viable child. Photographers now have film of embryos the size of a grape, oddly human, flexing their fingers, sucking their thumbs. Women have amniocentesis to find out whether they are carrying a child with birth defects that they may choose to abort. Before the procedure, they must have a sonogram, one of those fuzzy black-and-white photos like a love song heard through static on the radio, which shows someone is in there.

I have taped on my VCR a public-television program in which somehow, inexplicably, a film is shown of a fetus in utero scratching its face, seemingly putting up a tiny hand to shield itself from the camera's eye. It would make a potent weapon in the arsenal of the antiabortionists. I grow sentimental about it as it floats in the salt water, part fish, part human being. It is almost living, but not quite. It has almost turned my heart around, but not quite turned my head.

—Anna Quindlen

QUESTIONS ABOUT THE READING

PURPOSE

- In addition to comparison/contrast, what other development strategies support the purpose of this essay?
- Does the essay succeed in making a difference with readers? If so, how?

CONTENT

- In your own words, restate the point of the comparison in a complete sentence.
- Does Quindlen establish credibility for making her evaluations? If so, how?

ORGANIZATION

- Does this comparison follow a block pattern, a point-by-point pattern, or a combination? Comment on the effectiveness of the pattern.
- Do both sides of the issue receive balanced treatment? Explain.
- Does Quindlen order her points for greatest emphasis? Explain.
- Does she offer a final judgment? If so, is it based convincingly on the evidence she presents?

STYLE

- Is the tone appropriate for the audience and purpose? Explain.

RESPONDING TO YOUR READING

Explore your reactions to Anna Quindlen's essay by using the questions on page 158. Then respond with an essay, *based on your own experience or observations*, that evaluates competing positions on some controversial issue. Try to arrive at a reasonable conclusion about which position seems preferable. Be sure your essay supports a clear and definite thesis. If you select some highly emotional issue, such as euthanasia, school prayer, or nationwide standards for high school graduation, be sure to avoid preaching. Let your examples convey your point instead, as does Quindlen.

CASE STUDY

RESPONDING TO READING

After reading and analyzing Quindlen's essay, John Manning decides to evaluate both sides of an issue very familiar to him: the pros and cons of online education.

John presents an implied comparison here, focusing on the benefits and drawbacks of an online "classroom," which is the less familiar item in this comparison. He can reasonably expect readers to visualize for themselves the familiar, traditional classroom.

NOTE	*Even though comparison/contrast is the dominant rhetorical strategy in John's essay, other strategies, such as narration, illustration, and causal analysis, play supporting roles.*

Title gives an immediate forecast Defines the unfamiliar item in the comparison

IS ONLINE EDUCATION TAKING US ANYWHERE?

As a growing alternative to the traditional classroom, we hear more and more about Internet-based learning, variously known as "cybereducation," "online education," and "virtual education." In this model, each student's computer is "wired" to an instructor's Web site at which course material and assignments are transmitted, posted, and discussed electronically. "Virtual universities" even offer entire degrees online. After taking two of these courses, I asked myself this question: Compared with a physical classroom setting, what is gained and lost in a "virtual" classroom? *While the actual benefits are undeniable, the drawbacks or potential consequences also are worth considering.*

Writer establishes his credibility on this topic Thesis announces the basis for comparison: benefits and drawbacks. Point-by-point comparison of benefits and drawbacks First benefit (or criterion): access and convenience. Next benefit: economy and efficiency.

In terms of access and convenience, online education definitely holds the winning edge. This is especially true in Canada and Australia or parts of the American West in which relatively small populations are scattered thinly over a vast land mass. Students working online from any location now benefit from an endless variety of courses that require no travel whatsoever. Even though I live in a suburb, I personally enjoyed the luxury of commuting by computer.

Online education also is more economical and efficient than traditional schooling. The "school" itself has no need to maintain a physical structure with classrooms, faculty offices, and other expensive facilities. In the face of rising tuitions and room and board costs, the potential savings passed along to students are tremendous. Also students can participate and do most of their work at their convenience—without the time constraints of regularly scheduled classes. With work and family commitments in addition to my student responsibilities, I found this aspect especially appealing.

Major benefit: student interest. Uses causal analysis

Gives vivid examples throughout

In terms of student interest, online courses stimulate concentration and interactivity on the student's part. Motivated students can focus their energies on the computer screen, in the relative peace and quiet of their own room, without the usual distractions in an actual classroom. Shy students might feel more comfortable about interacting in a chatroom atmosphere. Also, the Web's graphics capabilities are more dynamic than the static pages of a textbook—in a medium that today's college-age students have grown up with (video games, e-mail, net surfing, and so on). I found the graphics especially useful in my online course, Introduction to Statistics.

First drawback: lack of interpersonal relations.

Gives equal attention to "benefits" and "drawbacks"— with criteria for each ranked in order of increasing importance.

Despite all these benefits, does the online learning experience itself carry interpersonal drawbacks? I personally missed the "human element" of getting to know my teachers, and having an advisor to turn to whenever some problem arises. I also missed face-to-face discussions. It seems easier to absorb what others are saying from hearing their actual voice and seeing their faces rather than reading their words from a computer screen. (Think of a poetry reading, for example.) For me, an inspiring lecture or a heated class discussion can only happen "in person."

Writer uses narrative examples throughout to reinforce his credibility. Next drawback: practical problems.

I also worry about some practical drawbacks. For instance, online courses demand a strong desire to learn and the self-discipline and skills—and confidence—to manage one's education on one's own. I wonder how many students are ready to do this. (It was extremely hard for me.) Also, some people could abuse the system. For example, how can anyone know for sure whether other people are doing a student's work or whether unqualified students are walking away with degrees based on work others have done for them? And what about studying a language online—how does one learn pronunciation without live conversation?

Major drawback: social costs.

My biggest concern is with the potential social costs of online education. While online dollar costs for access are low, those for training and equipment are high—in terms of fairly high-level computer skills and expensive hardware. For example, it takes nearly a top-of-the-line computer to run Web-browsing software—a computer that soon becomes obsolete. This investment in skills and equipment automatically rules out those people who can't afford it. Once again, it seems that the affluent will get another leg up based on this technology while the have-nots stay down in the dark.

Conclusion refocuses on the main question. Sums up the comparison.

All in all, do the benefits of online courses outweigh the drawbacks? On the plus side, the convenience, price, and dynamics of online education can't be beat. On the minus side, for people who come to school looking for human contact, transacting exclusively online seems awfully impersonal. Also, it's hard keeping up the motivation and self-discipline needed to do all one's work online. Finally, we have to consider the potential for creating an educated elite and even greater social division between the haves and have-nots. And so, while online education seems a powerful *supplement* to live classrooms, it's scary to think of it as a complete *substitute.*

Closes with a judgment based on the evidence

—*John Manning*

OPTIONS FOR ESSAY WRITING

1. If you had your high school years to relive, what would you do differently?

2. During your years in school you've had much experience with both good teaching and bad. Based on your experiences, what special qualities are necessary for good teaching? Use a series of contrasts to make your point.

Work Cited

Kelley-Reardon, Kathleen. *They Don't Get It, Do They?: Communication in the Workplace—Closing the Gap Between Women and Men.* Boston: Little, 1995.

CHAPTER 16

Explaining the Exact Meaning: Definition

All successful writing shares one feature—clarity. Clear writing begins with clear thinking; clear thinking begins with an understanding of what all the terms mean. Therefore, clear writing depends on definitions that both reader and writer understand.

What readers of definition want to know

- *What is it?*
- *What is its dictionary meaning?*
- *What personal meaning(s) does it suggest?*

Words can signify two kinds of meaning: *denotative* and *connotative*. Denotations—the meanings in a dictionary—usually appear in referential writing. A word's denotation means the same thing to everyone. *Apple* denotes the firm, rounded, edible fruit of the apple tree.

But words have connotations as well, overtones or suggestions beyond their dictionary meanings. A word can have different connotations for different people. Thus, *apple* might connote Adam and Eve, apple pie, Johnny Appleseed, apple polisher, or good health. These meanings play an important part in persuasive writing, as writers use the possible meanings audiences find in words to elicit their emotions or to share a viewpoint.

USING DENOTATIVE DEFINITIONS TO EXPLAIN

Denotative definitions either explain a term that is specialized or unfamiliar to your readers or convey your exact definition of a word that has more than one meaning.

Most fields have specialized terms. Engineers talk about *pre-stressed concrete, tolerances,* or *trusses;* psychologists refer to *sociopathic behaviour* or *paranoia;* lawyers discuss *liens, easements,* and *escrow accounts.* For readers outside the field, these terms must be defined.

Sometimes a term will be unfamiliar to some readers because it is new or no longer in use (*future shock, meltdown,* and *uptalk*) or a slang word (*bad, diss, freak*).

Some readers, though, are unaware that more familiar terms such as *guarantee, disability, lease,* or *consent* take on very specialized meanings in some contexts. What *consent* means in one situation is not necessarily what it means in another. Denotative definition then becomes crucial if all parties are to understand.

This next definition explains the meaning of a slang term no longer in use.

A DENOTATIVE DEFINITION

Main point (1)

Contrast and division (2)

[1]During my teen years I never left the house on my Saturday night dates without my mother slipping me a few extra dollars—Mad Money, it was called. [2]I'll explain what it was for the benefit of the new generation in which people just sleep with each other: the fellow was supposed to bring me home, lead me safely through the asphalt jungle, protect me

Division (3)

from slithering snakes, rapists, and the like. [3]But my mother and I knew that young men were apt to drink too much, to slosh down so many rye-and-gingers that some hero might well lead me in front of an oncoming bus, smash his daddy's car into Tiffany's window, or, less gallantly, throw up on my dress. [4]Mad Money was for getting home on your own, no matter what form of insanity your date happened to evidence. [5]Mad Money was also a wallflower's rope ladder; if a guy you came with suddenly fancied someone else, you didn't have to stay there and suffer; you could go home.

Cause-effect (sentence definition) (4)
Cause-effect as analogy (5)

—Anne Roiphe

USING CONNOTATIVE DEFINITIONS TO MAKE A POINT

A denotative definition cannot communicate the personal or special meaning a writer may intend. But connotative definitions explain terms that hold personal meanings for the writer.

In the next paragraph, the denotative definition of house (a structure serving as a dwelling) is replaced by a more personal, artistic, and spiritual definition:

A CONNOTATIVE DEFINITION

Main Point (1)
Analogies (2–4)

[1]What is a house? [2]A house is a human circumstance in Nature, like a tree or the rocks of the hills; a good house is a technical performance where form and function are made one; a house is integral to its site, a grace, not a disgrace, to its environment, suited to elevate the life of its individual inhabitants; a house is therefore integral with the nature of the methods and materials used to build it. [3]A house to be a good home has throughout what is most needed in American life today—integrity. [4]Integrity, once there, enables those who live in that house to take spiritual root and grow.

—Frank Lloyd Wright

Connotative definition is especially useful when we want people to accept a particular definition of a term that carries multiple, conflicting meanings (*freedom, love, patriotism*, or the like), and especially when the meaning we advocate is unconventional or controversial.

Unless you are sure that readers know the exact or special meaning you intend, always define a term the first time you use it.

CHOOSING THE LEVEL OF DETAIL IN A DEFINITION

How much detail will readers need to understand a term or a concept? Can you use a synonym (a term with a similar meaning)? Will you need a sentence, a paragraph—or an essay?

Parenthetical Definition

Often, you can clarify the meaning of an unfamiliar word by using a more familiar synonym or a clarifying phrase:

Parenthetical
definitions

To **waffle** means to be evasive and misleading.

The **leaching field** (sieve-like drainage area) requires 40 centimetres of crushed stone.

NOTE   *Be sure that the synonym clarifies your meaning instead of obscuring it.*

Don't say:

A tumour is a neoplasm.

Do say:

A tumour is a growth of cells that occurs independently of surrounding tissue and serves no useful function.

Sentence Definition

More complex terms may require a sentence definition (which may be stated in more than one sentence). These definitions follow a fixed pattern: (1) the name of the item to be defined, (2) the class to which the item belongs, and (3) the features that differentiate the item from all others in its class.

Elements of
sentence definitions

Term	Class	Distinguishing features
carburetor	a mixing device	in gasoline engines that blends air and fuel into a vapour for combustion with the cylinders
diabetes	a metabolic disease	caused by a disorder of the pituitary or pancreas and characterized by excessive urination, persistent thirst, and inability to metabolize sugar
brief	a legal document	containing all the facts and points of law pertinent to a case and filed by a lawyer before the case is argued in court
stress	an applied force	that strains or deforms a body

These elements are combined into one or more complete sentences:

A complete
sentence definition

Diabetes is a metabolic disease caused by a disorder of the pituitary or pancreas and characterized by excessive urination, persistent thirst, and inability to metabolize sugar.

Sentence definition is especially useful if you need to stipulate your precise definition for a term that has several possible meanings. For example, *qualified buyer* can have different meanings for different readers in construction, banking, or real estate.

Expanded Definition

The sentence definition of *carburetor* on page 257 is adequate for a general reader who simply needs to know what a carburetor is. An instruction manual for mechanics, however, would define *carburetor* in much greater detail; these readers need to know how a carburetor works, how it is made, what conditions cause it to operate correctly, and so on.

Your choice of parenthetical, sentence, or expanded definition depends on the amount of information your readers need. Consider the two examples that follow.

A SENTENCE DEFINITION

It [paranoia] refers to a psychosis based on a delusionary premise of self-referred persecution or grandeur (e.g., "The Knights of Columbus control the world and are out to get me"), and supported by a complex, rigorously logical system that interprets all or nearly all sense impressions as evidence for that premise.

This definition is part of an article published in *Harper's*, a magazine whose general readership will require a more detailed definition of this specialized term. The expanded version below uses several explanatory strategies.

EXPANDED DEFINITION OF A SPECIALIZED TERM

Main point (1)
Sentence definition (2)

[1]Paranoia is a word on everyone's lips, but only among mental-health professionals has it acquired a tolerably specific meaning. [2]It refers to a psychosis based on a delusionary premise of self-referred persecution or grandeur (e.g., "The Knights of Columbus control the world and are out to get me"), and supported by a complex, rigorously logical system that interprets all or nearly all sense impressions as evidence for that premise.

Effect-cause analysis (3)
Process analysis (4)

[3]The traditional psychiatric view is that paranoia is an extreme measure for the defense of the integrity of the personality against annihilating guilt. [4]The paranoid (so goes the theory) thrusts his guilt outside himself by denying his hostile or erotic impulses and projecting them onto other people or onto the whole universe.

Cause-effect analysis (5–7)

[5]Disintegration is avoided, but at high cost; the paranoid view of reality can make everyday life terrifying and social intercourse problematical. [6]And paranoia is tiring. [7]It requires exhausting mental effort to construct trains of thought demonstrating that random events or details "prove" a wholly unconnected premise.

Contrast (8)

[8]Some paranoids hallucinate, but hallucination is by no means obligatory; paranoia is an interpretive, not a perceptual, dysfunction.

—Hendrik Hertzberg and David C. K. McClelland

General readers are much more likely to understand this expanded definition than the sentence definition alone.

As we have seen in earlier chapters, synonyms and sentence definitions are part of most writing. But notice in turn how various development strategies from earlier chapters are employed in an expanded definition.

The expanded definition on page 260 from *Words First: An Evolving Terminology Relating to Aboriginal Peoples in Canada* establishes terminology and usage for the term "Indian" as preferred by Indian and Northern Affairs Canada.

GUIDELINES FOR DEFINITION

1. *Decide on the level of detail.* Definitions vary greatly in length and detail, from a few words in parentheses to a complete essay. How much does this audience need in order to follow your explanation or grasp your point?

2. *Classify the term precisely.* The narrower your class, the clearer your meaning. *Stress* is classified as an applied force; to say that stress "is what . . ." or "takes place when . . ." fails to reflect a specific classification. Diabetes is precisely classified as a *metabolic disease*, not as a *medical term*.

3. *Differentiate the term accurately.* If the distinguishing features are too broad, they will apply to more than this one item. A definition of *brief* as a "legal document used in court" fails to differentiate brief from all other legal documents (*wills, affidavits*, and the like).

4. *Avoid circular definitions.* Do not repeat, as part of the distinguishing feature, the word you are defining. "Stress is an applied force that places stress on a body" is a circular definition.

5. *Expand your definition selectively.* Begin with a sentence definition and select from a combination of the following development strategies: description/narration; illustration; division/classification; process analysis, cause/effect analysis; and comparison/contrast.

6. *Use negation to show what a term does not mean.* For example:

   Raw data is not "information"; data only becomes information after it has been evaluated, interpreted, and applied.

7. *Explain the term's etymology (its origin).* For example:

   "Biological control" of insects is derived from the Greek "bio," meaning life or living organism, and the Latin "contra," meaning against or opposite.

   Biological control, then, is the use of living organisms against insects. Check your college dictionary or, preferably, *The Oxford English Dictionary* (or its Web site).

EXPANDED DEFINITION OF A FAMILIAR TERM WITH A SPECIAL MEANING

The term *Indian* collectively describes all the Indigenous people in Canada who are not Inuit or Metis. Indian peoples are one of three recognized as Aboriginal in the *Constitution Act, 1982*. It specifies that Aboriginal people in Canada consist of the Indian, Inuit, and Metis. There are three categories of Indians in Canada: Status Indians, Non-Status Indians, and Treaty Indians. Status Indians are people who are entitled to have their names included on the Indian Register, an official list maintained by the federal government. Certain criteria determine who can be registered as a Status Indian. Only Status Indians are recognized as Indians under the *Indian Act*, which defines an Indian as "person who, pursuant to this Act, is registered as an Indian or is entitled to be registered as an Indian." Status Indians are entitled to certain rights and benefits under the law. Non-status Indians are people who consider themselves to be Indians or members of a First Nation but whom the Government of Canada does not recognize as Indians under the *Indian Act*, either because they are unable to prove their status or have lost their status rights. Many Indian people in Canada, especially women, lost their Indian rights through discriminatory practices in the past. Non-status Indians are not entitled to the same rights and benefits available to Status Indians. A Treaty Indian is a Status Indian who signed a treaty with the Crown. The term "Indian" is considered to be outdated by many people who prefer the term "First Nation."

This definition is designed to answer one question: *What is the difference between a Status Indian, a Non-Status Indian, and a Treaty Indian?*

NOTE *Because they are designed to draw readers into the writer's complex, private associations, connotative definitions almost always call for expanded treatment.*

APPLICATION 16-1

Sentence definitions require precise classification and detailed differentiation. Is each of these definitions adequate for a general reader? Rewrite those that seem inadequate. If necessary, consult dictionaries and specialized encyclopedias.

1. A bicycle is a vehicle with two wheels.
2. A transistor is a device used in transistorized electronic equipment.
3. Surfing is when one rides a wave to shore while standing on a board specifically designed for buoyancy and balance.
4. Mace is a chemical aerosol spray used by the police.
5. A Geiger counter measures radioactivity.
6. A cactus is a succulent.

7. In law, an indictment is a criminal charge against a defendant.

8. Friction is a force between two bodies.

9. Hypoglycemia is a medical term.

10. A computer is a machine that handles information with amazing speed.

APPLICATION 16-2

PARAGRAPH WARM-UP: DENOTATIVE DEFINITION THAT EXPLAINS

Using denotative definition, write a paragraph explaining the meaning of a term that is specialized, new, or otherwise unfamiliar to your reader. List in the margin the strategies for expansion you've used. Begin with a formal sentence definition (term—class—differentiation). Select a term from one of the lists below, from your major (defined for a nonmajor), or from your daily conversation with peers (defined for an elderly person). Identify clearly the situation, the audience, and your purpose.

Specialized terms	Slang terms
summons	jock
generator	Yuppie
dew point	nerd
capitalism	geek
economic recession	sweet
microprocessor	to break
T-square	awesome

APPLICATION 16-3

PARAGRAPH WARM-UP: CONNOTATIVE DEFINITION THAT MAKES A POINT

Using connotative definition, write a paragraph explaining the special meaning or associations that a term holds for you. Select a term from the list below, or provide your own. List in the margin the expansion strategies you've used. Identify clearly the situation, the audience, and your purpose.

patriotism	education	freedom
trust	marriage	courage
friendship	God	peace
progress	guilt	morality
beauty	the perfect date	happiness
adult	sex appeal	fear

APPLICATION **16-4**

 Computer Application: Consult a computer manual, a computer publication, or a newsgroup for computer enthusiasts. Find at least five technical terms that you—and probably most of your classmates—aren't familiar with or don't fully understand. Research these terms and then, for your classmates, write both sentence and expanded definitions for two of them. Some possibilities: FTP, MOO, MUD, IRC, HTML, memory bus, firewall, RISC, LAN, CGI, Javascript.

APPLICATION **16-5**

Compare two Internet dictionaries on the basis of specific criteria such as the following:

- search page (interface) is easy to use
- searches rapidly
- offers links to other dictionaries and language resources
- provides good navigational aids
- offers good Help, FAQ, and Search Tips pages
- entries are easy to browse

Be sure to specify the criteria you have chosen.

SAMPLE DICTIONARIES:

Dictionary.com **www.dictionary.com**

WWWebster Dictionary **www.m-w.com/netdict.htm**

Encyberpedia Dictionary and Glossary
www.encyberpedia.com/ glossary.htm

Wordsmyth English Dictionary-Thesaurus **www.wordsmyth.net**

APPLICATION **16-6**

ESSAY PRACTICE

In this next selection from *Canadian Geographic*, Briony Penn offers a connotative definition of Saltspring Island so that her audience understands what the island means to her. As you read, identify the various development strategies used to expand this definition.

ESSAY FOR ANALYSIS AND RESPONSE

GREEN WINTERS ON THE SALISH SEA
[1]On Saltspring Island, snow falls mostly in front of the word berry—snowberry, the lacy-stemmed bush festooned with the only globules of

white in our forests. We have less than one word for snow—slush. It is an occasional word that drips into our conversations when a slurry of white porridge slides off the leathery leaves of the arbutus.

[2]I live in a place that has never joined the North American Plate. Around 130 million years ago, a large chunk of land called Wrangellia crashed into North America after its long wander from the South Pacific. A shallow sea flooded between the continent and Wrangellia, and I live on an island in the middle between Vancouver Island and the British Columbia coast, protected from the buffeting of the Pacific and the tyranny of the continental winter. I have never learned to skate, and I didn't know who "The Rocket" was. Plans for an ice rink on the island are always defeated, and I don't own a toque. As the snow swirls over the rest of Canada, reinforcing the culture of battling the elements, I dream up 101 words for green.

[3]My great-granny, like me, was an errant artist who painted watercolours of this island. She wrote notes on her paintings to get the right greens. "For arbutus leaves, mix burnt umber with tea and cobalt blue." That's Saltspring in a clamshell: everyone is an artist; we make do with what is at hand; we drink a lot of tea. And in November, when you paint the landscape, the greens are at their best: lichen green, Douglas fir green, seaweed green, red cedar green, swordfern green, electrified cattail moss green.

[4]Geography books say we are the Mediterranean-of-the-West: mild wet winters, dry hot summers. That's Saltspring in a butter clamshell. Everything is named after something far away—Spanish midshipmen's hometowns, English captains' mistresses or mad German kaisers who never pondered Garry oak green. Kaiser Wilhelm I drew a line on a map and divided the sea, in front of my island, to settle a dispute between the British and the Americans. We named the Canadian half the Strait of Georgia, after another king, who was far from straight. I've joined a cross-border campaign to nominate Salish Sea as the single official name. It is a way to honour the Salish-speaking people who discovered, over thousands of years, that political boundaries are powerless to control such things as orcas, oystercatchers, germs, draft dodgers, hummingbirds, herring, currents, tourists, pollution, and continental drift.

[5]My friends who live ferry-rides away share further obsessions about this place. Every winter, we wage campaigns to save the herring—the cornerstone of sea life. Visitors think that we are a bit eccentric, enduring slush, ferries, and border crossings to save a small, greasy fish from corporate greed. That's Saltspring in a horse clamshell: there's time to be eccentric and fight causes, because you don't have 10 months of 101 types of snow to survive. As far as striking alliances around the sea to defend things, people have been doing that since the last ice left 9,000 years ago. There are mad kings in every generation.

[6]Also since the ice left, people have been calling November the "Shaking Time." Southeasterlies shake the huge leaves of the bigleaf maple that turn gold during "Golden Time" (October). My next campaign is to relinquish the Mediterranean month names for the local ones that honour the bigleaf. It's a

tree that defines my place in Canada so well. It's still a maple, but its roots are tied to the Salish Sea. Sewn onto a Canadian flag, the huge floppy golden leaf reflects less of a struggle in a snowstorm and more of a campaign for golden times. My retribution for not having to endure winters is that sweet maple sap will never run from this tree, for the same reason that I never learned to skate and we have less than one word for snow.

—*Briony Penn*

QUESTIONS ABOUT THE READING

Refer to the general questions on page 157 and the specific ones here.

PURPOSE

- Does Penn succeed in making her point? If so, how?

CONTENT

- What is the primary expansion (or development) strategy in this definition? Which additional strategies can you identify?
- Penn offers various connotations of Saltspring Island. Which ones seem most credible? Explain.

ORGANIZATION

- Trace the line of thought in this essay. Is this the most effective order? Explain.
- Does the organization make the expansion strategies easier to follow? Explain.

STYLE

- Identify the major devices that increase coherence.
- What attitude does the author express toward her subject? How do we know? Where are the signals?

RESPONDING TO YOUR READING

Explore your reactions to "Green Winters on the Salish Sea" by using the questions on page 158. Then respond with your own essay that examines the connotations of a familiar term that evokes positive or negative feelings. For instance, you might define a term of recent vintage, such as *rap, grunge,* or *skater,* or you might examine the connotations of *fraternity, sorority, commuter, jock, remedial course,* or some other campus-related term. Or perhaps you belong to an in-group that uses words in ironic or special ways to connote meanings that could be appreciated only by members of that particular group.

Your essay should make a clear and definite point about the larger meaning behind the examples you provide.

RESPONDING TO READING

After reading "Green Winters on the Salish Sea," Lois Shea settles on a practical goal for her own essay: As an editor of her campus newspaper, she decides to prepare the following editorial comparing the relative connotations of two names for an important campus building.

While planning, drafting, and revising, Lois relies on the Definition Guidelines and the Revision Checklist on page 58 to produce the following final draft.

NOTE

As Lois's essay illustrates, expanded definition relies on a rich combination of development strategies.

*Title gives a general preview of the topic
Classifies and differentiates the term
Orienting sentence announces the exact topic
Gives background
Thesis*

*First connotative definition
Negation
Examples
Causal analysis
Comparison follows a block pattern and emphatic order
Analyzes effects
Vivid description throughout
Second connotative definition
Analyzes effects
Examples
Sums up the distinction*

Process analysis

"CAMPUS CENTRE" VERSUS "STUDENT UNION"

We refer to the school building that houses the core of student activities at our school as the "Campus Centre." Is this an accurate term for the space that provides the nucleus of university life?

Until four years ago, the building was known as the "Student Union," a term appropriate to the place where students socialize, plan events, and debate issues. "A rose by any other name is still a rose," you may be thinking. *But to re-christen the building as "Student Union" would be good for our campus.*

"Campus Centre" connotes a mere physical location, bureaucratic and impersonal, assigning no real meaning to the hub of so much student activity. The phrase calls to mind passive things: the large-screen TV and the couch potatoes who watch it all day, the video arcade, the billiard room—people just hanging around. "Campus Centre". . . repeat it a few times, and it sounds official, almost militaristic, controlled by forces reminiscent of some sort of police state—perhaps the headquarters for Orwell's Thought Police. This university's poured-concrete architecture already resembles a missile-launching site, and so why throw around labels that further this effect?

"Student Union," on the other hand, carries active connotations, sounding as if people *do* things there. "Student Union" points to the dynamic organizations housed in the building. When we think "Student Union," we think student action: the student Senate, the newspaper, WUSM Radio, the Women's Centre, the Gender Issues Centre, and so on. Whereas "Campus Centre" is a value-neutral term that seems to connote the apathy student organizers so often condemn, "Student Union" reminds us of our unity and alliance as a decisive force within the university. The "Student Union" belongs to us. The "Campus Centre" belongs to someone else.

To revive the use of "Student Union" would be easy enough. We would merely be reversing a change made once before. Our newspaper and radio station have the tools to put "Student Union" back into our

Conclusion re-emphasizes main idea Focuses on the larger meaning

campus vocabulary. If we use the term in conversation, in announcements, on memos and posters, we might be surprised how quickly our peers pick it up and pass it on.

Instead of focusing on the building as a place for hanging around, the name would focus on the ideals embodied in the building and its organized student activities. "Student Union" reminds us that we as students have a say in what goes on.

—*Lois Shea*

OPTION FOR ESSAY WRITING

Along with changing times come changes in our way of seeing. Some terms that held meanings for us two or three years ago may have acquired radically different meanings by now. If we once defined *success* narrowly as social status and income bracket, we might now define it in broader words: leading the kind of life that puts us in close touch with ourselves and the world around us. Similarly, the meanings of many other terms (*education, friendship, freedom, maturity, self-fulfillment, pain, love, home, family, career, patriotism*) may have changed. Although some terms take on more positive meanings, others acquire more negative ones. Your connotations of *marriage* may depend on whether you have witnessed (or experienced) marriages that have been happy and constructive or bitter and destructive. And quite often an entire society's definition of something changes, *marriage* being a good example.

Identify something that has changed in meaning, either for you individually or for our society as a whole—such as the term "*The Canadian Dream.*" Discuss both the traditional and the new meanings (choose a serious, ironic, or humorous point of view) in such a way that your definition makes a specific point or commentary, either stated or implied, about society's values or your own.

CHAPTER 17

Using Multiple Strategies in a Persuasive Argument

s we have seen, the strategies in Chapters 10–16 can be used to draw readers into the writer's special viewpoint. This purpose can be called "persuasive," because it asks readers to agree with particular viewpoints such as these:

- mature students experience different challenges than younger students (page 191)
- the "wifely" stereotype persists in today's generation (page 163)
- children spend too much time doing homework (page 234)
- living on Saltspring Island is just about as good as it gets (page 262)

Writing for the *primary* goal of persuasion often takes a stand on even more controversial topics—issues on which people always disagree. Examples: Do the risks of nuclear power outweigh its advantages? Should your school require athletes to maintain good grades? Should your residence floor be co-ed? We write about these issues in hopes of winning readers over to our side—or at least inducing them to appreciate our position. Although these arguments employ various development strategies (description, comparison/contrast, and so on), their underlying goal is to persuade readers to see things the writer's way.

In a free society, you can expect some readers to disagree with your stand on a controversy no matter how long and how brilliantly you argue. But even though you won't change *everyone's* mind, a strong persuasive argument can make a difference to *some people.*

ANTICIPATING AUDIENCE RESISTANCE

Argument focuses on its audience; it addresses issues in which people are directly involved. But people rarely change their minds about such issues without good reason. Expect resistance from your readers and defensive questions such as these:

What readers of argument want to know

- *Why should I even read this?*
- *Why should I change my mind?*
- *Can you prove it?*
- *How do you know?*
- *Says who?*

Getting readers to admit *you* might be right means getting them to admit *they* might be wrong. The more strongly they identify with their position, the more resistance you can expect. To overcome this resistance, you have to put yourself in your audience's position and see things their way before you argue for your way. The persuasiveness of any argument ultimately depends on how convincing it is to its *audience.*

Making a good argument requires that you bring together all the strategies you've learned so far, along with features specific to any type of argumentative writing:

1. a main point or claim that the audience finds debatable
2. convincing support for the claim
3. a clear and unmistakable line of thought
4. a good relationship with the audience
5. attention to the ethics of argument

HAVING A DEBATABLE POINT

The main point in an argument must be debatable (something open to dispute, something that can be viewed from more than one angle). Statements of fact are not debatable:

A fact is something whose certainty is established

Several near-disastrous accidents have occurred recently in nuclear power plants.

Women outlive men.

Economic policies of this government have led to increases in student loan programs.

More than 50 percent of traffic deaths are alcohol related.

Because these statements can be verified (shown to be true or accurate—at least with enough certainty so that reasonable people would agree), they cannot be debated. Questions of taste or personal opinion never can be debated, because they rest on no objective reasons:

Personal taste or opinion is based on preference, belief, or feeling—instead of fact.

I love oatmeal.

Catholics are holier than Baptists.

Professor Dreary's lectures put me to sleep.

I hate the taste of garlic.

Even many assertions that call for expository support are not debatable for most audiences:

Once reasonable people know the facts, they would have to agree with these claims

During the last two years, the Canadian Alliance has gained political influence.

Competition for good jobs is now fiercer than ever.

Police roadblocks help deter drunk driving.

Lowering the drinking age increases alcohol-related traffic fatalities.

Writing that demonstrates the truth of these assertions is primarily referential. Once the facts are established, the audience almost certainly will agree, "Yes, it's true."

What, then, is a *debatable point?* It is *one that cannot be proved true, but only more or less probable.* For example, few readers would debate the notion that electronic games have altered the play habits of thousands of Canadian children. But some would disagree that electronic games are dominating children's lives.

No amount of evidence can prove or disprove these claims

> The political popularity of Pierre Elliott Trudeau has never been surpassed by another Canadian prime minister.
>
> Schools should place more emphasis on competition.
>
> Police roadblocks are a justifiable deterrent against drunk driving.
>
> All provinces should maintain the drinking age at nineteen.

Even though the rightness or wrongness of these controversial issues can never be proved, writers may argue (more or less persuasively) for one side or the other. And—unlike an assertion of personal opinion or taste—an arguable assertion can be judged by the quality of support the writer presents. How does the assertion hold up against *opposing* assertions?

Always state your arguable point directly and clearly as a thesis. While other development strategies (especially description and narration) may allow the thesis merely to be implied, argumentative writing almost never does. Let readers know exactly where you stand.

SUPPORTING YOUR CLAIM

Chapter 5 shows how any credible assertion rests on opinions derived from facts. But facts out of context can be interpreted in various ways. Legitimate argument offers convincing reasons, reliable sources, careful interpretation, and valid conclusions.

Offer Convincing Reasons

Any argument is only as convincing as the reasons that support it. Before readers will change their minds, they need to know why. They expect you to complete a version of this statement, in which your reasons follow the "because":

> My position is _____ because _____.

Arguing effectively means using *only* those reasons likely to move your specific audience. Assume, for instance, that all students living on your campus have a meal plan with a 15-meal requirement (for weekdays), costing $1800 yearly. You belong to a group trying to reduce the required meals to 10 weekly. Before seeking students' support and lobbying the administration, your group constructs a list of reasons for its position. A quick brainstorming session produces this list:

Subjective support offers reasons that matter to the writer—but not always to the reader.

> The number of required weekly meals should be reduced to 10 per week because:
>
> 1. Many students dislike the food.
> 2. Some students with only afternoon classes like to sleep late and should not have to rush to beat the 9:00 a.m. breakfast deadline.
> 3. The cafeteria atmosphere is too noisy, impersonal, and dreary.
> 4. The food selection is too limited.
> 5. The price of a yearly meal ticket has risen unfairly and is now more than 5 percent higher than last year's price.

You quickly spot a flaw in this list: All these reasons rest almost entirely on *subjective* grounds, on personal taste or opinion. For every reader who dislikes the food or sleeps late, another may like the food or rise early—and so on. Your intended audience (students, administrators) probably won't think these reasons very convincing. Your reasons should be based on *objective* evidence and on goals and values you and your readers share.

Provide Objective Evidence

Evidence (factual support from an outside source) is objective when it can be verified (shown to be accurate) by everyone involved. Common types of objective evidence include factual statements, statistics, examples, and expert testimony.

A *fact* is something that can be demonstrated by observation, experience, research, or measurement—and that your audience is willing to recognize:

Offer the facts

> Each residence suite has its own kitchen.

Be selective. Decide which facts best support your case (page 79).

Numbers can be highly convincing. Many readers are interested in the "bottom line" (percentages, costs, savings, profits):

Cite the numbers

> Roughly 30 percent of the 500 students we surveyed in the cafeteria eat only two meals per day.

But numbers can mislead. Your statistics must be accurate, trustworthy, and easy to understand and verify (see pages 368–371). Always cite your source.

Examples help people visualize and remember the point. For instance, the best way to explain what you mean by "wasteful" is to show "waste" occurring:

Show what you
mean

| From 20 to 25 percent of the food prepared is never eaten.

Use examples that your audience can identify with and that fit the point they are designed to illustrate.

Expert testimony—if it is unbiased and the expert is recognized—lends authority and credibility to any claim:

Cite the experts

Food service directors from three Ontario universities point out that their schools' optional meal plans have been highly successful.

See page 324 for the limits of expert testimony.

Appeal to Shared Goals and Values

Evidence alone isn't always enough to change a reader's mind. Identify at least one goal you and your audience have in common. In the meal plan issue, for example, we can assume that everyone wants to eliminate wasteful practices. A persuasive argument will therefore take this goal into account:

Appeal to shared
goals

These changes in the meal plan would eliminate waste of food, labour, and money.

People's goals are shaped by their values (qualities they believe in, ideals they stand for): friendship, loyalty, honesty, equality, fairness, and so on (Rokeach 57–58). Look for a common, central goal. In the meal plan case, *fairness* might be an important value:

Appeal to shared
values

| No one should have to pay for meals she or he doesn't eat.

Here is how your group's final list of reasons might read:

Persuasive claims
are backed up by
reasons that matter
to the reader

The number of required weekday meals should be reduced to ten per week because:

1. No one should have to pay for meals she or he doesn't eat.
2. Roughly 30 percent of the 500 students we surveyed in the cafeteria eat only two meals per day.
3. From 20 to 25 percent of the food prepared is never eaten—a waste of food, labour, and money.
4. Each residence suite has its own kitchen, but these are seldom used.
5. Between kitchen suites and local restaurants, students on only the Monday-through-Friday plan do survive on weekends. Why couldn't they survive just as well during the week?
6. Food service directors from three Ontario universities point out that their schools' optional meal plans have been highly successful.

Reasonable audiences should find the above argument compelling because each reason is based on a verifiable fact or (as in item 1) good sense. Even audience members not moved to support your cause will understand why you've taken your stand.

Give your audience reasons that have meaning for *them* personally. For example, in a recent study of teenage attitudes about smoking, respondents listed these reasons for not smoking: bad breath, difficulty concentrating, loss of friends, and trouble with adults. No respondents listed dying of cancer—presumably because this last reason carries little meaning for young people personally (Bauman et al. 510–30).

Finding objective evidence to support a claim often requires that we go beyond our own experience by doing some type of research (see Section Four).

SHAPING A CLEAR LINE OF THOUGHT

Like all writing, persuasive writing has an introduction, body, and conclusion. But within this familiar shape, your argument should do some special things as well. Readers need to follow your reasoning; they expect to see how you've arrived at your conclusions. The following model lays out a standard shape for arguments, but remember that virtually no argument rigidly follows the order of elements shown in the model. Select whatever shape you find most useful—as long as it reveals a clear line of thought.

STANDARD SHAPE FOR AN ARGUMENT

INTRODUCTION

Attract and Invite Your Readers and Provide a Forecast

- Identify the issue clearly and immediately. Show the audience that your essay deserves their attention.
- Acknowledge the opposing viewpoint accurately and concede its merit.
- Offer at least one point of your own that your audience can share.
- Offer significant background material so that your readers are fully prepared to understand your position.
- State a clear, concrete, and definite thesis. Never delay your thesis without good reason. For example, if your thesis is highly controversial, you might want to delay it until you've offered some convincing evidence.
- Keep the introduction short—no more than a few paragraphs.

BODY

Offer the Support and Refutation

- Use reasons that rest on impersonal grounds of support.

- In one or more paragraphs each, organize your supporting points for best emphasis. If you think your audience has little interest, begin with the more powerful material. Sometimes you can sandwich weaker points between stronger points. But if all your points are equally strong, begin with the most familiar and acceptable to your audience—to elicit some early agreement. In general, try to save the strongest points for last.

- Develop each supporting point with concrete, specific details (facts, examples, narratives, quotations, or other evidence that can be verified empirically or logically).

- Using transitions and other connectors, string your supporting points and their evidence together to show a definite line of reasoning.

- In at least one separate paragraph, refute opposing arguments (including any anticipated readers' objections to your points).

CONCLUSION

Sum Up Your Case and Make a Direct Appeal

- Summarize your main points and refutation, emphasizing your strongest material. Offer a short-and-sweet view of the Big Picture.

- End by appealing directly to readers for a definite action (where appropriate).

- Let readers know what they should do, think, or feel.

CONNECTING WITH YOUR AUDIENCE

In any persuasive writing, the audience is the main focus. Whenever you set out to influence someone's thinking, remember this principle:

No matter how brilliant, any argument rejected by its audience is a failed argument.

If readers dislike what you have to say or decide that what you have to say has no meaning for them personally, they reject your argument. Connecting with an audience means being able to see things from their perspective. The guidelines on page 275 can help you make that connection.

CONSIDERING THE ETHICAL DIMENSION

Arguments can "win" without being ethical if they "win" at any cost. For instance, advertisers effectively win customers with an implied argument that "our product is just what you need!" Some of their more specific claims can be: "Our artificial sweetener is made of proteins that occur naturally in the human body [amino acids]" or "Our potato chips contain no cholesterol." Such claims are technically accurate, but misleading: amino acids in artificial sweeteners can alter body chemistry to cause headaches, seizures, and possibly brain tumours; potato chips often contain saturated fat—from which the liver produces cholesterol.

We often are tempted to emphasize anything that advances our case and to ignore anything that impedes it. But a message is unethical if it prevents readers from making their best decision. To ensure that your writing is ethical, answer the questions on page 276.

GUIDELINES FOR PERSUASION

1. *Be clear about what you want.* Diplomacy is important, but don't leave people guessing about your purpose.

2. *Never make a claim or ask for something you know people will reject outright.* People never accept anything they consider unreasonable. Be sure readers can live with whatever you're requesting or proposing. Get a realistic sense of what is *achievable* in this particular situation by asking what people are thinking.

3. *Anticipate your audience's reaction.* Will people be defensive, surprised, annoyed, angry? Try to neutralize big objections beforehand. Express your judgments ("We could do better") without blaming people ("It's all your fault").

4. *Project a likable and reasonable persona.* **Persona** is the image or impression the writer projects in her or his tone. Resist the urge to preach or "sound off." Audiences tune out aggressive people—no matter how sensible the argument. Don't expect perfection from anyone—including yourself. Admit the imperfections in your case. A little humility never hurts.

5. *Find points of agreement with your audience.* What does everyone involved want? To reduce conflict, focus early on a shared value, goal, or concern. Emphasize your similarities.

6. *Never distort the opposing position.* A sure way to alienate people is to cast the opponent in more of a negative light than the facts warrant.

7. *Concede* something *to the opponent.* Readers expect a balanced argument. Admit the merits of the opposing case before arguing the merits of your own. Show empathy and willingness to compromise.

8. *Stick to your best material.* Some points are stronger than others. Decide which material—from your *audience's* view—best advances your case.

9. *Stick to claims or assertions you can support.* Show people what's in it for them—but never distort the facts just to please the audience.

10. *Use your skills responsibly.* The obvious power of persuasive skills creates tremendous potential for abuse. People who feel they have been bullied or manipulated or deceived most likely will become your enemies.

REVISION CHECKLIST ✔

ETHICS CHECKLIST FOR PERSUASIVE WRITING

☐ Do I avoid exaggeration, understatement, sugar-coating, or any distortion or omission that leaves readers at a disadvantage?

☐ Do I make a clear distinction between "certainty" and "probability"?

☐ Have I explored all sides of the issue and all possible alternatives?

☐ Are my information sources valid, reliable, and unbiased?

☐ Am I being honest and fair with everyone involved?

☐ Am I reasonably sure that what I'm saying will harm no innocent persons or damage their reputation?

☐ Am I respecting all legitimate rights to privacy and confidentiality?

☐ Do I provide enough information and interpretation for readers to understand the facts as I know them?

☐ Do I state the case clearly, instead of hiding behind fallacies or generalities?

☐ Do I inform readers of the consequences or risks (as I am able to predict) of what I am advocating?

☐ Do I credit all contributors and sources of ideas and information?

VARIOUS ARGUMENTS FOR VARIOUS GOALS

Arguments can differ considerably in what they ask readers to do. The goal of an argument might be to influence readers' opinions, seek readers' support, propose some action, or change readers' behaviour. Let's look at arguments that seek different levels of involvement from readers.

Arguing to Influence Readers' Opinions

An argument intended to change an opinion asks for minimal involvement from its readers. Maybe you want readers to agree that specific books and films should be censored, that more women should be hired as firefighters, that grades are a detriment to education. The specific goal behind any such argument is merely to get readers to change their thinking, to say "I agree."

Arguing to Enlist Readers' Support

In seeking readers' support for our argument, we ask readers not only to agree with a position but also to take a stand. Maybe you want readers to vote for a candidate, lobby for additional computer equipment at your school, or help enforce residence or library "quiet" rules. The goal in this kind of argument is to get readers actively involved, to get them to ask, "How can I help?"

Making a Proposal

The world is full of problems to solve. And proposals are designed precisely to solve problems. The type of proposal we examine here typically asks readers to take some form of direct action (to improve residence security, fund a new campus organization, or improve working conditions). But before you can induce readers to act, you must fulfill these preliminary persuasive tasks:

1. spell out the problem (and its causes) in enough detail to convince readers of its importance
2. point out the benefits of solving the problem
3. offer a realistic solution
4. address objections to your solution
5. give reasons why your readers should be the ones to act

Arguing to Change Readers' Behaviour

Persuading readers to change their behaviour is perhaps the biggest challenge in argument. Maybe you want your boss to treat employees more fairly, or a friend to be less competitive, or a teacher to be more supportive in the classroom. Whatever your goal, readers are bound to take your argument personally. And the more personal the issue, the greater resistance you can expect. You're trying to get readers to say, "I was wrong. From now on, I'll do it differently."

The four writing samples shown in Applications 17-1 through 17-4 are addressed to readers who have an increasing stake or involvement in the issue. Comparing these essays will show how writers in various situations can convey their way of seeing.

APPLICATION **17-1**

ESSAY PRACTICE: ARGUING TO INFLUENCE READERS' OPINIONS

The following essay from the *Miami Herald* argues that "trash" fiction (about Tarzan, Nancy Drew, Conan the Barbarian, and so on) offers children a good preparation for reading great literature. Read the essay, and answer the questions that follow. Then (as your instructor requests) select one of the essay assignments.

ESSAY FOR ANALYSIS AND RESPONSE

> **ON READING TRASH**
> [1]If you want kids to become omnivorous readers, let them read trash. That's my philosophy, and I speak from experience.

[2]I don't disagree with The National Endowment for the Humanities, which says every high school graduate should have read 30 great works of literature, including the Bible, Plato, Shakespeare, Hawthorne, the "Declaration of Independence," "Catcher in the Rye," "Crime and Punishment" and "Moby Dick."

[3]It's a fine list. Kids should read them all, and more. But they'll be better readers if they start off on trash. Trash? What I mean is what some might call "popular" fiction. My theory is, if you get kids interested in reading books—no matter what sort—they will eventually go on to the grander literature all by themselves.

[4]In the third grade I read my first novel, a mystic adventure set in India. I still recall the sheer excitement at discovering how much fun reading could be.

[5]When we moved within walking distance of the public library a whole new world opened. In the library I found that wonder of wonders, the series. What a thrill, to find a favorite author had written a dozen or more other titles.

[6]I read a series about frontiersmen, learning about Indian tribes, beef jerky and tepees. A Civil War series alternated young heroes from the Blue and the Gray, and I learned about Grant and Lee and the Rock of Chickamauga.

[7]One summer, in Grandpa Barrow's attic, I discovered the Mother Lode, scores of dusty books detailing the adventures of Tom Swift, The Rover Boys, The Submarine Boys, The Motorcycle Boys and Bomba the Jungle Boy. It didn't matter that some were written in 1919; any book you haven't read is brand new.

[8]Another summer I discovered Edgar Rice Burroughs. I swung through jungles with Tarzan, fought green Martians with John Carter, explored Pellucidar at the Earth's core, flew through the steamy air of Venus with Carson Napier. Then I came across Sax Rohmer and, for book after book, prowled opium dens with Nayland Smith, in pursuit of the insidious Fu Manchu.

[9]In the seventh grade, I ran across Booth Tarkington's hilarious Penrod books and read them over and over.

[10]My cousin went off to war in 1942 and gave me his pulp magazines. I became hooked on Doc Savage, The Shadow, G8 and His Battle Aces, The Spider, Amazing Stories. My folks wisely did not object to them as trash. I began to look in second-hand book shops for past issues, and found a Blue Book Magazine, with an adventure story by Talbot Mundy. It led me back to the library, for more of Mundy's Far East thrillers. From Mundy, my path led to A. Conan Doyle's "The Lost World," Rudyard Kipling's "Kim," Jules Verne, H. G. Wells and Jack London.

[11]Before long I was whaling with Herman Melville, affixing scarlet letters with Hawthorne and descending into the maelstrom with Poe. In due course came Hemingway, Dos Passos, "Hamlet," "The Odyssey," "The Iliad," "Crime and Punishment." I had discovered "real" literature by following the trail of popular fiction.

¹²When our kids were small, we read aloud to them from Doctor Dolittle and Winnie the Pooh. Soon they learned to read, and favored the "Frog and Toad" and "Freddie the Pig" series.

¹³When the old Doc Savage and Conan the Barbarian pulps were reissued as paperbacks, I brought them home. The kids devoured them, sometimes hiding them behind textbooks at school, just as I had. They read my old Tarzan and Penrod books along with Nancy Drew and The Black Stallion.

¹⁴Now they're big kids. Each kid's room is lined with bookshelves, on which are stacked, in an eclectic mix, Doc Savage, Plato, Louis L'Amour westerns, Thomas Mann, Gothic romances, Agatha Christie, Sartre, Edgar Allan Poe, science-fiction, Saul Bellow, Shakespeare, Pogo, Greek tragedies, Hemingway, Kipling, Tarzan, Zen and the Art of Motorcycle Maintenance, F. Scott Fitzgerald, Bomba the Jungle Boy, Nietzsche, the Iliad, Dr. Dolittle, Joseph Conrad, Fu Manchu, Hawthorne, Penrod, Dostoevsky, Ray Bradbury, Herman Melville, Conan the Barbarian . . . more. Some great literature, some trash, but all good reading.

—Bob Swift

QUESTIONS ABOUT THE READING

PURPOSE

- Who is Swift's intended audience here? How do we know?
- Does Swift succeed in connecting with his audience? If so, how?

CONTENT

- What is the primary development strategy used here? Which other strategies can you identify?
- Does the writer acknowledge the opposing viewpoint? If so, where?
- Does the thesis grow out of sufficient background details? Explain.

ORGANIZATION

- Is the material arranged in the best order? Explain.
- Are most paragraphs too short? Explain.

STYLE

- How would you characterize the tone? Is it appropriate for the audience and purpose?
- Does the writer appear likable? Is he ever too extreme? Explain.

RESPONDING TO YOUR READING

Explore your reactions to "On Reading Trash" by using the questions on page 158. You might wish to challenge the author's view by arguing your own ideas about what constitutes worthwhile reading. You might support his view by citing evidence from your own experience. Or you might set out to influence reader opinion on some other topic of interest. Decide carefully on your audience and on what you want these readers to do, think, or feel after reading your essay. Be sure your essay supports a clear and definite point.

Be sure your essay has a clear thesis and addresses a specific audience affected by the issue in some way. Although this essay will make an emotional appeal, your argument should not rest solely on subjective grounds (how you feel about it), but also on factual details.

CASE STUDY

RESPONDING TO READING

After reading and analyzing Swift's essay, Julia Schoonover decides to persuade fellow students that credit cards can be far more dangerous than they appear.

While planning, drafting, and revising, Julia refers to the Persuasion Guidelines, the Model Outline for Argument, and the Revision Checklist on page 58.

NOTE

Like most arguments, Julia's piece relies on multiple development strategies, especially causal analysis, process analysis, and illustration.

Title announces the essay's purpose
Opens directly with the thesis
Acknowledges opposing view
Vivid examples help establish agreement and neutralize objections
Transition to upcoming refutation
Cause/effect analysis
Process analysis

Uses examples as objective evidence
Process analysis

Gives striking statistics

CREDIT CARDS: LEAVE HOME WITHOUT THEM

Credit cards are students' best friends and potentially their worst enemy. Credit cards provide a convenient means of purchasing much-needed textbooks, food, and residence room essentials. Credit cards enable students to purchase plane tickets to fly home or to Bermuda for spring break. Credit cards even make money available for those "little" extras that mom and dad would never buy—like a state-of-the-art stereo system or a new wardrobe. Long distance calls and Christmas shopping are also made a lot easier by credit cards.

Although credit cards can be very helpful to the struggling student, they also can spell big trouble. The most obvious danger comes from their misuse: that is, the temptation to go on a spending spree. It is very easy for students to run up huge debt because credit card companies don't require cardholders—indeed, they don't *want* cardholders—to pay off their debts when the bill comes in at the end of each month. Although these cards are promoted with a teaser "low interest rate," that rate soon triples. As a result, many students end up owing more than they originally borrowed, even with regular minimum monthly payments.

Three co-workers of mine who are also students know what it's like to be in debt to credit card companies. Ron, in his final year at Grant MacEwan College, owes more than $5200 to credit card companies. Ron claims that when he first got a card he "went crazy" with it. He bought exercise equipment, a couch, a CD player, and clothes for himself and his girlfriend. Ron now makes about $120 weekly at his part-time job, goes to school full-time, and knows that because the interest rate for each of his three cards is around 17 percent and he pays only the $98 monthly minimum, it will take him about ten years to repay his debt. By then, Ron will have paid the credit card companies almost double the amount he charged.

Gives additional examples readers can identify with

Another co-worker, Jane, a second-year student at NAIT (Northern Alberta Institute of Technology), says she owes $1300 on one card and $1100 on another. Jane says most of the money she owes is from last Christmas. She tries to pay the minimum combined charge of $40 monthly but even $40 takes a big chunk out of her $64 weekly salary after she pays for meals, movies, gas, and a steep phone bill (her boyfriend goes to Bishops University). Dave, a third-year student at the University of Alberta, worries how he will ever pay his $3500 credit card debt on his $70 weekly paycheque. Dave can't even remember what he spent this money on. "You spend it here and there and it adds up fast." Meanwhile, Dave's debt is increasing at the rate of 18.9 percent yearly.

Gives striking quotation
Gives striking statistic
Projects a reasonable, empathetic persona throughout.
Cause/effect analysis
Cites an expert
Process analysis

Because of the immediate money problems that credit cards seem to solve, it's easy to ignore the long-term effects of a bad credit history. According to accountant John Farnes, former mortgage officer at the Bank of Montreal, when people apply for any type of loan, the bank immediately obtains a credit report, which lists the applicant's number of credit cards, total debt, and the amount that person is eligible to borrow. The report also shows whether the applicant has ever "maxed out" all credit cards or missed any minimum monthly payments. Applicants who have missed payments—or have been late with a payment—usually are rejected. Even people who make all minimum payments but still have outstanding or excessive credit card debt are turned down for loans. Farnes cautions that students who "run up credit card bills" can dig a big hole for themselves—a hole from which they might never climb out.

Acknowledges opposing view
Relies on visual details throughout

Granted, the temptation is hard to refuse. Credit card companies marketing on campus offer free cards and sign-up gifts "with no obligation." The "gifts" might include candy, coffee mugs, T-shirts, sports squeeze bottles, hip bags, and other paraphernalia. The process seems so easy and harmless: Just fill in your social insurance number and other personal information, take your pick from the array of gifts, and cancel the card when it arrives.

Conclusion refutes opposing view and re-emphasizes the main point
Appeals directly to readers

But these companies know exactly what they're doing. They know that misusing the card is often easier than cancelling it. They know that many of us work part time and are paid little. They know that most of us will be unable to pay more than the minimum balance each month—meaning big-time interest for years. Don't be seduced by instant credit.

—Julia Schoonover

OPTIONS FOR ESSAY WRITING

1. Argue for or against this assertion: Parents have the right to make major decisions in the lives of their teenagers.

2. Are grades an aid to education?

3. Sally and Sam have two children, ages two and five. Sally, a lawyer, is currently not working but has been offered an attractive full-time job. Sam believes Sally should not work until both children are in school. Should Sally take the job?

4. Recently, voters in several communities defeated or repealed bylaws protecting homosexuals from discrimination in housing and employment. Defend or attack these public decisions.

5. Should scholarships be awarded for academic achievement or promise rather than for financial need?

6. During your more than twelve years in school, you've undoubtedly developed legitimate gripes about the quality of Canadian education. Based on your experiences and perceptions and research, think about one specific problem in Canadian education and argue for its solution. Remember, you are writing an argument, not an attack; your goal is not to offend but to persuade readers—to move them to your way of seeing.

After making sure you have enough inductive evidence to support your main generalization, write an editorial essay for your campus newspaper: identify the problem; analyze its cause(s); and propose a solution. Possible topics:

- too little (or too much) attention given to remedial students
- too little (or too much) emphasis on practical education (career training)
- too little (or too much) emphasis on competition
- teachers' attitudes
- parents' attitudes
- students' attitudes

APPLICATION **17-2**

ESSAY PRACTICE: ARGUING TO ENLIST READERS' SUPPORT

Read the essay, and answer the questions that follow. Then (as your instructor requests) select one of the essay assignments.

ESSAY FOR ANALYSIS AND RESPONSE

SPRING BEAR HUNT*

[1]The spring bear hunt took place each year from April 15 to June 15 in most areas of Ontario—until last spring. On January 15, 1999, Natural Resources Minister John Snobelen announced the elimination of the spring bear hunt, effective immediately. The government's decision was based on

concern for the young cubs orphaned each spring by hunters who mistakenly shot female lactating bears. While the decision was welcomed by many naturalist and ecological groups, it angered outfitters whose livelihood benefited from the hunt, and hunters who feared further restrictions. Numerous organizations have called for the reinstatement of the spring bear hunt, and public pressure may force the Ministry of Natural Resources to reconsider the issue.

[2]Unfortunately, many outfitters will lose revenue from the cancellation of the spring bear hunt. In Ontario especially, outfitters profited from the high number of American tourists frequenting their camps. Because most U.S. states have already banned this hunt, more than 75 percent of Ontario bears killed in the spring were killed by U.S. hunters who were unable to continue the practice at home. While the practice of spring bear hunting continues in British Columbia, Alberta, Saskatchewan, Manitoba, New Brunswick, and Newfoundland, Ontario outfitters were privy to one of the largest bear populations in North America, resulting in a larger harvest maximum. Naturally, removing these privileges came as a shock to both hunters and outfitters alike and their resistance is not surprising. Groups opposing the spring bear hunt cancellation have also claimed that it infringes on the recreational rights of hunters, and that it has caused an increase in the number of nuisance bears.

[3]However, more than 4000 bears were killed each year in the Ontario spring bear hunt, of which one-third were females. Every spring, bears are at their most vulnerable as they emerge from their long winter hibernation. They must feed themselves and feed and protect their newborn cubs. When a nursing mother is killed, her cubs become particularly susceptible to predators and starvation. Several hundred bear cubs were orphaned each spring in Ontario.

[4]In response to outfitters' financial concerns, the provincial government established an assistance program to help businesses affected by the closure of the hunt and to promote new tourism opportunities. Eligible spring bear hunt operators received $250 per hunter who had used their services the previous year. Furthermore, to make up for some of the lost revenue, the government extended the fall bear-hunting season by opening the season two weeks earlier in most regions. Operators were also encouraged to make the transition to other less consumptive tourism revenue sources—an effort that was aided by both the government and many non-profit organizations, such as the International Fund for Animal Welfare. Many of these same organizations have pointed out that since bears are much more susceptible in the spring, the hunters' job becomes that much easier—raising an ethical issue of whether or not hunters are taking advantage of, rather than practising the skills of, their "sport."

---

*Facts and statistics came from the following sources: Ministry of Natural Resources, International Fund for Animal Welfare, Ontario Federation of Anglers and Hunters, Ontario Society for the Prevention of Cruelty to Animals, and the Legislative Library.

[5]Claims of nuisance bears have been similarly discredited by the fact that most biologists agree that there are no such things as nuisance bears, but rather nuisance people. Studies have shown that the number of incidents involving nuisance bears increases and decreases in proportion to the abundance of human garbage in an area, and to the environmental conditions at the time. For example, a campground where careless campers have left their garbage at the campsite and where it has been particularly dry (inhibiting the growth of natural food sources) will experience more instances of nuisance bears, even though the actual bear population may be lower than average.

[6]The only argument remaining in favour of the spring bear hunt is that the number of bears in Ontario is so large that the hunt cannot be detrimental to the population. However, the bear population can only be estimated at best, and the only studies available have been done by partisan organizations such as the Ontario Federation of Anglers and Hunters. Granted, the lack of scientific evidence neither supports nor opposes the spring bear hunt, but is it not better to err on the side of caution until further information is known?

[7]For these reasons, the Ontario government cancelled the spring bear hunt. Now because of protestations by hunters and outfitters, the Ministry of Natural Resources may be forced to reverse its decision. It may be true that the cancellation was originally based on public opinion and not on fact, but the reality is that the decision was ecologically and economically sound, and we should not let popular opinion reverse the decision.

—*Skye Lantinga*

QUESTIONS ABOUT THE READING

PURPOSE

- Does Lantinga succeed in making her point? If so, how?

CONTENT

- Does the writer acknowledge the opposing viewpoint, and does she address opponents' biggest objections to her position?
- Where is the thesis? Is it easily found?
- Does the writer offer sound reasons for her case? Explain.
- Does the writer offer impersonal (as well as personal) support? Explain.

ORGANIZATION

- Is the introduction effective? Which of the tasks on page 273 does it perform? Explain.
- Is the strongest material near the beginning or the end of the essay? Is this placement effective?
- How does the writer achieve coherence and smooth transitions between paragraphs?

STYLE

- Does the writer avoid an extreme persona here (say, sounding like a righteous environmentalist)? Explain.

RESPONDING TO YOUR READING

Explore your reactions to "Spring Bear Hunt" by using the questions on page 158. Then respond with your own essay supporting or opposing the author's view. Your goal is to get readers involved. Perhaps you will want to argue from the viewpoint of hunters affected by the cancellation.

Or, you might argue for and or against other hunting and fishing issues, such as the rights of Aboriginals to hunt and fish year round.

Whatever your position, be sure that your essay has a clear thesis and that you address a specific audience whose support you seek. In order to be persuasive, base your support not only on personal grounds (how you feel about it), but on impersonal grounds (verifiable evidence), as well.

CASE STUDY

RESPONDING TO READING

After reading and analyzing Lantinga's essay, Suzanne Gilbertson thinks about a controversy at her university: In an age when jobs require increasing specialization, the importance of the liberal arts are under question. Some people argue that students in career-oriented majors such as computer science and engineering actually are hurt by the university's humanities, social science, and language requirements, because these students are prevented from taking enough courses in their specialties. Beyond advocating that such requirements be dropped, some people argue that certain majors (such as fine arts and philosophy) and upper-level courses should be eliminated, thereby freeing more resources for career programs.

Suzanne decides to refute the assertion that the liberal arts have become an unaffordable luxury at her school. Her essay will be published in the campus newspaper as an open letter to faculty, administrators, trustees, and students.

NOTE

In shaping her argument, Suzanne combines a rich array of development strategies.

Title announces the argument's purpose
Opens with a familiar question
Gives visual examples readers can identify with

Projects a reasonable persona throughout

SAVE LIBERAL ARTS

You may be one of them. As a child you never could give a confident answer to the question "What do you want to be when you grow up?" In high school, while your friends fingered through various issues of *National Geographic* during study hall in the library, you hovered near the Fiction section or lost yourself in *The Last Days of Pompeii*. Once in university, you couldn't bring yourself to declare a major; instead, picking and choosing courses from an array of disciplines, you resembled a diner filling his or her plate at a breakfast buffet. Recognize the type? If you found yourself enjoying first-year English, if you register for beginning Spanish one semester and elementary Russian the next, or combine obscure philosophy courses with biology and write a poem on the similarities of the two, you might just be a "closet" liberal arts major.

Acknowledges opposing view without distorting it

Many folks tend to believe that education should provide the student with concrete skills that later can be applied to specific tasks. Historically, young children were apprenticed to a craftsperson to learn a skill by constant observation and imitation. Today, most people still prefer to specialize in a single field. They feel comfortable on a "career track." In our high-tech age, the liberal arts major seems to have lost its appeal. Some even label a liberal arts degree self-indulgent and impractical, and encourage students to take courses that will "guarantee" them employment after graduation.

Refutes opposing view

But some students find it harder to narrow their interests and sharpen their talents to fit a practical field. Are liberal arts majors simply choosing an easy or irrelevant way to a university degree?

Offers clear definitions

Maybe we need first to examine the meaning of "education" as opposed to "schooling." The "Renaissance person" is so named after the philosophers, poets, and artists who illuminated three centuries of Western civilization through a rebirth of classical learning. Such a person is characterized by an intense love of learning, a search for excellence. Far from being self-indulgent or withdrawn from worldly and practical affairs, the Renaissance person is committed to serving the needs of society by studying humanity and the life of citizens in society.

Defines by negation

Beyond merely imparting information or training, education in the Renaissance prepared students to be concerned citizens *in the world.* Career training alone was considered far inferior to a liberal education. Likewise today, a liberal education teaches us to observe the human condition, synthesize what we know of that condition from our study of history and philosophy, and verbalize and communicate our perception of the needs of others besides ourselves.

Thesis

The twentieth century has produced for us complex problems beyond the comprehension of Renaissance thinkers, such as da Vinci, Galileo, or Thomas More. Our world seems smaller and more crowded. We are threatened by poisons in our air and water. Many nations are hungry and oppressed. We live under the constant fear of the ultimate weapons of destruction we have created to protect our freedoms. We continue to need skilled doctors to cure our ills, dedicated farmers to feed us, and politicians and managers to lead us. And the advanced technology at the disposal of our specialists may well be the key to our survival.

Offers a contrast

Gives objective evidence to support the contrast

Offers points of agreement

Expands on above points Cause/effect analysis

Yet, in order to understand and cope with the challenges of the twenty-first century, we must first be able to see where we have come from. Even our present technological breakthroughs are made possible because of the questions first asked by the scholars of the Renaissance: Are there any limits to what humanity can accomplish? What are the possibilities for human achievement? How can we best take advantage of our human and natural resources?

Offers vivid examples throughout

Appeals to shared goals and values

In the Renaissance tradition, the liberal arts graduate is well equipped to meet the broadest challenges of our technological society. Now, more than ever, we need people who can step back and monitor our "progress." We need minds that can synthesize our many achievements and our aspirations, to guide us toward a safe and improved existence. In

Re-emphasizes the main idea

the end, what will bind us together will be our ability to formulate and question our goals and to communicate our global needs. Questioning, synthesizing, and communicating—these are the broad skills liberal arts graduates bring to the enrichment of their world.

—Suzanne Gilbertson

OPTIONS FOR ESSAY WRITING

1. Respond to the assertion that the liberal arts have become an unaffordable luxury. Be sure to consider the arguments for and against specialized vocational education versus a broadly humanistic—but less "practical"—education.

2. Your school is thinking of abolishing core requirements. Write a letter to the dean in which you argue for or against this change.

3. Should first-year composition be required at your school? Argue your position to the faculty senate.

4. Should your school (or institute) drop students' evaluations of teachers? Write to the student and faculty senates.

5. Perhaps you belong to a fraternity, a sorority, or some other organized group. Identify an important decision your group faces. In a letter, present your position on the issue to the group.

6. The Cultural Affairs Committee at your school has decided to sponsor a concert next fall, featuring some popular singer or musical group. Although the committee (mostly faculty) is aware that today's music reflects great diversity in personal taste and musical style, the committee members are uncertain about which performer or group would be a good choice for the event. In fact, most committee members admit to being ignorant of the characteristics that distinguish one performance or recording from another. To help in the decision, the committee has invited the student body to submit essays (not letters) arguing for a performer or group. Free tickets will be awarded to the writer of the best essay. Compose your response.

7. Should your school have an attendance policy?

8. In a letter to the school newspaper, challenge an attitude or viewpoint that is widely held on your campus. Maybe you want to persuade your classmates that the time required to earn a Bachelor's degree should be extended to four years. Or maybe you want to claim that the campus police should (or should not) wear guns. Or maybe you want to ask students to support a 10 percent tuition increase in order to make more computers and software available.

   What kind of resistance can you anticipate? How can you avoid outright rejection of your claim? What reasons will have meaning for your audience? What tone should you adopt?

APPLICATION **17-3**

Essay Practice: Making a Proposal

This proposal addresses a fairly common problem: a large television set in the campus centre is causing congestion and wasting students' time. One student confronts the problem by writing a proposal to the director of the campus centre.

Read the proposal carefully, and answer the questions that follow. Select one of the essay assignments if your instructor requests you to do so.

Essay for Analysis

A Proposal for Better Use of the Television Set in the Campus Centre

[1]Leaving the campus centre yesterday for class, I found myself stuck in the daily pedestrian jam on the second-floor landing. People by the dozens had gathered on the stairway for their daily dose of *General Hospital.* Fighting my way through the mesmerized bodies, I wondered about the appropriateness of the television set's location, and of the value of the shows aired on this set.

[2]Along with the recent upsurge of improvements at our school (in curriculum and standards), we should be considering ways to better use the campus centre television. The tube plays relentlessly, offering soap operas and game shows to the addicts who block the stairway and main landing. Granted, television for students to enjoy between classes is a fine idea, but no student needs to attend university to watch soap operas. By moving the set and improving the programs, we could eliminate the congestion and enrich the learning experience.

[3]The television needs a better location: out of the way of people who don't care to watch it, and into a larger, more comfortable setting for those who do. Background noise in the present location makes the set barely audible; and the raised seating in front of the set places the viewers on exhibit to all who walk by. A far better location would be the back wall of the North Lounge, outside the Sunset Room—a large, quiet, and comfortable space. Various meetings sometimes held in this room could be moved instead to the browsing area of the library.

[4]More important than the set's location is the quality of its programs. Videotaped movies might be a good alternative to the shows now aired. Our audiovisual department has a rich collection of excellent movies and educational programs on tape. People could request the shows they would like to see, and a student committee could be responsible for printing showtime information.

[5]The set might also serve as a primary learning tool by allowing communications students to create their own shows. Our school has the videotaping and sound equipment and would need only a faculty advisor to supervise the project. Students from scriptwriting, drama, political science, and journalism classes (to name a few) could combine their

talents, providing shows of interest to their peers. We now have a student news program that is aired evenings on a local channel, but many who live some distance off campus cannot receive this channel on their sets at home. Why not make the program accessible to students during the day, here on campus?

[6]With resources already in our possession, we can make a few changes that will benefit almost everyone. Beyond providing more efficient use of campus centre space, these changes could really stimulate people's minds. I urge you to allow students and faculty to vote on the questions of moving the television set and improving its programs.

—*Patricia Haith*

QUESTIONS ABOUT THE READING

CONTENT

- Does the proposal fulfill the tasks outlined on page 277? Explain.
- Does the writer offer the best reasons for her primary audience? Explain.
- For a different audience (say, students who avidly follow the soap operas), would the writer have to change her material? Explain.
- Is this argument primarily inductive or deductive?
- Does the writer establish agreement with the reader? If so, where?

ORGANIZATION

- Which expository strategy is mainly used in this essay?
- Is the narrative introduction effective? Explain.
- Does the conclusion perform all the tasks on page 274?

STYLE

- How do the outstanding style features of this essay contribute to its tone?
- Should the tone of this essay be more or less formal for this audience and purpose? Or is it appropriate? Explain.
- Is the writer's voice likable? Explain.

OPTIONS FOR ESSAY WRITING

Identify a problem in your school, community, family, or job. Develop a proposal for solving the problem. Stipulate a definite audience for your proposal. Here are some possible subjects:

- improving living conditions in your residence
- improving security in your residence
- creating a day-care centre on campus
- saving labour, materials, or money at your job
- improving working conditions
- improving the services of your university library
- improving the food service on campus
- establishing more equitable use of computer terminals on campus

Be sure to spell out the problem, explain the benefits of change, offer a realistic plan, and urge your readers to definite action. Decide exactly what you want your readers to do.

APPLICATION **17-4**

ESSAY PRACTICE: CHANGING THE READER'S BEHAVIOUR

This essay, a complaint letter from an employee to her boss, illustrates the challenge of trying to influence another person's behaviour. Read it carefully, and answer the questions that follow. Then select one of the essay assignments.

ESSAY FOR ANALYSIS

LETTER TO THE BOSS

[1]For several months I have been hesitant to approach you about a problem that has caused me great uneasiness at work. More recently, however, I've found that several other employees are equally upset, and I feel, as one of your close friends, that I should explain what's wrong. With you as our boss, we all have an exceptional employer-employee relationship, and I'd hate to see one small problem upset it.

[2]John, when you have criticism about any one of us at work, you never seem to deal directly with that specific person. When the chefs were coming in late, you didn't confront them directly to express your displeasure; instead, you discussed it with the other employees. When you suspected Alan's honesty and integrity as a bartender, you came to me rather than to Alan. I learned yesterday from the coat-checker that you are unhappy with the waitpersons for laughing and joking too much. And these are just a few of many such incidents.

[3]I understand how difficult it is to approach a person with constructive criticism—in fact, it's taken me several months to mention this problem to you! Having been on the receiving end of grapevine gossip, though, I would accept the complaint much more gracefully if it came directly from you. Many of the employees are needlessly upset, and our increasing dissatisfaction harms the quality of our work.

[4]Because I've never been a supervisor, I can only imagine your difficulty. I'm sure your task is magnified because when you bought this restaurant last spring, we employees all knew one another, but you knew none of us. You've told me many times how important it is for you to be a friend to all of us, but sometimes friendship can stand in the way of communication.

[5]Our old boss used to deal with the problem of making constructive suggestions in this way: Every other Saturday evening we would have a meeting at which he would voice his suggestions and we would voice ours. This arrangement worked out well, because none of us felt singled out for criticism, and we all had the chance to discuss problems openly.

[6]I value your friendship, and I hope you will accept this letter in the sincere spirit in which it's offered. I'm sure that with a couple of good conversations we can work things out.

—*Marcia White*

QUESTIONS ABOUT THE READING

CONTENT

- Bracket all facts in this letter, and underline all statements of opinion (see Chapter 5). Are all opinions supported by facts? Explain.
- Does the writer acknowledge the opposing viewpoint? Explain.
- Does the writer admit the imperfections in her case? Explain.

ORGANIZATION

- In the introductory paragraph, is the writer guilty of "beating around the bush"? Explain.
- Which body paragraph spells out the problem?
- Is the final body paragraph too indirect? Explain.
- Which is the most concrete paragraph? Explain its function.

STYLE

- In the second and third body paragraphs, identify one example of coordination. How does this structure reinforce the writer's meaning?
- Is the tone appropriate for the situation, audience, and purpose? Identify three sentences that contribute to this tone.
- Identify three sentences in which the writer expresses empathy with her reader.

OPTIONS FOR ESSAY WRITING

1. Everyone has habits that annoy others or are harmful in some way. Identify the bad habit of a friend, relative, co-worker, or someone you spend a lot of time with, and write a letter trying to persuade the person to break that habit. Suggest specific actions your reader might take to overcome it. (Stay away from the classic cigarette smoking.) Keep in mind you're writing to someone close to you; you want to sound like an honest friend, not a judge. Your reader will be defensive; how can you defuse that defensiveness while getting your message across?

2. Think of a situation in which you recently encountered problems—in a job, in a school, or as a consumer. Choose something about which you have a major complaint. Write a letter to the person who is in charge or is otherwise responsible, laying out the issues and suggesting appropriate changes.

APPLICATION **17-5**

Computer Application: The standard shape for an argument on pages 273–274 suggests an effective arrangement for your thesis, your response to opposing views, your support paragraphs, and your conclusion. But throughout this book, we have seen that the standard shape can be varied in many productive ways. Try out different placements for the various elements of one of your argumentative essays by cutting and pasting. (Be sure to change the file name for each version!) What happens if you position the thesis after the response to opposing arguments instead of before it? What if you place the response to your opposition after the support? Get feedback from classmates about the various options. In particular, notice how different arrangements call for different transitions (pages 102–104) between paragraphs and sections. Be sure to refine these transitions in the final version of this essay you select.

APPLICATION **17-6**

Collaborative/Computer Project: Select one of the types of essays presented in this chapter. Using your *listserv* or e-mail, collaborate with a group of classmates on a joint paper addressed to an appropriate audience. Use the Guidelines for Writing Collaboratively on pages 38–39 (Section One) to brainstorm electronically for a topic, thesis, and support. Then distribute writing tasks, exchange and peer review your work, and construct a draft using transitions to knit the sections together. Submit edited versions to the list and confer electronically about final decisions. As you work, take notes for a future paper about how the electronic process makes working together easier, more complex, or both.

APPLICATION **17-7**

Which of these statements are debatable, and why? (Review pages 269–270.)

1. Grades are an aid to education.
2. Forty percent of incoming first-year students at our school never graduate.
3. Physically and psychically, women are superior to men.
4. Pets should not be allowed on our campus.
5. Computer courses are boring.
6. Every student should be required to become computer literate.
7. The computer revolution is transforming business.
8. French wines are better than domestic wines.

9. French wines generally are more subtle and complex than domestic wines.

10. The price of French wines has risen 20 percent in the past two years.

APPLICATION **17-8**

Using your own subjects or those following, develop five arguable assertions. (Review pages 269–270.)

Examples

[sex] The sexual revolution has created more problems than it has solved.

[education] The heavy remedial emphasis at our school causes many introductory courses to be substandard.

education	law	pollution
sex	music	jobs
drugs	war	residence life

Works Cited

Bauman, K. E., et al. "Three Mass Media Campaigns to Prevent Adolescent Cigarette Smoking." *Preventative Medicine* 17 (1988): 510–30.

Rokeach, Milton. *The Nature of Human Values.* New York: Free Press, 1973.

CHAPTER 18

Special Issues in Persuasion

A persuasive argument connects with readers by appealing to their reason and, often, to their emotions as well.

APPEALING TO REASON

Although argument relies on some combination of description, narration, and exposition, many persuasive arguments are built around one or both of these specific reasoning patterns: *induction* (reasoning from specific evidence to a general conclusion) and *deduction* (applying a proven generalization to a specific case).

Just about any daily decision (including the ones you're asked to make in this book) is the product of inductive or deductive reasoning, or both. Consider this example: You suffer from a bad case of math anxiety. One registration day you're trying to decide on a course to fulfill your math requirement. After speaking with friends and reviewing your available evidence, you immediately decide to register for Math 101 with Professor Digit. Let's trace the reasoning that led to your decision.

First, you reasoned inductively, from this specific evidence to a generalization:

Inductive evidence

- *Fact:* Your older brother, a poor mathematician but a hard worker, took Professor Digit's course two years ago, mastered his own anxiety, and earned a B-minus.
- *Fact:* Although his course is demanding, Professor Digit is known for being friendly, encouraging, and for always being willing to help his students.
- *Fact:* The students you've talked to all praise Professor's Digit's ability to make math "fun and understandable."
- *Fact:* Many of Professor Digit's students go on to take his upper-level math courses as electives.

Based on the above evidence, you reached this generalization about Professor Digit's teaching skills:

A generalization based on inductive evidence

Professor Digit seems to be an excellent math teacher.

The evidence led you to an informed opinion (a probability, not a fact). You reached this opinion through inductive reasoning. You then used deductive reasoning to move from this generalization to a conclusion:

Generalization

Students willing to work hard succeed in Professor Digit's Math 101 course.

Specific instance

I am a hard worker.

Conclusion

I am likely to succeed in Professor Digit's course.

This conclusion led you to register for his section.

We use induction and deduction repeatedly, often unconsciously. Specific facts, statistics, observations, and experiences lead us inductively to generalizations such as these:

Other inductively based generalizations

> Pre-med majors must compete for the highest grades.
>
> Politicians can't always be trusted.
>
> Big cities can be dangerous.
>
> A university degree alone does not ensure success.

On the other hand, deductive reasoning leads us from generalizations to specific instances to conclusions.

Generalization

Specific instance

Conclusion

> Big cities can be dangerous.
>
> Montreal is a big city.
>
> Montreal can be dangerous.

Generalization

Specific instance

Conclusion

> Pre-med majors must compete for the highest grades.
>
> Brigitte will be a pre-med major next year.
>
> Brigitte will have to compete for the highest grades.

When we write to persuade others, we need to use these processes deliberately and consciously.

Using Induction

We use induction in two situations: (1) to move from specific evidence to a related generalization, or (2) to establish the cause or causes of something. Assume you've been dating a Significant Other for a while, but recently you've made these observations:

Reviewing the evidence

> My Significant Other (SO) hasn't returned my phone calls in a week.
>
> My SO always wants to go home early.
>
> My SO yawns a lot when we're together.
>
> My SO talks to everyone but me at parties.

This evidence leads to an inductive generalization:

Generalizing from the evidence

> My SO is losing interest in me.

The same kind of reasoning establishes the possible or probable causes of your SO's aloofness. As you reflect on the relationship, you recall a number of inconsiderate things you've done recently:

Establishing the
cause

> I've been awfully short-tempered lately.
>
> I forgot all about my SO's birthday last week.
>
> I'm usually late for our dates.
>
> A few times, I've made wisecracks about my SO's creepy friends.

And so you conclude that your own inconsiderate behaviour probably damaged the relationship.

Although generalizations aren't proof of anything, the better your evidence, the more likely it is that your generalizations are accurate. Avoid generalizing from too little evidence. That your Significant Other yawns a lot would not be a sufficient basis to conclude that she or he is losing interest. (Maybe he or she's ill or tired!) Or if your SO had yawned during only one evening, that fact alone would not support the hasty generalization that your relationship is on the rocks. Provide enough facts, examples, statistics, and informed opinions to make your assertions believable.

Consider the inductive reasoning employed by Justice Thomas R. Berger in his book *A Long and Terrible Shadow: White Values, Native Rights in the Americas*. The following excerpts demonstrate the effective use of inductive reasoning to argue two issues. On the issue of the movement to boycott seal fur, Berger cites Thomas Coon, a Cree from northern Quebec, who, in 1987, asked:

AN INDUCTIVE ARGUMENT

> How would you feel if 60 per cent, 80 per cent, or 90 per cent of your income was taken away from you? How would you feel when you have little children, a family to support? Killing a market is just like taking the food away from a family's table. Those people were poor before the ban, and today they are poorer . . . . Taking a life is definitely cruelty. No matter how we die as human beings, no matter how we take life, it is a cruelty. Killing a culture, killing a society, and killing a way of life is definitely a cruelty. My culture will die in agony.

On the issue of Aboriginal title, Berger quotes Professor Wilson Duff, who describes in his book *The Indian History of British Columbia* the concept of Aboriginal title as understood by the Aboriginal community:

> It is not correct to say that the [Aboriginal peoples*] did not own land but only roamed over the face of it and used it. The patterns of ownership and utilization which they imposed upon the lands and waters were different from those recognized by our system of law, but were nonetheless clearly defined and mutually respected. Even if they didn't subdivide and cultivate the land, they did recognize ownership of plots used for village sites, fishing places, berry and root patches, and similar purposes. Even if they

*The term *Aboriginal peoples* has replaced the term Indian in the quotation out of respect for our Aboriginal communities.

didn't subject the forests to wholesale logging, they did establish ownership of tracts used for hunting, trapping, and food gathering. Even if they didn't sink mine shafts into the mountains, they did own peaks and valleys for mountain goat hunting and sources of raw materials. Except for barren and inaccessible areas which are not utilized even today, every part of the province was formerly within the owned and recognized territory of the [Aboriginal*] tribes.

Notice how the inductive arguments are organized: Thomas Coon leads up to his premise (my culture will die in agony) by starting with two specific rhetorical questions directed toward his non-Native audience, asking them how they would feel if someone took away the majority of their income when they had children to support and then moving into the cruelty of taking lives by taking away a way of life. Wilson Duff leads up to his premise (that the Natives once owned the whole province of British Columbia) by starting with the smaller premise that their patterns of ownership were different from the white man's patterns and then using three examples of farming, logging, and mining to compare the differences in ownership patterns to support his conclusion.

Using Deduction

You reason deductively when you use generalizations to arrive at specific conclusions. Once the generalization "Killing a way of life is definitely a cruelty" is established inductively (and accepted), one can argue deductively by applying the generalization to a specific instance:

Generalization	Killing a way of life is definitely a cruelty.
	↓
Specific instance	Boycotting the hunting for seal fur has killed a way of life.
	↓
Conclusion	Boycotting the hunting for seal fur is definitely a cruelty.

The conclusion is valid because (a) the generalization is accepted and (b) the specific instance is a fact. Both these conditions must exist in order for the conclusion to be sound.

Here is how you might use deductive reasoning daily:

Examples of deductive reasoning

- If you know that Professor Jones gives no make-up exams, and you sleep through her final, then you can expect to flunk her course.
- If you know that Batmobiles need frequent repairs, and you buy a Batmobile, then you can expect many repairs.

The soundness of deductive reasoning can be measured by sketching an argument in the form of a *syllogism*, the basic pattern of deductive arguments. Any syllogism has three parts: a major premise, a minor premise, and a conclusion:

A valid syllogism

> All humans are mortal. [*Major premise*]
> ↓
> Feliciana is human. [*Minor premise*]
> ↓
> Feliciana is mortal. [*Conclusion*]

If readers accept both premises, they also must accept your conclusion. For the conclusion to be valid, the major premise must state an accepted generalization and the minor premise must state a factual instance of that generalization. Moreover, the conclusion must express the same degree of certainty as the premises (that is, if a "usually" appears in a premise, it must appear in the conclusion as well). Finally, the syllogism must be stated correctly, the minor premise linking its subject with the subject of the major premise; otherwise, the syllogism is faulty:

A faulty syllogism

> All humans are mortal.
> ↓
> John is mortal. [*Minor premise is stated incorrectly; all creatures are mortal, but not all are human.*]
> ↓
> John is human.

Each premise in a syllogism actually is derived from inductive reasoning. Because every human being we've known so far has been mortal, we can reasonably conclude that all human beings are mortal. And once we have examined John thoroughly and classified him as human, we can connect the two premises to arrive at the conclusion that John is mortal.

Illogical deductive arguments may result from a faulty major premise (or generalization). We usually can verify a minor premise (as in the previous example, merely by observing John, to determine if he is human). But the major premise is a generalization; unless we have enough inductive evidence, the generalization can be faulty. How much evidence is enough? Let your good judgment tell you. Base your premise on *reasonable* evidence, so that your generalization reflects reality as discerning people would recognize it. Avoid unreasonable premises such as these:

Faulty generalizations

> All men are male chauvinists.
> School is boring.
> Long-haired men are drug addicts.
> People can't be trusted.
> Frailty, thy name is woman.

Notice the problem when one such generalization serves as the major premise in an argument:

What happens when the major premise is faulty

> People can't be trusted. [*Major premise*]
>   ↓
> My grandparents are people. [*Minor premise*]
>   ↓
> My grandparents can't be trusted. [*Conclusion*]

In ordinary conversation deductive arguments often are expressed as *enthymemes,* implicit syllogisms in which the generalizations are not stated explicitly; instead they are implied, or understood:

Enthymemes are implicit syllogisms

> Joe is ruining his health with cigarettes. [*Implied generalization: Cigarette smoking ruins health.*]
>
> Sally's low verbal scores on her university entrance exam suggest that she will need remedial help in composition. [*Implied generalization: Students with low verbal scores need extra help in composition.*]

Here's what happens to the conclusion when the unstated generalization is faulty:

Faulty enthymemes

> Martha is a feminist, and so she obviously hates men. [*All feminists hate men.*]
>
> He's a member of the clergy, and so what he says must be true. [*Clergy members never are mistaken or dishonest.*]

Another danger in deductive arguments is the overstated generalization; that is, making a limited generalization apply to all cases. Be sure to modify your assertions with qualifying words such as **usually, often, sometimes,** and **some,** instead of absolute words such as **always, all, never,** and **nobody:**

Overstated generalizations

> All Dobermans are vicious. [*Revised: "Some can be . . . ."*]
>
> Politicians never keep their promises. [*Revised: "Some politicians seldom . . . ."*]

In such cases, remember that the conclusion that follows must also be qualified.

A DEDUCTIVE ARGUMENT

> By focusing more on bits of knowledge rather than on critical thinking skills, standardized tests tend to hinder, rather than encourage, student achievement. Critics claim that standardized tests place excessive emphasis on recall and rote learning at the expense of analysis, judgment, inspiration, and reflection. Such tests encourage students to be passive

> learners who need only to recognize—not to construct—answers and solutions. They also promote the misleading impression that every problem or question has one, single, right answer. Finally, they trivialize knowledge and skill development by reducing whatever is taught to a fill-in-the-best-choice format. Aware of these objections, progressive learning communities nationwide are working to develop testing tools that stimulate the student's analytical and imaginative powers.
>
> —*Cheryl Hebert*

The deductive argument in the above paragraph runs like this:

Implied generalization

Specific instance

Conclusion

> Tests that focus on bits of knowledge rather than on critical thinking seem to do more harm than good.
>
> Standardized tests often focus on bits of knowledge.
>
> Therefore, standardized tests often do more harm than good.

The argument is valid because it meets these criteria:

- The major premise is acceptable.
- The minor premise is verifiable.
- The argument is not overstated. Notice the limiting words: "tend to" [not *do*]; "critics claim" [not *critics have proven*].
- The author limits her argument to *one* problem: How such tests may be defeating the aims of education (not how they might provide inaccurate assessment, or favour certain groups, or the like).

RECOGNIZING INVALID OR DECEPTIVE REASONING

Errors in inductive or deductive reasoning are called *fallacies*. Fallacies weaken an argument by (1) breaking the chain of logic or (2) evading the issue.

Fallacies That Break the Chain of Logic

In any valid reasoning pattern, one element logically follows from another (say, when a generalization is derived from credible evidence). But that logical chain can be broken by reasoning errors such as the following.

Faulty Generalizations. When we jump to conclusions on the basis of limited evidence, we commit the error of *hasty generalization*.

Hasty generalization

> My ex-boss was trained at University of Calgary's Business School; she fired everyone in my department; therefore, I dislike everyone from Calgary.

When we overestimate the extent to which the evidence reveals some larger truth, we commit the error of *overstated generalization*.

Overstated generalization	I flunked my first university exam; therefore, I can expect to fail in university.

Consider this extended example: A study in Greece on the role of fruits, vegetables, and olive oil in lowering breast cancer risk was widely publicized in 1995 because of the alleged benefits of olive oil for women who consume olive oil twice or more daily. Subsequent analysis of this study revealed that data about the women's food consumption covered only one year and were based on a single questionnaire asking women to estimate their previous year's diet. (Estimates of this type tend to be highly inaccurate.) Also, the study did not identify the quantities of olive oil individual users consumed. In this instance, then, the study's generalization about olive oil was shown to be *hasty* (based on insufficient evidence).

Further analysis revealed that only 99 respondents (of the nearly 2500 surveyed) claimed to have consumed olive oil twice or more daily ("Olive oil" 1). In this instance, the study's generalization was shown to be *overstated* (a limited generalization applied to all cases). Something true in one instance need not be true in other instances.

Although this particular study was flawed, many other studies support the generalization that fruits and vegetables do help lower the risk of cancer. Generalizing is vital and perfectly legitimate—when it is warranted. How true are these generalizations?

Faulty generalizations	Blondes have more fun.
	Television is worthless.
	Humanities majors rarely get good jobs.

A common version of faulty generalization is *stereotyping*, the simplistic and trite assignment of characteristics to groups.

Stereotypes	All politicians are crooks.
	Mounties are rigid.
	The Irish are big drinkers.

Faulty Causal Reasoning. Causal reasoning tries to explain *why* something happened or *what* will happen, often very complex questions. Anything but the simplest effect is likely to have multiple causes. Faulty causal reasoning oversimplifies or distorts the cause-effect relationship through errors like these:

Ignoring other causes	Investment builds wealth. [*Ignores the role of knowledge, wisdom, timing, and luck in successful investing.*]
Ignoring other effects	Running improves health. [*Ignores the fact that many runners get injured, and that some even drop dead while running.*]
Inventing a causal sequence	Right after buying a rabbit's foot, Felix won the provincial lottery. [*Posits an unwarranted causal relationship merely because one event follows another—the* post hoc *fallacy.*]

Confusing correlation with causation	Poverty causes disease. [*Ignores the fact that disease, while highly associated with poverty, has many causes unrelated to poverty.*]
Rationalizing	My grades were poor because my exams were unfair. [*Denies the real causes of one's failures.*]

Slippery-Slope. We ski the slippery slope when we make some overstated prediction that one action will initiate other actions or events that produce dire consequences.

Slippery-slope assertions	Distributing condoms to high school students will lead to rampant promiscuity.
	Unless we prevent Quebec from seceding, Canada will no longer be a country.

Faulty Analogy. Our analogies are faulty when they overstate the similarities between the two items being compared.

Faulty analogies	All my friends' parents are allowing them to hitchhike across the country. Why can't I?
	In many instances, cancer cells can be eliminated by the appropriate treatment. Since violent criminals are a societal cancer, they should be eliminated by capital punishment.

Question Begging. You beg the question when you base your argument on a claim that remains to be proven. In other words, you commit the fault of circular reasoning by "begging" readers to automatically accept an unproven premise:

Assertions that beg the question	Useless subjects like composition should not be required.
	Voters should reject Candidate X's unfair accusation.
	Books like X and Y, which destroy the morals of our children, should be banned from school libraries.

If a subject is useless, obviously it should not be required. But a subject's uselessness is precisely what has to be established. Likewise, Candidate X's accusation has to be proven unfair, and books such as X and Y have to be proven corrupting.

Either/Or Thinking. You commit the either/or fallacy when you reduce an array of choices to a dilemma: only two extreme positions or sides—black or white—even though other choices exist.

False dilemmas	Students deserve the opportunity to do their best work. But deadlines force students to hand in something not carefully done, just to make sure it's on time. [*Ignores the possibility of doing it on time and doing it well.*]

We have the choice between polluting our atmosphere or living without energy. [*Leaves out the possibility of generating clean energy.*]

Marry me or I'll join the monastery.

Arguing from Ignorance. We argue from ignorance when we contend that an assertion is true because it has not been proven false—or that the assertion is false because it has not been proven true.

Arguments from ignorance

Drunk-driving laws are absurd: I know loads of people who drink and drive and who have never had an accident.

Since the defendant can't offer evidence to prove her innocence, she must be guilty.

Fallacies That Evade the Issue

A deceptive argument clouds the main issue with fallacies such as the following.

Red Herring. Named after the practice of dragging a dead herring across a game trail to distract hunting dogs from their prey, this strategy aims at deflecting attention from the main issue. The distraction commonly involves an attempt to rationalize one's bad action by making it seem insignificant or by pointing to similar actions by others.

Trivializing one's bad action

Asserting that two wrongs make a right

Except for my drunk driving arrest, I've always been a law-abiding citizen.

Sure, I bought my term paper from the CollegeSucks Web site, but so do lots of other students.

Bandwagon Appeal. The bandwagon approach urges readers to climb aboard by claiming that everyone else is doing it.

Bandwagon appeals

This book is a best-seller. How could you ignore it?

More Cadillac owners are switching to Continental than ever before. [*Of course, if the numbers provided real evidence, the assertion would be legitimate.*]

Irrational Appeals to Emotion. As we will see in the next section, some appeals to emotions (pity, fear, and the like) are perfectly legitimate. But you avoid the question when you distract readers from the real issue with material that is irrelevant or that obscures the issue by making an irrational appeal to emotions.

An appeal to pity

He should not be punished for his assault conviction because as a child he was beaten severely by his parents. [*Has no legal bearing on the real issue: his crime.*]

An appeal to fear	If we outlaw guns, only outlaws will have guns. [*Ignores the deaths and injuries caused by "legally owned" guns.*]
An appeal to normalcy	She is the best person for the teaching job because she is happily married and has two lovely children. [*Has nothing to do with the real issue: her qualifications as a teacher.*]
An appeal to flattery	A person with your sophistication surely will agree that marriage is outmoded. [*Has nothing to do with the conclusion that remains to be verified.*]
An appeal to authority or patriotism	Ottawa stands behind savings bonds. [*Ignores the question of whether savings bonds are a good investment: Although they are safe, they pay lower interest than many other investments.*]

The snob appeal to emotion persuades readers to accept your assertion because they want to be identified with respected or notable people.

| Snob appeal | "I want to be like Mike." [*Has nothing to do with the quality of the sneakers or hamburgers or other items being marketed.*] |
| | No All-Canadian sports hero could be guilty of such a horrible crime. [*Ignores the evidence.*] |

Attacking Your Opponent. Another way to ignore the real question is by attacking your opponent through name-calling or derogatory statements about this person on the basis of age, gender, political or sexual orientation, or the like (ad hominem argument):

Ad hominem attacks	The effete intellectual snobs in academia have no right to criticize our increase in military spending. [*Calling people names does not discredit their argument.*]
	How could any man be expected to understand a woman's emotional needs?
	University students are too immature to know what they want, so why should they have a say in the curriculum?

Instead of attacking the person, focus on refuting the argument.

Attacking a Strawperson. You commit a Strawperson fallacy when you distort your opponent's position on the issue and then use that distortion as a basis for attack.

| Strawperson fallacy | Feminists won't be satisfied until males are powerless. |
| | People oppose Affirmative Action because they refuse to give up their own, long-standing privilege. |

When you set out to refute an argument, be sure to represent the opposing position accurately.

APPEALING TO EMOTION

Emotion is no substitute for reason, but some audiences are not persuaded by reason alone. In fact, the audience's attitude toward the writer is often the biggest factor in persuasion—no matter how solid the argument. Audiences are more receptive to people they like, trust, and respect.

Appeals to honesty, fairness, humour, and common sense are legitimate ways of enhancing a supportable argument. On the other hand, appeals to closed-mindedness, prejudice, paranoia, and ignorance (as in the logical fallacies covered earlier) merely hide the fact that an argument offers no authentic support.

Emotional transactions between writer and reader are complex, but the following strategies offer some guidance.

GUIDELINES FOR MAKING EMOTIONAL APPEALS

1. *Try to identify—empathize—with the reader's feelings.*
2. *Show respect for the reader's views.*
3. *Try to appear reasonable.*
4. *Know when and how to be forceful or satirical.*
5. *Know when to be humorous.*

Showing Empathy

To show empathy is to identify with the reader's feelings and to express genuine concern for the reader's welfare. Consider the lack of empathy in this next paragraph.

A MESSAGE THAT LACKS EMPATHY

Dear Buck,

After a good deal of thought I've decided to write to you about your weight problem. Let's face it: You're much too fat. Last week's shopping trip convinced me of that. Remember the bathing suit you liked, the one that came only in smaller sizes? If you lost weight, you might be able to fit into those kinds of suits. In addition to helping you look attractive, the loss of 15 or 20 kilograms of ugly fat would improve your health. All you have to do is exercise more and eat less. I know it will work. Give me a call if you need any more help or suggestions.

This writer's superior tone can't help but alienate the reader. In this next version, he makes a distinct effort to empathize.

A MORE EMPATHETIC VERSION

Dear Buck,

Remember that great bathing suit we saw in Stuart's the other day, the one you thought would be perfect for the beach party but that didn't come in your size? Because the party is still three weeks away, why not begin dieting and exercising so you can buy the suit? I know that losing weight is awfully hard, because I've had to struggle with that problem myself. Buck, you're one of my best friends, and you can count on me for support. A little effort on your part could make a big difference in your life.

Empathy is especially important in arguments that try getting the reader to *do* something.

Acknowledging Opposing Views

Before making your case, acknowledge the opposing case. This next writer takes a controversial position on a turning point in the high school experience. But by showing respect for the traditional view, she decreases readers' resistance to her own position.

AN ACKNOWLEDGMENT OF OPPOSING VIEWS

Orienting statement
(1)
Acknowledgment
of opposing view
(2–3)

Writer's argument
(4)

[1]From our first steps into high school we learn to anticipate an essential rite of passage: the grad formal—one of those memories that last a lifetime. [2]Traditionally, grad night suggests a magical time when it's fun to get dressed up, have pictures taken with your date, enjoy a fancy dinner, and party with your friends; then, after a perfect evening, you kiss your date goodnight and go home. [3]This fairy tale chain of events is how our parents recount their long-ago experiences and it persists as part of the grad formal image. [4]But this benign image too often masks the reality of a night polluted by drugs and sex, a night based on competition and looks, a night hyped to unbelievable proportions, only to become a total letdown.

—*Julia Schoonover*

Maintaining a Moderate Tone

People are more inclined to accept the viewpoint of someone they *like*—someone who seems reasonable. Never overstate your case to make your point. Stay away from emotionally loaded words that boil up in the heat of argument. This next writer is unlikely to win converts:

VOICE OF THE HOTHEAD

Scientists are the culprits responsible for the rape of our environment. Although we never see these beady-eyed, amoral eggheads actually destroying our world, they are busy in their laboratories scheming new ways for industrialists and developers to ravage the landscape, pollute the air, and turn all our rivers, lakes, and oceans into stinking sewers. How anybody with a conscience or a sense of decency would become a scientist is beyond me.

Granted, this piece is forceful and sincere and does suggest the legitimate point that scientists share responsibility—but the writer doesn't seem very likable. The paragraph is more an attack than an argument. Besides generalizing recklessly and providing no evidence for the assertions, the writer uses emotionally loaded words (**eggheads, stinking sewers**) that overstate the position and surely will make readers skeptical.

Here is another version of this paragraph. Understating the controversial point makes the argument more convincing:

A MORE REASONABLE TONE

[1]It might seem unfair to lay the blame for impending environmental disaster at the doorstep of the scientists. [2]Granted, the rape of the environment has been carried out, not by scientists, but by profiteering industrialists and myopic developers, with the eager support of a burgeoning population greedy to consume more than nature can provide and to waste more than nature can clear away. [3]But to absolve the scientific community from complicity in the matter is quite simply to ignore that science has been the only natural philosophy the western world has known since the age of Newton. [4]It is to ignore the key question: who provided us with the image of nature that invited the rape, and with the sensibility that licensed it? [5]It is not, after all, the normal thing for people to ruin their environment. [6]It is extraordinary and requires extraordinary incitement.

—*Theodore Roszak*

Notice how the above argument begins by acknowledging the opposing view (sentences 1–2). The tone is firm yet reasonable. When the writer points the blame at scientists, in sentences 3–4, he offers evidence.

Roszak softens his tone while making his point by using a rhetorical question in sentence 4. *Rhetorical questions* are really statements in the form of questions; because the answer is obvious, readers are invited (or challenged) to provide it for themselves. A rhetorical question can be a good way of impelling readers to confront the issue (as does the question in sentence 2 of the letter to Buck, page 307) without offending them.

But use rhetorical questions with caution. They can easily alienate readers, especially if the issue is personal.

RHETORICAL QUESTIONS USED OFFENSIVELY

Your constant tardiness is an inconvenience to everyone. It's impossible to rely on a person who is never on time. Do you know how many times I've waited in crummy weather for you to pick me up? What about all the appointments I've been late for? Or how about all the other social functions we haven't "quite" made it to on time? It's annoying to everyone when you're always late.

The tone above seems far too aggressive for the situation.

Some strong issues may deserve the emotional emphasis created by rhetorical questions. This is another kind of decision you need to make continually about your audience and purpose.

Using Satire in Appropriate Circumstances

Satire can be one vehicle for expressing forceful anger, frustration, or outrage without alienating readers. No one enjoys being "told off" or ridiculed, but sometimes a jolt of lucid observation—"telling it like it is"—might help readers overcome denial in order to face an issue realistically.

Satire usually relies on irony and sarcasm. *Irony* is a form of expression that states one thing while clearly meaning another. *Sarcasm* employs a more blatant form of irony to mock or to ridicule. For instance, in the essay that follows, Mark Reynolds takes a hard look at the sportsmanship involved in both pro wrestling and big-game hunting.

As you read, think about how the satirical perspective forces a re-examination of attitudes.

SATIRE AS A PERSUASIVE STRATEGY

ALBERTA ELK ASSOCIATION

This summer, the Alberta Elk Association announced it would travel the province to raise support to allow "pen hunting," in which wild animals are stalked within an enclosed area for "sport."

The following is a letter from Mike Norman, Strategic Investments, Canadian Pro Wrestling, to Ron Schmidt, Alberta Elk Association.

First of all, let me thank you for the box of elk steaks enclosed with your proposal—they were a big hit around the office. We would like to know where we can pick up some more for the next inter-league barbecue.

Congratulations on getting approval for pen hunting in Alberta. We believe it has a lot of investment potential. But, before we commit to putting Canadian Pro Wrestling behind your operation, our corporate team would like you to consider the following ideas for improving the entertainment value of what we're tentatively calling "X-treme Elk Kombat."

You propose a hunting pen of 20 hectares. For television production and live audiences, that's simply too large. We suggest the area be reduced to the size of the standard hockey rink. With a proper bulletproof enclosure, this set-up would allow indoor matches at arenas around the world.

To make up for what will likely be called an unfair advantages for the human participant in such a small area of competition, we recommend the addition of obstacles and handicaps. Smoke machines, strobe lighting, and automated "dummy" elk would help even the playing field and heighten the "drama" for the audience.

Though we understand that elk are nimble creatures and a challenging hunt, they lack saleability for television and have too many cuddly associations with Bambi. We were thinking we could add more aggressive animals such as cougars and bears. Unfortunately, the licensing required to import lions and elephants is impossible—as we learned with *Wrestle Madness XII.*

A big part of the success of Canadian Pro Wrestling is the attachment our fans feel for our competitors. This requires personal conflict and drama, what we call "story." To emulate this in pen hunting, we need to create a chief "bad guy"—an uber-elk, if you will. Would it be possible to train one of your animals to use a firearm—perhaps mounted on the antlers—in order to seek revenge for the deaths of his fellow creatures? With the proper special effects, he could "wound" his human pursuers, who would then make it their quest to defeat him.

Although we agree that the recent success of *Gladiator* makes the association tempting, a marketing campaign based on "Lions and Christians II: Now it's our turn" is too highbrow for our target audience. We were thinking of a simpler tag line: "Man against Beast—plus tons of ammo."

Let us know what you think. We look forward to working with you in this exciting endeavour.

—*Mark Reynolds*

Some readers might feel offended or defensive about Mark Reynolds's harsh assessment; however, satire deliberately seeks confrontation. So be sure that you understand its potential effect on your audience before deciding on a satirical perspective in your own writing.

Adding Humour Where Appropriate

Sometimes a bit of humour can rescue an argument that might cause hard feelings. In this next paragraph, the writer wanted to call attention to the delicate issue of his roommate's sloppiness.

HUMOUR AS A PERSUASIVE STRATEGY

Jack,

If you never see me alive again, my body will be at the bottom of your dirty clothes pile that rises like a great mountain in the centre of our room. How did I end up there? Well, while doing my math I ran out of paper and set out for my desk to get a few pieces—despite the risk I knew I was taking. I was met by a two-metre wall of dirty laundry. You know how small our room is; I could not circumnavigate the pile. I thought I'd better write this note before going to the janitor's room for a shovel to dig my way through to my desk. The going will be tough and I doubt I'll survive. If the hard work doesn't kill me, the toxic fumes will. Three years from now, when you finally decide to do your wash, just hang my body up as a reminder to stash your dirty clothes in your closet where they will be out of sight and out of smell.

—*Your dead roommate*

Again, anticipate how your audience will react; otherwise, humour can backfire.

Whichever strategies you employ, don't allow your tone to be voiceless. Readers need to sense a real person behind the words.

APPLICATION **18-1**

The statements below are followed by false or improbable conclusions. What specific supporting evidence would be needed to justify each conclusion so that it is not a specious generalization? (First, you need to infer the missing generalization or premise; then you have to decide what evidence would be needed for the premise to be acceptable.) (Review pages 298–299.)

EXAMPLE

> Only 60 percent of incoming first-year students eventually graduate from this university. Therefore, the university is not doing its job.

To consider this conclusion valid, we would have to be shown that:

  a. All first-year students want to attend university in the first place.

  b. They are all capable of university-level work.

  c. They did all assigned work promptly and responsibly.

  1. Abner always speeds but never has an accident. Therefore, he must be an excellent driver.
  2. Fifty percent of last year's university graduates did not find the jobs they wanted. Therefore, university is a waste of time and money.
  3. Olga never sees a doctor. Therefore, she must be healthy.
  4. This house is expensive. Therefore, it must be well built.
  5. Felix is flunking first-year composition. Therefore, he must be stupid.

APPLICATION **18-2**

PARAGRAPH WARM-UP: INDUCTIVE REASONING

Using the Justice Berger paragraphs (pages 297–298) as models, write a paragraph in which you use inductive reasoning to support a general conclusion about one of these subjects (after you have narrowed it) or about one of your own choice.

highway safety	minorities
a university core requirement	the legal drinking age
the changing role of women	credit cards

Identify your audience and purpose. Provide enough evidence so that readers can follow your line of reasoning to its conclusion.

APPLICATION **18-3**

PARAGRAPH WARM-UP: DEDUCTIVE REASONING

Select an accepted generalization from this list or choose one of your own as the topic statement in a paragraph using deductive reasoning. (Review pages 298–301.)

- "Beauty is in the eye of the beholder."
- "That person is richest whose pleasures are the cheapest."
- Some teachers can have a great influence on a student's attitude toward a subject.
- A university degree doesn't guarantee career success.

APPLICATION **18-4**

Identify the fallacy in each of these sentences and revise the assertion to eliminate the error. (Review pages 301–305.)

EXAMPLE

Faulty   Television is worthless. [*sweeping generalization*]
Revised   Commercial television offers too few programs of educational value.

1. Big Goof received this chain letter, sent out twenty copies, and three days later won the lottery. Little Goof received this chain letter, threw it away, and fell off a cliff the next day.
2. Because our product is the best, it is worth the high price.
3. Canada—love it or leave it.
4. Three of my friends praise their Jettas, proving that Volkswagen makes the best car.
5. My grades last semester were poor because my exams were unfair.
6. Anyone who was expelled from university for cheating could not be trusted as a politician.
7. Until university students contribute to our society, they have no right to criticize our government.
8. Because Angela is a devout Christian, she will make a good doctor.
9. Anyone with common sense will vote for this candidate.
10. You should take up tennis; everyone else around here plays.
11. Hubert, a typical male, seems threatened by feminists.
12. Convex running shoes caused Karl Crane to win the Regina Marathon.
13. My doctor said "Mylanta."

14. How could voters expect any tax-and-spend liberal to know or understand the concerns of working people like us?

15. Sky diving is perfectly safe. After thirty dives it hasn't killed me yet!

16. If non-smokers think their lungs are being violated by smokers, it's a fact of life. Fumes from vehicles, woodstoves, and incinerators all damage everyone's lungs. Should we ban these things, too?

17. Vote for me, or our nation is doomed.

18. How could we trust any promise made by that radical, rightwing nut?

19. Smoking on buses and in elevators is a crime; therefore, smoking in bingo halls should also be a crime.

20. If Canadian-trained teachers keep leaving the country, soon our education system will be suffering severe staff shortages.

21. Gay-rights activists won't be satisfied until schools promote gay lifestyles for all students.

22. If everyone else filed honest tax returns, I would, too.

APPLICATION **18-5**

Revise this next paragraph so that its tone is more moderate and reasonable, more like an intelligent argument than an attack. Feel free to add personal insights that might help the argument.

> People who argue that marijuana should remain outlawed are crazy. Beyond that, many of them are mere hypocrites—the boozers of our world who squander their salary in bars and come home to beat the wife and kids. Any intelligent person knows that alcohol burns out the brain, ruins the body, and destroys the personality. Marijuana is definitely safer: it leaves no hangover; it causes no physical damage or violent mood changes, as alcohol does; and it is not psychologically or physically addictive. Maybe if those redneck jerks who oppose marijuana would put down the beer cans and light a joint, the world would be a more peaceful place.

APPLICATION **18-6**

In his May 2001 paper entitled "'Scutwork': The Marginalization of Writing within Canadian Universities," presented to ACCUTE (Association of Canadian College and University Teachers of English), Dr. Kim Fedderson addresses the issue of how the privileging of reading over writing shapes curriculums at the university, college, and high school levels. Part of his analysis is as follows:

> Finally, this same curricular hierarchy provides the conceptual underpinning for the high school curriculum, and there the role it plays in

reproducing class structures is particularly odious. Last fall, the Ontario government implemented a new high school curriculum, which was reshaped to better prepare students for the 21st-century workplace. The curriculum content in the three new streams—university, community college, and the workplace—is oriented to the post-graduation destination the student has chosen: courses for the university-bound have a greater theoretical orientation, those for the college-bound are more practical, and those for the workplace are focused on specific skill sets. As it undertook the reforms, the Harris government very deliberately reshaped the English curriculum to make it more responsive to the labour market. The variations in the curriculum, while predicated on differences in students' goals upon graduation, in fact, serve to reinforce class distinctions and perpetuate a division of labour. Students reading largely canonical literature in the university stream are offered a curriculum that has a modest historical orientation. As we move from the university to the workplace stream, history disappears. Students studying media in the university stream are introduced to media theory: theory is all but absent in the workplace stream. More significantly, students learning to write in the university stream "focus on using a **voice** suitable to forms studied and used in university programs" (Ontario English Curriculum 22). Even those in the college stream, "focus on using a **voice** suitable to forms studied and used in college programs" (OEC 22). But, voice, the capacity for independent thought and expression, drops out in the workplace stream, where the focus is merely "on using the forms related to the workplace" (OEC 37). The underlying assumption is that those in the workplace do not have the same need of voice as those in other streams. Here our conceptual hierarchy intersects with the government's acceptance of an existing class structure to produce forms of English instruction that will perpetuate that class structure.

—*Dr. Kim Fedderson*

1. Is the argument inductive or deductive? Explain.
2. What kind of evidence does the author use to support his premise?
3. Is his point arguable?

APPLICATION 18-7

Computer Application: "Lurk" on a newsgroup for a couple of days and find examples of faulty logic used by some of the people who post.

APPLICATION **18-8**

Computer Application: Look at the advertisements on the Web and discuss the types of arguments (and fallacies) used.

Work Cited

"Olive Oil and Breast Cancer: How Strong a Connection?" *University of California at Berkeley Wellness Letter* 11.7 (1995): 1–2.

SECTION FOUR

The Research Process

Introduction—Thinking Critically about the Research Process[*]

[*]Thanks to University of Massachusetts Dartmouth librarian Shaleen Barnes for inspiring this introduction.

We do research to obtain facts or expert opinions or to understand issues. For example, we might want to inquire about the prices of building lots on Grand Manan Island, the latest findings in AIDS research, or what experts are saying about global warming. Or, suppose you learn that your well water is contaminated with benzene. Should you merely ask your neighbour's opinion about the dangers, or should you track down the answers for yourself?

In the workplace, professionals need to locate all kinds of information daily (*How do we market this product? How do we avoid accidents like this one? Are we headed for a recession?*). We all have to know where and how to look for answers, and how to communicate them *in writing*. Research is the way to find your own answers; a research report records and discusses your findings.

A *research report* involves a lot more than cooking up any old thesis, settling for the first material you happen to find, and then blending in a few juicy quotations and paraphrases to "prove" you've done the assigned work. Research is a deliberate form of inquiry, a process of *problem solving*. And we cannot begin to solve the problem until we have clearly defined it.

Parts of the research process follow a recognizable sequence. The following steps shown in Figure IV.1 are treated in these chapters:

FIGURE IV.1
Procedural stages in the research process

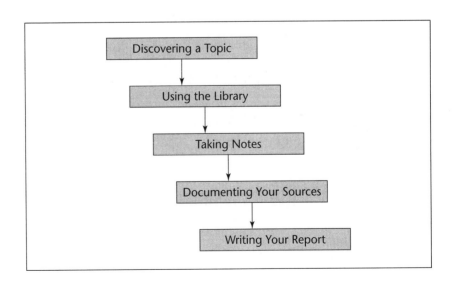

But research writing is never merely a "by-the-number" set of procedures ("First, do this; then do that"). The procedural stages depend on the many careful decisions that accompany any legitimate inquiry, depicted in Figure IV.2.

FIGURE IV.2
Inquiry stages in
the research
process

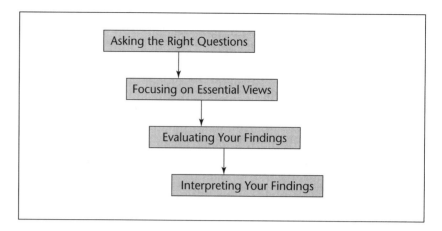

Let's consider how these inquiry stages of the research process lead to the kind of inquiry that makes a real difference.

ASKING THE RIGHT QUESTIONS

The answers you uncover will depend on the questions you ask. Suppose, for instance, you've decided to research the following topic.

DEFINING AND REFINING A RESEARCH QUESTION

The problem of violent crime on campuses has received a good deal of recent publicity. So far your own school has been spared but, as a precautionary measure, campus decision makers are considering doubling the police force and allowing police to carry guns. Some groups are protesting, claiming that guns pose a needless hazard to students or that funding for additional police should be devoted to educational programs instead. On the student senate you and your colleagues have discussed the controversy, and you have been appointed to prepare a report that examines the trends regarding violent crime on campuses nationwide. Your report will form part of a document to be presented to the student and faculty senates in six weeks.

First, you need to identify the exact question or questions you want answered. Before settling on a definite question, you need to navigate a long list of possible questions, like those in the Figure IV.3 tree chart. Any *one* of the questions could serve as the topic of a worthwhile research report on such a complex topic.

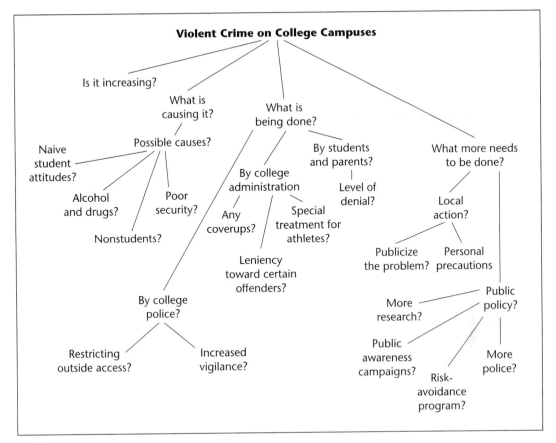

FIGURE IV.3
How the right questions help define a research problem

EXPLORING A BALANCE OF VIEWS

Instead of settling for the most comforting or convenient answer, pursue the *best* answer. Even "expert" testimony may not be enough, because experts can disagree or be mistaken. To answer fairly and accurately, you are ethically obligated to consider a balance of perspectives from up-to-date and reputable sources (Figure IV.4).

Let's say you've chosen this question: *Violent crimes on campuses: How common is it?* Now you can consider sources to consult (journals, reports, news articles, Internet sites, database searches, and so on). Figure IV.5 lists some likely sources of information on college crime.

FIGURE IV.4
Effective research
considers multiple
perspectives

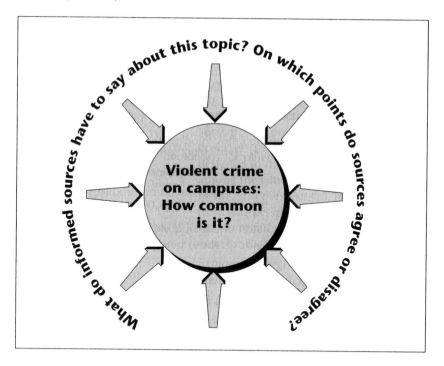

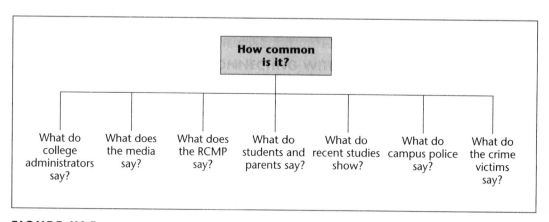

FIGURE IV.5
A range of essential viewpoints

NOTE   *Recognize the difference between "balance" (sampling a full range of opinions)
and "accuracy" (getting at the facts). The media, for example, might present a
more negative view than the facts warrant. Not every source is equal, nor
should we report points of view as if they were equal (Trafford 137).*

ACHIEVING ADEQUATE DEPTH IN YOUR SEARCH*

Balanced research examines a *broad range* of evidence; thorough research, however, examines that evidence in sufficient *depth*. Different sources of information have different levels of detail and dependability (Figure IV.6).

1. At the surface layer are items from the popular press (newspapers, radio, TV, magazines, certain Internet newsgroups and Web sites). Designed for general consumption, this layer of information often merely skims the surface of an issue.

2. At the next level are trade and business publications or Web sites (*Law Enforcement Digest, The Chronicle of Higher Education,* Internet *Listservs,* and so on). Designed for readers who range from moderately informed to highly specialized, this layer of information focuses more on practice than on theory, on items considered newsworthy to group members, on issues affecting the field, and on public relations. While the information is usually accurate, viewpoints tend to reflect a field's particular biases.

3. At a deeper level is the specialized literature (journals from professional associations: academic, medical, legal, engineering, and so on). Designed for practising professionals, this layer of information focuses on theory as well as practice: on descriptions of the latest studies

FIGURE IV.6
Effective research achieves adequate depth

The depth of a source often determines its quality

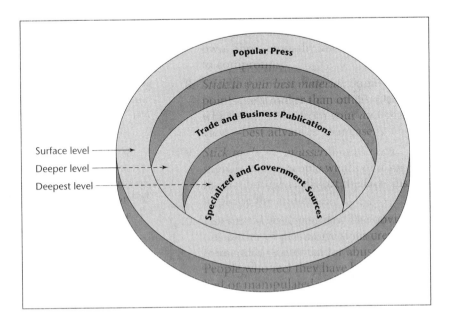

Surface level
Deeper level
Deepest level

Popular Press
Trade and Business Publications
Specialized and Government Sources

*Thanks to University of Massachusetts Dartmouth librarian Ross LaBaugh for inspiring this section.

(written by the researchers themselves and scrutinized by others for accuracy and objectivity), on debates among scholars and researchers, and on reviews and critiques of prior studies and publications.

Also at this deeper level are government sources (studies and reports by CCIW, CIDA, CWS, the RCMP, the House of Commons) and corporate documents available through the *Access to Information Act* (page 337). Designed for anyone willing to investigate its complex resources, this layer of information offers hard facts and highly detailed and (in many instances) *relatively* impartial views.

Most of these sources are accessible via the Internet, through specialized search engines such as Lexis Nexis. Ask your librarian.

NOTE   *Web pages, of course, offer links to increasingly specific levels of detail, but the actual "depth" and quality of information from a particular Web site ultimately depend on the sponsorship and reliability of that site (page 362).*

How "deep" is deep enough? This depends on your topic. But the real story and the hard facts more likely reside at deeper levels. Research on college crime, for instance, would need to look beneath popular "headlines," focusing instead on studies done by experts.

GUIDELINES FOR EVALUATING EXPERT INFORMATION

To use expert information effectively, follow these suggestions:

1. *Look for common ground.* When opinions conflict, consult as many experts as possible and try to identify those areas in which they agree (Detjen 170).

2. *Consider all reasonable opinions.* Science writer Richard Harris notes that "Often [extreme views] are either ignored entirely or given equal weight in a story. Neither solution is satisfying. . . . Putting [the opinions] in balance means . . . telling . . . where an expert lies on the spectrum of opinion. . . . The minority opinion isn't necessarily wrong—just ask Galileo" (Harris 170).

3. *Be sure the expert's knowledge is relevant in this context.* Don't seek advice about a brain tumour from a podiatrist.

4. *Don't expect certainty.* In complex issues, experts cannot *eliminate* uncertainty; they can merely help us cope with it.

5. *Don't expect objectivity in all cases.* For example, the expert might have a financial or political stake in the issue or might hold a radical point of view.

6. *Expect special interests to produce their own experts to support their position.*

7. *Learn all you can about the issue before accepting anyone's final judgment.*

EVALUATING YOUR FINDINGS

Not all findings have equal value. Some information might be distorted, incomplete, or misleading. Information might be tainted by *source bias,* in which a source might understate or overstate certain facts, depending on whose interests that source represents—say, university administrators, or students, or a reporter seeking headlines.

Questions for Evaluating a Particular Finding

- *Is this information accurate, reliable, and relatively unbiased?*
- *Can the claim be verified by the facts?*
- *How much of it (if any) is useful?*
- *Is this the whole or the real story?*
- *Do I need more information?*

Remember, ethical researchers don't try to prove the "rightness" of some initial assumptions; instead, they research to find the *right* answers. And only near the end of your inquiry can you settle on a *definite* thesis based on what the facts suggest.

INTERPRETING YOUR FINDINGS

Once you have decided which of your findings seem legitimate, you must decide what they mean.

Questions for Interpreting Your Findings

- *What are my conclusions?*
- *Do any findings conflict?*
- *Are other interpretations possible?*
- *Should I reconsider the evidence?*
- *What, if anything, should be done?*

Even the best research can produce contradictory or indefinite conclusions. For example (Lederman 5): What does a reported increase in violent crime on U.S. and Canadian college campuses mean—especially in light of national statistics that show violent crime decreasing?

- That college students are becoming more violent?
- That some drugs and guns in high schools end up on campuses?
- That off-campus criminals see students as easy targets?

Or could these findings mean something else entirely?

FIGURE IV.7
Critical thinking in the research process

No single stage is complete until all stages are complete

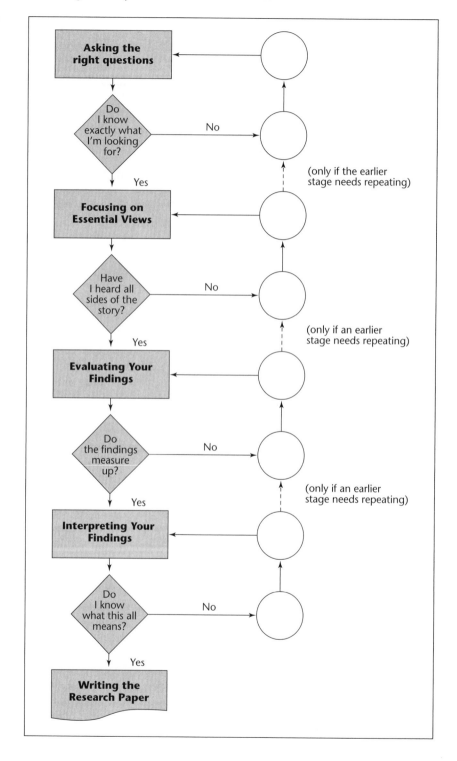

- That increased law enforcement has led to more campus arrests—and thus greater recognition of the problem?
- That crimes actually have not increased, but fewer now go unreported?

Depending on our interpretation, we might conclude that the problem is worsening—or improving!

Figure IV.7 shows the critical-thinking decisions crucial to worthwhile research: asking the right questions about your topic, your sources, your findings, and your conclusions. Like the writing process (Figure 1.2 on page 16), the research process is *recursive:* stages are revisited and repeated as often as necessary.

NOTE   *Never force a simplistic conclusion on a complex issue. Sometimes the best you can offer is an indefinite conclusion. A wrong conclusion is far worse than no definite conclusion at all.*

Works Cited

Detjen, Jim. "Environmental Writing." *A Field Guide for Science Writers.* Eds. Deborah Blum and Mary Knudson. New York: Oxford, 1997. 173–79.

Harris, Richard F. "Toxics and Risk Reporting." *A Field Guide for Science Writers.* Eds. Deborah Blum and Mary Knudson. New York: Oxford, 1997. 166–72.

Lederman, Douglas. "Colleges Report Rise in Violent Crime," *Chronicle of Higher Education* 3 Feb. 1995, sec. A: 31–42.

Trafford, Abigail. "Critical Coverage of Public Health and Government." *A Field Guide for Science Writers.* Eds. Deborah Blum and Mary Knudson. New York: Oxford, 1997. 131–41.

CHAPTER 19

Asking Questions and Finding Answers

DECIDING ON A RESEARCH TOPIC

A crucial step in developing a research report is deciding on a worthwhile topic. Begin with a subject with real meaning for you, and then decide on the specific question you want to ask about it. Pages 320–327 show how the subject of campus crime might be narrowed. Now let's try another subject.

GUIDELINES FOR CHOOSING A RESEARCH TOPIC

1. *Avoid topics that are too broad for a six- to twelve-page research report.* The topic "Do food additives and preservatives affect children?" would have to include children's growth and development, their intelligence, their susceptibility to diseases, and so on.

2. *Avoid topics that limit you to a fixed viewpoint before you've done your research:* "Which behaviour disorders in children are caused by food additives and preservatives?" Presumably, you haven't yet established that such chemicals have any harmful effects. Your initial research is meant to find the facts, not to prove some point. Allow your thesis to grow from your collected facts, instead of manipulating the facts to fit your thesis.

3. *Avoid topics that have been exhausted:* abortion, capital punishment, gun control—unless, of course, you can approach such topics in a fresh way: "Could recent technological developments to help a fetus survive outside the womb change our laws on abortion?"

4. *Avoid topics that can be summed up in an encyclopedia entry or in any one source:* "The Life of Thoreau," "How to Cross-Country Ski," or "The History of

Microwave Technology." From a different angle, of course, any of these areas might allow you to draw your own, more interesting conclusions: "Was Thoreau Ever in Love?"; "How Do Injury Rates Compare Between Cross-Country and Downhill Skiing?"; "How Safe are Microwave Ovens?"

5. *Avoid religious, moral, or emotional topics that offer no objective basis for informed conclusions:* "Is Euthanasia Moral?"; "Will Jesus Save the World?"; "Should Prayer Be Allowed in Public Schools?" Questions debated throughout the ages by philosophers, judges, and social thinkers are unlikely to be definitively answered in your research paper.

6. *Consider narrowing your focus electronically.* For example, browse through subject and subtopic lists catalogued on *Yahoo!* www.yahoo.com. Continue exploring subtopics until you locate the right topic and the listing of related Web sites. Or explore subject categories at *WWW Virtual Library* www.vlib.org. Or scan more than 4000 research topics listed in the *Idea Directory* at *Researchpaper.com* (www.researchpaper.com).

Let's say you're disturbed about all the chemicals used to preserve or enhance flavour and colour in foods—*food additives and preservatives.* What specific part of this subject would you like to focus on? This will be your *topic,* and it should be phrased as a question. To identify the possible questions you might ask, develop a tree chart (as on page 321). Your interests might lead you to this question: *What effects, if any, do food additives and preservatives have on children's behaviour?*

NOTE *Far more important than the topic you choose is the question you decide to ask about it. Plan to spend many hours in search of the right question.*

PRIMARY VERSUS SECONDARY SOURCES

How primary and secondary sources differ

For many topics, you will want *primary* as well as *secondary* sources. Primary research is a firsthand study of the topic from observation, questionnaires, interviews, inquiry letters, works of literature, or personal documents. If your topic is the love life of Thoreau, a good primary source will be his poems, journals, and letters—or an interview with a specialist in the English department. Secondary research is based on information and conclusions that other researchers—by their primary research—have compiled in books and articles. Secondary sources are *about* primary sources. Whenever possible, combine these approaches.

HARD COPY VERSUS ELECTRONIC SOURCES

Although electronic searches for information are becoming the norm, a *thorough* search often requires careful examination of hard copy sources as well. Advantages and drawbacks of each search medium (Table 19.1) often provide good reason for exploring both.

Benefits of hard copy sources

Hard copy libraries offer the judgment and expertise of librarians who organize and search for information. Compared with electronic files (on disks, tapes, hard drives), hard copy is easier to protect from tampering and to preserve from aging. (An electronic file's life span can be as brief as ten years.)

NOTE *For many automated searches, a manual search of hard copy is usually needed as well. A manual search provides the whole "database" (the bound index or abstracts). As you browse, you often randomly discover something useful.*

Drawbacks of hard copy sources

Manual searches (flipping pages by hand), however, are time-consuming and inefficient: books can get lost; relevant information has to be pinpointed and retrieved or "pulled" by the user. Also, hard copy cannot be updated easily.

Benefits of electronic sources

Compared with hard copy, electronic sources are more current, efficient, and accessible. Sources are updated rapidly. Ten or fifteen years of an index can be reviewed in minutes. Searches can be customized: for example, narrowed to specific dates or topics. They also can be broadened: a

Table 19.1   HARD COPY VERSUS ELECTRONIC SOURCES: BENEFITS AND DRAWBACKS

	Benefits	Drawbacks
Hard Copy Sources	• organized and searched by librarians • often screened by experts for accuracy • easier to preserve and keep secure	• time-consuming and inefficient to search • offer only text and images • hard to update
Electronic Sources	• more current, efficient, and accessible • searches can be narrowed or broadened • can offer material that has no hard copy equivalent	• access to recent material only • not always reliable • user might get lost

keyword search (page 342) can uncover material that a hard copy search might have overlooked; Web pages can provide links to material of all sorts—much of which exists in hard copy form.

Drawbacks of electronic sources

Drawbacks of electronic sources include the fact that databases rarely contain entries published before the mid-1960s and that material, especially on the Internet, can change or disappear overnight or be highly unreliable. Also, given the potential for getting lost in cyberspace, a thorough electronic search calls for a preliminary conference with a trained librarian.

NOTE

One recent study found greater than 50 percent inconsistency among database indexers. Thus, even an electronic search by a trained librarian can miss improperly indexed material (Lang and Secic 174–75).

EXPLORING HARD COPY SOURCES

Where you begin your hard copy search depends on whether you are searching background and basic facts or the latest information. Library sources appear in Figure 19.1.

If you are an expert in the field, you might simply do a computerized database search or browse through specialized journals and *listservs*. If you have limited knowledge or you need to focus your topic, you probably will want to begin with general reference sources.

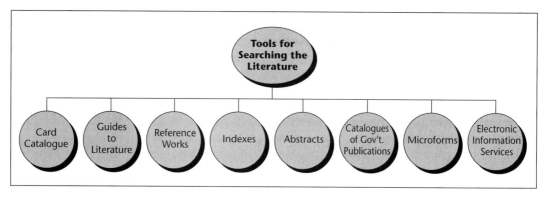

FIGURE 19.1
Ways you can search the literature

NOTE	*University of Massachusetts, Dartmouth, librarian Ross LaBaugh suggests beginning with the popular, general literature, then working toward journals and other specialized sources: "The more accessible the source, the less valuable it is likely to be."*

Reference Works

Reference sources provide background information

Reference works include encyclopedias, almanacs, handbooks, dictionaries, histories, and biographies. These provide background and bibliographies that can lead to more specific information. Make sure the work is current by checking the last copyright date.

Bibliographies. These comprehensive lists of publications about a subject are issued yearly, or even weekly. However, others can quickly become dated.

Annotated bibliographies (which include an abstract for each entry) are most helpful. Sample listings (with annotations):

Bibliographies

MLA International Bibliography. The basic research tool for the humanities, published annually by the Modern Language Association.

Bibliographic Index. A list (by subject) of bibliographies that contain at least 50 citations; to see which bibliographies are published in your field, begin here.

Guide to Canadian Government. A comprehensive list of Government of Canada publications.

Health Hazards of Video Display Terminals: An Annotated Bibliography. One of many bibliographies focused on a specific subject.

Bibliographies often can be searched electronically via your school's Web site. Ask your reference librarian or browse the library's home page.

Encyclopedias. Encyclopedias provide basic information (which might be outdated). Sample listings:

Encyclopedias

Cassell's Encyclopedia of World Literature

Encyclopedia of Social Sciences

Encyclopedia of Food Technology

Most Web encyclopedias, except for *Britannica,* charge a monthly access fee, but many schools subscribe, thereby giving students free access. *Encarta* offers summarized versions of articles at no charge.

The *Encyclopedia of Associations* lists over 30 000 professional organizations worldwide (Canadian Federation of Humane Societies, Institute of Electrical and Electronics Engineers, Canadian Association of Disabled Skiing).

Dictionaries. Dictionaries can be generalized or they can focus on specific disciplines or give biographical information. Sample listings:

Dictionaries

Dictionary of Engineering and Technology

Dictionary of Telecommunications

Dictionary of Scientific Biography

Handbooks. These research aids amass key facts (formulas, tables, advice, examples) about a field in condensed form. Sample listings:

Handbooks

Business Writer's Handbook

Civil Engineering Handbook

The McGraw-Hill Computer Handbook

Almanacs. Almanacs contain factual and statistical data. Sample listings:

Almanacs

World Almanac and Book of Facts

Scott's Canadian Sourcebook

Almanac of Business and Industrial Financial Ratios

Directories. In directories you will find updated information about organizations, companies, people, products, services, or careers, often including addresses and phone numbers. Sample listings:

Directories

The Career Guide: Dun's Employment Opportunities Directory

Directory of Canadian Scientific and Technical Data Bases

The Internet Directory

Reference works increasingly are accessible by computer. Some, such as the *Free Online Dictionary of Computing,* are wholly electronic.

NOTE

Many of the reference works listed above are accessible at no charge via the Internet. Go to the Internet Public Library at www.ipl.org or consult "Appendix C: Useful Web Sites and Electronic Library Resources" (page 482).

The Card Catalogue

All books, reference works, indexes, periodicals, and other materials held by a library are usually listed in its card catalogue under three headings: *author, title,* and *subject.*

Most libraries are automating their card catalogues. These electronic catalogues offer additional access points (beyond *author, title,* and *subject*) including:

Access points for an electronic card catalogue

- *Descriptor:* For retrieving works on the basis of a keyword or phrase (for example, "electromagnetic" or "power lines and health") in the subject heading, in the work's title, or in the full text of its bibliographic record (its catalogue entry or abstract).
- *Document type:* for retrieving works in a specific format (videotape, audiotape, compact disk, motion picture).
- *Organizations and Conferences:* for retrieving works produced under the name of an institution or professional association (Brookings Institution or Canadian Heart and Stroke Association).
- *Publisher:* for retrieving works produced by a particular publisher (for example: Little, Brown, and Co.).
- *Combination:* for retrieving works by combining any available access points (a book about a particular subject by a particular author or institution). Through the Internet, a library's electronic catalogue can be searched from anywhere in the world. To search many different libraries easily, use the National Library of Canada Web site at www.nlc-bnc.ca/canlib/eindex.htm.

Guides to Literature

If you simply don't know which books, journals, indexes, and reference works are available for your topic, consult a guide to literature. For a general list of books in various disciplines, see Walford's *Guide to Reference Material* or Sheehy's *Guide to Reference Books.*

For scientific and technical literature, consult Malinowsky and Richardson's *Science and Engineering Literature: A Guide to Reference Sources.* Ask your librarian about literature guides for your discipline.

Indexes

Indexes offer current information

Indexes are lists of books, newspaper articles, journal articles, or other works on a particular subject.

Book Indexes. A book index lists works by author, title, or subject. Sample indexes:

Book indexes

Canadian Books in Print. An annual listing of all books published in Canada.

Books in Print. An annual listing of all books published in the United States.

New Technical Books. A selective list with descriptive annotations. Issued ten times yearly.

Medical and Healthcare Books and Serials in Print. An annual listing of works from medicine and psychology.

NOTE

No book is likely to offer the very latest information because of the time required to publish a book manuscript (from several months to over one year).

Newspaper Indexes. These indexes list articles from major newspapers by subject. Sample titles:

Newspaper indexes

Canadian News Index

The Christian Science Monitor Index

Wall Street Journal Index

Most newspapers and news magazines are searchable via their Web sites, and they usually charge a fee for searches of past issues.

Periodical Indexes. A periodical index provides sources from magazines and journals. First decide whether you seek general or specialized information. Two general indexes are the *Magazine Index,* a subject index on microfilm, and the *Readers' Guide to Periodical Literature,* which is updated every few weeks.

For specialized information, consult indexes that list journal articles in specific disciplines, such as *Ulrich's International Periodicals Directory,* the *General Science Index,* the *Applied Science and Technology Index,* or the *Business Periodicals Index.* Specific disciplines have their own indexes:

Periodical indexes

Biological and Agricultural Index

Canadian Business and Current Affairs Index

Canadian Music Periodicals Index

Ask your librarian about the best indexes for your topic and about the many indexes that can be searched by computer. For example, the *Expanded Academic Index,* searchable by CD-ROM, provides listings from some 1200 journals, including the full text and images from many of these works.

Citation Indexes. Citation indexes enable researchers to trace the development and refinement of a published idea. Using a citation index, you can track down the specific publications in which the original material has been cited, quoted, applied, critiqued, verified, or otherwise amplified. In short, you can answer this question: *Who else has said what about this idea?*

The *Science Citation Index* cross-references articles on science and technology worldwide. Both the *Science Citation Index* and its counterpart, the *Social Science Citation Index,* are searchable by computer.

Indexes to Conference Proceedings. Many of the papers presented at the more than 10 000 yearly professional conferences are collected and then indexed in printed or computerized listings such as these:

Indexes to confer-
ence proceedings

Proceedings in Print

Index to Scientific and Technical Proceedings

*Engineering Meetings (*an *Engineering Index* database*)*

The very latest ideas or explorations or advances in a field often are presented during such proceedings, before appearing as journal publications. Check your library's electronic resources to see which indexes are searchable by computer.

Abstracts

By indexing and also summarizing each article, an abstract can save you from going all the way to the journal to decide whether to read the article or to skip it. Abstracts usually are titled by discipline:

Collections of
abstracts

Biological Abstracts

Computer Abstracts

Forestry Abstracts

Readers' Guide Abstracts

For some current research, you might consult abstracts of doctoral dissertations in *Dissertation Abstracts International.* Abstracts increasingly are searchable by computer. Check your library's electronic resources.

Access Tools for Canadian and U.S. Government Publications

Federal governments publish maps, periodicals, books, pamphlets, manuals, monographs, annual reports, research reports, and a bewildering array of other information, often searchable by computer. A few of the countless titles available:

Government
publications

Geological Survey of Canada, Current Research

Basic Labour Force Statistics for Canada from Stats Canada's CANSIM

Major Oil and Gas Fields of the Free World

Your best bet for tapping this complex resource is to request assistance from the librarian in charge of government documents. Here are the basic access tools for documents issued or published at government expense, as well as for many privately sponsored documents.

Access tools

- *Weekly Checklist of Canadian Government Publications*, a major pathway to government publications and reports.
- *The Monthly Catalog of the United States Government*, the major pathway to U.S. government publications and reports.
- *Directory of Statistics in Canada*, a single source for bibliographic records of Canadian statistical publications.

Finally, the government also publishes bibliographies on hundreds of subjects, from "Accidents and Accident Prevention" to "Home Gardening of Fruits and Vegetables."

Many unpublished documents are available, in Canada, under the *Access to Information Act*. This act grants public access to all federal agency records except for classified documents, trade secrets, certain law enforcement files, records protected by the *Privacy Act*, and similar categories of exempted information.

Publicly accessible government records

Suppose you want to read individual appeals and applications for refugee status redetermination made before January 1, 1989, to the former Immigration Appeals Board. In this case, the Canadian Immigration and Appeals Board keeps such information available. Or, you have heard that a university student has claimed that his financial aid providers failed to accommodate his disability. You can find the details under the Canadian Human Rights Commission. Or if you want to know if the RCMP has a file on you, then you can access this information as well. (Sources of Federal Government Information 2001/2002)

Contact the agency that would hold the data you seek: for fact sheets on various species of fish and shellfish produced in Canada, Agriculture and Agri-food Canada; for a wide range of medical conditions that result from exposure to various hazards on the job, the Canadian Centre for Occupational Health and Safety.

Government information increasingly is posted to the Internet or the World Wide Web. For example, the Transportation Safety Board of Canada posts its annual transportation occurrence statistics on accidents in the four transportation modes (air, marine, rail, and pipeline). Health Canada posts information on the effects of fetal alcohol syndrome and air and water contaminants.

Ask your reference librarian for electronic addresses of government agencies. A good starting point is the Canadian Government Information in the Internet (CGII) home page at igci.gc.ca/index-e.html and the Library of Congress World Wide Web Home Page at http://lcWeb.loc.gov. See Appendix C for other useful Web sites.

Microforms

Microform technology allows vast quantities of printed information to be stored on microfilm or microfiche. (This material is read on machines that magnify the reduced image.)

EXPLORING ONLINE SOURCES

The hard copy sources discussed earlier are increasingly available in electronic form, accessible through your library or the Internet and the World Wide Web.

Compact Disks

A single CD-ROM disk stores the equivalent of an entire encyclopedia and serves as a portable database.

One useful CD-ROM for business information is ProQuest™: its *ABI/INFORM* database indexes over 800 journals in management, marketing, and business published since 1989; its *UMI* database indexes major newspapers. A keyword search of ProQuest's subject headings, titles, and abstracts yields a listing of relevant titles. You then can obtain the full bibliographic record, including the abstract, for each title of interest.

A useful CD-ROM for information about psychology, nursing, education, and social policy is SilverPlatter™, whose databases are easily accessed via keyword searches. Both ProQuest and SilverPlatter databases are updated frequently and subscribers (libraries and other organizations) receive revised disks regularly.

Consult Appendix C for a listing of CD-ROM resources commonly accessible from a university library, and check your library's holdings.

NOTE *In many cases, CD-ROM access via the Internet is restricted to users who have their own passwords for entering a particular library's information system.*

Mainframe Databases

University and college libraries subscribe to online retrieval services that can access thousands of databases stored on centralized computers. From a library terminal or personal computer (using a password) you can access indexes, journals, books, monographs, dissertations, and reports. Compared with CDs, mainframe databases are usually more specialized and more current, often updated daily (as opposed to the weekly, monthly, or quarterly updating of CD databases).

Online retrieval services offer three types of databases: bibliographic, full-text, and factual (Lavin 14):

Types of online
databases

- *Bibliographic databases* list publications in a particular field and sometimes include abstracts of each entry.
- *Full-text databases* display the entire article or document (usually excluding graphics) directly on the computer screen, and then will print the article on command.
- *Factual databases* provide facts of all kinds: global and up-to-the-minute stock quotations, weather data, lists of new patents filed, and credit ratings of major companies, to name a few.

The following sections discuss three popular database services.

OCLC and RLIN. You easily can compile a comprehensive list of works on your subject at any library that belongs to the Online Computer Library Center (OCLC) or the Research Libraries Information Network (RLIN). OCLC and RLIN databases store millions of records of the same information in a printed card catalogue. Using a networked terminal, you type in author or title. You will then get a listing of the publication you seek and information about where to find it.

DIALOG. Many libraries subscribe to DIALOG, a network of more than 150 independent databases covering a broad range of subjects. You retrieve information by typing in key terms; the computer scans bibliography lists for titles containing those terms. Say you need information on possible *health hazards* from *household electrical equipment.* You instruct the computer to search MEDLINE®, a medical database, for titles including *health hazards* or synonymous words, such as *risk, danger, appliances.* The system provides full bibliographies and abstracts of the most recent medical articles on your topic.

Here are a few of DIALOG's databases:

DIALOG databases   *Conference Papers Index*

Electronic Yellow Pages (for retailers, services, manufacturers)

Enviroline

Comprehensive databases such as DIALOG are accessible via the Internet for a fee (or, via password, through your school's library network at no cost). Specialized databases, such as MEDLINE or ENVIROLINE, offer bibliographies and abstracts free, and for a fee copies of the full text can be ordered.

Check on the databases accessible through your library.

NOTE   *Never assume that computers yield the best material. University of Massachusetts Dartmouth database specialist Charles McNeil points out that "the material in the computer is what is cheapest to put there." Reference librarian Ross LaBaugh warns of a built-in bias in databases: "The company that assembles the bibliographic or full-text database often includes a disproportionate number of its own publications." Like any collection of information, a database can reflect the biases of its assemblers.*

EXPLORING INTERNET SOURCES

Today's Internet connects computer users by the tens of millions, and Web sites and addresses (uniform resource locators, or URLs) numbering in the hundreds of millions continue to multiply across the globe.

Internet service providers (ISPs), including commercial services such as *Compuserve, America Online,* and *Microsoft Network,* provide Internet access via "gateways," along with aids for navigating its many resources (see Figure 19.2).

FIGURE 19.2
Various parts of the Internet

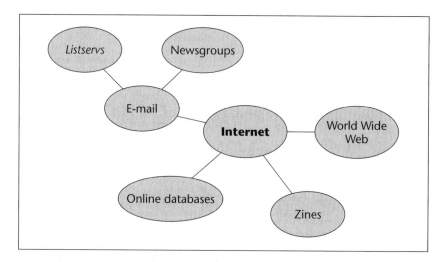

Usenet

Usenet denotes a worldwide system for online discussions via newsgroups, a type of electronic bulletin board at which users post and share information and discuss topics of common interest via e-mail. Newsgroups offer public access to countless topics ranging from rain-forest preservation to intellectual property laws to witchcraft.

Newsgroups are either *moderated* or *unmoderated*. In a moderated group, all contributions are reviewed by a moderator who must approve the material before it can be posted. In an unmoderated group, all contributions are posted. Most newsgroups are unmoderated. Also available are *newsfeed* newsgroups, which gather and post news items from wire services such as the Associated Press.

Newsgroups typically publish answers to "frequently asked questions" (*FAQ lists*) about their particular topic of interest (acupuncture, AIDS research, sexual harassment, etc.). While these can be a good source of any group's distilled wisdom, FAQs reflect the biases of those who contribute to and edit them (Busiel and Maeglin 5). A group's particular convictions might politicize information and produce all sorts of inaccuracies (Snyder 90).

For a comprehensive index of newsgroups go to www.liszt.com/news.

Listservs

Like newsgroups, *listservs* are special-interest groups for e-mail discussion and information sharing. In contrast to newsgroups, *listserv* discussions usually focus on specialized topics, with discussions usually among experts (say, cancer researchers), often before their findings or opinions appear in published form. Many *listservs* include a FAQ listing of answers to frequently asked questions.

Listserv access is available to subscribers who receive mailings automatically via e-mail. Instead of delivering messages to a newsgroup bulletin board, *listservs* deliver to each subscriber's electronic "mailbox." Like a newsgroup, a *listserv* may be moderated or unmoderated, but subscribers/ contributors are expected to observe proper Internet etiquette and to stick to discussion of the topic, without digressions or "flaming" (attacking someone) or "spamming" (posting irrelevant messages). Some lists allow anyone to subscribe, while others require that subscription requests be approved by the list owner. In general, only subscribers can post messages to the list.

To find *listservs* relevant to your topic, begin by visiting a comprehensive list directories such as www.liszt.com or http://tile.net/lists.

Electronic Magazines (Zines)

Zines offer information available only in electronic form. Despite the broad differences in quality among different zines, this online medium offers certain benefits over hard copy magazines (Brody 40):

Benefits of online magazines

- links to related information
- immediate access to earlier issues
- interactive forums for discussions among readers, writers, and editors
- rapid updating and error correction.

Major news publications such as *The Globe and Mail* offer interactive editions online. See Appendix C for listings.

E-mail Inquiries

The global e-mail network is excellent for contacting knowledgeable people in any field worldwide. E-mail addresses are increasingly accessible via locator programs that search various local directories listed on the Internet (Steinberg 27). But unsolicited and indiscriminate e-mail inquiries might offend the recipient.

World Wide Web

The Web is a global network of databases, documents, images, and sounds. All types of information from anywhere in the Web network can be accessed and explored through search engines known as "browsers," such as *Lynx, Netscape Navigator,* or *Microsoft Internet Explorer.* Hypertext links among Web resources enable users to explore information along different paths by clicking on key words or icons that reveal additional paths for browsing and discovery.

Each Web site has its own *home page* that serves as introduction to the site and is linked to additional "pages" that individual users can explore according to their information needs.

Through your campus or office network, or using a modem, a phone line, and an Internet service provider, you can search Internet files and databases. You can participate in various Internet newsgroups, subscribe to discussion lists, send e-mail inquiries to NASA or your Member of Parliament, and gain access to publications that exist only in electronic form. Using browsing tools such as *Netscape Navigator,* you can explore sites on the World Wide Web, locate experts in all types of specialties, read the latest articles in journals, such as *Nature* or *Science,* or the latest newspaper listings of jobs in your specialty. For online databases in your field, ask your librarian.

Consult Appendix C for a listing of search engines suitable for academic work.

NOTE *Assume that any material obtained from the Internet is protected by copyright. Before using this material anyplace other than in a college paper (properly documented), obtain written permission from its owner.*

KEYWORD SEARCHES USING BOOLEAN OPERATORS

Most engines that search by key word allow the use of Boolean* operators (commands such as "AND," "OR," "NOT," and so on) to define relationships among various key words. Table 19.2 shows how these commands can expand a search or narrow it by generating fewer "hits."

Boolean commands also can be combined, as in

(additives *OR* preservatives) *AND* (health *OR* behaviour)

The hits produced here would contain any of these combinations:

additives and health, additives and behaviour, preservatives and health, preservatives and behaviour

Using *truncation* (cropping a word to its root and adding an asterisk), as in *preserv**, would produce a broad array of hits, including these:

preserves, preservation, preservatives . . .

Different search engines use Boolean operators in slightly different ways; many include additional options (such as NEAR, to search for entries that contain search terms within ten or twenty words of each other). Click on the HELP option of your search engine to see which strategies it supports.

Table 19.2   USING BOOLEAN OPERATORS TO EXPAND OR LIMIT A SEARCH

If you enter these terms . . .	The computer searches for . . .
food preservatives *AND* health	only entries that contain both terms
food preservatives *OR* health	all entries that contain either term
food preservatives *NOT* health	only entries that contain term 1 and do not contain term 2
food preserv*	all entries that contain this root within other words

---

*British mathematician and logician George Boole (1815–1864) developed the system of symbolic logic (Boolean logic) now widely used in electronic information retrieval.

GUIDELINES FOR RESEARCHING ON THE INTERNET*

1. *Focus your search beforehand.* The more precisely you identify the information you seek, the less your chance of wandering through cyberspace.

2. *Select keywords or search phrases that are varied and technical, rather than general.* Some search terms generate better hits than others. In addition to "food additives," for example, try "monosodium glutamate," "sugar and hyperactivity," or "attention deficit disorder." Specialized terms (for example, *vertigo* versus *dizziness*) offer the best access to sites that are reliable, professional, and specific. Always check your spelling.

3. *Look for Web sites that are specific.* Compile a *hotlist* of sites that are most relevant to your needs and interests. (Specialized newsletters and trade publications offer good site listings.)

4. *Set a time limit for searching.* Set a 10–15 minute time limit, and avoid tangents.

5. *Expect limited results from any search engine.* Each search engine (*Alta Vista, Excite, Hot Bot, Infoseek, WebCrawler*—see Appendix C) has strengths and weaknesses. Some are faster and more thorough while others yield more targeted and updated hits. Some search titles only—instead of full text—for key words. No single search engine can index more than a fraction of rapidly increasing Web content. Broaden your coverage by using multiple engines.

6. *Use bookmarks and hotlists for quick access to favourite Web sites.* Mark a useful site with a bookmark and add it to your hotlist.

7. *Expect material on the Internet to have a brief life span.* Site addresses can change overnight; material is rapidly updated or discarded. If you find something of special value, save or print it before it changes or disappears.

8. *Be selective about what you download.* Download only what you need. Unless they are crucial to your research, omit graphics, sound, and video files because these consume time and disk space. Focus on text files only.

9. *Never download copyrighted material without written authorization from the copyright holder.* It can be a crime to possess or give out electronic copies of copyrighted material without permission. Only material in the public domain is exempted. Such crimes are punishable by heavy fines and prison sentences.

   Before downloading *anything* from the Internet, ask yourself: "Am I violating someone's privacy (as in forwarding an e-mail or a newsgroup entry)?" or "Am I decreasing, in any way, the value of this material for the person who owns it?" Obtain permission beforehand, and cite the source.

10. *Consider Using Information Retrieval Services.* An electronic service such as *Inquisit* or *Dialog* protects copyright holders by selling access to all materials in its database. For a monthly fee and or per-page fee, users can download full texts of articles. Subscribers to these Internet-accessible databases include companies and educational institutions. Check with your library. One drawback is that these retrieval services do not catalogue material that exists only in electronic form (E-

GUIDELINES FOR RESEARCHING ON THE INTERNET* (continued)

zines, newsgroup and *listserv* entries, and so on). Therefore, these databases exclude potentially valuable material (such as research studies not yet available in hard copy) accessible only through a general Web search.

*Guidelines adapted from Baker 57+; Branscum 78; Busiel and Maeglin 39–40, 76; Fugate 40–41; Kawasaki 156; Matson 249–52.

USING ELECTRONIC MAIL

E-mail benefits for writers and researchers

Among the most widely used applications on or off the Internet, electronic mail connects to discussion forums on *Listserv* and *Usenet* and countless other networked locations across the globe.

Compared to phone, fax, or conventional mail (or even face-to-face conversation, in some cases), e-mail offers real advantages:

E-mail facilitates communication and collaboration

- *E-mail is fast, convenient, efficient, and relatively non-intrusive.* Unlike conventional mail, e-mail travels instantly. Moreover, e-mail makes for efficiency by eliminating "telephone tag." It is less intrusive than the telephone, offering recipients the choice of when to read a message or respond.
- *E-mail can foster creative thinking.* E-mail dialogues involve a give-and-take, much like a conversation. Writers feel encouraged to express their thoughts spontaneously as they write and respond—without worrying about page design, paragraph structure, or perfect phrasing. This relatively free exchange of views can lead to new insights or ideas (Bruhn 43).
- *E-mail is an excellent tool for collaborative work and research.* Collaborative teams keep in touch via e-mail, and researchers contact people who have the answers they need. Documents or electronic files of any length can be attached and sent for downloading by the receiver.

INFORMATIVE INTERVIEWS

An excellent source for information unavailable in any publication is the *personal interview*. Much of what an expert knows may never be published (Pugliano 6). Also, a respondent might refer you to other experts or sources of information.

Of course, an expert's opinion can be just as mistaken or biased as anyone else's (page 324). As medical patients, for example, we would seek second opinions about serious medical conditions. As researchers, we should seek a balanced range of expert opinions about a complex problem or controversial issue. For example, in assessing safety measures at a local nuclear power plant, we would question not only company spokespersons and environmentalists, but also independent and presumably more objective third parties such as a professor or journalist who has studied the issue.

GUIDELINES FOR USING E-MAIL

Recipients who consider an e-mail message poorly written, irrelevant, offensive, or inappropriate will only end up resenting the sender. These guidelines offer suggestions for effective e-mail use.[*]

1. *Check and answer your e-mail daily.* Like an unreturned phone call, unanswered e-mail is annoying. If you're really busy, at least acknowledge receipt and respond later.

2. *Check your distribution list before each mailing.* Verify that your message will reach all intended recipients—but no unintended ones.

3. *Assume your e-mail correspondence is permanent and could be read by anyone anytime.* Don't write anything you couldn't say to another person face-to-face. Avoid *spamming* (sending junk mail) and *flaming* (making rude remarks).

4. *Don't use e-mail to send confidential information.* Avoid complaining, criticizing, or evaluating people, or saying anything private.

5. *Before you forward an incoming message to other recipients, obtain permission from the sender.* Assume that any material you receive via e-mail is the private property of the sender.

6. *Limit your message to a single topic.* Remain focused and concise. (Yours may be one of many messages confronting the recipient.)

7. *Limit your message to a single screen, if possible.* Don't force readers to scroll needlessly.

8. *Use a clear subject line to identify your topic.* ("Subject: Request for Make-up Exam in English 201.") Recipients can scan subject lines in deciding which new mail to read immediately. Messages also are easier to file and retrieve for later reference.

9. *Refer clearly to the message to which you are responding.* ("Here are the available meeting dates you requested on Oct. 10.")

10. *Keep sentences and paragraphs short, for easy reading.*

11. *Don't write in FULL CAPS—unless you want to SCREAM at the recipient!*

[*]Adapted from Bruhn 43; Goodman 33–35, 167; Kawasaki 286; Munger; Nantz and Drexel 45–51; Peyser and Rhodes 82.

GUIDELINES FOR INFORMATIVE INTERVIEWS*

Planning the Interview

1. *Focus on your purpose.* Determine exactly what you hope to learn from this interview. Write out your purpose.

Purpose statement

> I will interview Carol Bono, campus police chief, to ask her about specific campus safety measures being proposed and implemented.

2. *Do your homework.* Learn all you can about the topic beforehand. If the respondent has published anything relevant, read it before the interview. Be sure the information this person might provide is unavailable in print.

3. *Request the interview at your respondent's convenience.* Give the respondent ample notice and time to prepare, and ask whether she/he objects to being quoted or taped. If possible, submit a list of questions well before the actual interview.

Preparing the Questions

1. *Make each question unambiguous and specific.* Avoid questions that can be answered with a simple "yes" or "no."

An unproductive question

> In your opinion, can campus safety be improved?

Instead, phrase your question to elicit a detailed response:

A productive question

> Of the various measures being proposed or considered, which do you consider most effective?

This is one instance in which your earlier homework pays off.

2. *Avoid loaded questions.* A loaded question invites or promotes a particular bias:

A loaded question

> Wouldn't you agree that campus safety problems have been overstated?

An impartial question does not lead the interviewee to respond in a certain way.

An impartial question

> In your opinion, have campus safety problems been accurately stated, overstated, or understated?

3. *Save the most difficult, complex, or sensitive questions for last.* Leading off with your toughest questions might annoy respondents, making them uncooperative.

4. *Write out each question on a separate notecard.* Use the notecard to summarize the responses during the interview.

Conducting the Interview

1. *Make a good start.* Arrive on time; thank your respondent; restate your purpose; explain why you believe he/she can be helpful; explain exactly how the information will be used.

2. *Ask questions clearly, in the order you prepared them.*

3. *Let the respondent do most of the talking.* Keep opinions to yourself.

4. *Be a good listener.* Don't fidget, stare out the window, or doodle.

5. *Stick to your interview plan.* If the respondent wanders, politely nudge the conversation back on track (unless the additional information is useful).

6. *Ask for clarification or explanation.* If you don't understand an answer, say so. Request an example, an analogy, or a simplified version—and keep asking until you understand.

Clarifying questions

- Could you go over that again?

- Is there a simpler explanation?

7. *Keep checking on your understanding.* Repeat major points in your own words and ask if the details are accurate and if your interpretation is correct.

8. *Be ready with follow-up questions.* Some answers may reveal new directions for the interview.

Follow-up questions

- Why is it like that?

- Could you say something more about that?

- What more needs to be done?

- What happened next?

9. *Keep note taking to a minimum.* Record statistics, dates, names, and other precise data, but don't record every word. Jot key terms or phrases that later can refresh your memory.

Concluding the Interview

1. *Ask for closing comments.* Perhaps the respondent can lead you to additional information.

Concluding questions

- Would you care to add anything?

- Is there anyone else I should talk to?

- Is there anyone who has a different point of view?

- Are there any other sources you are aware of that might help me better understand this issue?

2. *Invite the respondent to review your version.* If the interview is to be published, ask the respondent to check your final draft for accuracy and to approve it before you quote him or her in print. Offer to provide copies of any document in which this information appears.

3. *Thank your respondent and leave promptly.*

4. *As soon as you leave the interview, write a complete summary* (or record one verbally). Do this while responses are fresh in your memory.

*Several guidelines are adapted from Blum 88; Dowd 13–14; Hopkins-Tanne 23, 26; Kotulak 147; McDonald 190; Rensberger 15; Young 114, 115, 116.

SURVEYS AND QUESTIONNAIRES

Surveys help us to develop profiles and estimates about the concerns, preferences, attitudes, beliefs, or perceptions of a large, identifiable group (a *target population*) by studying representatives of that group (a *sample group*).

- Do consumers prefer brand A or brand B?
- How many students on this campus are "nontraditional"?
- Is public confidence in technology increasing or decreasing?

The tool for conducting surveys is the questionnaire. While interviews allow for greater clarity and depth, questionnaires offer an inexpensive way to survey a large group. Respondents can answer privately and anonymously—and often more candidly than in an interview.

INQUIRY LETTERS, PHONE CALLS, AND E-MAIL INQUIRIES

Letters, phone calls, or e-mail inquiries to experts listed in Web pages are handy for obtaining specific information from government agencies, legislators, private companies, university research centres, trade associations, and research foundations such as the Brookings Institution and the Rand Corporation (Lavin 9). Keep in mind that unsolicited inquiries, especially by phone or e-mail, can be intrusive and offensive.

PUBLIC RECORDS AND ORGANIZATIONAL PUBLICATIONS

The Access to Information Act and provincial public record laws grant access to an array of government, corporate, and organizational documents. Obtaining these documents from provincial or federal agencies takes time, but in them, you can find answers to questions like these:

Public records may hold answers to tough questions

- What have been specific child support rulings based on federal guidelines regarding the determination of income?
- What is Canada's Sustainable Development Policy?
- What are the results of the Walkerton inquiry?

Most organizations publish pamphlets, brochures, annual reports, or prospectuses for consumers, employees, investors, or voters.

NOTE

Be alert for bias in company literature. In evaluating the safety measures at a local nuclear power plant, you would want the complete picture. Along with the company's literature, you would want studies and reports from government agencies and publications from environmental groups.

PERSONAL OBSERVATION

If possible, amplify and verify your findings with a firsthand look. Observation should be your final step, because you now know what to look for. Know how, where, and when to look, and jot down observations immediately. You might even take photos or make drawings.

NOTE   *Even direct observation is not foolproof: For instance, you might be biased about what you see (focusing on the wrong events or ignoring something important), or, instead of behaving normally, people being observed might behave in ways they believe you expect that they should (Adams and Schvaneveldt 244).*

APPLICATION **19-1**

Prepare a research report by completing these steps. (Your instructor might establish a timetable for your process.)

PHASE ONE: PRELIMINARY STEPS

1. Choose a topic of immediate practical importance, something that affects you or your community directly. Develop a tree chart to help you ask the right questions.

2. Identify a specific audience and its intended use of your information.

3. Narrow your topic, checking with your instructor for approval and advice.

4. Identify the various viewpoints that will lead to your own balanced viewpoint.

5. Make a working bibliography to ensure sufficient primary and secondary resources. Don't delay this step!

6. List the information you already have about your topic.

7. Submit a clear statement of purpose to your instructor.

8. Make a working outline.

PHASE TWO: COLLECTING, EVALUATING, AND INTERPRETING DATA

Read Chapter 20 in preparation for this phase.

1. In your research, move from the general to the specific; begin with general reference works for an overview.

2. Skim the sources, looking for high points.

3. Evaluate each finding for accuracy, reliability, fairness, and completeness.

GUIDELINES FOR DEVELOPING A QUESTIONNAIRE

1. *Decide on the types of questions* (Adams and Schvaneveldt 202–12; Velotta 390). Questions can be *open-ended* or *closed-ended*. Open-ended questions allow respondents to express exactly what they're thinking or feeling in a word, phrase, sentence, or short essay:

Open-ended questions

- How much do you know about crime at our school?

- What do you think should be done about crime at our school?

Closed-ended questions

Are you interested in joining a group of concerned students?

YES _____   NO _____

Rate your degree of concern about crime problems at our school.

HIGH _____   MODERATE _____

LOW _____   NO CONCERN _____

Circle the number that indicates your view about the administration's proposal to allow campus police to carry handguns.

1 . . . . 2 . . . . 3 . . . . 4 . . . . 5 . . . . 6 7

STRONGLY   NO OPINION   STRONGLY
DISAPPROVE   APPROVE

Respondents may be asked to *rate* one item on a scale (from high to low, best to worst), to *rank* two or more items (by importance, desirability), or to select items from a list. Other questions measure percentages or frequency:

How often do you . . . ?

ALWAYS _____   OFTEN _____

SOMETIMES _____   RARELY _____

NEVER _____

Although they are easy to answer, tabulate, and analyze, closed-ended questions create the potential for biased responses. Some people, for instance, automatically prefer items near the top of a list or the left side of a rating scale (Plumb and Spyridakis 633). Also, respondents are prone to agree rather than disagree with assertions in a questionnaire (Sherblom, Sullivan, and Sherblom 61).

2. *Design an engaging introduction and opening questions.* Persuade respondents that the survey relates to their concerns, that their answers matter, and that their anonymity is assured. Explain how respondents will benefit from your findings, or offer an incentive (say, a copy of your final report).

A survey introduction

Your answers will enable our Member of Parliament to convey your views about handguns for the campus police. Results of this survey will appear in our campus newspaper. Thank you.

Researchers often include a cover letter with the questionnaire. Begin with the easiest questions. Once respondents commit to these, they are likely to complete later, more difficult questions.

3. *Make each question unambiguous.* All respondents should be able to interpret identical questions in the same manner.

An ambiguous question

Do you favour weapons for campus police?

YES _____   NO _____

"Weapons" might mean tear gas, clubs, handguns, all three, or two out of three. Consequently, responses to the above question would produce a misleading statistic, such as "Over 95 percent of students favour handguns for campus police," when the accurate conclusion might really be "Over 95 percent of students favour some form of weapon." Moreover, the limited choice ("yes/no") reduces an array of possible opinions to an either/or response.

A clear and incisive question

Do you favour (check all that apply):

_____ Having campus police carry mace and a club?

_____ Having campus police carry non-lethal "stun guns"?

_____ Having campus police store handguns in their cruisers?

_____ Having campus police carry small-calibre handguns?

_____ Having campus police carry large-calibre handguns?

_____ Having campus police carry no weapons?

_____ Don't know

To ensure a full range of possible responses, include options such as "Other _____," "Don't know," "Not Applicable," or include an "Additional Comments" section.

4. *Make each question unbiased.* Avoid loaded questions that invite or advocate a particular viewpoint or bias:

A loaded question

Should our campus tolerate the needless endangerment of innocent students by lethal weapons?

YES _____   NO _____

Emotionally loaded and judgmental words ("endangerment," "innocent," "tolerate," "needless," "lethal") in a survey are unethical because their built-in judgments manipulate people's responses (Hayakawa 40).

5. *Keep the questionnaire as short as possible.* Try to limit questions and their response spaces to two sides of a single page.

4. Take notes *selectively*. Use notecards or electronic file software.

5. Decide what your findings mean.

6. Settle on your thesis.

7. Use the checklist on page 373 to assess your methods, interpretations, and reasoning.

PHASE THREE: ORGANIZING YOUR DATA AND WRITING THE REPORT

1. Revise your working outline, as needed.

2. Follow the introduction-body-conclusion format.

3. Fully document all sources of information.

4. Write your final draft according to the checklist on page 402.

5. Proofread carefully.

DUE DATES

- List of possible topics due: _____
- Final topic due: _____
- Working bibliography and working outline due: _____
- Notecards due: _____
- Revised outline due: _____
- First draft of report due: _____
- Final draft of report with full documentation due: _____

Works Cited

Adams, Gerald R., and Jay D. Schvaneveldt, *Understanding Research Methods.* New York: Longman, 1985.

Baker, Russ. "Surfer's paradise." *Inc.* Nov. 1997: 57+.

Blum, Deborah. "Investigative Science Journalism." *Field Guide for Science Writers.* Eds. Deborah Blum and Mary Knudson. New York: Oxford, 1997. 86–93.

Branscum, Deborah. "bigbrother@the.office.com." *Newsweek* 27 Apr. 1998: 78.

Brody, Herb. "Clicking onto Webzines." *Technology Review* Aug./Sept. 1995: 24–35.

Bruhn, Mark J. "E-Mail's Conversational Value." *Business Communication Quarterly* 58.3 (1995): 43–44.

Busiel, Christopher, and Tom Maeglin. *Researching Online.* New York: Addison, 1998.

Dowd, Charles. "Conducting an Effective Journalistic Interview." *INTERCOM* May 1996: 12–14.

Fugate, Alice E. "Mastering Search Tools for the Internet." *INTERCOM* Jan. 1998: 40–41.

Goodman, Danny. *Living at Light Speed.* New York: Random, 1994.

Hayakawa, S. I. *Language in Thought and Action.* 3rd ed. New York: Harcourt, 1972.

Hopkins-Tanne, Janice. "Writing Science for Magazines." *A Field Guide for Science Writers.* Eds. Deborah Blum and Mary Knudson. New York: Oxford, 1997. 17–26.

Kawasaki, Guy. "Get Your Facts Here." *Forbes* 23 Mar. 1998: 156.

———. "The Rules of E-Mail." *MACWORLD* Oct. 1995: 286.

Kotulak, Ronald. "Reporting on Biology of Behavior." *A Field Guide for Science Writers.* Eds. Deborah Blum and Mary Knudson. New York: Oxford, 1997. 142–51.

Lang, Thomas A., and Michelle Secic. *How to Report Statistics in Medicine.* Philadelphia: American College of Physicians, 1997.

Lavin, Michael R. *Business Information: How to Find It. How to Use It.* 2nd ed. Phoenix, AZ: Oryx, 1992.

Matson, Eric. "(Search) Engines." *Fast Company* Oct./Nov. 1997: 27–31.

McDonald, Kim A. "Covering Physics." *A Field Guide for Science Writers.* Eds. Deborah Blum and Mary Knudson. New York: Oxford, 1997. 188–95.

Munger, David. Unpublished review.

Nantz, Karen S., and Cynthia L. Drexel. "Incorporating Electronic Mail with the Business Communication Course." *Business Communication Quarterly* 58.3 (1995): 45–51.

"Online." *Chronicle of Higher Education* 14 Oct. 1992: sec. A:1.

Peyser, Marc, and Steve Rhodes. "When E-Mail Is Oops-Mail." *Newsweek* 16 Oct. 1995: 82.

Plumb, Carolyn, and Jan H. Spyridakis. "Survey Research in Technical Communication: Designing and Administering Questionnaires." *Technical Communication* 39.4 (1992): 625–38.

Pugliano, Fiore. Unpublished review.

Rensberger, Bayce. "Covering Science for Newspapers." *A Field Guide for Science Writers.* Eds. Deborah Blum and Mary Knudson. New York: Oxford, 1997. 7–16.

Sherblom, John C., Claire F. Sullivan, and Elizabeth C. Sherblom. "The What, the Whom, and the Hows of Survey Research." *Bulletin of the Association for Business Communication* 56:12 (1993): 58–64.

Snyder, Joel. "Finding It on Your Own." *Internet World* June 1995: 89–90.

Steinberg, Stephen. "Travels on the Net." *Technology Review* July 1994: 20–31.

Velotta, Christopher. "How to Design and Implement a Questionnaire." *Technical Communications* 38.3 (1991): 387–92.

Weinstein, Edith. Unpublished review.

Young, Patrick. "Writing about Articles for Science Journals." *A Field Guide for Science Writers.* Eds. Deborah Blum and Mary Knudson. New York: Oxford, 1997. 110–16.

CHAPTER 20

Recording, Evaluating, and Interpreting Your Findings

TAKING NOTES

Many researchers take notes on a laptop computer, using electronic file programs or database management that allows notes to be filed, shuffled, and retrieved by author, title, topic, date, or key words. You can also take notes in a single word processing file, then use the "find" command to locate notes quickly. Whether you use a computer or notecards, your notes should be easy to organize and reorganize.

GUIDELINES FOR RECORDING RESEARCH FINDINGS

1. *Make a separate bibliography listing for each work you consult.* Record that work's complete entry (see Figure 20.1), using the citation format that will appear in your report. (See pages 377–398 for sample entries.) Record the information accurately so that you won't have to relocate a source at the last minute. When searching an online catalogue, you often can print out the full bibliographic record for each work, thereby ensuring an accurate citation.

2. *Skim the entire work to locate relevant material.* Look over the table of contents and the index. Check the introduction for an overview or thesis. Look for informative headings.

3. *Go back and decide what to record.* Use a separate entry for each item.

4. *Be selective.* Don't copy or paraphrase every word. (See the Guidelines for Summarizing on page 360.)

5. *Record the item as a quotation or a paraphrase.* When quoting others directly, be sure to record words and punctuation accurately. When restating material in your own words, preserve the original meaning and emphasis.

FIGURE 20.1
Bibliography entry

Record each bibliographic citation exactly as it will appear in your final report

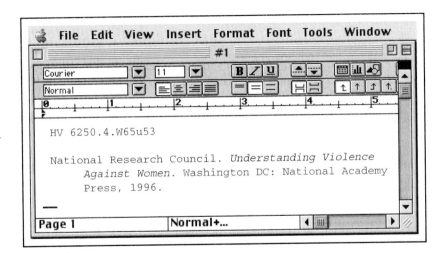

```
HV 6250.4.W65u53

National Research Council. Understanding Violence
     Against Women. Washington DC: National Academy
     Press, 1996.
```

QUOTING THE WORK OF OTHERS

You must place quotation marks around all exact wording you borrow, whether the words were written or spoken (as in an interview or presentation) or whether they appeared in electronic form. Even a single borrowed sentence or phrase, or a single word used in a special way, needs quotation marks, with the exact source properly cited.

GUIDELINES FOR QUOTING THE WORK OF OTHERS

1. *Use a direct quotation only when absolutely necessary.* Sometimes a direct quotation is the only way to do justice to the author's own words—as in these instances:

   Expressions that warrant direct quotation

   "Writing is a way to end up thinking something you couldn't have started out thinking" (Elbow 15).

   Think of the topic sentence as "the one sentence you would keep if you could keep only one" (USAF Academy 11).

   Consider quoting directly for these purposes:

   Reasons for quoting directly

   - to preserve special meaning or emphasis
   - to preserve special phrasing or emphasis
   - to preserve precise meaning
   - to preserve a striking or colourful example
   - to convey the authority of expert opinion
   - to convey the original's voice, sincerity, or emotional intensity

2. *Ensure accuracy.* Copy the selection word for word; record the exact page numbers; and double-check that you haven't altered the original expression in any way (Figure 20.2).

3. *Keep the quotation as brief as possible.* For conciseness and emphasis, use ellipses: Use three spaced periods (. . .) to indicate each omission within a single sentence. Use four periods (. . . .) to indicate each omission that includes the end of a sentence or sections of multiple sentences.

   Ellipses within and between sentences

   Use three . . . periods to indicate each omission within a single sentence. . . . [and] four . . . to indicate. . . .

   The elliptical passage must be grammatical and must not distort the original meaning. (For additional guidelines, see page 473.)

4. *Use brackets to insert your own clarifying comments or transitions.* To distinguish your words from those of your source, place them inside brackets:

Plagiarism often is
unintentional

If your notes don't identify quoted material accurately, you might forget to credit the source. Even when this omission is unintentional, writers face the charge of *plagiarism* (misrepresenting as one's own the words or ideas of someone else). Possible consequences of plagiarism include expulsion from school, the loss of a job, and a lawsuit.

The perils of buying plagiarized work online

It's no secret that any cheater can purchase essays, reports, and term papers on the Web. But anti-plagiarism Web sites such as Plagiarism.org (at www.plagiarism.org) now enable professors to cross-reference a suspi-

---

Brackets setting off words within a quotation

"This occupation [campus police officer] requires excellent judgment."

Note also the bracketed transition in example 3, preceding.

5. *Embed quoted material in your sentences clearly and grammatically.* Introduce integrated quotations with phrases such as "*Jones argues that,*" or "*Gomez concludes that.*" More important, use a transitional phrase to show the relationship between the quoted idea and the sentence that precedes it:

An introduction that unifies a quotation with the discussion

One investigation of sexual assault on college campuses found that "college athletes and fraternity men are a protected species." (Johnson, 1991, p. 34).

Your integrated sentence should be grammatical:

Quoted material integrated grammatically with the writer's words

"Alcohol has become the social drug of choice at American colleges," reports

Mathews, "and a fuel for campus crime" (1993, p. 41).

(For additional guidelines, see pages 472–473.)

6. *Quote passages four lines or longer in block form.* Avoid relying on long quotations except in these instances:

Reasons for quoting a long passage

- to provide an extended example, definition, or analogy
- to analyze or discuss a particular idea or concept

Double-space a block quotation and indent the entire block ten spaces. Do not indent the first line of the passage, but do indent first lines of subsequent paragraphs three spaces. Do not use quotation marks.

7. *Introduce the quotation and discuss its significance.*

An introduction to quoted material

Here is a corporate executive's description of some audiences you can expect to address. . . .

8. *Cite the source of each quoted passage.*

FIGURE 20.2
Entry for a
quotation

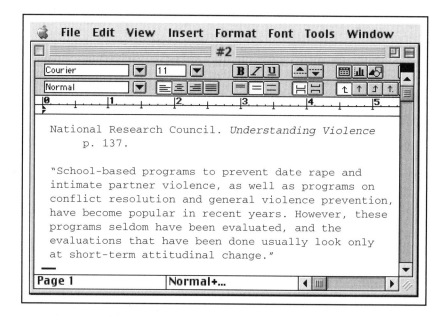

Place quotation
marks around all
directly quoted
material

cious paper against previously published material, flagging and identifying each plagiarized source.

Research writing is a process of independent thinking in which you work with the ideas of others in order to reach your own conclusions; unless the author's exact wording is essential, try to paraphrase, instead of quoting, borrowed material.

PARAPHRASING THE WORK OF OTHERS

Paraphrasing means more than changing or shuffling a few words; it means restating the original idea in your own words—sometimes in a clearer, more direct, and emphatic way—and giving full credit to the source.

Faulty paraphrasing
is a form of
plagiarism

To borrow or adapt someone else's ideas or reasoning without properly documenting the source is plagiarism. To offer as a paraphrase an original passage only slightly altered—even when you document the source—also is plagiarism. Equally unethical is offering a paraphrase, although documented, that distorts the original meaning.

Figure 20.3 shows an entry paraphrased from the passage in Figure 20.2. Paraphrased material is not enclosed within quotation marks, but it is documented to acknowledge your debt to the source.

PREPARING SUMMARIES AND ABSTRACTS

As we record our research findings, we summarize and paraphrase to capture the main ideas in compressed form. Also, researchers and readers who

FIGURE 20.3
Entry for a para-phrase

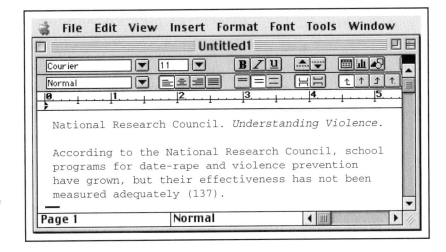

Signal the beginning of the para-phrase by citing the author, and the end by citing the source.

must act on information need to identify quickly what is most important in a long document. An abstract is a type of summary that does three things: (1) shows what the document is all about; (2) helps readers decide whether to read all of it, parts of it, or none of it; and (3) gives readers a framework for understanding what follows.

Whether you summarize your own writing (like the sample on page 404) or someone else's, readers expect these qualities:

What readers expect from an abstract

- *Accuracy:* Readers expect an abstract to precisely sketch the content, emphasis, and line of reasoning from the original.
- *Completeness:* Readers expect to consult the original document only for more detail—but not to make sense of the main ideas and their relationships.

GUIDELINES FOR PARAPHRASING THE WORK OF OTHERS

1. *Refer to the author early in the para-phrase, to indicate the beginning of the borrowed passage.*

2. *Retain keywords from the original, to preserve its meaning.*

3. *Restructure and combine original sentences, for emphasis and fluency.*

4. *Delete needless words from the original for conciseness.*

5. *Use your own words and phrases to explain the author's ideas, for clarity.*

6. *Cite (in parentheses) the exact source to mark the end of the borrowed passage and to give full credit.*

7. *Be sure to preserve the author's original intent* (Weinstein 3).

- *Readability:* Readers expect an abstract to be clear and straightforward—easy to follow and understand.
- *Conciseness:* Readers expect an abstract to be informative yet brief, and they may stipulate a word limit (say, 200 words).

For college papers, the abstract normally appears on a separate page right before the text of the paper or report. Although the abstract is written last, it is read first; take the time to do a good job.

EVALUATING THE SOURCES

Not all sources are equally dependable. A source might offer information that is out-of-date, inaccurate, incomplete, mistaken, or biased.

"Is the source up-to-date?"

— *Determine the currency of the source.* Certain types of information become outdated more quickly than others. For topics that focus on *technology* (Internet censorship, alternative cancer treatments), infor-

---

GUIDELINES FOR SUMMARIZING INFORMATION AND PREPARING AN ABSTRACT

1. *Be considerate of later users.* Unless you own the book, journal, or magazine, work from a photocopy.

2. *Read the entire original.* When summarizing someone else's work, grasp the total picture before picking up your pencil.

3. *Reread and underline.* Identify the issue or need that led to the article or report. Focus on the main ideas: thesis, topic sentences, findings, conclusions, and recommendations.

4. *Pare down your underlined material.* Omit lengthy background, examples, technical details, explanations, or anything not essential to the overall meaning. In abstracting the writing of others, avoid quotations; if you must quote some crucial word or phrase directly, use quotation marks.

5. *Rewrite in your own words.* Even if this first draft is too long, include everything that seems essential for this version to stand alone; you can trim later. If a direct quotation is absolutely necessary, be sure to place quotation marks around the author's own words.

6. *Edit for conciseness.* Once your draft contains everything readers need, find ways to trim the word count. (Review pages 119–124.)

   a. Cross out all needless words—but keep sentences clear and grammatical:

   Needless words omitted

   ~~As far as~~ artificial intelligence ~~is concerned, the~~ technology is only in its infancy.

mation more than a few months old may be outdated. But for topics that focus on *people* (student motivation, gender equality), historical perspectives often help.

NOTE   *The most recent information is not always the most reliable—especially in scientific research, a process of ongoing inquiry in which what seems true today may be proven false tomorrow (Taubes 76). Consider, for example, the recent discoveries of fatal side effects from some of the latest "miracle" weight-loss drugs.*

"Is the printed source dependable?"

— *Assess the reputation of a printed source.* Some sources are more reputable, unbiased, and authoritative than others. For research on alternative cancer treatments, you could depend more on reports in the *New England Journal of Medicine* or *Scientific American* than on those in scandal sheets or movie magazines. Even researchers with expert credentials, however, can disagree or be mistaken.

Assess a publication's reputation by checking its copyright page. Is the work published by a university, professional society, museum, or respected news organization? Do members of the editorial and

---

b. Cross out needless prefaces:

Needless prefaces omitted

The writer argues that . . .
Also discussed is . . .

c. Combine related ideas (page 126) and rephrase to emphasize important connections:

Disconnected and Rambling

A recent study emphasized job opportunities in the computer field. Fewer of tomorrow's jobs will be for programmers and other people who know how to create technology. More jobs will be for people who can use technology—as in marketing and finance (Ross 206).

Connected and concise

A recent study predicts fewer jobs for programmers and other creators of technology, and more jobs for users of technology—as in marketing and finance (Ross 206).

d. Use numerals for numbers, except to begin a sentence.

7. *Check your version against the original.* Verify this version's accuracy and completeness. Add no personal comments.

8. *Rewrite your edited version.* In this final draft, strive for readability and conciseness. Respect any stipulated word limit.

9. *Document your source.* Cite the full source (see Chapter 21) below any abstract not accompanied by its original.

advisory board all have distinguished titles and degrees? Is the publication *refereed* (all submissions reviewed by experts before acceptance)? Does the bibliography or list of references indicate how thoroughly the author has researched the issue (Barnes)? Many periodicals also provide brief biographies or descriptions of authors' earlier publications and achievements.

GUIDELINES FOR EVALUATING SOURCES ON THE WEB*

1. *Consider the site's domain and sponsor.* In these two typical addresses, both are domains for North American universities: www.umass.edu and www.utoronto.ca. The .edu signifies a U.S. university or educational institution, whereas .ca is the domain from which academic information can be retrieved in Canada. Below are some standard domains:

   .com = business/commercial organization

   .ca = site originating in Canada

   .edu = educational institution (U.S.)

   .gov = government organization (U.S.)

   .mil = military organization (U.S.)

   .net = any group or individual with simple software and Internet access

   .org = nonprofit organization

   The domain type might signal a certain bias or agenda that could skew the data. For example, at a .com site, you might find accurate information, but also a sales pitch. At an .org site, you might find political or government information such as Access to Canada's Justice Network at www.acjnet.org or Frequently Asked Questions About the Law in Canada at www.law-faqs.org. Knowing a site's sponsor can help you evaluate the credibility of its postings.

2. *Identify the purpose of the page or message.* Decide whether the message is intended simply to relay information, to sell something, or to promote a particular ideology or agenda.

3. *Look beyond the style of a site.* Fancy graphics, video, and sound do not always translate into dependable information. Sometimes the most reliable material resides in the less attractive, text-only sites.

4. *Assess the site's/material's currency.* An up-to-date site should indicate when the material was created or published, and when it was posted and updated.

5. *Assess the author's credentials.* Learn all you can about the author's reputation, expertise on this topic, institutional affiliation (a university, Fortune 500 Company, reputable environmental group). Do this by following links to other sites that mention the author or by using search engines to track the author's name. Newsgroup postings often contain "a signature file that includes the author's name, location, institutional or organizational affiliation, and often a quote that suggests

— *Assess the dependability of an Internet or database source.* The Internet offers information that never appears in other sources, for example from *listservs* and *newsgroups*. But much of this information may reflect the bias of the special-interest groups that provide it. Moreover, anyone can publish almost anything on the Internet—including a great deal of misinformation—without having it verified,

something of the writer's personality, political leanings, or sense of humor" (Goubril-Gambrell 229–30).

6. *Compare the site with other sources.* Check related sites and publications to compare the quality of information and to discover what others might have said about this site or author. Comparing many similar sites helps you create a benchmark, a standard for evaluating any particular site. Ask a librarian for help.

7. *Decide whether the assertions/claims make sense.* Decide where, on the spectrum of informed opinion and accepted theory, this author's position resides. Is each assertion supported by convincing evidence? Never accept any claim that seems extreme without verifying it through other sources, such as a professor, a librarian, or a specialist in the field.

8. *Look for other indicators of quality:*

   ■ *Worthwhile content:* The material is technically accurate. All sources of data presented as "factual" are fully documented (see Chapter 21).

   ■ *Sensible organization:* The material is organized for the user's understanding, with a clear line of reasoning.

■ *Readable style:* The material is well written (clear, concise, easy to understand) and free of typos, misspellings, and other mechanical errors.

■ *Objective coverage:* Debatable topics are addressed in a balanced and impartial way, with fair, accurate representation of opposing views. The tone is reasonable, with no "sounding off."

■ *Expertise:* The author refers to related theory and other work in the field and uses specialized terminology accurately and appropriately.

■ *Peer review:* The material has been evaluated and verified by related experts.

■ *Links to reputable sites:* The site offers a gateway to related sites that meet quality criteria.

■ *Follow-up option:* The material includes a signature block or a link for contacting the author or the organization.

*Guidelines adapted from Barnes; Busiel and Maeglin 39; Elliot; Fackelmann 397; Grassian; Hall 60–61; Hammett; Harris; Stemmer.

edited, or reviewed for accuracy. Don't expect to find everything you need on the Internet. (Pages 362–363 offer suggestions for evaluating sources on the Web.)

Even in a commercial database such as DIALOG, decisions about what to include and what to leave out depend on the biases, priorities, or interests of those who assemble that database.

"Who sponsored the study, and why?"

— *Consider the sponsorship and the motives for the study.* Much of today's research is paid for by private companies or special-interest groups, which have their own agendas (Crossen 14, 19). Medical research may be sponsored by drug or tobacco companies; nutritional research, by food manufacturers; environmental research, by oil or chemical companies. Instead of a neutral and balanced inquiry, this kind of "strategic research" is designed to support one special interest or another (132–34).

Furthermore, those who pay for strategic research are not likely to publicize findings that contradict their original claims or opinions or beliefs. Research consumers need to know exactly what the sponsors of a particular study stand to gain or lose from the results (234).

NOTE *Keep in mind that any research ultimately stands on its own merits. Thus, funding by a special interest should not automatically discredit an otherwise valid and reliable study.*

"What are similar sources saying?"

— *Cross-check the source against other, similar sources.* Instead of relying on a single source or study, seek a consensus among various respected sources (Cohn 106).

NOTE *Some issues (the need for defence spending or causes of inflation) always are controversial and will never be resolved. Although we can get verifiable data and can reason persuasively on some subjects, no close reasoning by any expert and no supporting statistical analysis will "prove" anything about a controversial subject. Some problems simply are more resistant to solution than others, no matter how dependable the sources.*

EVALUATING THE EVIDENCE

Evidence is any finding used to support or refute a particular claim. While evidence can serve the truth, it also can create distortion, misinformation, and deception. For example:

Questions that invite distorted evidence

- How much money, material, or energy does recycling really save?
- How well are public schools educating children?
- Which automobiles are safest?

Competing answers to such questions often rest on evidence that has been stacked to support a particular view or agenda. As consumers of research we have to assess for ourselves the quality of evidence presented.

"Is there enough evidence?"

— *Determine the sufficiency of the evidence.* Evidence is sufficient when nothing more is needed to reach an accurate judgment or a conclusion. Say you are researching the benefits of low-impact aerobics for reducing stress among employees at a fireworks factory. You would need to interview or survey a broad sample: people who have practised aerobics for a long time; people of both genders, different ages, different occupations, different lifestyles before they began aerobics, and so on. Even responses from hundreds of practitioners might be insufficient unless those responses were supported by laboratory measurements of metabolic and heart rates, blood pressure, and so on.

NOTE

Although anecdotal evidence ("This worked great for me!") might offer a good starting point for investigation, your personal experience rarely provides enough evidence from which to generalize. No matter how long you might have practised aerobics, for instance, you need to determine whether your experience is representative.

"Can the evidence be verified?"

— *Differentiate hard from soft evidence.* Hard evidence consists of factual statements, expert opinion, or statistics that can be verified. Soft evidence consists of uninformed opinion or speculation, data that were obtained or analyzed unscientifically, and findings that have not been replicated or reviewed by experts.

INTERPRETING YOUR FINDINGS

Interpreting means trying to reach an overall judgment about what the findings mean and what conclusion or action they suggest.

Unfortunately, research does not always yield answers that are clear or conclusive. Instead of settling for the most *convenient* answer, we pursue the most *reasonable* answer by examining critically a full range of possible meanings.

Identify Your Level of Certainty

Research can yield three distinct and very different levels of certainty:

1. The ultimate truth—the *conclusive answer*:

A practical definition of "truth"

Truth is *what is so* about something, as distinguished from what people wish, believe, or assert to be so. In the words of Harvard philosopher Israel Scheffler, truth is the view "which is fated to be ultimately agreed to by all who investigate."* The word *ultimately* is important. Investigation may produce a wrong answer for years, even for centuries. For example, in the second century A.D., Ptolemy's view of the universe placed the earth at its center—and though untrue, this judgment was based on the best informa-

* From *Reason and Teaching.* New York: Bobbs-Merrill, 1973.

tion available at that time. And Ptolemy's view survived for 13 centuries, even after new information had discredited this belief. When Galileo proposed a more truthful view in the fifteenth century, he was labeled a heretic.

One way to spare yourself any further confusion about truth is to reserve the word *truth* for the final answer to an issue. Get in the habit of using the words *belief, theory,* and *present understanding* more often. (Ruggiero 21–22)

2. The *probable answer:* the answer that stands the best chance of being true or accurate—given the most we can know at this particular time. Probable answers are subject to revision in the light of new information.

3. The *inconclusive answer:* the realization that the truth of the matter is more elusive or ambiguous or complex than we expected.

Exactly how certain are we?

We need to decide what level of certainty our findings warrant. For example, we are *highly certain* about the perils of smoking, *reasonably certain* about the health benefits of fruits and vegetables, but *less* certain about the perils of coffee drinking or the benefits of vitamin supplements.

Can you think of additional examples of information about which we are *highly, reasonably,* or *barely* certain?

Be Alert for Personal Bias

Personal bias is a fact of life

When the issue is controversial, our own bias might cause us to overestimate (or deny) the certainty of our findings.

> Expect yourself to be biased, and expect your bias to affect your efforts to construct arguments. Unless you are perfectly neutral about the issue, an unlikely circumstance, at the very outset . . . you will believe one side of the issue to be right, and that belief will incline you to . . . present more and better arguments for the side of the issue you prefer. (Ruggiero 134)

Because personal bias is hard to transcend, *rationalizing* often becomes a substitute for *reasoning:*

Reasoning versus rationalizing

> You are reasoning if your belief follows the evidence—that is, if you examine the evidence first and then make up your mind. You are rationalizing if the evidence follows your belief—if you first decide what you'll believe and then select and interpret evidence to justify it. (Ruggiero 44)

Personal bias often is unconscious until we examine our own value systems, attitudes long held but never analyzed, notions we've inherited from our backgrounds, and so on. Recognizing our own biases is a crucial first step in managing them.

Examining the Underlying Assumptions

Assumptions are notions we take for granted, things we accept without proof. The research process rests on assumptions like these: that a sample group accurately represents a larger target group, that survey respondents remember certain facts accurately, that mice and humans share enough biological similarities for meaningful research. For a particular study to be valid, the underlying assumptions have to be accurate.

Assume, for instance, you are an education consultant evaluating the accuracy of IQ testing as a predictor of academic performance. Reviewing the evidence, you perceive an association between low IQ scores and low achievers. You then check your statistics by examining a cross-section of reliable sources. Should you feel justified in concluding that IQ tests do predict performance accurately? This conclusion might be invalid unless you could verify the following assumptions:

1. That neither parents nor teachers nor the children tested had seen individual test scores and had thus been able to develop biased expectations.

2. That, regardless of their IQ scores, all children had been exposed to an identical pace, instead of being "tracked" on the basis of individual scores.

The evidence could be evaluated and interpreted only within the framework of these underlying assumptions.

NOTE *Assumptions are often easier to identify in someone else's thinking and writing than in our own. During collaborative discussions, ask group members to help you identify your own assumptions (Maeglin).*

AVOIDING STATISTICAL FALLACIES

How numbers can mislead

The purpose of statistical analysis is to determine the meaning of a collected set of numbers. Surveys and questionnaires often lead to some kind of numerical interpretation. ("What percentage of respondents prefer X?" "How often does Y happen?") In our own research, we often rely on numbers collected by survey researchers.

Numbers seem more precise, more objective, more scientific, and less ambiguous than words. They are easier to summarize, measure, compare, and analyze. But numbers can be totally misleading. For example, radio or television phone-in surveys produce grossly distorted data: although 90 percent of callers might express support for a particular viewpoint, people who call tend to be those with the greatest anger or extreme feelings about the issue—representing only a fraction of overall attitudes (Fineman 24). Mail-in surveys can produce similar distortion because only people with certain attitudes might choose to respond.

Before relying on any set of numbers, we need to know exactly where they come from, how they were collected, and how they were analyzed (Lavin 275–276). Are the numbers accurate and, if so, what do they mean?

Common Statistical Fallacies

Faulty statistical reasoning produces conclusions that are unwarranted, inaccurate, or deceptive. Here are some typical fallacies:

"Exactly how well are we doing?"

- *The sanitized statistic.* Numbers are manipulated (or "cleaned up") to obscure the facts. For example, many Canadian universities claim that they attract better students because their minimum admission average is 70 percent, even though that percentage does not represent the quality of teaching and learning provided in every school or school board across the country. The fact is that the percentage is meaningless in terms of defining a high-quality student.

"How many rats was that?"

- *The meaningless statistic:* Exact numbers are used to quantify something so inexact or vaguely defined that it should only be approximated (Huff 247; Lavin 278): "Halifax has 3 247 561 rats." "Zappo detergent makes laundry 10 percent brighter." An exact number looks impressive, but it can hide the fact that certain subjects (child abuse, cheating in college, virginity, drug and alcohol abuse on the job, eating habits) cannot be quantified exactly because respondents don't always tell the truth (because of denial or embarrassment or merely guessing). Or they respond in ways they think the researcher expects.

"Why is everybody griping?"

- *The undefined average:* The mean, median, and mode are confused in determining an average (Huff 244; Lavin 279). The *mean* is the result of adding up the value of each item in a set of numbers, and then dividing by the number of items. The *median* is the result of ranking all the values from high to low, then choosing the middle value (or the 50th percentile, as in calculating test scores). The *mode* is the value that occurs most often in a set of numbers.

Each of these three measurements represents some kind of average. But unless we know which "average" is being presented, we cannot interpret the figures accurately. Assume, for instance, that we are computing the average salary among female vice presidents at XYZ Corporation (ranked from high to low):

Vice President	Salary
"A"	$90 000
"B"	$90 000
"C"	$80 000
"D"	$65 000
"E"	$60 000
"F"	$55 000
"G"	$50 000

In the above example, the mean salary (total salaries divided by people) equals $70 000; the median salary (middle value) equals $65 000; the mode (most frequent value) equals $90 000. Each is, legitimately, an "average," and each could be used to support or refute a particular assertion (for example, "Women receive too little" or "Women receive too much").

Research expert Michael R. Lavin sums up the potential for bias in reporting averages:

> Depending on the circumstances, any one of these measurements may describe a group of numbers better than the other two. . . . [But] people typically chose the value which best presents their case, whether or not it is the most appropriate to use. (279)

Although the mean is the most commonly computed average, this measurement is misleading when one or more values on either end of the scale deviate excessively from the normal distribution (or spread) of values. Suppose, for instance, that Vice President "A" (above) was paid $200 000: because this figure deviates so much from the normal range of salary figures for "B" through "G," it distorts the average for the whole group—increasing the "mean salary" by more than 20 percent (Plumb and Spyridakis 636).

"Is 51 percent really a majority?"

■ *The distorted percentage figure:* Percentages are reported without explanation of the original numbers used in the calculation (Adams and Schvaneveldt 359; Lavin 280); "Seventy-five percent of respondents prefer our brand over the competing brand"—without mention that only four people were surveyed. Another fallacy in reporting percentages occurs when the *margin of error* is ignored. This is the margin within which the true figure lies, based on estimated sampling errors in a survey. For example, a claim that most people surveyed prefer Brand X might be based on the fact that 51 percent of respondents expressed this preference; but if the survey carried a 2 percent margin of error, the real figure could be as low as 49 percent or as high as 53 percent. In a survey with a high margin of error, the true figure may be so uncertain that no definite conclusion may be drawn.

"Which car should we buy?"

■ *The bogus ranking:* This happens when items are compared on the basis of ill-defined criteria (Adams and Schvaneveldt 212; Lavin 284): "Last year, the Batmobile was the number-one selling car in North America"—without mention that some competing car makers actually sold *more* cars to private individuals, and that the Batmobile figures were inflated by hefty sales to rental-car companies and corporate fleets. Unless we know how the ranked items were chosen and how they were compared (the criteria), a ranking can produce a scientific-seeming number based on a completely unscientific method.

"Does X actually cause Y?"

- *Confusion of correlation with causation: Correlation* is the measure of association between two variables (between smoking and increased lung cancer risk or between education and income). *Causation* is the demonstrable production of a specific effect (smoking causes lung cancer). Correlations between smoking and lung cancer or education and income signal a causal relationship that has been proven by many studies. But not every correlation implies causation. For instance, a recently discovered correlation between moderate alcohol consumption and decreased heart disease risk offers no sufficient proof that moderate drinking *causes* less heart disease.

  Many highly publicized correlations are the product of "data dredging": In this process, computers randomly compare one set of variables (say, eating habits) with another set (say, a range of diseases). From these countless comparisons, certain relationships reveal themselves (say, between coffee drinking and pancreatic cancer risk). As dramatic as such isolated correlations may be, they constitute no proof of causation and often lead to hasty conclusions (Ross 135).

"How have assumptions influenced this computer model?"

- *The fallible computer model:* Complex assumptions form the basis of computer models designed to predict or estimate costs, benefits, risks, or probable outcomes. But answers produced by any computer model depend on the assumptions (and data) programmed in. Assumptions might be influenced by researcher bias or the sponsors' agenda. For example, a prediction of human fatalities from a nuclear reactor meltdown might rest on assumptions about availability of safe shelter, evacuation routes, time of day, season, wind direction, and the structural integrity of the containment unit. But these assumptions could be manipulated to overstate or understate the risk (Barbour 228). For computer-modelled estimates of accident risk (oil spill, plane crash) or of the costs and benefits of a proposed project or policy (a new stadium, health-care reform), consumers rarely know the assumptions behind the numbers.

"Is this good news or bad news?"

- *Misleading terminology:* The terms used to interpret statistics sometimes hide their real meaning. For instance, the widely publicized figure that people treated for cancer have a "50 percent survival rate" is misleading in two ways; (1) *Survival* to laypersons means "staying alive," but to medical experts, staying alive for only five years after diagnosis qualifies as survival; (2) the "50 percent" survival figure covers *all* cancers, including certain skin or thyroid cancers that have extremely high *cure rates,* as well as other cancers (such as lung or ovarian) that rarely are curable and have extremely low *survival rates* ("Are We" 6).

  Even the most valid and reliable statistics require us to interpret the reality behind the numbers. For instance, the overall cancer rate today is "higher" than it was in 1910. What this may mean is that people are living longer and thus are more likely to die of cancer and that cancer today rarely is misdiagnosed—or mislabelled because of stigma ("Are We" 4). The finding that rates for certain cancers "double" after prolonged exposure to electromagnetic waves may really mean that cancer risk actually increases from 1 in 10 000 to 2 in 10 000.

These are only a few examples of statistics and interpretations that seem highly persuasive but that in fact cannot always be trusted. Any interpretation of statistical data carries the possibility that other, more accurate interpretations have been overlooked or deliberately excluded (Barnett 45).

GUIDELINES FOR CRITICALLY ANALYZING INFORMATION

Evaluate the Sources

1. *Check the source's date of posting or publication.* Although the latest information is not always the best, it's important to keep up with recent developments.

2. *Assess the reputation of each printed source.* Check the copyright page, for background on the publisher; the bibliography, for the quality and extent of research; and (if available) the author's brief biography, for credentials.

3. *Assess the quality of each electronic source.* See page 362 for evaluating Internet sources. Don't expect comprehensive sources on any single database.

4. *Identify the study's sponsor.* If the study acclaims the crash-worthiness of the Batmobile, but is sponsored by the Batmobile Auto Company, be skeptical.

5. *Look for corroborating sources.* Usually, no single study produces dependable findings. Learn what other sources say.

Evaluate the Evidence

1. *Decide whether the evidence is sufficient.* Evidence should surpass mere personal experience, anecdote, or news reports. It should be substantial enough for reasonable and informed observers to agree on its value, relevance, and accuracy.

2. *Look for a reasonable and balanced presentation of evidence.* Suspect any claims about "breakthroughs," or "miracle cures," as well as loaded words that invite emotional response or anything beyond accepted views on a topic. Expect a discussion of drawbacks as well as benefits.

3. *Do your best to verify the evidence.* Examine the facts that support the claims. Look for replication of findings. Go beyond the study to determine the direction in which the collective evidence seems to be leaning.

Interpret Your Findings

1. *Don't expect "certainty."* Most complex questions are open-ended and a mere accumulation of "facts" doesn't "prove" anything. Even so, the weight of solid evidence usually points toward some reasonable conclusion.

2. *Examine the underlying assumptions.* As opinions taken for granted, assumptions are easily mistaken for facts.

GUIDELINES FOR CRITICALLY ANALYZING INFORMATION (continued)

3. *Identify your personal biases.* Examine your own assumptions. Don't ignore evidence simply because it contradicts your way of seeing, and don't focus only on evidence that supports your assumptions.

4. *Consider alternate interpretations.* Consider what else this evidence might mean. Instead of settling for the most convenient conclusion, seek out the most reasonable one.

Check for Weak Spots

1. *Scrutinize all generalizations.* Decide whether the "facts" are indeed facts or merely assumptions, and whether the evidence supports the generalization (page 299). Suspect any general claim not limited by some qualifier ("often," "sometimes," "rarely," or the like).

2. *Treat causal claims skeptically.* Differentiate correlation from causation, as well as possible from probable or definite causes (pages 225–229). Consider confounding factors (other explanations for the reported outcome). For example, studies indicating that regular exercise improves health might be overlooking the fact that healthy people tend to do more exercise than those in poor health ("Walking" 3–4).

3. *Look for statistical fallacies.* Determine where the numbers come from, and how they were collected and analyzed—information that legitimate researchers routinely provide. Note the margin of error.

4. *Consider the limits of computer analysis.* Data mining (dredging) often produces intriguing but random correlations; a computer model is only as accurate as the assumptions and data programmed into it.

5. *Look for misleading terminology.* Examine terms that beg for precise definition in their specific context: "survival rate," "success rate," "customer satisfaction," "average increase," "risk factor," and so on.

6. *Interpret the reality behind the numbers.* Consider the possibility of alternative, more accurate, interpretations of these numbers. For example, "Saabs and Volvos are involved in 75 percent fewer fatal accidents than average." Is this only because of superior engineering or also because people who buy these cars tend to drive carefully ("The Safest" 72)?

7. *Consider the study's possible limitations.* Small, brief studies are less reliable than large, extended ones; epidemiologic studies are less reliable than laboratory studies (that also carry flaws); animal or human exposure studies are often not generalizable to larger human populations; "masked" (or blind) studies are not always as objective as they seem; measurements are prone to error.

8. *Look for the whole story.* Consider whether bad news may be underreported; good news, exaggerated; bad science, camouflaged and sensationalized; or research on promising but unconventional topics (say, alternative energy sources), ignored.

ASSESSING YOUR INQUIRY

The inquiry phases of the research process present a minefield of potential errors in where we search, how we interpret, and how we reason. So before preparing the actual report, examine critically your methods, interpretations, and reasoning with the checklist below.

REVISION CHECKLIST FOR THE RESEARCH PROCESS ✔

(Numbers in parentheses refer to the first page of discussion.)

METHODS

☐ Did I ask the right questions? (320)

☐ Are the sources appropriately up-to-date? (360)

☐ Is each source reputable, trustworthy, relatively unbiased, and borne out by other, similar sources? (361–364)

☐ Does the evidence clearly support the conclusions? (325)

☐ Can all the evidence be verified? (364)

☐ Is a fair balance of viewpoints presented? (321)

☐ Has my research achieved adequate depth? (323)

REASONING

☐ Am I reasonably certain about the meaning of these findings? (365)

☐ Can I rule out other possible interpretations or conclusions? (371)

☐ Am I reasoning instead of rationalizing? (366)

☐ Am I confident that my causal reasoning is correct? (302)

☐ Can all the numbers and statistics be trusted? (367)

☐ Have I resolved (or at least acknowledged) any conflicts among my findings? (325)

☐ Have I decided whether my final answer is definitive, probable, or inconclusive? (365)

☐ Is this the most reasonable conclusion (or merely the most convenient)? (365)

☐ Have I accounted for all sources of bias, including my own? (366)

☐ Should the evidence be reconsidered? (373)

Works Cited

Adams, Gerald R., and Jay D. Schvaneveldt. *Understanding Research Methods.* New York: Longman, 1985.

"Are We in the Middle of a Cancer Epidemic?" *University of California at Berkeley Wellness Letter* 10.9 (1994): 4–5.

Barbour, Ian. *Ethics in an Age of Technology.* New York: Harper, 1993.

Barnes, Shaleen. "Evaluating Sources Checklist." Information Literacy Project. 10 June 1997. Online Posting. 23 June 1998 <www.2lib.umassd.edu/library2/INFOLIT/prop.html>.

Barnett, Arnold. "How Numbers Can Trick You." *Technology Review* Oct. 1994: 38–45.

Busiel, Christopher, and Tom Maeglin. *Researching Online.* New York: Addison, 1998.

Cohn, Victor. "Coping with Statistics." *A Field Guide for Science Writers.* Eds. Deborah Blum and Mary Knudson. New York: Oxford, 1997. 102–09.

Crossen, Cynthia. *Tainted Truth: The Manipulation of Fact in America.* New York: Simon, 1994.

Elbow, Peter. *Writing without Teachers.* New York: Oxford, 1973.

Elliot, Joel. "Evaluating Web Sites: Questions to Ask." 18 Feb. 1997. Online Posting. List for Multimedia and New Technologies in Humanities Teaching. 9 Mar. 1997 <www.learnnc.org/documents/webeval.html>.

Facklemann, Kathleen. "Science Safari in Cyberspace." *Science News* 152.50 (1997): 397–98.

Fineman, Howard. "The Power of Talk." *Newsweek* 8 Feb. 1993: 24–28.

Goubril-Gambrell, Patricia. "Designing Effective Internet Assignments in Introductory Technical Communication Courses." *IEEE Transactions on Professional Communication* 39.4 (1996): 224–31.

Grassian, Esther. "Thinking Critically Aabout World Wide Web Resources." 1 April 1999. UCLA College Library. 12 Nov. 1999 <www.library.ucla.edu/libraries/college/instruct/critical.htm>.

Hall, Judith. "Medicine on the Web: Finding the Wheat, Leaving the Chaff." *Technology Review* Mar./Apr. 1998: 60–61.

Hammett, Paula. "Evaluating Web Resources." 29 Mar. 1997. Ruben Salazar Library. Sonoma State University. 26 Oct. 1997 <www.libweb.sonoma.edu/resources/eval.html>.

Harris, Robert. "Evaluating Internet Research Sources." 17 Nov. 1997. Online. 23 June 1998 <www.sccu.edu/faculty/R_Harris/evalu8it.htm>.

Huff, Darrell. *How to Lie with Statistics.* New York: Norton, 1954.

Lavin, Michael R. *Business Information: How to Find It, How to Use It.* 2nd ed. Phoenix, AZ: Oryx, 1992.

Maeglin, Tom. Unpublished review.

Plumb, Carolyn, and Jan H. Spyridakis. "Survey Research in Technical Communication: Designing and Administering Questionnaires." *Technical Communication* 39.4 (1992): 625–38.

Ross, Philip E. "Enjoy It While It Lasts." *Forbes* 27 July 1998: 206.

———. "Lies, Damned Lies, and Medical Statistics." *Forbes* 14 Aug. 1995: 130–35.

Ruggiero, Vincent R. *The Art of Thinking.* 3rd ed. New York: Harper, 1991.

"The Safest Car May Be a Truck." *Fortune* 21 July 1997: 72.

Stemmer, John. "Citing Internet Sources." 4 Mar. 1997. Online Posting. Political Science Research and Teaching List. 22 Apr. 1997 <polpsrt@h-met.msu.edu>.

Taubes, Gary. "Telling Time by the Second Hand." *Technology Review* May/June 1998: 30+.

U.S. Air Force Academy. *Executive Writing Course.* Washington: GPO, 1981.

"Walking to Health." *Harvard Men's Health Watch* 2.12 (1998): 3–4.

Weinstein, Edith K. Unpublished review.

C H A P T E R   2 1

Documenting Your Sources

Documenting research means acknowledging one's debt to each information source. Proper documentation satisfies professional requirements for ethics, efficiency, and authority.

WHY YOU SHOULD DOCUMENT

Documentation is a matter of *ethics,* for the originator of borrowed material deserves full credit and recognition. Moreover, all published material is protected by copyright law. Failure to credit a source could make you liable to legal action, even if your omission was unintentional.

Documentation also is a matter of *efficiency.* It provides a network for organizing and locating the world's recorded knowledge. If you cite a particular source correctly, your reference will enable interested readers to locate that source themselves.

Finally, documentation is a matter of *authority.* In making any claim (say, "A Mercedes-Benz is more reliable than a Ford Taurus") you invite challenge: "Says who?" Data on road tests, frequency of repairs, resale value, workmanship, and owner comments can help validate your claim by showing its basis in *fact.* A claim's credibility increases in relation to the expert references supporting it. For a controversial topic, you may need to cite several authorities who hold various views, as in this next example, instead of forcing a simplistic conclusion on your material:

Citing a balance of views

> Opinion is mixed over whether or not Lake Superior's North Shore should become a National Marine Conservation area. Those in favour want to protect the pristine area from overcamping, abuse of campsites, and overfishing (Gilchrist 1999). Those opposed fear the loss of freedom to access areas they have enjoyed for years because of Parks Canada constraints (Parks Canada 2001). However, careful planning and management will protect the land and its resources and create educational and recreational opportunities for visitors (Dearden and Rollins 1993).

Readers of your research paper expect the *complete picture.*

WHAT YOU SHOULD DOCUMENT

Document any insight, assertion, fact, finding, interpretation, judgment or other "appropriated material that readers might otherwise mistake for your own" (Gibaldi and Achtert 155)—whether the material appears in published form or not. Specifically you must document these sources:

Sources that require documentation

- any source from which you use exact wording
- any source from which you adapt material in your own words
- any visual illustration: charts, graphs, drawings, or the like

In some instances, you might have reason to preserve the anonymity of unpublished sources: say, to allow people to respond candidly without fear of reprisal (as with employee criticism of the company), or to protect their privacy (as with certain material from e-mail inquiries or electronic newsgroups). You still must document the fact that you are not the originator of this material by providing a general acknowledgment in the text ("A number of faculty expressed frustration with . . . ") along with a general citation in your list of References or Works Cited ("Interviews with campus faculty, May 1996").

You don't need to document anything considered *common knowledge:* material that appears repeatedly in general sources. In medicine, for instance, it has become common knowledge that foods containing animal fat (meat, butter, cheese, whole milk) contribute to blood cholesterol levels. And so in a research report on fatty diets and heart disease, you probably would not need to document that well-known fact. But you would document information about how the fat-cholesterol connection was discovered, subsequent studies (say, of the role of saturated versus unsaturated fats), and any information for which some other person could claim specific credit. If the borrowed material can be found in only one specific source, and not in multiple sources, document it. When in doubt, document the source.

HOW YOU SHOULD DOCUMENT

Cite borrowed material twice: at the exact place you use that material, and at the end of your paper. Documentation practices vary widely, but all systems work almost identically: a brief reference in the text names the source and refers readers to the complete citation, which enables the source to be retrieved.

This chapter illustrates citations and entries for two styles widely used for documenting sources in college writing:

■ Modern Language Association (MLA) style, for the humanities
■ American Psychological Association (APA) style, for social sciences

Unless your audience has a particular preference, either of these styles can be adapted to most research writing. Use one style consistently throughout your paper.

MLA DOCUMENTATION STYLE

Use this alternative
to footnotes and
bibliographies

Traditional MLA documentation used superscripted numbers (like this:[1]) in the text, followed by complete citations at page bottom (footnotes) or at document's end (endnotes) and, finally, by a bibliography. But a more current form of documentation appears in the *MLA Style Manual and Guide to Scholarly Publishing,* 2nd ed., New York: Modern Language Association,

1998. Footnotes or endnotes are now used only to comment on material in the text or on sources or to suggest additional sources. (Place these notes at page bottom or in a "Notes" section at document's end.)

Cite a source briefly in your text and fully at the end

In current MLA style, in-text parenthetical references briefly identify the source(s). The complete citation then appears in a "Works Cited" section at the paper's end.

A parenthetical reference usually includes the author's surname and the exact page number(s) of the borrowed material:

Parenthetical reference in the text

> Recent data provided by 796 colleges indicate that violent crime on campus is increasing (Lederman 31).

Readers seeking the complete citation for Lederman can refer easily to Works Cited, listed alphabetically by author:

Full citation at paper's end

> Lederman, Douglas. "Colleges Report Rise in Violent Crime." <u>Chronicle of Higher Education</u> 3 Feb. 1995, sec. A: 31–42.

This complete citation includes page numbers for the entire article.

MLA Parenthetical References

How to cite briefly in your text

For clear and informative parenthetical references, observe these guidelines:

- If your discussion names the author, do not repeat the name in your parenthetical reference; simply give the page number(s):

Citing page numbers only

> Lederman points out that data provided by 796 colleges indicate that violent crime on campus is increasing (31).

- If you cite two or more works in a single parenthetical reference, separate the citations with semicolons:

Three works in a single reference

> (Jones 32; Leduc 41; Gomez 293–94)

- If you cite two or more authors with the same surname, include the first initial in your parenthetical reference to each author:

Two authors with identical surnames

> (R. Jones 32) (S. Jones 14–15)

- If you cite two or more works by the same author, include the first significant word from each work's title, or a shortened version:

Two works by one author

> (Lamont, <u>Biophysics</u> 100–01) (Lamont, <u>Diagnostic Tests</u> 81)

- If the work is by an institutional or corporate author or if it is unsigned (that is, author unknown), use only the first few words of the institutional name or the work's title in your parenthetical reference:

Institutional, corporate, or anonymous author

> (American Medical Assn. 2) ("Distribution Systems" 18)

To avoid distracting the reader, keep each parenthetical reference as brief as possible. (One method is to name the source in your discussion, and to place only the page number[s] in parentheses.)

Where to place a parenthetical reference

For a paraphrase, place the parenthetical reference *before* the closing punctuation mark. For a quotation that runs into the text, place the reference *between* the final quotation mark and the closing punctuation mark. For a quotation set off (indented) from the text, place the reference two spaces *after* the closing punctuation mark.

MLA Works-Cited Entries

How to space and indent entries

The Works Cited list includes each source that you have paraphrased or quoted. In preparing the list, type the first line of each entry flush with the left margin. Indent the second and subsequent lines one-half inch. Double-space within and between each entry. Use one character space after any period, comma, or colon.

How to cite fully at the end

Following are examples of complete citations as they would appear in the Works Cited section of your report. Shown below each citation is its corresponding parenthetical reference as it would appear in the text. Note capitalization, abbreviations, spacing, and punctuation in the sample entries.

INDEX TO SAMPLE ENTRIES FOR MLA WORKS-CITED LIST

What to include in
an MLA book
citation
MLA Works-Cited Entries for Books. Any citation for a book should contain the following information (found on the book's title and copyright pages): author, title, editor or translator, edition, volume number, and facts about publication (city, publisher, date).

1. Book, Single Author—MLA

Clark, Matthew. <u>A Matter of Style</u>. Don Mills, ON: Oxford UP, 2002.

Parenthetical reference: (Clark 10–11)

Identify the state or province of publication by postal abbreviations. If the city of publication is well known (Boston, Toronto, and so on), omit the postal abbreviation. If several cities are listed on the title page, give only the first. For all other countries, include an abbreviation of the country name.

2. Book, Two or Three Authors—MLA

Hoffman, S., and J. Harris. <u>Introduction to Kinesiology: Studying Physical Activity</u>. Windsor, ON: Human Kinetic Publishers Inc., 2000.

Parenthetical Reference: (Hoffman and Harris 40)

Shorten publishers' names, as in "Simon" for Simon & Schuster, "GPO" for Government Printing Office, or "McGill-Queen's UP" for McGill-Queen's University Press. For page numbers having more than two digits, give only the final two digits for the second number if both first digits are identical.

3. Book, Four or More Authors—MLA

Santos, Ruth J., et al. <u>Environmental Crises in Developing Countries</u>. New York: Harper, 1998.

Parenthetical reference: (Santos et al. 9)

"Et al." is the abbreviated form of the Latin "et alia," meaning "and others."

4. Book, Anonymous Author(s)—MLA

<u>Structured Programming</u>. Boston: Meredith, 1999.

Parenthetical reference: (<u>Structured</u> 67)

5. Multiple Books, Same Author(s)—MLA

Chang, John W. <u>Biophysics</u>. Boston: Little, 1999.

—. <u>Diagnostic Techniques</u>. New York: Radon, 1994.

Parenthetical references: (Chang, <u>Biophysics</u> 123–26) (Chang, <u>Diagnostic</u> 87)

When citing more than one work by the same author, do not repeat the author's name; simply type three hyphens followed by a period. List the works alphabetically by title.

6. Book, One or More Editors—MLA

Dearden, P., and R. Rollins, eds. <u>Parks and Protected Areas in Canada</u>. Toronto: Oxford UP, 1993.

Parenthetical reference: (Dearden and Rollins 24)

For more than three editors, name only the first, followed by "et al."

7. Book, Indirect Source—MLA

Kline, Thomas. <u>Automated Systems</u>. Boston: Rhodes, 1992.

Stubbs, John. <u>White-Collar Productivity</u>. Miami: Harris, 1999.

Parenthetical reference: (qtd. in Stubbs 116)

When your source (as in Stubbs, above) has quoted or cited another source, list each source in its appropriate alphabetical place in the Works Cited list. Use the name of the original source (here, Kline) in your text and begin the parenthetical reference with "qtd. in," or "cited in" for a paraphrase.

8. Anthology Selection or Book Chapter—MLA

Bowman, Joel P. "Electronic Conferencing." <u>Communication and Technology: Today and Tomorrow</u>. Ed. Al Williams. Denton, TX: Assn. for Business Communication, 1994. 123–42.

Parenthetical reference: (Bowman 129)

The page numbers in the complete citation are for the selection cited from the anthology.

What to include in an MLA periodical citation

MLA Works-Cited Entries for Periodicals. Give all available information in this order: author, article title, periodical title, volume and issue, date (day, month, year), and page numbers for the entire article—not just pages cited.

9. Article, Magazine—MLA

Borts, Andrea. "Extremely Sporty Women." <u>Campus.ca</u> March/April 2002: 14–19.

Parenthetical reference: (Borts 15)

No punctuation separates the magazine title and date. Nor is the abbreviation "p." or "pp." used to designate page numbers. If no author is given, list all other information:

"Video Games for the Next Decade." <u>Power Technology Magazine</u> 18 Oct.
    2000: 18+.

Parenthetical reference: ("Video Games" 18)

This article began on page 18 and then continued on page 21. When an
article does not appear on consecutive pages, give only the number of the
first page, followed immediately by a plus sign. A three-letter abbreviation
denotes any month spelled with five or more letters.

10. Article, Journal with New Pagination Each Issue—MLA

Bonen, A. "Benefits of Exercise for Type II Diabetics: Convergences of
    Epidemiologic, Physiologic, and Molecular Evidence." <u>Canadian
    Journal of Applied Physiology</u> 20.3 (1995): 261–279.

Parenthetical reference: (Bonen 262).

Because each issue for that year will have page numbers beginning with
"1," readers need the number of this issue. The "20" denotes the volume
number; the "3" denotes the issue number. Omit "The" or "A" or any other
introductory article from a journal or magazine title.

11. Article, Journal with Continuous Pagination—MLA

Barnstead, Marion H. "The Writing Crisis." <u>Journal of Writing Theory</u> 12
    (1998): 415–33.

Parenthetical reference: (Barnstead 418)

When page numbers continue from issue to issue for the full year, readers won't need the issue number, because no other issue in that year
repeats these same page numbers. (Include the issue number if you think
it will help readers retrieve the article more easily.) The "12" denotes the
volume number.

12. Article, Newspaper—MLA

Avery, Jefferson. "Environmentalists Fear Forest Sell-Out." <u>Globe and Mail</u>.
    13 Aug. 1997, Metro Edition, sec A: 8.

Parenthetical reference: (Avery 8)

When a daily newspaper has more than one edition, cite the specific edition after the date. Omit any introductory article in the newspaper's name
(not <u>The Globe and Mail</u>). If no author is given, list all other information.
If the newspaper's name does not contain the city of publication, insert it,
using brackets: "<u>Daily News</u> [Truro NS]."

What to include in
an MLA citation for
a miscellaneous
source

MLA Works-Cited Entries for Other Sources. Miscellaneous sources range
from unsigned encyclopedia entries to conference presentations to government publications. A full citation should give this information (as
available): author, title, city, publisher, date, and page numbers.

13. Encyclopedia, Dictionary, Other Alphabetical Reference—MLA

"Communication." The Business Reference Book. 1998 ed.

Parenthetical reference: ("Communication")

Begin a signed entry with the author's name. For any work arranged alphabetically, omit page numbers in the complete citation and the parenthetical reference. For a well-known reference book, include only an edition (if stated) and a date. For other reference books, give the full publication information.

14. Report—MLA

Indian and Northern Affairs Canada. "Aboriginal Awareness." Aboriginal Workforce Participation Initiative (AWPI) Employer Toolkit. (Report No. QS-3593-002-EE-A1). Ottawa: Public Works and Government Services. 1998. 5-1-5-45.

Parenthetical reference: (Indian and Northern Affairs Canada 5-33)

If no author is given, begin with the organization that sponsored the report.

For any report or other document with group authorship, as above, include the group's abbreviated name in your first parenthetical reference, and then use only that abbreviation in any subsequent reference.

15. Conference Presentation—MLA

Smith, Abelard A. "Multicultural Stereotypes in Elizabethan Prose Fiction." First British Symposium in Multicultural Studies. London, 11–13 Oct. 1998. Ed. Anne Hodkins. London: Harrison, 1999. 106–21.

Parenthetical reference: (Smith 109)

The above example shows a presentation that has been included in the published proceedings of a conference. For an unpublished presentation, include the presenter's name, the title of the presentation, and the conference title, location, and date, but do not underline or italicize the conference information.

16. Interview, Personally Conducted—MLA

Nasson, Gamela. Chief of Campus Police. Rangeley, ME. 2 Apr. 1999.

Parenthetical reference: (Nasson)

17. Interview, Published—MLA

Lescault, James. "The Future of Graphics," Executive Views of Automation. Ed. Karen Prell. Miami: Haber, 2000. 216–31.

Parenthetical reference: (Lescault 218)

The interviewee's name is placed in the entry's author slot.

18. Letter, Unpublished—MLA

Rogers, Leonard. Letter to the author. 15 May 1998.

Parenthetical reference: (Rogers)

19. Questionnaire—MLA

Taynes, Lorraine. Questionnaire sent to 61 college administrators. 14 Feb. 2000.

Parenthetical reference: (Taynes)

20. Brochure or Pamphlet—MLA

Sexual Assault and Drug Issues: What Should I Know To Protect Myself. Toronto: Hoffman La Roche in collaboration with the University of Toronto, Faculty of Nursing, and Ontario Network of Sexual Assault Care and Treatment Centres, 2002.

Parenthetical reference: (Sexual)

If the work is signed, begin with its author.

21. Lecture—MLA

Keller, Michael. "The Pleasures and Pains of Synthetic Non-Viral Gene Delivery Vectors." Lecture, Lakehead University, 1 May, 2002.

Parenthetical reference: (Keller)

If the lecture title is not known, write Address, Lecture, or Reading but do not use quotation marks. Include the sponsor and the location if they are available.

22. Government Document—MLA

If the author is unknown, begin with the information in this order: name of the government, name of the issuing agency, document title, place, publishers, and date.

Ontario, Ontario Universities' Application Centre. Info: The Guide to Ontario Universities for High School Students. Guelph: Standing Committee on Secondary Liaison of the Ontario Universities Registrars' Association, the Council of Ontario Universities, and the Ontario Universities' Application Centre, Fall 1999.

Parenthetical reference: (Ontario Universities' Application Centre 40–41)

For any Parliamentary document, start with the House of Commons or the Senate before the title and then provide the remaining information

House of Commons Canada. Standing Committee on Fisheries and
Oceans. <u>Central Canada's Freshwaters Fisheries Report</u>. Ottawa:
The Committee. November 1998.

Parenthetical reference: (Standing Committee on Fisheries and Oceans 7)

23. Document with Corporate Authorship—MLA

Hermitage Foundation. <u>Global Warming Scenarios for the Year 2030</u>.
Washington: Natl. Res. Council, 2000.

Parenthetical reference: (Hermitage Foun. 123)

24. Photograph or Other Visual Aid—MLA

<u>A Burned Mature Stand Near Saint-Alphonse, Que</u>. Photo. FERIC
Silvicultural Operations Newsletter. Pointe-Claire, Quebec: Forest
Engineering Research Institute of Canada, Spring 1998.

Parenthetical reference: (<u>Burned Mature</u> 14)

If the creator of the visual is listed, list that name first. Identify the type of
visual (Photo, Map, Graph, Table, Diagram) immediately following its title.

25. Miscellaneous Items (Unpublished Report, Dissertation, and so on)—MLA

Author (if known), title (in quotes), sponsoring organization or publisher,
date, page number(s).

For any work that has group authorship (corporation, committee, task
force), cite the name of the group or agency in place of the author's name.

What to include in an MLA electronic source citation

MLA Works-Cited Entries for Electronic Sources. Citation for an electronic source with a printed equivalent should begin with that publication information (see relevant sections above). But whether or not a printed equivalent exists, any citation should enable readers to retrieve the material electronically.

The following models demonstrate the guidelines for citing electronic sources according to the 1998 *MLA Style Manual and Guide to Scholarly Publishing* and the 2003 *MLA Handbook for Writers of Research Papers*. The MLA recommends these general guidelines:

PUBLICATION DATES For sources taken from the Internet, include the date the source was posted to the Internet or last updated or revised; give also the date the source was accessed. Include publication information for any print version of the source.

UNIFORM RESOURCE LOCATORS Include a full and accurate URL for any source taken from the Internet (with access-mode identifier—*http, ftp, gopher,* or *telnet*). If an URL is complex and very long, give the URL of the site's search page. Enclose URLs in angle brackets (< >). When an URL continues from one line to the next, break only after a slash. Do not add a hyphen.

PAGE NUMBERING Include page or paragraph numbers when given by the source.

26. Online Database Source—MLA

Sahl, J. D. "Power Lines, Viruses, and Childhood Leukemia." <u>Cancer Causes Control</u> 6.1 (Jan. 1995): 83. <u>MEDLINE</u>. Online. 7 Nov. 1995. Dialog.

Parenthetical reference: (Sahl 83)

For entries with a printed equivalent, begin with publication information, then the database title (underlined or italicized), the "Online" designation to indicate the medium, and the service provider (or URL or e-mail address) and the date of access. The access date is important because frequent updatings of databases can produce different versions of the material.

For entries with no printed equivalent, give the title and date of the work in quotation marks, followed by the electronic source information:

Argent, Roger R. "An Analysis of International Exchange Rates for 1999." <u>Accu-Data</u>. Online. Dow Jones News Retrieval. 10 Jan. 2000.

Parenthetical reference: (Argent 4)

If the author is not known, begin with the work's title.

27. Computer Software—MLA

<u>Virtual Collaboration</u>. Diskette. New York: Harper, 1994.

Parenthetical reference: (<u>Virtual</u>)

Begin with the author's name, if known.

28. CD-ROM Source—MLA

Canalte, Henry A. "Violent-Crime Statistics: Good News and Bad News." <u>Law Enforcement</u> Feb. 1995: 8. ABI/INFORM. CD-ROM. Proquest. Sept. 1995.

Parenthetical reference: (Canalte 8)

If the material also is available in print, begin with the information about the printed source, followed by the electronic source information: name of database (underlined), "CD-ROM" designation, vendor name, and electronic publication date. If the material has no printed equivalent, list its author (if known) and its title (in quotation marks), followed by the electronic source information. If you are citing merely an abstract of the complete work, insert "Abstract," followed by a period, immediately after the work's page number(s)—as in "8" in the previous entry.

For CD-ROM reference works and other material that is not routinely updated, give the work title followed by the "CD-ROM" designation, place, electronic publisher, and date:

Time Almanac. CD-ROM. Washington: Compact, 1994.

Parenthetical reference: (Time Almanac 74)

Begin with the author's name, if known.

29. *Listserv*—MLA

Kosten, A. "Major update of the WWWVL Migration and Ethnic Relations." 7 April 1998. Online posting. ERCOMER News. 7 Apr. 1998 <www.ercomer.org/archive/ercomer-news/002.html>.

Begin with the author's name (if known), followed by the title of the work (in quotation marks), publication date, the Online posting designation, name of discussion group, date of access, and the URL. The parenthetical reference includes no page number because none is given in an online posting.

30. Usenet—MLA

Dorsey, Michael. "Environmentalism or Racism." 25 Mar. 1998. Online posting. 1 Apr. 1998 <news: alt.org.sierra-club>.

31. E-mail—MLA

Wallin, John Luther. "Frog Reveries." E-mail to the author. 12 Oct. 1999.

Cite personal e-mail as you would printed correspondence. If the document has a subject line or title, enclose it in quotation marks.

For publicly posted e-mail (say, a newsgroup or discussion list) include the address and the date of access.

32. Web Site—MLA

Montelpare, William. "An Online Course in Introductory Statistics." 31 May 2002. Lakehead University Online. 14 June 2002. <de.lakeheadu.ca:8910/Script/kine3030ade02/scripts/serve_home>

Parenthetical reference: (Montelpare)

Begin with the author's name (if known), followed by title of the work (in quotation marks), the posting date, name of Web site, date of access, and Web address (in angle brackets). Note that a Web address that continues from one line to the next is broken only after slash(es). No hyphen is added.

33. Article in an Online Periodical—MLA

Khan, Aliya, and John Bilezikian. "Primary Hyperparathyroidism:
Pathophysiology and Impact on Bone." *Canadian Medical Journal*
163.2 (2000): 1–9. 25 July 2000. <www.cmaj.ca>.

Parenthetical reference: (Khan and Bilezikian 6)

Information about the printed version is followed by the date of access to
the Web site and the electronic address.

34. Real-Time Communication—MLA

Synchronous communication occurs in a "real-time" forum and
includes MUDs (multiuser dungeons), MOOs (MUD object-oriented
software), IRC (Internet relay chat), and FTPs (file transfer protocols). The
message typed in by the sender appears instantly on the screen of the
recipient, as in a personal interview.

Mendez, Michael R. Online debate. "Solar Power versus Fossil Fuel Power."
3 Apr. 1998. CollegeTownMoo. 3 Apr. 1998
<telnet://next.cs.bvc.edu.777>.

Parenthetical reference: (Mendez)

Begin with the name of the communicator(s) and indicate the type of
communication (personal interview, online debate, and so on), topic title,
posting date, name of forum, access date, and electronic address.

MLA Sample List of Works Cited

Place your "Works Cited" section on a separate page at document's end.
(See pages 450–452.) Arrange entries alphabetically by author's surname.
When the author is unknown, list the title alphabetically according to its
first word (excluding introductory articles). For a title that begins with a
digit ("5," "6," etc.), alphabetize the entry as if the digit were spelled out.

APA DOCUMENTATION STYLE

One popular alternative to MLA style appears in the *Publication Manual of
the American Psychological Association*, 5th ed. Washington, DC: American
Psychological Association, 2001. APA style is useful when writers wish to
emphasize the publication dates of their references. A parenthetical reference in the text briefly identifies the source, date, and page number(s):

Reference cited in
the text

Recent data provided by 796 colleges indicate that violent crime on campus is increasing (Lederman, 1995, p. 31).

The full citation then appears in the alphabetical listing of "References" at
the paper's end:

Lederman, D. (1995). Colleges report rise in violent crime. *Chronicle of Higher Education*, pp. 31–42.

Full citation at
paper's end

Because it emphasizes the date, APA style (or any similar author-date style) is preferred in the sciences and social sciences, where information quickly becomes outdated.

APA Parenthetical References

How APA and
MLA parenthetical
references differ

APA's parenthetical references differ from MLA's (pages 378–379) as follows: the citation includes the publication date; a comma separates each item in the reference; and "p." or "pp." precedes the page number (which is optional in the APA system). When a subsequent reference to a work follows closely after the initial reference, the date need not be included. Here are specific guidelines:

- If your discussion names the author, do not repeat the name in your parenthetical reference; simply give the date and page number(s):

Author named in
the text

Lederman points out that recent data provided by 796 colleges indicate that violent crime on campus is increasing (1995, p. 31).

When two authors of a work are named in your text, their names are connected by "and," but in a parenthetical reference their names are connected by an ampersand: "&."

- If you cite two or more works in a single reference, list the authors in alphabetical order and separate the citations with semicolons:

Two or more
works in a single
reference

(Jones, 1994; Gomez, 1992; Leduc, 1997)

- If you cite a work with three to five authors, try to name them in your text, to avoid an excessively long parenthetical reference:

A work with three
to five authors

Franks, Oblesky, Ryan, Jablar, and Perkins (1993) studied the role of electromagnetic fields in tumour formation.

In any subsequent references to this work, name only the first author, followed by "et al." (Latin abbreviation for "and others").

- If you cite two or more works by the same author published in the same year, assign a different letter to each work:

Two or more works
by the same author
in the same year

(Lamont 1994a, p. 135) (Lamont 1994b, pp. 67–68)

Other examples of parenthetical references appear with their corresponding entries in the following discussion of the reference-list entries.

APA Reference-List Entries

How to space and indent entries

The APA reference list includes each source you have cited in your paper. In preparing the list of references for a student paper, type the first line of each entry flush with the left margin. Indent the second and subsequent lines one-half inch. Double-space within and between each entry. Skip one character space after any period, comma, or colon.

Following are examples of complete citations as they would appear in the "References" section of your paper. Shown immediately below each entry is its corresponding parenthetical reference as it would appear in the text. Note the capitalization, abbreviation, spacing, and punctuation in the sample entries.

INDEX TO SAMPLE ENTRIES FOR APA REFERENCES

Books

1. Book, single author
2. Book, two to five authors
3. Book, six or more authors
4. Book, anonymous author
5. Multiple books, same author(s)
6. Book, one to five editors
7. Book, indirect source
8. Anthology selection or book chapter

Periodicals

9. Article, magazine
10. Article, journal with new pagination for each issue
11. Article, journal with continuous pagination
12. Article, newspaper

Other Sources

13. Encyclopedia, dictionary, alphabetical reference
14. Report

15. Conference presentation
16. Interview, personally conducted
17. Interview, published
18. Personal correspondence
19. Brochure or pamphlet
20. Unpublished lecture
21. Government document
22. Miscellaneous items (unpublished manuscript, dissertation, and so on)

Electronic Sources

23. Online database abstract
24. Online database article
25. Computer software or software manual
26. CD-ROM abstract
27. CD-ROM reference work
28. Electronic bulletin boards, discussion lists, e-mail
29. Web site
30. Article in an online periodical

What to include in an APA citation for a book

APA Entries for Books. Any citation for a book should contain all applicable information in the following order: author, date, title, editor or translator, edition, volume number, and facts about publication (city and publisher).

1. Book, Single Author—APA

Clark, M. (2002). *A matter of style.* Don Mills: Oxford UP.

Parenthetical reference: (Clark, 2002, pp.7–8)

Use only initials for an author's first and middle name. Capitalize only the first words of a book's title and subtitle and any proper names. Identify a later edition in parentheses between the title and the period.

2. Book, Two to Five Authors—APA

Hoffman, S., & Harris J. (2002). *Introduction to kinesiology: Studying physical activity.* Windsor ON: Human Kinetic Publishers Inc.

Parenthetical reference: (Hoffman & Harris, 2002)

Use an ampersand (&) before the name of the final author listed in an entry. As an alternative parenthetical reference, name the authors in your text and include date (and page numbers, if appropriate) in parentheses.

3. Book, Six or More Authors—APA

Fogle, S. T., et al. (1998). *Hyperspace technology.* Boston: Little, Brown.

Parenthetical reference: (Fogle, et al., 1998, p. 34)

"Et al." is the Latin abbreviation for "et alia," meaning "and others."

4. Book, Anonymous Author—APA

Structured programming. (1995). Boston: Merideth Press.

Parenthetical reference: (*Structured Programming,* 1995, p. 67)

In your list of references, place an anonymous work alphabetically by the first key word (not "The," "A," or "An") in its title. Capitalize only the first word in the title and subtitle. In your parenthetical reference, capitalize all key words" in a book, article, or journal title.

5. Multiple Books, Same Author(s)—APA

Chang, J. W. (1997a). *Biophysics.* Boston: Little, Brown.

Chang, J. W. (1997b). *MindQuest.* Chicago: John Pressler.

Parenthetical reference: (Chang, 1997a) (Chang, 1997b)

Two or more works by the same author not published in the same year are distinguished by their respective dates alone, without the added letter.

6. Book, One to Five Editors—APA

Dearden, P., & Rollins, R. (Eds.). (1993). *Parks and protected areas in Canada.* Toronto: Oxford UP.

Parenthetical reference: (Dearden & Rollins, 1993, p. 24)

For more than five editors, name only the first, followed by "et al."

7. Book, Indirect Source

Stubbs, J. (1998). *White-collar productivity.* Miami: Harris.

Parenthetical reference: (cited in Stubbs, 1998, p. 47)

When your source (as in Stubbs, above) has cited another source, list only this second source, but name the original source in your text: "Kline's study (cited in Stubbs, 1996, p. 47) supports this conclusion."

8. Anthology Selection or Book Chapter—APA

Bowman, J. (1994). Electronic conferencing. In A. Williams (Ed.),
    Communication and technology: Today and tomorrow. (pp.
    123–142). Denton, TX: Association for Business Communication.

Parenthetical reference: (Bowman, 1994, p. 126)

The page numbers in the complete reference are for the selection cited from the anthology.

What to include in an APA citation for a periodical

APA Entries for Periodicals. A citation for an article should give this information (as available), in order: author, publication, date, article title (without quotation marks), volume or number (or both), and page numbers for the entire article—not just the page(s) cited.

9. Article, Magazine—APA

Borts, A. (2002, March/April). Extremely sporty women. *Campus.ca,* 14–19.

Parenthetical reference: (Borts, 2002, p. 15)

If no author is given, provide all other information. Capitalize only the first words in an article's title and subtitle. Capitalize all key words in a periodical title.

10. Article, Journal with New Pagination for Each Issue—APA

Bonen, A. (1995). Benefits of exercise for type II diabetics: Convergences of
    epidemiologic, physiologic, and molecular evidence. *Canadian
    Journal of Applied Physiology, 20*(3), 261–279.

Parenthetical reference: (Bonen, 1995, p. 262)

Because each issue for a given year has page numbers that begin at "1," readers need the issue number (in this instance, "1"). The "20" denotes the volume number, which is italicized.

11. Article, Journal with Continuous Pagination—APA

Barnstead, M. H. (1999). The writing crisis. *Journal of Writing Theory, 12,*
    415–433.
Parenthetical reference: (Barnstead, 1999, pp. 415–416)

The "*12*" denotes the volume number. When page numbers continue from issue to issue for the full year, readers won't need the issue number, because no other issue in that year repeats these same page numbers. (You can include the issue number if you think it will help readers retrieve the article more easily.)

12. Article, Newspaper—APA

Avery, J. (1997, August 13). Environmentalists fear forest sell-out. *The Globe and Mail* (Metro Edition), p. A8.

Parenthetical reference: (Avery, 1997, p. A8)

In addition to the year of publication, include the month and date. If the newspaper's name begins with "The," include it in your citation. Include "p." or "pp." before page numbers. For an article on nonconsecutive pages, list each page, separated by a comma.

What to include in an APA citation for a miscellaneous source

APA Entries for Other Sources. Miscellaneous sources range from unsigned encyclopedia entries to conference presentations to government documents. A full citation should give this information (as available); author, publication date, work title, city, publisher (or volume and issue number), and page numbers (if applicable).

13. Encyclopedia, Dictionary, Alphabetical Reference—APA

Communication. (1998). In *The business reference book.*

Parenthetical reference: (Communication, 1998)

For an entry that is signed, begin with the author's name and publication date.

14. Report—APA

Indian and Northern Affairs Canada (INAC). (1998). Aboriginal awareness. *Aboriginal Workforce Participation Initiative (AWPI) Employer Toolkit.* (Report No. QS-3593-002-EE-A1). Ottawa: Public Works and Government Services, pp. 5–1 to 5–45.

Parenthetical reference: (Indian and Northern Affairs Canada [INAC], 1998, p. 5–33)

If authors are named, list them first, followed by the publication date. When citing a group author, as above, include the group's abbreviated name in your first parenthetical reference, and use only that abbreviation in any subsequent reference. When the agency (or organization) and publisher are the same, list "Author" in the publisher's slot.

15. Conference Presentation—APA

Smith, A. A. (1999). Multicultural stereotypes in Elizabethan prose fiction. In A. Hodkins (Ed.), *First British Symposium on Multicultural Studies* (pp. 106–121). London: Harrison Press, 2000.

Parenthetical reference: (Smith, 1999, p. 109)

In parentheses is the date of the presentation. The name of the symposium is a proper name, and so is capitalized. Following the publisher's name is the date of publication.

For an unpublished presentation, include the presenter's name, year and month, title of the presentation (italicized), and all available information about the conference or meeting: "Symposium held at . . . . " Do not italicize or underline this last information.

16. Interview, Personally Conducted—APA

This material is considered a "nonrecoverable" source, and so is cited in the text only, as a parenthetical reference:

Parenthetical reference: (G. Nasson, personal interview, April 2, 1999)

If you name the interviewee in your text, do not repeat the name in your citation.

17. Interview, Published—APA

Jable, C. K. (1998, June 7). The future of graphics. [Interview with James Lescault]. In K. Prell (Ed.), *Executive views of automation* (pp. 216–231). Miami: Haber Press, 1999.

Parenthetical reference: (Jable, 1998, pp. 218–223)

Begin with the name of the interviewer, followed by the interview date and title (if available), the designation (in brackets), and the publication information, including the date.

18. Personal Correspondence—APA

This material is considered nonrecoverable data and so is cited in the text only, as a parenthetical reference:

Parenthetical reference: (L. Rogers, personal correspondence, May 15, 1998).

If you name the correspondent in your text, do not repeat the name in your citation.

19. Brochure or Pamphlet—APA

Sexual assault and drug issues: What I should know to protect myself. (2002). Toronto: Hoffman La Roche in collaboration with the

University of Toronto, Faculty of Nursing, and Ontario Network of Sexual Assault Care and Treatment Centres.

Parenthetical reference: (Sexual, 2002)

20. Unpublished Lecture—APA

Keller, M. (2002, May 1). *The pleasures and pains of synthetic non-viral gene delivery vectors.* Lecture presented at Lakehead University, Thunder Bay.

Parenthetical reference: (M. Keller, 2002)

If you name the lecturer in your text, do not repeat the name in your citation.

21. Government Document—APA

If the author is unknown, present the information in this order: name of the issuing agency, publication date, document title, place, and publisher.

Ontario Universities' Application Centre. (1999, Fall). *Info: The guide to Ontario universities for high school students.* Guelph, ON: Standing Committee on Secondary Liaison of the Ontario Universities Registrars' Association, the Council of Ontario Universities, and the Ontario Universities' Application Centre.

Parenthetical reference: (Ontario Universities Application Centre, 1999)

For any Parliamentary document, identify the House of Commons or the Senate before the title and then provide the remaining information.

House of Commons Canada. Standing Committee on Fisheries and Oceans. (1998). *Central Canada's freshwater fisheries report.* Ottawa: The Committee.

Parenthetical reference: (Standing Committee on Fisheries and Oceans, 1998)

22. Miscellaneous Items (Unpublished manuscript, Dissertation, and so on)—APA

Author (if known), date of publication, title of work, sponsoring organization or publisher, page numbers.

For any work that has group authorship (corporation, committee, and so on), cite the name of the group or agency in place of the author's name.

What to include in an APA citation for an electronic source

APA Entries for Electronic Sources. APA documentation standards for electronic sources continue to be refined and defined. A sampling of currently preferred formats is presented below. Any citation for electronic media should enable readers to identify the original source (printed or electronic) and provide an electronic path for retrieving the material.

Begin with the publication information for the printed equivalent. Then name the electronic source ([Online], [CD-ROM], [Computer software]), the protocol* (Bitnet, Dialog, FTP, Telnet), and any other items that define a clear path (service provider, database title, and access code, retrieval number, or site address).

23. Online Database Abstract—APA

Sahl, J. D. (1995). Power lines, viruses, and childhood leukemia [Online]. *Cancer Causes Control, 6*(1), 83. Abstract from DIALOG File: MEDLINE Item: 93–04881

Parenthetical reference: (Sahl, 1995)

Note the absence of closing punctuation. Any punctuation added to the availability statement could interfere with retrieval.

24. Online Database Article—APA

Alley, R. A. (1999, January). Social influences on worker satisfaction [29 paragraphs]. *Industrial Psychology* [Online serial], *5*(11). Available FTP: Hostname:publisher.com Directory:pub/journals/industrial. psychology/1999

Parenthetical reference: (Alley, 1999)

Give the length of the article [in paragraphs] after its title. Add no terminal punctuation to the availability statement.

25. Computer Software or Software Manual—APA

Virtual collaboration [Computer software]. (1994). New York: HarperCollins Publishers.

Parenthetical reference: (Virtual, 1994)

For citing a manual, replace the "Computer software" designation in brackets with "Software manual."

26. CD-ROM Abstract—APA

Canalte, H. A. (1995, February). Violent-crime statistics: Good news and bad news [CD-ROM]. *Law Enforcement, 8.* Abstract from: Proquest File: ABI/Inform Item: 978032

Parenthetical reference: (Canalte, 1995)

The "8" in the above entry denotes the page number of this one-page article.

---

*A protocol is a body of standards that ensure compatibility among the different products designed to work together on a particular network.

27. CD-ROM Reference Work—APA

Time almanac. (1994). Washington Compact, 1994.

Parenthetical reference: (*Time almanac,* 1994)

If the work on CD-ROM has a printed equivalent, APA currently prefers that it be cited in its printed form. As more works appear in electronic form, this convention may be revised.

28. Electronic Bulletin Boards, Discussion Lists, E-mail—APA

Parenthetical reference: Fred Flynn (personal communication, May 10, 1999) provided these statistics.

This material is considered personal communication in APA style. Instead of being included in the list of references, it is cited directly in the text. According to APA's current standards, material from discussion lists and electronic bulletin boards has limited research value because it does not undergo the kind of review and verification process used in scholarly publications.

29. Web Site—APA

Montelpare, William. (2002). *An online course in introductory statistics* [Online Web site]. Available de.lakeheadu.ca8910/Script/ kine3030ade02/scripts/serve_home

Parenthetical reference: (Montelpare, 2002)

If the Web address continues from one line to the next, divide it only after the slash(es).

30. Article in an Online Periodical—APA

Khan, Aliya, & Bilezikian, J. (2000). "Primary hyperparathyroidism: Pathophysiology and impact on bone. *Canadian Medical Journal, 163*(2), 1–9. Retrieved July 25, 2000 from www.cmaj.ca

Parenthetical reference: (Khan & Bilezikian, 2000, p. 7)

APA Sample List of References

APA's "References" section is an alphabetical listing (by author) equivalent to MLA's "Works Cited" section (page 388). Like Works Cited, the References section includes only those works actually cited. (A bibliography usually would include background works or works consulted as well.) In one notable difference from MLA style, APA style calls for only "recoverable" sources to appear in the reference list. Therefore, personal interviews, e-mail messages, and other unpublished materials are cited in the text only.

APPLICATION **21-1**

Computer Project: Both MLA and APA have issued new guidelines (pages 387, 397) for documenting sources from the Internet or Web.

But electronic documentation presents special problems. First, authors or sponsoring organizations for material posted directly to the Internet can be hard to find. Material on the Internet may have appeared somewhere else first, and this original source is sometimes not indicated clearly. Internet addresses won't take you back to the same site if you fail to copy them exactly—even though they may be several lines long. Pages often aren't numbered. Finally, it's sometimes hard to verify the quality of Internet sources, since on the Internet, *anyone* can claim to be an expert.

As you conduct your own electronic searches, use the list of problems above as a starting point and compile your own list of documentation issues in electronic research. For your classmates, compose a set of guidelines that will help them deal with these difficulties. Then examine the MLA and APA formats for electronic documentation. Which seems most useful? Why? Can you suggest changes that will make the formats more effective for students like you as they try to document their work?

Work Cited

Gibaldi, Joseph, and Walter S. Achtert. *MLA Handbook for Writers of Research Papers.* 3rd ed. New York: Modern Language Assn., 1988.

CHAPTER 22

Composing the
Research Paper

DEVELOPING A WORKING THESIS AND OUTLINE

Don't expect to arrive at your thesis until you have evaluated and interpreted your findings (as discussed on pages 360–373). Your thesis should emerge from the most accurate and reliable information you have been able to find.

You have phrased your topic as this question:

Research topic

Liberal Arts Degrees: Are They Career Dead Ends or Tickets to Success?

Near the completion of your research, you should have at least a tentative answer to that question:

Tentative thesis

Liberal arts graduates possess the skills and knowledge they will require to succeed in our very competitive society.

As your research proceeds, you might revise this tentative thesis any number of times.

Now you need a road map—a working outline. Perhaps your topic itself or your reading suggests a rough, working outline:

A working outline

I. The extent of the problem
    A. Liberal arts disciplines
    B. Employment opportunities
    C. Science and technology disciplines
    D. Differences between degrees

II. Specific causes of society's views towards liberal arts degrees
    A. Historical views of benefits of liberal arts education
    B. Current views of skills required by society
    C. Benefits of liberal arts to science and technology
    D. Role of government funding of liberal arts

III. Solutions to improving status of liberal arts
    A. More government funding and support
    B. More private sector funding and support
    C. More student support through course enrollments

Of course, by the time you compose your final outline, the shape of your paper may have changed radically (see pages 403–417).

DRAFTING YOUR PAPER

When you have collected and reviewed your material, organized your notecards, and settled on a workable thesis, you are ready to write the first draft of your paper.

Begin by revising your working outline. At this stage, try to develop a detailed formal outline, using at each level either topic phrases (page 400) or full sentences (page 426).

A formal outline needs logical notation and consistent format. Notation is the system of numbers and letters marking the logical divisions; format is the arrangement of your material on the page (indention, spacing, and so on). Proper notation and format show the subordination of some parts of your topic to others. The general pattern of outline notation goes like this:

The logical divisions of a formal outline

I.
   A.
      1.
      2.*
   B.
      1.
      2.
         a.
         b. (1)†
            (2)
   C.
II. etc.

(For a discussion of a sample formal outline, see page 427.) When your outline is complete, check your tentative thesis to make sure it promises exactly what your report will deliver.

Now you can begin to write. Students often find this the most intimidating part of research: pulling together a large body of information. Don't frantically throw everything on the page simply to get done. Concentrate on only one section at a time.

Begin by classifying your notecards or electronic notes in groups according to the section of your outline to which each note is keyed. Next, arrange the notes for your introduction in order. You are ready to write your first section. As you move from subsection to subsection, provide commentary and transitions, and document each source.

---

*Note each level of division yields at least two items. If you cannot divide a major item into at least two subordinate items, retain only your major heading.

†Carry further subdivisions as far as needed, but keep notation for each level individualized and consistent.

REVISING YOUR PAPER

After completing and documenting a first draft, use the Revision Checklist for essays in Chapter 4, along with the following Research Paper checklist, to revise the paper.

REVISION CHECKLIST FOR THE RESEARCH PAPER ☑

(Numbers in parentheses refer to the first page of discussion.)

CONTENTS

☐ Does the paper grow from a clear thesis? (400)

☐ Does the title offer an accurate forecast? (45)

☐ Does the evidence support the conclusion? (325)

☐ Is the paper based on reliable sources and evidence? (360, 364)

☐ Is the information complete? (325)

☐ Does the paper avoid reliance on a single source? (321)

☐ Is the evidence free of weak spots? (325)

☐ Are all data clearly and fully interpreted? (365)

☐ Can anything be cut? (355)

☐ Is anything missing? (365)

ORGANIZATION

☐ Does the introduction state clearly the purpose and thesis? (400)

☐ Does the paper follow the outline? (400)

☐ Is each paragraph focused on one main thought? (91)

☐ Is the line of reasoning clear and easy to follow? (31)

DOCUMENTATION

☐ Is the documentation consistent, complete, and correct? (376)

☐ Is all quoted material marked clearly throughout the text? (356)

☐ Are all sources not considered common knowledge documented? (377)

☐ Are direct quotations used sparingly and appropriately? (356)

☐ Are all quotations accurate and integrated grammatically? (357)

☐ Is the paper free of excessively long quotations? (356)

☐ Are all paraphrases accurate and clear? (358)

☐ Are electronic sources cited clearly and appropriately? (385, 395)

Figure 22.1 shows the completed report, documented according to the APA style guidelines discussed in Chapter 21.

A SAMPLE PAPER IN APA STYLE

The following paper was written in APA style. As you refer to the paper, evaluate its content, organization, and documentation by referring to the Checklist above.

Liberal Arts 1

Liberal Arts Degrees:
Career Dead Ends or Tickets to Success?

Terry-Lynn Fero

1 0177777

Professor D. Parsons

English 1500 YI

April 8, 2002

FIGURE 22.1
A research paper in APA style

2

ABSTRACT

The fallacy that liberal arts degrees result in career dead ends has been blindly accepted as truth by society in general. In comparison to their counterparts—business, science, and technology degrees—liberal arts degrees do differ in terms of what they offer in the way of employment opportunities, salaries, and skills. Universities, facing declining government funding, have shifted their attention from offering a well-balanced education to pursuing alternate funding sources. Often in the form of private donations, bequests, and corporate contributions, these funding sources have combined with an increasingly market-driven society to shape the types of higher-education programs that universities and colleges now offer. To some people, the liberal arts have lost their value. However, the facts do not support the claims of naysayers that the liberal arts do not have a role to play in one's future success. Increasing government financial support and intensifying university and college public-relations efforts will help to restore value to liberal arts degrees.

FIGURE 22.1
A research paper in APA style (continued)

DISCUSSION OF RESEARCH PAPER IN APA STYLE

APA FRONT MATTER (ITEMS THAT PRECEDED THE REPORT): 1–2

1. *Title Page:* Centre the title and all other lines. Do not underline the title or use all capital letters. Number the title page and all subsequent pages in the upper-right corner and include a shortened title as a running head for each page.

2. *Abstract:* Papers in APA style usually contain a one-paragraph abstract (roughly 100 words) that previews the main points and shows how they are related. Place the abstract on a separate page, following the title page. Centre the heading; double-space the abstract; use no paragraph indent. (To prepare an abstract, see pages 358–360).

3

4

5

6

7

8

9

LIBERAL ARTS DEGREES:
CAREER DEAD ENDS OR TICKETS TO SUCCESS?

There is a prevailing attitude in society that liberal arts degrees result in career dead ends. The results of a July 1998 Angus Reid poll clearly demonstrated this attitude—only 3 percent of respondents believed that having a Bachelor of Arts degree was the most valuable degree to have (Axelrod, 1999). However, enrollment numbers for the 1998–1999 university year followed the same trend as they had for the past thirty years—309 000 students, or 55 percent of those studying full time in Canadian universities, were enrolled in the social sciences and humanities (Renaud, 2002). Are all of these students wasting their time and money in pursuit of useless degrees? No, they are not. These students can face the future with confidence, secure in the knowledge that their education has equipped them with the skills necessary to succeed in our very competitive Canadian society.

Where Does the Negative Attitude
about Liberal Arts Degrees Originate?

So, where does this negative attitude toward the liberal arts originate? Supporters of the liberal arts claim that this negativity is the product of the current society, which favours globalization, privatization, institutional competition, and market-driven programming (Axelrod, 1999). The often intangible benefits of a liberal arts education—the development of intellect, good judgment, character, and citizenship—have lost favour to what is considered by some people to be the more market-worthy benefits of scientific, technical, and business knowledge. In order to understand why one degree is assumed to be more valuable than the other, one must first learn what they are both about.

FIGURE 22.1
A research paper in APA style (continued)

APA Body Elements: 3–9

3. Include the shortened title as a running head on each page and continue the page numbering.

4. Repeat the title exactly as it appears on the title page and centre it.

5. The left margin should be 4 cm ($1^1/_2$ in.) to allow for any form of binding. The top, bottom, and right margins should be 2.5 cm (1 in.). Begin the first paragraph two lines below the title and use double spacing throughout. Use one-half inch indent for the first line of each paragraph. Do not hyphenate words at the right margin or justify the right margin (i.e., do not make even).

6. Use the introduction to invite readers in and present your main idea. Show readers that your topic has meaning for them personally. University students, particularly those enrolled in humanities and social science courses and programs, would be particularly interested in this topic.

7. Use statistics and cited material from experts to support your thesis.

8. Write your thesis or point of view clearly and logically.

9. Use section headings to orient readers and show them what to expect. If you use questions as headings, phrase them the way readers might ask them. Phrase all section headings consistently.

Liberal Arts 4

Liberal arts degrees cover a wide range of study within the social sciences and humanities, including languages, philosophy, sociology, political studies, English, and anthropology (Charbonneau, 2001). Among the many important skills learned within these fields of study are the ability to define problems and tasks, to organize ideas and solutions, to think creatively, and to communicate clearly and effectively (Corcodilos, 2002). Savvy corporate leaders recognize the flexibility of these skills and value the power they impart on a Canadian workforce that finds itself in a constant state of change (Wetmore et al., 2002).

Because the liberal arts teach skills that have such broad applications and are not restricted to just one or two particular fields, graduates may find that in order to locate employment, they may have to learn how to market their skills. Once these graduates learn how to promote their talents, they will find that employment opportunities are as varied and as diverse as they want them to be. Besides the traditional teaching, writing, and publishing occupations, liberal arts graduates find work in advertising, architecture, business administration, all levels of civil service, politics, law, and entertainment. Some examples of successful Canadians with liberal arts degrees are Sheila Copps, federal cabinet minister; Tomson Highway, playwright and novelist; Al Waxman, actor; Annie Woods, cofounder of Kids Can Press; Jane Siberry, singer/songwriter; and Silken Lauman, Olympic medal-winning rower (Anderson, 2002). Examples of Americans with liberal arts degrees are Sally Ride, astronaut and first woman in space; John F. Kennedy, 35th president of the United States; and David Letterman, entertainer.

Science, technology, and business degrees cover fields of study such as engineering, geophysics, and accounting. Graduates in these fields of study are trained to apply specific technologies, strategies, and formulas to solve problems. The skills and talents that these people possess are critical

10

FIGURE 22.1
A research paper in APA style (continued)

APA Body Element: 10

10. Use examples, such as successful celebrities who hold liberal arts degrees, to validate your thesis.

to keeping Canada competitive within the global marketplace.

There are numerous differences between what these two university degrees have to offer graduates.

Among other areas, differences can be found in the availability of employment, level of income, and ability to generalize skills. Immediately after graduation, liberal arts graduates may experience some initial difficulty in obtaining employment, especially within their chosen field of study. In a survey of graduates from January 1993 to December 1997, those with liberal arts degrees were found to have averaged one week more of unemployment than graduates with science, technology, or business degrees (Giles and Drewes, 2001). These latter graduates tend to have an easier time finding employment immediately after graduation, whereas liberal arts graduates may experience some difficulty finding employment.

Also of note is the disparity in earnings between graduates with the two degrees. Although liberal arts graduates initially earn less money than the other graduates, earning levels do even out over time. In many instances, liberal arts graduates eventually enjoy an even higher rate of earnings than the others (Lewington, 1998). According to a report by University of British Columbia labour economist Robert Allen, sponsored by the Social Science and Humanities Research Council, men who graduated with science, technology, and business degrees saw their earnings increase an average of 78 percent in the 30-year span from their twenties to their fifties. For male liberal arts graduates during the same time period, their earnings rose an average of 106 percent (Lewington, 1998).

The skills learned in the liberal arts have broad applications far beyond the original field of study. In addition, these skills do not quickly become dated (Anderson, 2000). Instead, they continue to develop over time and form what some people consider to be a firm foundation for further specialized education. A study that examined how graduates evaluated the

11

FIGURE 22.1
A research paper in APA style (continued)

APA BODY ELEMENT: 11

11. Use statistics and examples to support general premises.

skills they were taught at school and their relation to what was demanded by their jobs found that during the first year after graduation, 62.5 percent of respondents considered their skills to be related; 31 percent said they were somewhat related (Liddell, 1994, pp. 120–121). The longer these people were in the work force, the more relevant they considered their skills to be. Conversely, the skills taught in science, technology, and business do become dated. These graduates must continually re-educate themselves in order to remain current with the latest information available.

What Skills Do Canadians Deem to Be Valuable?

One possible reason for the negative attitude toward the successful futures of liberal arts graduates may be found in a change of what Canadians deem to be valuable. Liberal arts graduates were once viewed as valuable, contributing members of a successful, well-balanced society. Throughout the years, changes within our economy and educational system have resulted in a society that values education for economic gain and undervalues education for the purpose of human development. Does this mean that our inherent desire for personal growth will be permanently suppressed in favour of financial gain?

In today's workplace, employers value employees who possess skills on which an easily recognizable market value can be placed. It is much easier to assign a value to the skills of science, technology, and business graduates than it is to place one on the less tangible cognitive skills of liberal arts graduates. Liberal arts graduates were once valued because it was believed that they possessed the skills necessary to make them better thinkers, better citizens, and better parents. Unfortunately, these skills have been devalued. According to some, Canada's future rests in the hands of science, technology, and business graduates.

FIGURE 22.1
A research paper in APA style (continued)

Canadians need to acknowledge the fact that these two kinds of degrees complement each other. Neither one is more important than the other. According to Lakehead University's Associate Professor Livio Di Matteo, "While science graduates can provide technical solutions to problems, only individuals trained in human science can deal with the economic, ethical, cultural, and social implications of these solutions" (Di Matteo, 1999). Only by recognizing the vital role that liberal arts graduates play in this partnership will we have the chance to return them to the high level of esteem that they were once held in.

Every sector of Canadian society that is reliant on government funding has had to find ways to compensate for funding gaps created by a decline in federal financial support. Cutbacks at the federal level of government have created a decrease in the direct transfer payments to universities from the provincial government. Universities are increasingly dependent on income derived from other sources, such as direct payments from students, private donations and bequests, and commercial enterprises (Storm, 1996, p. 164). As they grow increasingly dependent upon these outside funding sources, universities have had to face the fact that they have lost a great deal of their autonomy. Once the bastions of independent higher learning, universities now find that their programs are being shaped less by the desire to provide a well-rounded education and more by the unwelcome effects of fiscal instability.

In an effort to make up for reduced government funding, universities have had to increase tuition. Between 1980 and 1995, operating revenues derived from student tuition rose from 13 percent to 24.3 percent (Axelrod, 1999). In addition to their fixed portion of the cost of their education, students are now expected to partially cover the gap created by decreased government funding (Storm, 1996, p.168). For all but a few fortunate students, covering the complete cost of a university education is impossible. If tuition continues to rise at the same speed that it has in recent years, university education will become an elitist privilege, inaccessible to the majority of Canadians.

Funding from the private sector has become a welcome crutch for universities to lean on. However, this financial assistance comes with a price. Private funding tends to dictate university programming by virtue of the fact that this source has the freedom to place its money wherever it sees fit. With the majority of this funding going to research and to the further development of science, technology, and business, liberal arts programs have been virtually neglected. Although some corporations have stated that they recognize the valuable contributions that liberal arts graduates can make to their enterprises, when it comes down to placing their money on the table, they overwhelmingly support the other programs (Axelrod, 1999). It is understandable that universities accept private funding because it allows them to continue to operate today. It would not be understandable for them to allow private funding to permanently alter university education for tomorrow.

Another influence on the negative portrayal of liberal arts degrees is a breakdown in the distinctions between university education and college training. Because of the changes due to funding pressures, university administrators have had to alter the kind of education that they offer to fit into what may be considered a more utilitarian role (Fisher et al., 2000). In an effort to secure some of the available funding that goes with certain programs, universities have had to offer technical training courses that were once the sole domain of colleges. Conversely, colleges have become more concerned with producing a saleable product than they are with providing a well-rounded education.

FIGURE 22.1
A research paper in APA style (continued)

What Can Be Done to Ensure the Continued Development of Liberal Arts Programs?

There is no denying that cutbacks in government funding have dramatically affected university programs. Canadians have witnessed how the increased dependence upon private funding sources has shaped university education. It would be negligent for the government to allow this trend to continue. Canada needs a well-rounded, diversely educated population to ensure its future success. As difficult as it may be to find the additional money, the government must allocate more funds where they are needed. Not only must they provide adequate funding for universities, but they must also allow universities to decide for themselves where to allocate these funds. So far, Quebec has been the only province to demonstrate its support of liberal arts programs by increasing its provincial government funding for these programs (Renaud, 2002). The rest of the provincial governments would be wise to follow this example.

Government agencies such as the Social Science and Humanities Research Council (SSHRC), which is responsible for funding peer-reviewed research within the liberal arts, can use their clout to further promote liberal arts programs (Fisher et al., 2000). Agencies such as the SSHRC have been collecting data about the important contributions that liberal arts graduates have made to Canada's cultural and social well-being. Public relations programs targeting politicians and the general public can be used to promote the economic and social benefits of a liberal arts education. Pushing the value of these degrees into the public consciousness may persuade the next corporation, philanthropist, or politician to support these programs financially.

Students cannot afford to take a passive approach toward their education. They need to become informed about what exactly each

Liberal Arts 10

degree has to offer them and make an enlightened decision about which to pursue. By choosing to disregard society's misconceptions about the future of a liberal arts degree, they can elect to follow an educational path that best suits them. Enrollment figures clearly show that students are interested in the liberal arts. Without their continued support, these programs will be the first to go as universities face funding pressures.

Graduates of liberal arts programs should consider themselves extremely fortunate (Corcodilos, 2002). They possess fundamental skills, knowledge, and attributes that their competitors may lack. As opposed to the applied science graduate who goes directly to a position within a science research lab, or the business graduate who finds employment within a brokerage firm, liberal arts graduates are not restricted to their original field of study. In order to find employment, they may need to use some of the creative thinking skills they have learned. Learning to market their skills in unique ways to fit into a variety of employment situations will ensure that these graduates have the base for successful futures.

Is the question of whether or not liberal arts degrees result in career dead ends foremost in most students' minds? Probably not. The beauty of our society is that it allows us the freedom to choose who we want to be. So, in this atmosphere of free choice, why do those of us who feel drawn to languages or fine arts or history question our ability to earn a living through these degrees? Can it be that our society no longer values creative thinkers, problem solvers, or effective communicators? Does our emphasis on the more marketable science, technology, and business skills preclude all other skills? Perhaps it is the change in how universities receive their funding and the effects that change has had on programming. Certainly, all these factors have played a role in perpetuating the myth that a successful future cannot be found within the liberal arts. But it is just that—a myth, based on assumptions rather than on facts.

FIGURE 22.1
A research paper in APA style (continued)

Maybe someone should have informed her Excellency the Right Honourable Adrienne Clarkson that choosing to earn a Masters of English would result in her career hitting a dead end.

12

13

14

15

16

17

Liberal Arts 12

References

Anderson, J. (2000). Liberal arts: Pathway to brilliant careers. *Centre Point.*
[Online Web site]. Available www.uwo.ca/wnews/centre/centre99-00/
liberalarts.htm

Axelrod, P. (1999). The uncertain future of the liberal education. *Bulletin
Online.* [Online Web site]. Available www.caut.ca/English/Bulletin/
99_oct/commentary.htm

Charbonneau, L. (2001). AUCC launches campaign to promote the value
of an arts and science education. *Train your brain.* [Online Web site].
Available www.trainyourbrain.ca/english/media/press.htm

Corcodilos, N. (2002). Making the liberal arts degree pay off. *Train your
brain.* [Online Web site]. Available www.trainyourbrain.ca/english/
tools/hunter.html

Fisher, D. et al. (2000). Performance indicators: A summary. Centre for
Policy Studies in Higher Education and Training (CHET). [Database].

Giles, P. & Drewes, T. (2001). Liberal arts degrees and the labour market.
Statistics Canada. [Online Web site]. Available www.statcan.ca/
english/Pgdb/People/labour.htm

Lewington, J. (1998). Arts background no handicap in job search, study
finds. *The Globe and Mail National News.* [Online Web site]. Available
www.sfu.ca/arts/artsback.htm

Liddell, E. (1994). *Liberal studies in the Canadian context: The nature, the
need, the prospects.* St. Catharines: Brock University Liberal Studies
Program.

Di Matteo, L. (1999). Arts education does pay off. *Financial Post.* [Online
Web site]. Available www.sfu.ca/arts/doespay/htm

FIGURE 22.1
A research paper in APA style (continued)

APA LIST OF REFERENCES 12–17

12. Continue the running heads and page numbers. Use the same margins.

13. Centre the "references" title at the top of a new page. Include only the recoverable data (material readers can recover for themselves); cite personal interviews, unpublished letters and memos, electronic discussions lists, e-mail and other personal correspondence, such as telephone conversations, parenthetically in the text in this form: (B.K. Beaker, personal communication, June 30, 2002).

14. Double-space entries and order them alphabetically by author's last name (excluding A, An, or The). List initials only for author's first and middle names. Write out names of all months. Capitalize only the first word in article or book titles and subtitles, and any proper nouns. Capitalize all key words in magazine, journal, or newspaper titles. Do not enclose article titles in quotation marks. Italicize rather than underline titles.

15. Reference list entries are now shown with hanging indention rather than paragraph indention. If creating hanging indention is problematic, APA allows paragraph indention. Just be consistent throughout.

16. List all Web sites that directly contributed to your paper and provide the electronic address, especially for resources readers might wish to consult. If no author is named, list the organization sponsoring the Web site in the author slot. Omit punctuation at the end of an electronic address.

17. For more than one author or editor, use ampersands instead of spelling out "and." Use italics for a journal's title, volume number, and the comma. Give the issue number in parentheses only if each issue begins on page 1. Do not include "p." or "pp." before journal page numbers (only before page numbers from a newspaper). For page numbers of three or more digits, provide all digits in the second number.

Renaud, M. (2002). Some hard facts on "soft sciences." *Research Money.* [Online Web site]. Available www.sshrc.ca/english/resnews/presdesk/research_money_e.html

Storm, C. (1996). *Liberal education and the small university in Canada.* Montreal & Kingston: McGill-Queens University Press.

Wetmore, J. et al. (2002). Hi-tech CEO's say value of liberal arts is increasing. *Train your brain.* [Online Web site]. Available trainyourbrain.ca/english/tools/ceo.html

FIGURE 22.1
A research paper in APA style (continued)

Case Study:
A Sample Research Paper

This chapter will follow one student writer's problem solving, during the planning, researching, drafting, and revising stages.

DISCOVERING A WORTHWHILE TOPIC

Even though the research paper wasn't due until the end of March, Mike Dahlquist started thinking about a potential topic sometime in late October. As a first-year student living in residence, Dahlquist and his floormates had become aware of changes in their sleeping habits and patterns by the end of October. All of the students on that floor grew up with normal or reasonably normal sleep habits and patterns. Except for one or two days during exams and one or two weekends every three months, they had been averaging eight to nine hours of sleep a night. But, once they arrived at university and moved into residence, the noise, the parties, the nights at the bars, the bull sessions, the massive amount of material to read and the ten or so papers to write in 24 short weeks changed those normal sleep habits and patterns drastically. Sleep deprivation became the norm.

FOCUSING THE INQUIRY

To help himself focus his inquiry, Dahlquist designed a tree chart:

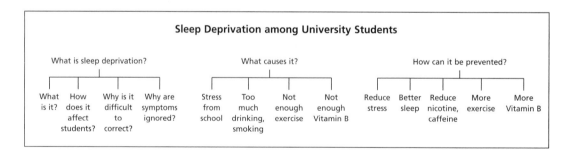

Once he knew what information he was looking for, Dahlquist focused on the various viewpoints that would give him a balanced picture:

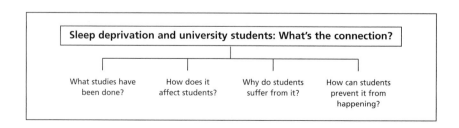

Now that Dahlquist knew what questions to ask and where to get the answers, he was ready to research.

SEARCHING THE LITERATURE

Sleep deprivation is a reasonably specific topic, so Dahlquist searched for his information using the standard methods of research. He used the electronic card catalogue looking for books on sleep and sleep deprivation. Those he found became entries on his working bibliography cards. Then, using the electronic resources as well as the electronic services librarian at his university, Dahlquist started a second search. He checked through the electronic indexes and abstracts, specifically the dissertation abstracts and the readers' guide abstracts, looking for current or recent dissertations and journal articles dealing with sleep and sleep deprivation. Consequently, he tapped into the Canadian Sleep Institute and the Stanford Sleep Laboratory, for example, as well as Statistics Canada for relevant information. Then, through Google, he searched for relevant articles on sleep and discovered a number of interesting and relevant data sources. Whatever information he deemed relevant became entries on his bibliography cards.

RECORDING AND REVIEWING FINDINGS

With the stack of working bibliography cards in hand, Dahlquist skimmed the most promising works, evaluating each finding for accuracy, reliability, fairness, appropriateness, and completeness. He recorded the information accurately and completely, ensuring that the author's or authors' points were correct both in content and emphasis. He recorded source and page numbers and quotations word for word. Because his audience would primarily be university or college students, he decided to structure his paper in this way:

PROBLEM ──────────▶ CAUSES ──────────▶ SOLUTIONS

SETTLING ON A THESIS

The evidence pointed toward a definite conclusion: University students suffer from sleep deprivation. So, he formulated his thesis statement:

> Many university students suffer from sleep deprivation because of lifestyle choices.

Dahlquist would refine his thesis later, if needed, but he now had a focal point for developing his paper.

WRITING AND DOCUMENTING THE PAPER IN MLA STYLE

Dahlquist continued with the writing process. He continued to read, record the information, and organize the material. Once he decided he had enough material and the outlined sections appeared complete, he was ready to write his first draft. Using the revision checklists, he reworked the first two drafts into his final draft that appears on the following pages. (Marginal numbers refer to the writer's decisions discussed on the facing pages.)

1

Sleep Deprivation among University Students

by

Mike Dahlquist

English 1500YE
Professor Parsons
April 8, 2002

FIGURE 23.1
A research paper in MLA style

Dahlquist i

2

Outline

Thesis: Many university students suffer from sleep deprivation because of lifestyle choices.

I. The Problem: Sleep deprivation causes a variety of disruptive symptoms, yet many students do not realize they suffer from the disorder.

    A. Sleep deprivation affects motivation and concentration.

    B. Social influences, such as smoking and drinking, can affect sleep.

    C. The symptoms of sleep deprivation are difficult to detect.

II. Specific Causes: Stress, smoke, alcohol, caffeine, exercise, and vitamin B affect sleep.

    A. School increases anxiety and affects sleep.

        1. School stress is caused by deadlines, exams, and finances.

        2. Stress results from balancing time between friends, work, and school.

    B. Agitation caused by nicotine in the blood prevents sleep.

    C. Alcohol fragments sleep, causing repeated waking.

        1. School events encourage drinking.

        2. Students drink to relieve stress.

    D. Students drink coffee and pop to stay awake.

    E. Students don't get enough regular exercise, affecting sleep.

    F. Most students don't get enough vitamin B.

III. Possible Solutions: Small adjustments to lifestyle can improve the quality and length of sleep.

    A. Students need to reduce the stress they experience.

    B. Students need to regulate their sleeping patterns.

    C. Students need to cut back on smoking and drinking.

    D. Students need to exercise regularly.

    E. Students need to include more vitamin B in their diet.

FIGURE 23.1
A research paper in MLA style (continued)

1. *Title Page:* Many reports for government, business, and industry are prefaced by a title page with these standard items: report title, author's name, course or department, intended reader's name, and date. Dahlquist centres and spaces these items for visual appeal. The title page is not numbered.

2. *Outline:* The running head for all pages consists of the author's last name, followed by one space and page number (small Roman numerals for outline, Arabic for paper). Dahlquist prefaces his sentence outline with his thesis, so that readers can understand his plan at a glance. His three major sections (*The Problem*, *Specific Causes*, and *Possible Solutions*) reveal a clear and sensible effect-to-cause development (see pages 227–228).

Notice that each level of division in the outline yields at least two parts.

3

The Problem: Sleep Deprivation

4

The clock on the desk read 3:00 a.m. Amanda leaned back in her chair and stretched. Papers were strewn across her desk with a half-drunk cup of coffee getting cold in the far corner. She rubbed her temples lightly and tried not to think about how late it really was. Her exam was at 8:30 a.m. and she had three more chapters to go. On a normal night, Amanda would be fast asleep by 11:30. Unfortunately, Amanda decided she needed a few

5

more hours of studying, rather than a few more hours of sleep. When she woke in the morning, Amanda felt groggy and fog-headed. She couldn't concentrate during her exam and became frustrated quickly. An hour into the exam, Amanda just wanted it to be over so she could go back to bed. After the exam, Amanda went home and slept for four hours.

Many students across Canada and the U.S. have experienced a situation similar to Amanda's. Sleep is such a natural and common occurrence that many students simply forget about its importance. As a result, many university students are at risk of experiencing sleep deprivation. Sleep deprivation affects memory and learning skills as well as concentration and motivation. Studies have shown that when people are deprived of sleep, they can still perform complicated tasks like solving puzzles and repairing things, but they make simple mistakes, particularly

6

when the task is boring, repetitive, and monotonous (Dawson). Students have been taught about nutrition and physical fitness, yet they have not been taught about sleep. Student drivers, for example, learn nothing

7

about the dangers of driving while drowsy; an astounding 55 percent of all drivers killed in sleep-related accidents are under the age of 25 (Dement 2). Motivation and concentration are important to students because they spend most of their day performing routine, often monotonous tasks such as reading textbooks and research articles, taking copious notes, and

FIGURE 23.1
A research paper in MLA style (continued)

3. *Headings and page numbering.* Because he uses a title page, Dahlquist does not repeat his title on page 1. Instead, he uses section headings to keep readers on track. Each page of the paper itself (including Works Cited) has an Arabic number after the author's last name as a running head.

4. *Opening Strategy:* Dahlquist decides to open with a specific example of a student who is depriving herself of sleep to cram for an early-morning exam. Using specific examples is a good technique for attracting and keeping his audience's attention and interest.

5. *Defining the problem:* Dahlquist defines the problem early to ensure that his audience sees the relevance of the topic.

6. *Citing authorities:* Dahlquist cites authorities to establish credibility and places each source inside the parentheses, including the page number for the non-electronic source.

7. *Using statistics and examples:* Dahlquist uses statistics and an example to make his point specific and emphatic.

Dahlquist 2

listening to hours of lectures. If students cannot concentrate on their work or cannot motivate themselves to do this work, then they cannot learn what they need to learn to be successful.

8

Common causes of sleep deprivation are stress; tobacco, alcohol, coffee, and pop consumption; lack of regular exercise; and lack of dietary vitamin B (Insomnia: What is Insomnia?). Students can resolve their sleep deprivation problems by reducing stress, cutting back on their smoking and drinking, increasing their exercise regimen, and eating more foods rich in vitamin B.

9

Unfortunately, students simply cannot avoid all the causes of sleep deprivation because too many of the causes are firmly ingrained in what it means to go to university and to be a university student. Students are under constant stress to perform well academically, frequently drink and smoke to excess, particularly when the universities sponsor events that encourage that behaviour, and develop poor nutritional habits. And even if students suffer from sleep deprivation, the symptoms are often difficult to detect. Because so many students suffer from sleep deprivation, other students have a difficult time identifying it. In the university culture, students are expected to ignore nature's signals to sleep. Yet, when the signals become too strong to ignore, students will simply fall asleep—in the library, in class, during an exam, or tragically, behind the wheel. Is a student yawning in an early afternoon class simply tired from a night partying or is he/she suffering from long-term sleep deprivation? Students need to educate themselves so that they can see the symptoms themselves, before something tragic does happen (Horne 88–90).

FIGURE 23.1
A research paper in MLA style (continued)

8. *Listing causes:* Dahlquist lists the common causes of sleep deprivation in parallel structures.

9. *Establishing thesis:* Rather than stating the thesis established clearly at the top of his outline explicitly, Dahlquist expresses it implicitly by talking about attitudes and lifestyles.

Dahlquist 3

Specific Causes of Sleep Deprivation

Sleep deprivation is caused by lack of sleep, but how much sleep do students actually need? Studies have shown that the average Canadian gets between six and nine hours of sleep per day, with an average of seven to eight hours (Urban 67). However, this number is just an average, so some students may require more or less sleep each night. Many students know how much sleep they need and adjust their sleep pattern accordingly. There are, however, many other factors that affect the quantity and quality of sleep that students do not take into consideration.

10

Stress is present in almost every aspect of student life. Few students can honestly say that they have not, at one time or another, felt burdened by the amount of stress placed on them (Table 1). Meeting deadlines, taking exams, completing projects, and managing money all contribute to student stress. Many students have to work part-time while enrolled to help pay for school; consequently, balancing time for work, school, and friends can lead students to believe that there are not enough hours in the day. Stress leads to agitation, which is very inhibiting towards sleep. Agitation prevents students from reaching the calm necessary to drift off into sleep. Thus, the amount of sleep they actually receive is much less than planned for. Students who overexert themselves after having a sleepless night generally do their work the next day while they are sleepy. The stress created produces another sleepless night, thus a vicious circle develops (Selye 425). Stress also increases the likelihood of nightmares, causing the sleeper to wake up during the night and then be unable to fall asleep again (Selye 177).

FIGURE 23.1
A research paper in MLA style (continued)

10. *Referring to a table.* Dahlquist has included a table in the body of the paper, so he referenced the table in text before the table appears to show the reader the relationship between the text and the table.

Dahlquist 4

11

TABLE 1: A Life-Events Scale for College Students*			
Event	Points	Event	Points
Death of close family member	63	Change in residence	20
Major personal injury or illness	53	Change in social activities	18
Death of a close friend	37	Loan of less than $10 000	17
Beginning or end of school	26	Change in sleeping habits	16
Change in work hours or conditions	20	Change in eating habits	15

12

*Researchers assigned point values to 43 specific life events and asked subjects to total points for recent events in their lives. Events that happened more than once would have the points multiplied by the number of times the event happened. Point totals over 150 indicated high stress levels.

13

SOURCE: Adapted from Holmes and Rahe, Table 3: 216.

Agitation, however, is not only caused by stress. Although smoking is often used as a stress reliever, in large amounts it can cause the opposite effect. High nicotine levels in the blood, caused by smoking or breathing in second-hand smoke, will cause a person to become agitated. Although smoking is on the decline among Canadians (19 percent, down from 23 percent in 1989), smoking among university students is still around 40 percent. As many as 75 percent of these smokers reported smoking four or more cigarettes per day (Steiff and Witham 34).

FIGURE 23.1
A research paper in MLA style (continued)

11. *Placing the table.* When placing tables in the text, the author ensures that the table is complete. The table number and title appear at the top of the table. Columns and rows complete the body.

12. *Footnoting.* Elements of the table can be footnotes. Dahlquist wanted to explain the title "A Life-Events Scale for College Students," so he placed an asterisk at the end. He then repeated the symbol below the field of the table and provided the textual explanation.

13. *Documenting the table:* Tables are documented when they are borrowed just as text is. The word SOURCE is fully capitalized and followed by a colon. If the table is adapted from the original, then the word "adapted" precedes the source and page number. The full bibliographic information is entered on the Works Cited page.

Dahlquist 5

14

Drinking, as much a part of university life as studying, also leads to sleep deprivation. Many university campuses across Canada have a bar located close to residence and often on the university grounds itself. Lakehead University's The Outpost is one of the biggest on-campus student pubs in Canada. Local bars offer no cover for students and set one night a week as "Student Pub Night." Not many students miss "Wednesday Night at Coyotes." At Lakehead, many university-sponsored events like "Pub Night" and "The Stimulator" encourage drinking by offering both free cover and reduced prices. Alcohol, unfortunately, has negative effects on the quality of sleep. First, alcohol fragments sleep, causing students to wake up several times during the night. Second, REM sleep (the deepest and most rewarding kind of sleep) occurs in the beginning of sleep after drinking and becomes shallow later. This pattern is unhealthy because students need deep sleep to be rested the following day. Third, after drinking, increased snoring and sleep apnea (the cessation of breathing for periods of time) may occur (Kosslyn and Rosenberg 132). Consequently, students who drink a lot rarely get a good night's sleep.

15

Coffee shops across Canada are also filled with students poring over papers and group projects. Many students cannot start their day until they have had that first cup of coffee. Caffeine, the main ingredient in coffee, is a stimulant students take to stay awake. But caffeine is not found only in coffee; chocolate and pop are also loaded with caffeine. Caffeine has a tendency to build up in the body and if any caffeine product is consumed as early as four hours before bed, troubled sleep will occur. Caffeine also poses another problem: it helps students keep irregular sleep cycles (Nordenberg 11). If students wake up drowsy in the morning, they just take coffee and get on with their day. They do not try to understand why they are drowsy when they wake up; they just take certain measures to

FIGURE 23.1
A research paper in MLA style (continued)

14. *Supporting claims:* Dahlquist decided to support his premise that universities contribute to students' drinking by describing university-sponsored events, in case university officials deny their involvement. The fact that universities have pubs on campus also supports his point of view.

15. *Defining Causes and Effects.* Dahlquist explains how ingesting large amounts of caffeine affects sleep patterns. Students need to understand this causal relationship, and the other causal relationships, if they are going to take the solutions seriously.

Dahlquist 6

stay awake. Keeping a regular sleep pattern is important, so relying on coffee too heavily will lead only to increased sleep problems in the future.

Since many students cannot even find the time for school work, finding time for exercise seems out of the question. The benefits from regular exercise are well known and far-reaching. Studies done at the Canadian Sleep Institute have shown that people who exercise one to three hours per day experience a higher percentage of deep sleep and fewer wakings. Exercising immediately before going to bed is discouraged because a high body temperature makes it harder to fall asleep (Dement 9).

Finally, vitamins also play a role in sleep deprivation, vitamin B in particular. Found in most vegetables and organ meats, vitamin B can lower fatigue, insomnia, and agitation (Horne 16). Taking vitamin B also can improve one's sleep/wake cycle. In 1974, a patient at Stanford University Sleep Disorders Clinic complained about his difficulties falling asleep. He would fall asleep in the early mornings and have difficulties waking up. The problem plagued him all through high school where he was always late for school and had problems staying awake when he got there. Using a process called *Chronotherapy* (extending sleep time each night so the patient wakes up earlier) and a diet rich in vitamin B12, the doctors were able to wean the patient onto an 11:00 p.m. to 7:00 a.m. sleep cycle (Coleman 86).

Possible Solutions

It seems as though a student's life is filled with causes of sleep deprivation. From the first day of school, students face pressure to perform well and to smoke and drink. Although many of the causes of sleep deprivation seem extreme and far reaching, small changes in lifestyle can improve the quantity and quality of sleep. None of these changes will dramatically alter a student's life, but the improved sleep certainly will. By reducing stress,

FIGURE 23.1
A research paper in MLA style (continued)

16. *Using clinical studies:* The Canadian Sleep Institute and the Stanford University Sleep Disorder Clinic are two world-class research facilities whose work on sleep deprivation adds scientific credibility to the paper's argument that students need to change their lifestyle to solve their sleep deprivation problems.

17. *Establishing solutions:* Here, Dahlquist re-establishes the premise that students start experiencing sleep deprivation from the first day of school. If the readers are still agreeing with the author, then they will accept the solutions with ease and confidence.

Dahlquist 7

regulating sleep patterns, consuming less alcohol and tobacco, exercising regularly, and improving their diets, students can almost guarantee a good night's sleep every night.

18

Stress, one of the leading causes of sleep deprivation, can actually be beneficial. Stress mobilizes the body to fight off the causes of stress or to run away from it. When stress occurs, the adrenal glands produce and release cortisol, a steroid hormone, to give the body energy and to reduce fatigue. Cortisol, the only hormone that is absolutely essential for life, also benefits those suffering from rheumatoid arthritis or hay fever and asthma (Jeffries). However, even though some stress is good stress, students should look for ways to reduce the bad stress that affects their lives.

19

The first step in reducing stress is often the easiest—planning ahead. Students should keep and update a school calendar and plan enough time to be fully prepared for each test and exam. Students who have good time management skills will avoid unnecessary surprises (McGinty 13). Gina Steiff, a student at Bethel College, encourages her fellow students to "[s]et realistic goals during the day so that you don't stay awake thinking about what you have not accomplished. Perfectionists and worriers tend to have more trouble sleeping" (Steiff 7).

20

The second step is putting things into perspective. From time to time, students need to step back, away from their daily lives, and examine everything objectively. Looking at how important daily stressors are in the long term is a good way to reduce stress. Many of life's problems are not as serious as they seem to be. Taking up a hobby or a sport is a great way to leave life for even a few hours a day or week. Hobbies and sports remind students that other parts of life do exist. Stress isn't something that has to spin out of control; it can be managed.

The third step is regulating sleeping patterns. A study performed at Stanford University looked at the effects of sleep patterns on a person's

FIGURE 23.1
A research paper in MLA style (continued)

18. *Distinguishing between good stress and bad stress.* Students need to understand that some stress is good and that the hormones produced by the body to fight stress are actually beneficial.

19. *Citing relevant sources:* College and university students probably would accept testimony from their peers more than from their elders, so Dahlquist included commentary from a student from Bethel College.

20. *Listing steps for reducing stress:* To help the readers, Dahlquist lists the steps to be followed to reduce stress. Of importance is the need to stay on the same sleep patterns on the weekends that they are on during the week.

biological clock. Volunteers were isolated from time cues, things like clocks, windows, radios, televisions, and telephones. They were told to avoid naps and only have one sleep period per day. Nearly all of the volunteers averaged a 25-hour day, meaning they would go to bed one hour later every night and sleep for approximately eight hours. By changing the time each volunteer wakes, scientists concluded that the 25-hour day can be reset two hours each day, meaning most people can function on a 23- to 27-hour day (Coleman 34). These results can be applied to a student's life as well. Most students who habitually sleep in on weekends complain that Monday is the worst day of the week. They are drowsy and irritable. They are tired because they were unable to sleep well Sunday night. By sleeping in on weekends and not worrying about getting up, most students go to a 25-hour day. Trying to go to sleep on Sunday at the regular time, however, is forcing the students to live a 21-hour day. Therefore, they have trouble falling asleep and wake tired and drowsy. So, to help maintain a sleep cycle, they should stay on a weekday pattern, even on weekends.

The fourth step is reducing smoking and drinking, as one usually accompanies the other. Unfortunately, asking students to cut back on their smoking and drinking would not produce the desired results. So, perhaps they would agree to a compromise. They would not drink during the week before tests, exams, or project due dates, but would save their drinking for after these events so they have time to readjust their sleep patterns.

The fifth step is improving their exercise schedules. Many students put off exercising until their daily lives settle down, which means they do

21

not exercise at all. According to a report found in *FDA Consumer Magazine* (March, 1998), "Exercise information, currently, is misrepresented and misunderstood; filled with gimmicks and programs to entice the consumer toward the easiest way to meet the minimum requirements" (Nordenberg

FIGURE 23.1
A research paper in MLA style (continued)

21. *Citing sources:* When quoting from a magazine, you can identify the magazine (with its month and date of publication in parentheses) before the quote and include the author and page number, in parentheses, after the quote.

34). All students have to do is find 20 minutes a day to do some running, walking, swimming, biking, or playing any sport that requires them to move, such as tennis, or basketball. Exercising at a pace that will allow continued activity for at least 20 minutes is preferred. That pace should produce a heart rate about 50 to 85 percent of the maximum heart rate that can be determined by the equation:

22

ideal heart rate = (resting heart rate) + (percentage)/100
((220 – age) – resting heart rate) (Witham 2).

Most students either love exercise or hate it. Therefore, some students overexert themselves while others become lazy and obese. Exercising, nevertheless, is a great way to feel better, sleep better, and perform better.

The final step is increasing vitamin B intake. Vitamin B, particularly B6, has the power to cure many forms of sleep deprivation. Converting tryptophan to serotonin (a hormone involved in sleep and relaxation), vitamin B6 is found in animal protein foods, spinach, broccoli, bananas, salmon, eggs, and sunflower seeds. Folic acid, found in green leafy vegetables, orange juice, sprouts, and sunflower seeds can help with fatigue and insomnia. Also, pantothenic acid can help and is found in most plant and animal tissues. When changing from a day shift to a night shift or coming back from a vacation, taking vitamin B12 will help establish normal sleep and wake patterns. Vitamin B12 is found in animal foods, especially organ meats, but not naturally in plant foods. Finally, when suffering from severe insomnia, a supplement of B3 may be required (Horne 34–35).

FIGURE 23.1
A research paper in MLA style (continued)

22. *Including an equation.* Sometimes, authors of physical fitness articles and reports include the equation in text for determining ideal heart rate. A colon follows the word "equation," which is then followed by the equation itself. The equation must be clearly set off from the surrounding text.

23

University students need to become more aware of the effects sleep has on their bodies. Sleep consumes over one-third of their 24-hour day for good reason. The body and the mind need sleep to stay healthy and to perform well. Sleep affects concentration, motivation, memory, health; nearly all functions can be related to sleep. Students have so many pressures in their lives that they should not make things worse by not getting enough sleep. And for those interested in testing their knowledge about sleep, they can try the Sleep IQ test in Appendix A.

FIGURE 23.1
A research paper in MLA style (continued)

23. *Concluding the paper.* The conclusion here is short and direct. Dahlquist restates his premise that students need to become more aware of the effects that sleep has on them and the main reasons why good sleep patterns are beneficial.

24

Appendix A: What's Your Sleep I.Q.?

"While the average adult needs eight to nine hours sleep a night, most get only seven, and nearly one-third of the 1,027 adults surveyed in late 1997 and early 1998 got six hours or less during the work week" (Brody). People may spend six to eight hours a day sleeping, but how many know what's happening when they are doing it?

The National Sleep Foundation, a nonprofit Washington organization, designed a 12-question "sleep IQ test" that only 14 percent of those tested passed. How will you do?

Questions

1. During sleep, your brain rests.
2. You cannot learn to function normally with one or two fewer hours a night than you need.
3. Boredom makes you feel sleepy, even if you have enough sleep.
4. Resting in bed with your eyes closed cannot satisfy your body's need for sleep.
5. Snoring is not harmful as long as it does not disturb others or wake you up.
6. Everyone dreams every night.
7. The older you get, the fewer hours of sleep you need.
8. Most people do not know when they are sleepy.
9. Raising the volume of your radio will help you stay awake while driving.
10. Sleep disorders are mainly due to worry or psychological problems.
11. The human body never adjusts to night shift work.
12. Most sleep disorders go away even without treatment (Brody).

Answers: 1F, 2T, 3F, 4T, 5F, 6T, 7F, 8T, 9F, 10F, 11T, 12F

FIGURE 23.1
A research paper in MLA style (continued)

24. *Including appendices:* Appendices are storage areas for data deemed not important enough for the body, but important for a thorough understanding of the topic. This appendix is a test on understanding one's Sleep IQ. The test's main purpose is to set aside people's misperceptions about sleep.

Dahlquist 12

25

Works Cited

26
27

Brody, Jane E. <u>Facing up to the Realities of Sleep Deprivation</u>. March 31, 1998. ,www.physics.ohio-state.edu/~wilkins/writing/Resources/essays/ sleeping.html.

Coleman, Richard M. <u>Wide Awake at 3:00 a.m.</u> New York: W. H. Freeman and Company, 1986.

28

Dawson, James B. <u>Ten Principles for Better Sleep</u>. Canadian Sleep Institute, Calgary, 1999. <www.csisleep.com>.

29

Dement, W. "What All Undergraduates Should Know about How Their Sleeping Lives Affect Their Waking Lives." Diss. Stanford University, 1997.

Holmes, Thomas H. and R. H. Rahe. "The Social Readjustment Scale." <u>Journal of Psychosomatic Research</u> 11 (1967): 213–218.

Horne, James A. <u>Why We Sleep: The Functions of Sleep in Humans and Other Mammals</u>. Oxford: The Oxford Press. 1998.

"Insomnia: What Is Insomnia?" <u>Reach Out: Factsheet</u> <reachout.socialchange.net.au/visible/factsheet/Insomnia_20000221. html>. Retrieved 22 Feb. 2002.

Jeffries, William, McK. <u>Safe Use of Cortisol</u>. 2nd ed. <members.aol.com/ jeffriesw/safeuses/safecor1.html>.

Kosslyn, Stephen M., and Robin S. Rosenberg. <u>Psychology: The Brain, the Person, the World</u>. Toronto: Allyn and Bacon, 2001.

McGinty, Alice B. <u>Staying Healthy: Sleep and Rest</u>. New York: Powerkids Press, 1995.

FIGURE 23.1
A research paper in MLA style (continued)

25. *Developing Works Cited page.* The Works Cited page lists all the sources of the material cited in text. The heading "Works Cited" is centred on the page, one inch from the top. All entries are listed alphabetically by the authors' last names. Each entry is double-spaced with second and subsequent lines indented one-half inch from the left margin. The page follows the numbering of the text pages.

26. *Italicizing or underlining.* Article titles appear in quotation marks; book or periodical titles are underlined or italicized. Articles, prepositions, or conjunctions are capitalized only if they come first or last. Three-letter abbreviations denote months having five or more letters. Volume numbers for magazines are not cited. No punctuation separates magazine title and date.

27. *Including date of access.* An entry for an online database or any electronic source that is updated periodically should include your date of access.

28. *Citing personal or professional Web site.* When citing from a personal or professional Web site, you should begin with the creator's name, followed by the work's title in quotation marks, if an article, or underlined, if a textbook, followed by the access data.

29. *Listing a dissertation.* When listing a dissertation, you should include the title in quotations, identify the work as a dissertation, and end with the date.

Dahlquist 13

Nordenberg, Tamar. "Tossing and Turning No More: How to Get a Good Night's Sleep." Canadian Food and Drug Administration, <u>FDA Consumer Magazine</u>, July–August, 1998: 8–12.

Selye, Hans. <u>The Stress of Life</u>. Rev ed. New York: McGraw-Hill Book Company, 1976.

Steiff, Gina, and Andrea Witham. "College Women in the Know: Sleep." Diss. Bethel College, 1998.

Urban, Chris. "Sleep Deprivation Not Unusual for Students." <u>The Tech</u>. June, 1991: 5.

FIGURE 23.1
A research paper in MLA style (continued)

APPENDIX A

Editing for Grammar, Punctuation, and Mechanics

he rear endsheets display editing and revision symbols and their page references. When your instructor marks a symbol on your paper, turn to the appropriate section for explanations and examples.

COMMON SENTENCE ERRORS

The following common sentence errors are easy to repair.

frag

Sentence Fragment

A sentence expresses a logically complete idea. Any complete idea must contain a subject and a verb and must not depend on another complete idea to make sense. Your sentence might contain several complete ideas, but it must contain at least one!

| [INCOMPLETE IDEA] | [COMPLETE IDEA] | [COMPLETE IDEA] |

Although Heidi was injured, she grabbed the line, and she saved the boat.

Omitting some essential element (the subject, the verb, or another complete idea) leaves only a piece of a sentence—a *fragment*.

Grabbed the line. [*a fragment because it lacks a subject*]

Although Heidi was injured. [*a fragment because—although it contains a subject and a verb—it needs to be joined with a complete idea to make sense*]

Igor an electronics technician.

This last statement leaves the reader asking, "What about Igor the electronics technician?" The verb—the word that makes things happen—is missing. Adding a verb changes this fragment to a complete sentence.

Simple verb	Igor **is** an electronics technician.
Verb plus adverb	Igor, an electronics technician, **works hard.**
Dependent clause, verb, and subjective complement	**Although he is well paid,** Igor, an electronics technician, **is not happy.**

Do not, however, mistake the following statement—which seems to contain a verb—for a complete sentence:

Igor being an electronics technician.

Such "-ing" forms do not function as verbs unless accompanied by such other verbs as **is, was,** and **will be.**

Igor, being an electronics technician, **was responsible for checking the circuitry.**

Likewise, the "to + verb" form (infinitive) is not a verb.

Fragment   To become an electronics technician.

Complete   To become an electronics technician, **Igor had to complete a two-year apprenticeship.**

Sometimes we inadvertently create fragments by adding subordinating conjunctions (**because, since, it, although, while, unless, until, when, where,** and others) to an already complete sentence.

Although Igor is an electronics technician.

Such words subordinate the words that follow them; that is, they make the statement dependent on an additional idea, which must itself have a subject and a verb and be a complete sentence. (See also "Subordination"—pages 115–116.) We can complete the subordinate statement by adding an independent clause.

Although Igor is an electronics technician, **he hopes to become an electrical engineer.**

NOTE   *Because the incomplete idea (dependent clause) depends on the complete idea (independent clause) for its meaning, you need only a pause (symbolized by a comma), not a break (symbolized by a semicolon).*

Here are some fragments from students' writing. Each is repaired in two ways. Can you think of other ways of making these statements complete?

Fragment   She spent her first week on the job as a researcher. **Selecting and compiling technical information from digests and journals.**

Revised   She spent her first week on the job as a researcher, selecting and compiling technical information from digests and journals.

In her first week on the job as a researcher, she selected and compiled technical information from digests and journals.

Fragment   **Because the operator was careless.** The new computer was damaged.

Revised   Because the operator was careless, the new computer was damaged.

The operator was careless; as a result, the new computer was damaged.

Fragment   **When each spool is in place.** Advance your film.

Revised   When each spool is in place, advance your film.

Be sure that each spool is in place before advancing your film.

Acceptable Fragments

A fragmented sentence is acceptable in commands or exclamations because the subject ("you") is understood.

> **Acceptable** Slow down.
> **fragments** Give me a hand.
> Look out!

Also, questions and answers sometimes are expressed as incomplete sentences.

> **Acceptable** How? By investing wisely.
> **fragments** When? At three o'clock.
> Who? Izzy.

In general, however, avoid fragments unless you have good reason to use one for special tone or emphasis.

APPLICATION **A-1**

Correct these sentence fragments by rewriting each in two ways.

1. Jonas is a terrible math student. But an excellent writer.
2. As they entered the haunted house. The floors began to groan.
3. Hoping for an A in biology. Johanna studied every night.
4. Although many students flunk out of this college. Its graduates find excellent jobs.
5. Three teenagers out of every ten have some sort of addiction. Whether it is to alcohol or drugs.

CS Comma Splice

In a comma splice, two complete ideas (independent clauses), which should be *separated* by a period or a semicolon, are incorrectly *joined* by a comma:

> Noni did a great job, she was promoted.

You can choose among several possibilities for repair:

1. Substitute a period followed by a capital letter:

> Noni did a great job. She was promoted.

2. Substitute a semicolon to signal a relationship between the two items:

| Noni did a great job; she was promoted.

3. Use a semicolon with a connecting (conjunctive) adverb (a transitional word):

| Noni did a great job; **consequently,** she was promoted.

4. Use a subordinating word to make the less important clause incomplete, thereby dependent on the other:

| **Because** Noni did a great job, she was promoted.

5. Add a connecting word after the comma:

| Noni did a great job, **and** she was promoted.

The following revisions show that your choice of construction will depend on the exact meaning or tone you wish to convey:

Comma splice	This is a fairly new product, therefore, some people don't trust it.
Revised	This is a fairly new product. Some people don't trust it.
	This is a fairly new product; therefore, some people don't trust it.
	Because this is a fairly new product, some people don't trust it.
Comma splice	Ms. Gomez was a strict supervisor, she was well liked by her employees.
Revised	Ms. Gomez was a strict supervisor. She was well liked by her employees.
	Ms. Gomez was a strict supervisor; **however,** she was well liked by her employees.
	Although Ms. Gomez was a strict supervisor, she was well liked by her employees.
	Ms. Gomez was a strict supervisor, **but** she was well liked by her employees.

APPLICATION **A-2**

Correct these comma splices by rewriting each in two ways.

1. Efforts are being made to halt water pollution, however, there is no simple solution to the problem.

2. Bill slept through his final, he had forgotten to set his alarm.

3. Signe must be a genius, she never studies yet always gets A's.

4. We arrived at the picnic late, there were no hamburgers left.

5. My part-time job is excellent, it pays well, provides good experience, and offers a real challenge.

ro   Run-On Sentence

The run-on sentence, a cousin to the comma splice, crams too many ideas without needed breaks or pauses.

Run-on   The hourglass is more accurate than the waterclock for the water in a waterclock must always be at the same temperature in order to flow with the same speed since water evaporates it must be replenished at regular intervals thus not being as effective in measuring time as the hourglass.

Revised   The hourglass is more accurate than the waterclock because water in a waterclock must always be at the same temperature to flow at the same speed. Also, water evaporates and must be replenished at regular intervals. These temperature and volume problems make the waterclock less effective than the hourglass in measuring time.

APPLICATION **A-3**

Revise these run-on sentences.

1. The gale blew all day by evening the sloop was taking on water.

2. Elena felt hopeless about passing English however the writing centre helped her complete the course.

3. The professor glared at John he had been dozing in the back row.

4. Our drama club produces three plays a year I love the opening nights.

5. Pets should not be allowed on our campus they are messy and sometimes dangerous.

agr sv   Faulty Agreement—Subject and Verb

The subject should agree in number with the verb. Faulty agreement seldom occurs in short sentences, where subject and verb are not far apart: "Jack eat too much" instead of "Jack eats too much." But when the subject is separated from its verb by other words, we sometimes lose track of the subject-verb relationship.

> **Faulty**   The lion's **share** of diesels **are** sold in Europe.

Although **diesels** is closest to the verb, the subject is **share,** a singular subject that needs a singular verb.

> **Revised**   The lion's **share** of diesels **is** sold in Europe.

Agreement errors are easy to correct once subject and verb are identified.

> **Faulty**   There **is** an estimated 29 000 **women** living in our city.
> **Revised**   There **are** an estimated 29 000 **women** living in our city.
> **Faulty**   A **system** of lines **extend** horizontally to form a grid.
> **Revised**   A **system** of lines **extends** horizontally to form a grid.

A second problem with subject-verb agreement occurs with indefinite subject pronouns such as **each, everyone, anybody,** and **somebody.** They usually take a singular verb.

> **Faulty**   **Each** of the crew members **were** injured during the storm.
> **Revised**   **Each** of the crew members **was** injured during the storm.
> **Faulty**   **Everyone** in the group **have** practised long hours.
> **Revised**   **Everyone** in the group **has** practised long hours.

Collective nouns such as **herd, family, union, group, army, team, committee,** and **board** can call for a singular or plural verb, depending on your intended meaning. When denoting the group as a whole, use a singular verb.

> **Correct**   The **committee meets** weekly to discuss new business.
> The editorial **board** of this magazine **has** high standards.

To denote individual members of the group, use a plural verb.

> **Correct**   The **committee disagree** on whether to hire Jim.
> The editorial **board are** all published authors.

When two subjects are joined by **either . . . or** or **neither . . . nor,** the verb is singular if both subjects are singular and plural if both subjects are plural. If one subject is plural and one is singular, the verb agrees with the one closer to the verb.

> **Correct**   Neither **Jarek** nor **Sebastian works** regularly.
> Either **apples** or **oranges are** good vitamin sources.
> Either Felix or his **friends are** crazy.
> Neither the boys nor their **father likes** the home team.

If, on the other hand, two subjects (singular, plural, or mixed) are joined by **both . . . and,** the verb will be plural.

> **Correct** **Both** Oscar and Kumbi **are** resigning.

A single **and** between subjects makes for a plural subject.

Faulty Agreement—Pronoun and Referent

A pronoun must refer to a specific noun (its referent or antecedent), with which it must agree in gender and number.

> **Correct** **Catia** lost **her** book.

The **students** complained that **they** had been treated unfairly.

When an indefinite pronoun such as **each, everyone, anybody, someone,** or **none** serves as the pronoun referent, the pronoun is singular.

> **Correct** **Anyone** can get **his** degree from that college.
> **Anyone** can get **his** or **her** degree from that college.
> **Each** candidate described **her** plans in detail.

APPLICATION **A-4**

Revise these sentences to make their subjects and verbs agree in number or their pronouns and referents agree in gender and number.

1. Ten years ago the mineral rights to this land was sold to a mining company.
2. Each of the students in our residence have a serious complaint about living conditions.
3. Neither the students nor the instructor like this classroom.
4. Neither Isaac nor Rachel expect to pass this course.
5. Anyone wanting to enhance their career should take a computer course.

Faulty Pronoun Case

A pronoun's case (nominative, objective, or possessive) is determined by its role in the sentence: as subject, object, or indicator of possession.

If the pronoun serves as the subject of a sentence (**I, we, you, she, he, it, they, who**), its case is *nominative*.

> **She** completed her graduate program in record time.
> **Who** broke the chair?

When a pronoun follows a version of the verb **to be** (a linking verb), it explains (complements) the subject, and so its case is nominative.

> The killer was **she.**
>
> The professor who perfected our new distillation process is **he.**

If the pronoun serves as the object of a verb or a preposition (**me, us, you, her, him, it, them, whom**), its case is *objective.*

Object of the verb	The employees gave **her** a parting gift.
Object of the preposition	To **whom** do you wish to complain?

If a pronoun indicates possession (**my, mine, our, ours, your, yours, his, her, hers, its, their, whose**), its case is *possessive.*

> The brown briefcase is **mine.**
>
> Her offer was accepted.
>
> **Whose** opinion do you value most?

Here are some frequent errors in pronoun case:

Faulty	**Whom** is responsible to **who?** [*The subject should be nominative and the object should be objective.*]
Revised	**Who** is responsible to **whom?**
Faulty	The debate was between Olesia and **I.** [*As object of the preposition, the pronoun should be objective.*]
Revised	The debate was between Olesia and **me.**
Faulty	**Us** students are accountable for our decisions. [*The pronoun accompanies the subject, "students," and thus should be nominative.*]
Revised	**We** students are accountable for our decisions.
Faulty	A group of **we** students will fly to California. [*The pronoun accompanies the object of the preposition, "students," and thus should be objective.*]
Revised	A group of **us** students will fly to California.

Deleting the accompanying noun from the two latter examples reveals the correct pronoun case ("We . . . are accountable . . ."; "A group of us . . . will fly . . .").

APPLICATION **A-5**

Select the appropriate pronoun case from each of these pairs (in parentheses).

1. By (who, whom) was the job offer made?
2. The argument was among Naseer, Amir, and (I, me).
3. A committee of (we, us) concerned citizens is working to make our neighbourhood safer.
4. (Us, we) students are being hurt by federal cuts in loan programs.
5. The liar is (he, him).

Sentence Shifts

Shifts in point of view damage coherence. If you begin a sentence or paragraph with one subject or person, do not shift to another.

Shift in person	When **one** finishes such a great book, **you** will have a sense of achievement.
Revised	When **you** finish such a great book, **you** will have a sense of achievement.
Shift in number	**One** should sift the flour before **they** make the pie.
Revised	**One** should sift the flour before **one** makes the pie. (*Or better: Sift the flour before making the pie.*)

Do not begin a sentence in the active voice and then shift to the passive voice.

Shift in voice	**He** delivered the plans for the apartment complex, and the building site **was also inspected by him.**
Revised	He **delivered** the plans for the apartment complex and also **inspected** the building site.

Do not shift tenses without good reason.

Shift in tense	She **delivered** the blueprints, **inspected** the foundation, **wrote** her report, and **takes** the afternoon off.
Revised	She **delivered** the blueprints, **inspected** the foundation, **wrote** her report, and **took** the afternoon off.

Do not shift from one verb mood to another (as from imperative to indicative mood in a set of instructions).

Shift in mood	**Unscrew** the valve and then steel wool **should be used** to clean the fittings.
Revised	**Unscrew** the valve and then **use** steel wool to clean the fitting.

APPLICATION **A-6**

Revise these sentences to eliminate shifts in person, mood, voice, tense, or number.

1. People should keep themselves politically informed; otherwise, you will not be living up to your democratic responsibilities.
2. Meilan made the Dean's List and the Junior Achievement award was also won by her.
3. As soon as he walked into his residence room, Ahmed sees the mess left by his roommate.
4. When one is being stalked by a bear, you should not snack on sardines.
5. First loosen the lug nuts; then you should jack up the car.

pct

EFFECTIVE PUNCTUATION

Punctuation marks are like road signs and traffic signals. They govern reading speed and provide clues for navigation through a network of ideas; they mark intersections, detours, and road repairs; they draw attention to points of interest along the route; and they mark geographic boundaries.

Let's review the four used most often. These marks can be ranked in order of their relative strengths.

1. *Period.* A period signals a complete stop at the end of an independent idea (independent clause). The first word in the idea following the period begins with a capital letter.

   Janus is a fat cat. His friends urge him to diet.

2. *Semicolon.* A semicolon signals a brief stop after an independent idea but does not end the sentence; instead, it announces that the forthcoming independent idea is **closely related** to the preceding idea.

   Janus is a fat cat; he eats too much.

3. *Colon.* A colon usually follows an independent idea and, like the semicolon, signals a brief stop but does not end the sentence. The colon and semicolon, however, are never interchangeable. A colon symbolizes "explanation to follow." Information after the colon (which need not be an independent idea) explains or clarifies the idea expressed before the colon.

   Janus is a fat cat: he weighs twenty kilograms. [*The information after the colon answers "How fat?"*]

   or

   Janus is a fat cat: twenty kilograms worth! [*The second clause is not independent.*]

4. *Comma.* The weakest of these four marks, a comma signals only a pause within or between ideas in the sentence. A comma often indicates that the word, phrase, or clause set off from the independent idea cannot stand alone but must rely on the independent idea for its meaning.

> Janus, a fat cat, is a jolly fellow.
> **Although he diets often,** Janus is a fat cat.

A comma is used between two independent clauses only if accompanied by a coordinating conjunction (**and, but, or, nor, yet**).

> **Comma splice**   Janus is a party animal, he is loved everywhere.
> **Correct**   Janus is a party animal, **and** he is loved everywhere.

End Punctuation

The three marks of end punctuation—period, question mark, and exclamation point—work like a red traffic light by signalling a complete stop.

Period. A period ends a sentence and is the final mark in some abbreviations.

> Ms.   Assn.   N.S.
> M.D.   Inc.   B.A.

Periods serve as decimal points for numbers.

> $15.95
> 21.4%

Question Mark. A question mark follows a direct question.

> Where is the essay that was due today?

Do not use a question mark to end an indirect question.

> **Faulty**   Professor Grey asked if all students had completed the essay?
> **Revised**   Professor Grey asked if all students had completed the essay.
> *or*
> Professor Grey asked, "Did all students complete the essay?"

Exclamation Point. Use an exclamation point only when expression of strong feeling is appropriate.

> **Appropriate**   Oh, no!
> Pay up!

Semicolon

Like a blinking red traffic light at an intersection, a semicolon signals a brief but definite stop.

Semicolons Separating Independent Clauses. Semicolons separate independent clauses (logically complete ideas) whose contents are closely related and are not connected by a coordinating conjunction.

> The project was finally completed; we had done a good week's work.

The semicolon can replace the conjunction-comma combination that joins two independent ideas.

> The project was finally completed, and we were elated.
> The project was finally completed; we were elated.

The second version emphasizes the sense of elation.

Semicolons Used with Adverbs as Conjunctions and Other Transitional Expressions. Semicolons must accompany conjunctive adverbs like **besides, otherwise, still, however, furthermore, moreover, consequently, therefore, on the other hand, in contrast,** or **in fact.**

> The job is filled; however, we will keep your résumé on file.
> Your background is impressive; in fact, it is the best among our applicants.

Semicolons Separating Items in a Series. When items in a series contain internal commas, semicolons provide clear separation between items.

> I am applying for summer jobs in Calgary, Alberta; Halifax, Nova Scotia; Montreal, Quebec; and Winnipeg, Manitoba.
> Members of the survey crew were Juan Jiminez, a geologist; Hector Lightfoot, a surveyor; and Mary Shelley, a graduate student.

Colon

Like a flare in the road, a colon signals you to stop and then proceed, paying attention to the situation ahead. Usually a colon follows an introductory statement that requires a follow-up explanation.

> We need this equipment immediately: a voltmeter, a portable generator, and three pairs of insulated gloves.
> She is an ideal colleague: honest, reliable, and competent.

Except for salutations in formal correspondence (e.g., Dear Ms. Jones:), colons follow independent (logically and grammatically complete) statements.

> **Faulty** My plans include: finishing college, travelling for two
> years, and settling down in Fredericton.

No punctuation should follow "include."
Colons can introduce quotations.

> The supervisor's message was clear enough: "You're fired."

A colon can replace a semicolon between two related, complete statements
when the second one explains or amplifies the first.

> Moira's reason for accepting the lowest-paying job offer was simple:
> she had always wanted to live in the Northwest.

APPLICATION **A-7**

Insert semicolons or colons as needed in these expressions.

1. June had finally arrived it was time to graduate.
2. I have two friends who are like brothers Pierre and Michel.
3. Raul did not get the job however, he was high on the list of finalists.
4. The wine was superb an 1898 Margaux.
5. Our student senators are Min-Sun Chen, a geology major Helen Simms, a nursing major and Henry Drew, an English major.

Comma

The comma is the most frequently used—and abused—punctuation mark. It works like a blinking yellow traffic light, for which you slow down briefly without stopping. Never use a comma to signal a *break* between independent ideas.

Comma as a Pause Between Complete Ideas. In a compound sentence in which a coordinating conjunction (**and, or, nor, for, but**) connects equal (independent) statements, a comma usually precedes the conjunction.

> This is an excellent course, **but** the work is difficult.

Comma as a Pause Between an Incomplete and a Complete Idea. A comma usually is placed between a complete and an incomplete statement in a complex sentence when the incomplete statement comes first.

> **Because he is a fat cat,** Lisle diets often.
> **When he eats too much,** Lisle gains weight.

When the order is reversed (complete idea followed by incomplete), the comma usually is omitted.

> Lisle diets often **because he is a fat cat.**
> Lisle gains weight **when he eats too much.**

Reading a sentence aloud should tell you whether or not to pause (and use a comma).

Commas Separating Items (Words, Phrases, or Clauses) in a Series. Use commas after items in a series, including the next to last item.

> **Helen, Edson, Marsha,** and **Sabah** are joining us on the term project.
> He works hard **at home, on the job,** and even **during his vacation.**
> The new employee complained **that the hours were long, that the pay was low, that the work was boring, and** that the supervisor was paranoid.

Use no commas if **or** or **and** appears between all items in a series.

> She is willing to study in Victoria or Vancouver or even in Edmonton.

Comma Setting Off Introductory Phrases. Infinitive, prepositional, or verbal phrases introducing a sentence usually are set off by commas, as are interjections.

Infinitive phrase	**To be or not to be,** that is the question.
Prepositional phrase	**In Rome,** do as the Romans do.
Participial phrase	**Being fat,** Lisle was slow at catching mice.
	Moving quickly, the army surrounded the enemy.
Interjection	**Oh,** is that the verdict?

Commas Setting Off Nonrestrictive Elements. A *restrictive* phrase or clause modifies or defines the subject in such a way that deleting the modifier would change the meaning of the sentence.

> All students **who have work experience** will receive preference.

Without **who have work experience,** which *restricts* the subject by limiting the category **students,** the meaning would be entirely different. All students will receive preference.

Because this phrase is essential to the sentence's meaning, it is *not* set off by commas.

A *nonrestrictive* phrase or clause could be deleted without changing the sentence's meaning and *is* set off by commas.

Our new manager, **who has only six weeks' experience,** is highly competent.

> **Modifier**   Our new manager is highly competent.
> **deleted**

This house, **riddled with carpenter ants,** is falling apart.

> **Modifier**   This house is falling apart.
> **deleted**

Commas Setting Off Parenthetical Elements. Items that interrupt the flow of a sentence (such as **of course, as a result, as I recall,** and **however**) are called parenthetical and are enclosed by commas. They may denote emphasis, afterthought, clarification, or transition.

> **Emphasis**   This deluxe model, **of course,** is more expensive.
> **Afterthought**   Your essay, **by the way,** was excellent.
> **Clarification**   The loss of my job was, **in a way,** a blessing.
> **Transition**   Our warranty, **however,** does not cover tire damage.

Direct address is parenthetical.

Listen, **my children,** and you shall hear . . .

A parenthetical expression at the beginning or the end of a sentence is set off by a comma.

> **Naturally,** we will expect a full guarantee.
> **My friends,** I think we have a problem.
> You've done a good job, **Eli.**
> **Yes,** you may use my name in your advertisement.

Commas Setting Off Quoted Material. Quoted items within a sentence are set off by commas.

The customer said, "I'll take it," as soon as he laid eyes on our new model.

Commas Setting Off Appositives. An appositive, a word or words explaining a noun and placed immediately after it, is set off by commas when the appositive is nonrestrictive. (See page 467.)

> Andrea Cloutier, **our new president,** is overhauling all personnel policies.
> Alpha waves, **the most prominent of the brain waves,** typically are recorded in a waking subject whose eyes are closed.
> Please make all cheques payable to Sam Sawbuck, **school treasurer.**

Commas Used in Common Practice. Commas set off the day of the month from the year, in a date.

May 10, 1989

Commas can be used to set off numbers in three-digit intervals.

11,215
6,463,657

In metric usage, however, three-digit intervals are set off with spaces.

11 215
6 463 657

Commas are used to set off street, city, and province in an address.

Mail the bill to J. B. Smith, 18 Sea Street, Corner Brook, Newfoundland A7A 2B6.

When the address is written vertically, however, the omitted commas are those that would otherwise occur at the end of each address line.

J. B. Smith
18 Sea Street
Corner Brook, Newfoundland A7A 2B6

Commas set off an address or date in a sentence.

Room 3C, Margate Complex, is my summer address.
June 15, 1987, is my graduation date.

They set off degrees and titles from proper nouns.

Roger P. Cayer, M.D.
Sandra Mello, Ph.D.

Commas Used Erroneously. Avoid needless or inappropriate commas. Read a sentence aloud to identify inappropriate pauses.

Faulty   The instructor told me, that I was late. [*separates the indirect from the direct object*]

The most universal symptom of the suicide impulse, is depression. [*separates the subject from its verb*]

This has been a long, difficult, semester. [*second comma separates the final adjective from its noun*]

Ian, Sean, and Meaghen, are joining us on the trip home. [*third comma separates the final subject from its verb*]

An employee, who expects rapid promotion, must quickly prove his or her worth. [*separates a modifier that should be restrictive*]

I spoke by phone with Gerrit, and Uta. [*separates two nouns linked by a coordinating conjunction*]

The room was, 8 metres long. [*separates the linking verb from the subjective complement*]

We painted the room, red. [separates the object from its *complement*]

APPLICATION **A-8**

Insert commas where needed in these sentences.

1. In modern society highways seem as necessary as food water or air.
2. Everyone though frustrated by pollution can play a part in improving the environment.
3. Professor Song who has written three books is considered an authority in her field.
4. Amanda Ford of course is the best candidate for mayor.
5. Terrified by the noise Serafina ran never looking back.
6. One book however will not solve all your writing problems.

APPLICATION **A-9**

Eliminate needless or inappropriate commas from these sentences.

1. Students, who smoke marijuana, tend to do poorly in school.
2. As I started the car, I saw him, dash into the woods.
3. This has been a semester of happy, exciting, experiences.
4. Ali mistakenly made dates on the same evening with Carlos, and Yves, even though she had promised herself to be more careful.
5. In fact, a writer's reaction to criticism, is often defensiveness.

ap/

Apostrophe

Apostrophes indicate the possessive, a contraction, and the plural of numbers, letters, and figures.

Apostrophe Indicating the Possessive. At the end of a singular word, or of a plural word that does not end in **s**, add an apostrophe plus **s** to indicate the possessive.

The people's candidate won.

The chainsaw was Emma's.

The women's locker room burned.

Normally, singular nouns that end in **s** take an apostrophe and an **s**.

> I borrowed Chris's book.
>
> I supported the business's objectives.

However, it is also acceptable not to add **s** following the apostrophe to words that already end in **s**; the key is to be consistent in your usage throughout each piece of writing.

Do not use an apostrophe to indicate the possessive form of either singular or plural pronouns.

> The book was hers.
>
> Ours is the best school in the county.
>
> The fault was theirs.

At the end of a plural word that ends in **s,** add an apostrophe only.

> the **cows'** water supply
>
> the **Jacksons'** wine cellar

At the end of a compound noun, add an apostrophe plus **s**.

> my **father-in-law's** false teeth

At the end of the last word in nouns of joint possession, add an apostrophe plus **s** if both own one item.

> **Joe and Sam's** lakefront cottage

Add an apostrophe plus **s** to both nouns if each owns specific items.

> **Pei-Mao's** and **Minoru's** passports

Apostrophe Indicating a Contraction. An apostrophe shows that you have omitted one or more letters in a phrase that is usually a combination of a pronoun and a verb.

> I'm   they're
>
> he's   you'd
>
> you're   who's

Don't confuse **they're** with **their** or **there.**

Faulty	there books
	their now leaving
	living their
Correct	their books
	they're now leaving
	living there

Remember the distinction this way:

> Their friend knows they're there.

It's means "it is." **Its** is the possessive.

> It's watching its reflection in the pond.

Who's means "who is," whereas **whose** indicates the possessive.

> Who's interrupting whose work?

Other contractions are formed from the verb and the negative.

> | isn't | can't |
> | don't | haven't |
> | won't | wasn't |

Apostrophe Indicating the Plural of Numbers, Letters, and Figures.

> The **6's** on this new printer look like smudged **G's, 9's** are illegible, and the **%'s** are unclear.

"/"   Quotation Marks

Quotation marks set off the exact words borrowed from another speaker or writer. The period or comma at the end is placed within the quotation marks.

| **Periods and commas belong within quotation marks** | "Hurry up," Aris whispered.
Aris told Felicia, "I'm depressed." |

The colon or semicolon always is placed outside quotation marks.

| **Colons and semicolons belong outside quotation marks** | Our student handbook clearly defines "core requirements"; however, it does not list all the courses that fulfill the requirement. |

When a question mark or exclamation point is part of a quotation, it belongs within the quotation marks, replacing the comma or period.

| **Some punctuation belongs within quotation marks** | "Help!" he screamed.
Fiona asked Kurt, "Can't we agree about anything?" |

But if the question mark or exclamation point pertains to the attitude of the person quoting instead of the person being quoted, it is placed outside the quotation mark.

Some punctuation belongs outside quotation marks   Why did Boris wink and whisper, "It's a big secret"?

Use quotation marks around titles of articles, paintings, book chapters, and poems.

Certain titles belong within quotation marks   The enclosed article, "The Job Market for College Graduates," should provide some helpful insights.

But titles of books, journals, or newspapers should be underlined or italicized.

Finally, use quotation marks (with restraint) to indicate your ironic use of a word.

Quotation marks to indicate irony   She is some "friend"!

APPLICATION **A-10**

Insert apostrophes and quotation marks as needed in these sentences.

1. Our countrys future, as well as the worlds, depends on everyone working for a cleaner environment.
2. Once you understand the problem, Professor Nisenholt explained, you find its worse than you possibly could have expected.
3. Can we help? asked the captain.
4. Its a shame that my dog had its leg injured in the accident.
5. All the players bats were eaten by the cranky beaver.

Ellipses

Three spaced dots in a row (. . .) indicate you have omitted material from a quotation. If the omitted words come at the end of the original sentence, a fourth dot indicates the period. (Also see page 356.)

> "Three dots . . . indicate . . . omitted . . . material. . . . A fourth dot indicates the period. . . ."

ital   ## Italics

In typing or longhand writing, indicate italics by underlining. On a word processor, use italic print for titles of books, periodicals, films, newspapers, and plays; for the names of ships; for foreign words or scientific names; sparingly, for emphasizing a word; and for indicating the special use of a word.

> The *Oxford English Dictionary* is a handy reference tool.
>
> The *Lusitania* sank rapidly.
>
> She reads the *Vancouver Sun* often.
>
> My only advice is *caveat emptor.*
>
> *Bacillus anthracis* is a highly virulent organism.
>
> *Do not* inhale these fumes under any circumstances!
>
> Our contract defines a *work-study student* as one who works a minimum of twenty hours weekly.

()/ Parentheses

Use commas normally to set off parenthetical elements, dashes to give some emphasis to the material that is set off, and parentheses to enclose material that defines or explains the statement that precedes it.

> An anaerobic (**airless**) environment must be maintained for the cultivation of this organism.
>
> The cost of running our college has increased by 15 percent in one year **(see Appendix A for full cost breakdown)**.
>
> This new calculator (**made by Ilco Corporation**) is perfect for science students.

Material between parentheses, like all other parenthetical material discussed earlier, can be deleted without harming the logical and grammatical structure of the sentence.

[]/ Brackets

Brackets in a quotation set off material that was not in the original quotation but is needed for clarification, such as an antecedent (or referent) for a pronoun. (Also see pages 356–357.)

> "She [**Amy**] was the outstanding candidate for the scholarship."

Brackets can enclose information taken from some other location within the context of the quotation.

> "It was in early spring [**April 2, to be exact**] that the tornado hit."

Use **sic** ("thus," or "so") when quoting an error in a quotation.

> The assistant's comment was clear: "He don't [**sic**] want any."

Dashes

Dashes can be effective—if not overused. Parentheses de-emphasize the enclosed material; dashes emphasize it.

> Have a good vacation—but watch out for sandfleas.
>
> Mary—a true friend—spent hours helping me rehearse.

APPLICATION **A-11**

Insert parentheses or dashes as appropriate in these sentences.

1. Writing is a deliberate process of deliberate decisions about a writer's purpose, audience, and message.
2. Have fun but be careful.
3. She worked hard summers at three jobs actually to earn money for agricultural school.
4. To achieve peace and contentment that is the meaning of success.
5. Fido a loyal pet saved my life during the fire.

EFFECTIVE MECHANICS

Correctness in abbreviation, hyphenation, capitalization, use of numbers, and spelling demonstrates your attention to detail.

ab Abbreviations

Avoid abbreviations in formal writing or in situations that might confuse your reader. When in doubt, write the word out.

Abbreviate some words and titles when they precede or immediately follow a proper name, but not military, religious, or political titles.

Correct Mr. Tayebi
Dr. Jekyll
Raymond Dumont, Jr.
Reverend Ormsby
Prime Minister Chrétien

Abbreviate time designations only when they are used with actual times.

Correct 400 B.C.

5:15 A.M.

Faulty Plato lived sometime in the B.C. period.

She arrived in the A.M.

Most dictionaries provide an alphabetical list of other abbreviations. For abbreviations in documentation of research sources, see pages 379–397.

Hyphen

Hyphens divide words at the right-hand margin and join two or more words used as a single adjective if they precede the noun but not if they follow it:

> com-puter
>
> the rough-hewn wood
>
> the all-too-human error
>
> The wood was rough hewn.
>
> The error was all too human.

Some other commonly hyphenated words:

- Most words that begin with the prefix self-. (Check your dictionary.)

  > self-reliance
  > self-discipline

- Combinations that might be ambiguous.

  > re-creation [*a new creation*]
  > recreation [*leisure activity*]

- Words that begin with **ex,** only if **ex** means "past."

  > ex-faculty member
  > excommunicate

- All fractions, along with ratios that are used as adjectives and that precede the noun (but not those that follow it), and compound numbers from twenty-one through ninety-nine.

  > a **two-thirds** majority
  >
  > In a **four-to-one** vote, the student senate defeated the proposal.
  >
  > The proposal was voted down **four to one.**
  >
  > **Thirty-eight** windows were broken.

Capitalization

Capitalize the first words of all sentences as well as titles of people, books, and chapters; languages; days of the week; the months; holidays; names of organizations or groups; races and nationalities; historical events; important documents; and names of structures or vehicles. In titles of books, films, and the like, capitalize the first word and all those following except articles or prepositions.

Items that are capitalized		
	Joe Schmoe	Russian
	A Tale of Two Cities	Labour Day
	Protestant	Dupont Chemical Company
	Wednesday	Senator Barbara Boxer
	the *Queen Mary*	France
	the Peace Tower	The War of 1812

Do not capitalize the seasons (**spring, winter**) or general groups (the **younger generation, the leisure class**).

Capitalize adjectives that are derived from proper nouns.

Chaucerian English

Capitalize titles preceding a proper noun but not those following.

Mayor Minoru Kawahora

Minoru Kawahora, mayor

Capitalize words such as **street, road, corporation,** and **college** only when they accompany a proper noun.

St. Mary's University

High Street

The Rand Corporation

Capitalize **north, south, east,** and **west** when they denote specific locations, not when they are simply directions.

the South

the Northwest

Turn east at the next set of lights.

Use of Numbers

Numbers expressed in one or two words can be written out or written as numerals. Use numerals to express larger numbers, decimals, fractions, precise technical figures, or any other exact measurements.

543	2 800 357
3¼	15 kilograms
50 kilowatts	4000 rpm

Use numerals for dates, census figures, addresses, page numbers, exact units of measurement, percentages, times with A.M. or P.M. designations, and monetary and mileage figures.

page 14	1:15 P.M.
18.4 pounds	9 metres
12 litres	$15

Do not begin a sentence with a numeral. If your figure needs more than two words, revise your word order.

Six hundred students applied for the 102 available jobs.

The 102 available jobs brought 780 applicants.

Do not use numerals to express approximate figures, time not designated as A.M. or P.M., or streets named by numbers less than 100.

about seven hundred fifty

four fifteen

108 East Forty-second Street

sp Spelling

Take the time to use your dictionary for all writing assignments. When you read, note the spelling of words that give you trouble. Compile a list of troublesome words.

APPLICATION **A-12**

In these sentences, make any needed mechanical corrections in abbreviations, hyphens, numbers, or capitalization.

1. Dr. Ishak, our english prof., drives a red maserati.
2. Eighty five students in the survey rated self-discipline as essential for success in college.
3. Since nineteen eighty seven, my goal has been to live in the northwest.
4. Senator tarbell has collected forty five hand made rugs from the middle east.
5. During my third year at Bishop's university, I wrote twenty three page papers on the Russian revolution.
6. 100 bottles of beer are on the wall.

APPENDIX B

Format Guidelines for Submitting Your Manuscript

Format is the look of a page, the visual arrangement of words and spacing. A well-formatted manuscript invites readers in, guides them through the material, and helps them understand it.

FORMAT GUIDELINES FOR SUBMITTING YOUR MANUSCRIPT

1. *Use the right paper and ink.* Print in black ink, on 21.5 × 28 cm low-gloss, high-quality, white computer paper. Use rag-bond paper with a high fibre content (25 percent minimum).

2. *Use high-quality type or print.* On typewritten copy, keep erasures to a minimum, and redo all smudged pages. On a computer, print your hard copy on a letter-quality printer, a laser printer, or a dot-matrix printer (with a fresh ribbon) in the letter-quality mode.

3. *Use standard type sizes and typefaces.* Standard type sizes for manuscripts run from 10 to 12 points—depending on the particular typeface. (Certain typefaces, such as "pica," usually call for a 10-point type size whereas others, such as "elite," call for a 12-point typesize.) Use other sizes only for headings, titles, or special emphasis.

   Word processing programs offer a variety of typefaces (or fonts). Except for special emphasis, use conservative typefaces; the more ornate ones are harder to read and inappropriate for most manuscripts.

4. *Number pages consistently.* Number your first and subsequent pages with Arabic numerals (1, 2, 3), 1 cm from the top of the page and aligned with the right margin or centred in the top or bottom margin. For numbering pages in a research report, see pages 405, 429.

5. *Provide ample margins.* Small margins make a page look crowded and difficult, and allow no room for peer or instructor comments. Provide margins of at least 2.5 cm top and bottom, and 2.5 cm right and left. If the manuscript is to be bound in some kind of cover, widen your left margin to at least 3.5 cm.

6. *Keep line spacing and indention consistent.* Double space within and between paragraphs. Indent the first line of each paragraph five spaces from the left margin. (Indent five spaces on a computer by striking the Tab key.)

7. *Design your first page.* If your instructor requires a title page, see pages 425, 427. For the first page of a manuscript without a separate title page, follow the format your instructor recommends.

8. *Cite and document each source.* Consult Chapter 21. For designing "Works Cited" pages in a documented essay, see pages 450–452.

9. *Proofread your final manuscript.* On a computer, spell checkers and grammar checkers can reveal certain errors, but are no substitute for your own careful evaluation.

How to Insert Corrections on Final Copy

If you need to make a few handwritten corrections on your final copy, use a caret (∧) to denote the insertion:

make

If you need to ∧ a few handwritten . . . .

Any page requiring more than three or four such corrections should be retyped or reprinted.

FORMAT GUIDELINES FOR SUBMITTING YOUR MANUSCRIPT (continued)

10. *Bind your manuscript for readers' convenience.* Do not use a cover unless your instructor requests one. Use a staple or large paper clip in the upper left-hand corner.

11. *Make a backup copy.* Print out or photocopy a backup paper, which you should keep—just in case the original you submit gets lost or misplaced.

FORMAT CHECKLIST ☑

Before submitting any manuscript, evaluate its format by using the following checklist.

☐ Do paper and ink meet quality standards?

☐ Is the type or print neat, crisp, and easy to read?

☐ Are type sizes and typefaces appropriate and easy to read?

☐ Are pages numbered consistently?

☐ Are all margins adequate?

☐ Are line spacing and indention consistent?

☐ Are the first and subsequent pages appropriately designed?

☐ Is each source correctly cited and documented?

☐ Has the manuscript been proofread carefully?

☐ Is the manuscript bound for readers' convenience?

☐ Has a backup copy been made?

APPENDIX C

Useful Web Sites and Electronic Library Resources

The following sites are available to anyone with Internet access.

Search Engines

AltaVista **www.altavista.ca** Offers a comprehensive Web catalogue.

Deja News **www.deja.com** Searches for newsgroup discussions by keyword.

Excite **www.excite.com** Includes Usenet postings.

Google **www.google.ca** Provides comprehensive Web catalogue.

Infoseek **www.infoseek.go.com** Fast and easy to use.

Liszt Directory of Mailing Lists **www.liszt.com** Searches for *listservs* by keyword.

Liszt Directory of Newsgroups **www.liszt.com/news** Searches for newsgroups by keyword.

Savvy Search **www.savvy search.com** Can search over one hundred engines at once.

WebCrawler **www.webcrawler.com** Easy to use and comprehensive.

Subject Directories (or Catalogues)

The Argus Clearinghouse **www.clearinghouse.net** A useful site for beginning a research project.

The Internet Public Library **www.ipl.org** The gateway for countless Web sites, including many in this listing.

WWW Virtual Library **www.vlib.org** An index listing hundreds of categories.

Yahoo! **www.yahoo.com** A popular and valuable tool for searching a subject on the Web.

Almanacs

The Almanac of Politics and Government **www.polisci.com** Focuses on U.S. and world political structures and history.

Global Statistics **www.stats.demon.nl** Provides worldwide statistical data.

Information Please Almanac **www.infoplease.com** A popular general almanac.

Associations and Organizations

Associations on the Net (AON) **www.ipl.org/ref/AON** Gateway to sites for countless associations and societies.

Idealist **www.idealist.org** Lists thousands of sites for nonprofit organizations.

International Organizations **www.library.nwu.edu/govpub/idtf/igo.html** Lists sites for organizations worldwide.

Business

Big Book **www.bigbook.com** A listing of U.S. businesses.

Europages **www.europages.com** A listing of European businesses.

Exportsource **www.exportsource.gc.ca**

SuperPages.ca **www.superpages.ca** Provides a listing of Canadian businesses.

Strategis **www.strategis.ic.gc.ca** Canada's most comprehensive business information Web site.

Student Connection Program **www.scp-ebb.com**

Dictionaries

Dictionary.com **www.dictionary.com** Considered the top online dictionary in English.

Encyberpedia Dictionary **www.encyberpedia.com/glossary.htm** Lists all types of dictionaries available on the Internet.

Roget's Thesaurus **www.thesaurus.com**

WWWebster Dictionary **www.m-w.com/netdict.htm**

Encyclopedias

The Canadian Encyclopedia **www.thecanadianencyclopedia.com** Available free.

Encyberpedia **www.encyberpedia.com/ency.htm** Lists the various specialized encyclopedias on the Web.

Microsoft Encarta Concise Encyclopedia **www.encarta.msn.com/find/default.asp?section=find** Available free.

Encyclopedia Brittanica **www.brittanica.com** Available free.

Grolier's Encyclopedia **www.grolier.com** Usually available via your school library's Web page.

Journal Articles

Carl UnCover **www.carl.org** Indexes millions of articles from thousands of journals. Faxed copies of articles can be ordered for a fee.

Kluwere Online **www.reference.kluwereonline.com** An index of 720 journals covering computational and mathematical sciences and earth and environmental sciences.

Publist.Com **www.publist.com** A comprehensive index of articles from publications worldwide.

News Organizations

CBC News **www.cbc.ca/news**

CBC Radio **www.cbc.ca/radioguide/index.jsp**

CTV News **www.ctvnews.ca**

The Globe and Mail **www.globeandmail.com**

Maclean's Magazine **www.macleans.ca**

MSNBC **www.msnbc.com/news/default.asp**

PBS Online NewsHour **www.pbs.org/newshour**

Time Magazine **pathfinder.com/time**

Vancouver Sun **www.vancouversun.com**

The Wire—News from the Associated Press **www.wire.sp.org** For breaking news from around the world.

Canadian Government Information

Government of Canada Information on the Internet (CGII) **igci.gc.ca/ index-e.html**

Government of Canada **canada.gc.ca**

Canadian Parliament **www.parl.gc.ca**

U.S. Government Information

Federal Gateway **www.fedgate.org** The gateway for information on federal, state, and local governments.

The National Security Archive **www.seas.gwu.edu/nsarchive** Provides access to formerly classified documents now available through the Freedom of Information Act.

Government Documents **www.sosu.edu/lib/govdocs** A guide to federal government information and publications.

Writing and Research Guides

Researchpaper.com **www.researchpaper.com** Offers ideas for topics, a chat room, and tips and guidelines for research and writing.

Purdue Online Writing Lab **www.owl.english.purdue.edu/introduction.html** Offers all kinds of writing help.

University of Toronto Writing Lab **www.utoronto.ca/writing/index.html** Provides many links to advice on research, grammar, and documentation.

University College of the Cariboo "Writing in the Disciplines" Website **www.cariboo.bc.ca/disciplines/** Offers writing advice specific to subject areas in the humanities, social sciences, sciences and business.

ELECTRONIC LIBRARY RESOURCES

The following databases are easily searchable through your school library, often on CD-ROM. Access is usually restricted to the school community via password. A sampling of likely databases in your library:

Applied Science and Technology Index

Art Index

Books in Print with Reviews

Canadian Periodicals Index

Canadian Business and Current Affairs Index

Contemporary Literary Criticism (InfoTRAC)

Expanded Academic ASAP (InfoTRAC) An excellent index to begin a search.

General Science Index

Humanities Index

MLA International Bibliography

Readers' Guide to Periodical Literature

Social Sciences Index

Ask your reference librarian about specific resources available at your school.

CREDITS

Anthony, John K. "Being a Mature Student."

Berger, Thomas A. Excerpt from *A Long and Terrible Shadow: White Values, Native Rights in the Americas.* Copyright © 1991 by Thomas A. Berger. Published by Douglas & McIntyre Ltd. Reprinted by permission of the publisher.

Bodell, Richard. "Plumbing The Brain Drain Problem" by Richard Bodell. Excerpt from the article that appeared in the September 2000 issue of *Studentbody*. Reprinted with permission of the author.

Brooks, John. Telephone: The First Hundred Years by John Brooks. New York: Harper & Row, Publishers, Inc., 1975, 1976.

Choyce, Lesley. "Thin Edge of the Wedge" by Lesley Choyce as appeared in the March/April issue of *Canadian Geographic*. Reprinted by permission of the author.

Cousins, Norman. "How to Make People Smaller Than They Are." Saturday Review, December 1978.

Cruickshank, Tom. "Heart's Content." Adapted from the copy in the April 1999 issue of *Harrowsmith Country Life*. Adapted with permission of the editor.

Dalquist, Mike. "Sleep Deprivation Among University Students."

Davies, Phillipa. "The Homework Debate: When Is It Too Much" by Phillipa Davies as appeared in the June 2001 issue of *Professionally Speaking*, the Magazine of the Ontario College of Teachers. Reprinted with permission of the Executive Coordinator.

Dillard, Annie. "Seeing" from Pilgrim at Tinker Creek by Annie Dillard. Copyright © 1974 by Annie Dillard. Reprinted by permission of HarperCollins Publishers, Inc.

Dowsett Johnston, Ann. "Measuring Excellence" by Ann Dowsett Johnston from *Maclean's*, November 20, 2000 issue. Excerpt used with permission of the Manager-Editorial Services.

Eighner, Lars. "On Dumpster Diving" from Travels with Lizbeth: Three Years On the Road and on the Streets by Lars Eighner. Copyright © 1993 by Lars Eighner. Reprinted by permission of St. Martin's Press LLC.

Fedderson, Kim. "Scutwork: The Marginalization of Writing Within Canadian Universities." Paper given May 2001 to ACCUTE (Association of Canadian College and University Teachers of English). Reprinted with permission of the author.

Fero, Terry. "Liberal Arts Degrees: Career Dead Ends or Tickets to Success."

Goleman, Daniel. "Why the Brain Blocks Daytime Dreams" by Daniel Goleman. Copyright © 1976 by Sussex Publishers, Inc. Reprinted with permission from Psychology Today Magazine.

Hemingway, Ernest. From "Bull Fighting: A Tragedy" by Ernest Hemingway in By-Line: Ernest Hemingway, edited by William White. Copyright © 1967 by Mary Hemingway. Reprinted by permission of Scribner, A Division of Simon & Schuster.

Hertzberg, Hendrick and David C. K. McClelland. "Paranoia" by Hendrick Hertzberg and David C. K. McClelland. Copyright © 1974 by Harper's Magazine. All rights reserved. Reproduced from the June issue by special permission.

Holmes, Thomas H. and R. H. Rahe. Table, "The Social Readjustment Rating Scale" by Thomas H. Holmes and R. H. Rahe from Journal of Psychosomatic Research 11(2), 1967: 213–218. Reprinted with permission from Elsevier Science.

487

Holt, John. "How Teachers Make Children Hate Reading" by John Holt. Copyright © 1967 by John Holt. Originally appeared in Redbook. This usage granted by permission.

Hugi, Maria M.D., and Susan Harris, M.D., eds. "Management of Breast Cancer Related Lymphedema" from *Abreast in the Nineties, Summer 98*" a quarterly newsletter of the BC and Yukon Breast Cancer Information Project which is a cooperative venture of the BC Cancer Agency and the Canadian Cancer Society. Permission to use granted by the editors in the newsletter.

Huxley, Aldous. Excerpt from Brave New World Revisited by Aldous Huxley. Copyright © 1958 by Aldous Huxley. Reprinted by permission of HarperCollins Publishers, Inc., Chatto & Windus Ltd., and Mrs. Laura Huxley.

Indian and Northern Affairs Canada.*Words First: An Evolving Terminology Relating to Aboriginal Peoples in Canada* (Catalogue No. R2-236/2002E-IN, ISBN 0-662-33143-5). www.ainc-inac.gc.ca/pr/pub/wf/index_e.html.

Kemelman, Harry. Common Sense in Education. New York: Crown Publishers, Inc., 1970, pp. 34–35.

King, Martin Luther, Jr. "Letter from Birmingham Jail" by Martin Luther King, Jr. Copyright © 1963 by Martin Luther King, Jr., copyright renewed 1991 by Coretta Scott King. Reprinted by arrangement with The Heirs to the Estate of Martin Luther King, Jr., c/o Writers House, Inc. as agent for the proprietor.

Lantinga, Skye. "Spring Bear Hunt."

Lindbergh, Anne Morrow. Gift from the Sea. Copyright © 1955 by Anne Morrow Lindbergh. Reprinted by permission of Pantheon Books, a division of Random House, Inc.

McCourt, Ann. "The Heart of My Neighbourhood."

Menninger, Karl. From The Crime of Punishment by Karl Menninger. Copyright 1966, 1968 by Karl Menninger. Used by permission of Viking Penguin, a division of Penguin Putnam Inc.

Milner, Philip. "These Hours Have 50 Minutes " by Philip Milner, Professor, Department of English, St. Francis Xavier University, Antigonish, Nova Scotia. Permission of the author.

Moody, Edward J. From "Urban Witches" by Edward J. Moody in Conformity and Conflict: Readings in Cultural Anthropology, Third Edition, edited by James P. Spradley and David W. McCurdy. Copyright © 1977. All rights reserved. Reprinted by permission of Allyn & Bacon.

Morgan, Ted. From On Becoming American by Ted Morgan. Copyright © 1978 by Ted Morgan. Reprinted by permission of Houghton Mifflin Company. All rights reserved.

Murray, Donald. A Writer Teaches Writing, Second Edition. Boston, MA: Houghton Mifflin Co.

Needles, Dan. "Hawk among the Chickens." by Dan Needles as appeared in the February 2000 issue of *Harrowsmith Country Life.* Reprinted with permission of the author.

Orwell, George. Excerpt from "Shooting an Elephant" in Shooting an Elephant and Other Essays by George Orwell. Copyright 1950 by Sonia Brownell Orwell and renewed 1978 by Sonia Pitt-Rivers. Reprinted by permission of Harcourt, Inc. and A. M. Heath & Co. Ltd., on behalf of Bill Hamilton as the Literary Executor of the Estate of the Late Sonia Brownell Orwell and Secker & Warburg Ltd.

Penn, Briony. "Green Winters on the Salish Sea" by Briony Penn as appeared in the November/December 2000 issue of *Canadian Geographic.* Reprinted with permission of the author.

Quindlen, Anna. "Abortion Is Too Complex to Feel All One Way About" by Anna Quindlen, The New York Times, November 1, 1986. Copyright © 1986 by The New York Times Co. Reprinted by permission.

Reynolds, Mark."Alberta Elk Association." by Mark Reynolds as appeared in the September/October issue of *Explore.* Reprinted with permission of the author.

Roiphe, Anne. "Mad Money" from "Confessions of a Female Chauvinist Sow" by Anne Roiphe, New York Magazine, 1972. Reprinted by permission of International Creative Management, Inc.

Roszak, Theodore. Where the Wasteland Ends. New York: Bantam Doubleday Dell.

Schooler, Lynn. "A Grizzly Tale: Tracker Translates Gritty Clues." by Lynn Schooler. An excerpt from the article as appeared in the June/July 1997 issue of *Equinox.* Used with permission of the editor.

Selye, Hans, M.D. The Stress of Life, Revised Edition. New York: McGraw-Hill Book Company, 1956, 1976.

Smith, Scott Earl. " Getting the Most Out of a Gun Dog," by Scott Earl Smith. An excerpt from the article that appeared in the October 2000 issue of *Angler and* Hunter. Used with permission of the author.

Swift, Bob. "On Reading Trash" by Bob Swift, The Miami Herald, April 28, 1988. Reprinted with permission of The Miami Herald.

Syfers, Judy Brady. "Why I Want a Wife" by Judy Brady Syfers as appeared in MS Magazine, December 31, 1971. Reprinted by permission of the author.

Thomas, David. "Banff: The Sacrificial Lamb" by David Thomas as appeared in the January/ February issue of *Explore*. Reprinted with permission of the author.

Viorst, Judith. "Friends, Good Friends–and Such Good Friends" by Judith Viorst. Copyright © 1977 by Judith Viorst. Originally appeared in Redbook. This usage granted by permission.

Watts, Alan. In My Own Way. New York: Pantheon Books.

Wright, Frank Lloyd. Excerpt adapted from Frank Lloyd Wright, "Away with the Realtor," Esquire Magazine, October 1958. Copyright © 1958 by Esquire Publishing Inc. Reprinted courtesy of Esquire and the Hearst Corporation.

Yantha, Brian. "Part of Muskoka."

INDEX

Editing and Revision Symbols

Symbol	Problem	Page*	Symbol	Problem	Page*
ab	incorrect abbreviation	475	ital	italics needed for emphasis	473
agr p	error in pronoun agreement	460	mod	a modifying word or phrase misplaced	110
agr sv	error in subject-verb agreement	458	neg	negative construction needs rephrasing	123
apl	missing or misused possessive apostrophe	470	nom	nominalization (nouns made from verbs)	112
av	active voice needed	116	num	error in the use of numbers	477
bias	biased language needs rephrasing	142	np	a needless phrase, creates wordiness	121
ca	pronoun in the wrong case	460	over	overstatement or exaggeration	133
cap	capital letter needed	476	par	parallel phrasing needed	113
cl	word that merely adds clutter	123	pct	error in punctuation	463
comb	choppy sentences need to be combined	126	[ ]/	brackets	474
cont	faulty contraction	471	:/	colon	465
coord	coordination needed or faulty	114	,/	comma	466
cs	comma splice, links two sentences only by a comma	456	--/	dash	475
			.../	ellipses	473
dgl	dangling modifier	111	!/	exclamation point	464
euph	euphemism that misleads	133	-/	hyphen	476
			( )/	parentheses	474
frag	a fragment used as a sentence	454	./	period	464
			?/	question mark	464
			"/"	quotation mark	472
			;/	semicolon	465

*Numbers refer to the first page of major discussion in the text.